Retail
Marketing
Strategy

Retail Marketing Strategy

PLANNING, IMPLEMENTATION, AND CONTROL

A. Coskun Samli

 Quorum Books

New York • Westport, Connecticut • London

Library of Congress Cataloging-in-Publication Data

Samli, A. Coskun.
  Retail marketing strategy : planning, implementation, and control /
  A. Coskun Samli.
      p.   cm.
  Bibliography: p.
  Includes index.
  ISBN 0-89930-249-1 (lib. bdg. : alk. paper)
  1. Retail trade.   2. Marketing.   I. Title.
HF5429.S275 1989
658.8′7—dc 19   87-37575

British Library Cataloguing in Publication Data is available.

Library of Congress Catalog Card Number: 87-37575
ISBN: 0-89930-249-1

First published in 1989 by Quorum Books

Greenwood Press, Inc.
88 Post Road West, Westport, Connecticut 06881

Printed in the United States of America

The paper used in this book complies with the
Permanent Paper Standard issued by the National
Information Standards Organization (Z39.48-1984).

10 9 8 7 6 5 4 3 2 1

To Stanley C. Hollander,
professor, mentor, friend, and scholar par excellence

Contents

Exhibits

Preface

Retailing is a very important aspect of the total business world. As consumers, we collect the fruits of economic development and industrial progress at the retail level by being able to buy more, better, and highly sophisticated products. Even though it may not be commonly realized, much of the manufacturers' marketing efforts either pays off or is wasted at the retail level. Thus, retailing is the firing line for most marketing planning and management decisions.

Despite its important role in the society and in the total distribution system, retailing has not been treated as effectively in the literature as other areas of marketing. If, for instance, one considers the elaborate models, research, and body of sophisticated knowledge accumulated in such areas as consumer behavior or marketing research, it becomes clear that retailing has been lagging behind.

Although the research methodology is not absent and in fact good research information is available on many aspects of retailing, previous retailing books have not focused on this wealth of knowledge. At least part of the reason is that almost all retailing courses are taught at junior college and undergraduate levels. Since, at these academic levels, the emphasis is on practical "how-to" approaches, much of the sophisticated research has been unnoticed, if not completely ignored.

A NEW ERA IN RETAILING

The premise of this book is that in the near future retailing will take its rightful place in the academic arena. There will be more retailing courses at the graduate level as well as greater use of research findings at the undergraduate level. Many retailers will hire young people with master's degrees in business, and many consulting firms will find themselves more involved in retailing research.

Although this book aims at graduate-level courses in retailing as well as some of tne more advanced graduate courses in marketing, it will appeal primarily to the young and ambitious retail decision makers who would like to do just a bit better than their competition. They understand the importance of research-based decision making. They realize the value of strategic decisions and strategy development as opposed to making decisions on a day-to-day basis. The book will also appeal to professional researchers and consultants, not because it has a very heavy research orientation but rather because it raises research-related issues and at times also imparts some new research findings.

By combining research findings and retail marketing strategy implementation we can achieve an important balance. This balance will address the often neglected finer points of marketing strategy development for retailers. In this sense this book will make a real contribution. The book raises many issues that will need further research. Hence, those who are pursuing research in the retailing area as well as those who are managing retail establishments will find it useful.

As stated above, most books on retailing have approached the subject as a craft, using a ''how-to-do-it'' method that has taken them away from elaborate planning in the marketing strategy area. By the same token, this approach has led retail decision makers in the direction of heavy emphasis on retail accounting, retail financing, and retail operations. However, as the retail competition gets keener and as the retailing environment becomes more and more adverse, success in retailing will be equated with the ability to develop effective retail marketing strategy rather than extensive emphasis on day-to-day operations. In developing a retail marketing strategy, this book proposes the concept of differential congruence as the basic philosophy of success. This concept is as applicable to large retailing giants as to small retailing establishments. Throughout this book, examples are given which are applicable to small firms. This orientation is somewhat neglected in many other retailing books. It must be emphasized at the outset that good understanding and implementation of retail marketing strategies are important for all retailers and not just for retailing giants.

This book is based on the notion that developing an effective retail marketing strategy involves three key phases: planning the strategy, implementing the strategy, and evaluating the performance (Exhibit P.1). The book comprises eighteen chapters. The introductory chapter presents an overview of retail marketing strategy development, and the first few chapters explore the externalities of retail marketing strategy development, namely, a theory of retail competition (Chapter 1) and major trends (Chapters 2 and 3). Chapter 4 delves into a more specific area: the downtown versus shopping center conflict as it relates to individual retailers.

Chapters 5, 6, and 7 bring external factors closer to the individual retail store. Whereas Chapter 5 explores market potentials and feasibility, Chapter 6 examines specific aspects of consumer behavior pertaining particularly to retail purchase behavior. Chapter 7 expands on the foundation established in Chapters 5 and 6.

Exhibit P.1
Three Phases of Retail Marketing Strategy Development

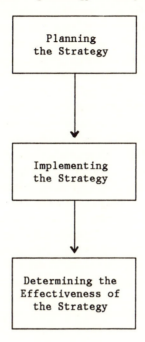

Chapter 7 explores segmentation not only as a strategic alternative but also as a fact of life in modern-day retailing.

Alternative retail marketing strategies are discussed in Chapter 8. Since effective retail management involves managing the store image, Chapter 9 provides a paradigm for managing the retail store image.

Since the market's perceived image often differs from that of management, Chapter 10 explores this dichotomy as a diagnostic tool. Store image is perceived differently by customers of the store and by the store management itself. This difference can be used to direct management to strengthen its strategic plans and their implementation.

If the perceived store image is in congruence with the self-image, then the store is successful in creating customer satisfaction and pursuant customer loyalty. This topic is examined in Chapter 11, and it is the key theme of the book, that is, differential congruence.

Retailing mixes are retail management's tools for implementing the overall strategy and for fulfilling the store objectives. Chapters 12, 13, and 14 discuss these mix components: (1) promotion, (2) merchandise mix, and (3) price mix. Thus, these chapters deal with implementation of the planned strategy.

Three of the last four chapters probe the question of how we can determine the effectiveness of the strategy implemented.

Store loyalty is one of the most important indicators of the effectiveness of strategy implementation. We cover this topic in Chapter 15 by using empirical data and different measurement concepts. The chapter on Retail Information Management Systems (RIMS), Chapter 16, delves into establishing a general system in order to ascertain the degrees of success or failure in implementing retail marketing strategies.

Chapter 17 explores a most important topic—control—describing retail control functions for specific and general purposes. Since the existing literature perhaps places too much emphasis on financial controls, this chapter attempts to balance this picture by giving equal attention to nonfinancial controls.

Finally, Chapter 18 points out some of the key areas of future research in retailing theory and practice. There are some significant gaps in our retailing knowledge, and this chapter seeks to identify some of them.

Whereas standard books on retailing usually contain a separate chapter on retailing research, retailing research topics and concepts are spread throughout this book. Thus, important research topics are handled as necessary in various chapters.

This book reflects many years of teaching, research, and consulting experience. All of the episodes and most of the examples relate to my field research and consulting activity. Although some of the chapters reflect some of my extensive research, others only pose questions and issues that still need to be thought out and researched.

Many people aided in the research and preparation of this book. It all started at Michigan State University where Stan Hollander planted the seeds of the importance of retailing in my mind. At California State University, Sacramento, I started my teaching and research career in retailing in 1961. In Blacksburg these activities accelerated, and ideas started taking a specific form and direction. Two students who are now successful professors and researchers, Robert Zimmer at California State, Fullerton, and Douglas Lincoln at Boise State University, worked with me during these formative years. Douglas wrote a dissertation under my direction which contributed both to the literature and to my general knowledge. In addition to making a major contribution to Chapters 8 and 10, he coauthored Chapter 16. Subsequently, Joseph Sirgy, a colleague, friend, and scholar par excellence, inspired me to do some sophisticated research in this area. He also assumed the major task of preparing two chapters in this book (Chapters 11 and 15). Perhaps no day has passed during the past few years that he and I have not discussed some esoteric problem related to retailing. My assistant, David Randall, performed invaluable research in relating my ideas to the literature. A colleague and a doctoral student, Ken Bahn and Fanis Varvoglis, respectively, are coauthors of Chapters 11 and 15.

A good friend and assistant, Rob Penn, did some valuable work in the early phases of this project. My doctoral student, Linda Edmunds of Dupont, conducted the major portion of research dealing with black and white professional women. Professor Jay Lindquist of Western Michigan was instrumental in developing the final chapter. Finally, a good friend and scholar, Edward M. Mazze of Temple University, reviewed the whole manuscript and made many valuable suggestions.

Hundreds of undergraduate and graduate students have interacted with me in my retailing classes and in so doing have made some valuable contributions by questioning many of my ideas. My friends who are members of Downtown Blacksburg, Inc., constantly fed me with new practical ideas as we discussed vital downtown redevelopment issues. My clients in various aspects of retailing taught me, both directly and indirectly, numerous important lessons that enabled me to bring theory and practice together.

Our secretaries at Virginia Polytechnic Institute and State University, Wanda Belcher, Becky Stoddard, Janice Blevins, and Linda Hills, patiently typed and retyped from my sometimes incomprehensible script. My department head, James Littlefield, and my dean, Richard Sorensen, were always supportive.

Finally, my wife, Jane Walter, sometimes by criticizing and sometimes by simply displaying how consumers behave, made many contributions to this project. My children, Evan, Ayla, Susan, and Gena, were sometimes patient, and they too were helpful by displaying the behavior of future retailing customers.

The theory of differential congruence is the working theme of this book. It is hoped that through this concept this book will contribute to the well-being of my friends in retailing as well as to my students in marketing. I cheerfully acknowledge full responsibility for this book and its contents.

Introduction: An Overview of Retail Marketing Strategy Development and Implementation

Dayton Hudson, one of the largest general mechandise retailers in the United States, has been following a growth strategy based on carrying merchandise that largely represents quality fashion and value. During a 14-year period it has grown from 100 stores to 1,000 stores (Macke 1983). Domino's Pizza, on the other hand, has scaled down its offering from a full-fledged Italian restaurant to just take-out pizza. In 1983 its nearly 2,000 units scattered throughout the country had an annual sales volume of $625 million (Whalen 1984).

These are just two strategies out of countless options that are open to retailers. However, unless the retailer thinks in terms of strategic planning and acts accordingly, the chances of survival, growth, and prosperity are rather limited in view of steadily increasing retail competition. Retail organizations, as a result of increasing competition, have been moving in the direction of planning certain marketing strategies.

When retail organizations make the shift from an old-fashioned merchandise management orientation to a strategic marketing orientation, the development of functional marketing plans gains in importance (Mason et al. 1985). As Mason et al. (1985, p. 162) state: "successful, well-managed retail companies are finding the marketing efforts of the consumer packaged-goods firms are equally applicable to retailing strategy formulation." This book is about retail marketing strategy formulation and development. May et al. 1986 (p. 32) posit that:

Retailing is facing a period of intensifying competition, a period in which it will become even more difficult to obtain and maintain a competitive advantage. They continue to say that the pursuit of a competitive advantage requires what is now skill not typically found in retail marketing.

The focus of this book is on developing this retail marketing skill. Retail marketing, as conceptualized here, goes beyond day-to-day activities, how-to approaches, or fail-safe recipes. Instead, retail marketing emphasizes strategic planning and the decision-making aspects of retailing. Consider, for instance, the May Department Store's company mission:

The May Company stands for excellence in retailing achieved through a premier organization, by leading our markets in innovative execution of superior merchandising skills and delivering a quality level of service to the customer. (Quoted from a mission statement presented at the American Marketing Association (AMA) Consortium on retailing, University of Alabama, July 1987.)

Here, the company is emphasizing excellence by developing and implementing superior merchandising skills and providing high-quality service. The May Company statement clearly displays the retail marketing concept and how it can be constructed to provide a competitive edge in retail markets.

A series of logical and research-based steps and major tasks must be performed if a retail establishment is to be viable and prosper (Miller 1981; Kerin and Miller 1981; Mason and Mayer 1984). By providing an overview of the sequential steps and tasks to be performed, this chapter seeks to present a general guideline for developing a successful retail marketing strategy. There are three key phases of successful retail marketing strategy: planning, implementation, and evaluation. This chapter highlights the development of retail marketing strategy which is the focal point of this book. As such, the chapter provides a basic summary for the book.

PLANNING

The first step in planning effectively is to establish goals. A retail establishment's goals begin with articulation of the retail objectives and positioning. Articulating retail objectives and positioning imply the unique ability to match external uncontrollable variables with internal controllable tools of management in such a way that the retail establishment achieves the competitive advantage. Certainly Neiman-Marcus, Bloomingdale's, and Sears have been successful in positioning themselves and achieving competitive advantage. However, in retailing, for each successful establishment that manages to establish proper goals, achieve effective positioning, and develop significant competitive advantage and differential congruence, many establishments do not have a chance to achieve any of these. They fail because they lack effective planning for successful marketing strategy development, implementation, and control.

The development of effective retail market strategy begins with adequate knowledge of externalities. In turn, this knowledge leads to the establishment of market opportunities. Market opportunities are based on total market potentials scaled down by the nature and intensity of competition. The retailer who is not

Exhibit I.1
Establishing Retail Objectives

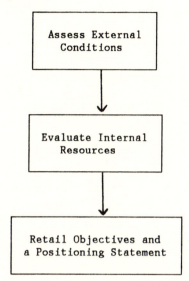

able to approximate the market potentials and who is not familiar with local trends cannot possibly succeed in assessing external conditions.

Once the external conditions are assessed, the retailer must take a good hard look at himself or herself (Exhibit I.1). This implies an evaluation of the firm's inventory, including the existing image, financial resources, merchandise mix, administrative know-how, personnel, location of existing inventory, delivery system, and other physical facilities, such as warehouse equipment.

Following the assessment of external conditions and internal evaluation of the firm's resources, it is possible to establish goals. For existing firms, instead of establishing goals, the revision of goals would be the next step. In either case, at this point the retail establishment knows where it wants to go, and, on this basis, it begins to formulate its marketing strategy.

Clearly defined retail targets and particular positioning goals are necessary prerequisites for effective planning. One retail establishment might consider itself a mass merchandiser and position itself between Sears and Penney's. Another retail establishment might aim at a differentiating status and position itself as an upper-middle-class apparel store for women. Yet a third retail store might be a segmenter, keying its imported gifts to primarily "cosmopolitans" in the community and positioning itself above Pier I Imports.

Ability to spell out the objectives and position goals facilitates the planning of the retailing effort. The planning process involves three specific executive actions: analysis, evaluation, and prediction. Exhibit I.2 illustrates the components and sequential ordering of retail marketing planning. The process involves

Exhibit I.2
The Planning Process in Retail Management

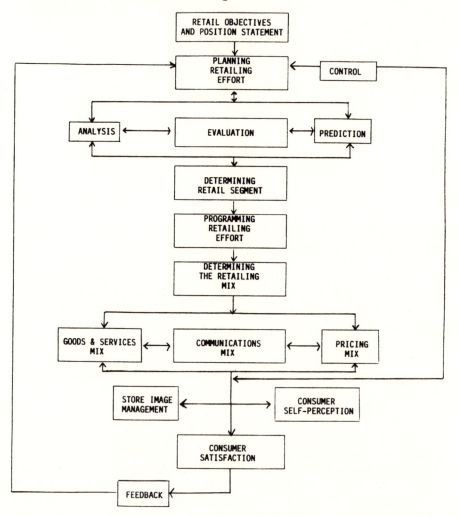

Exhibit I.3
Components of the Retail Mixes

Goods and Service Mix	Communication Mix	Pricing Mix
Merchandise	Advertising	Price Level
Variety and Assortment	Catalogues	Price Lines
Guarantees and Exchanges	Store Layout	Mark Down
Customer Services	Public Relations	Mark Up
Credit	Internal Displays	Price Perceived
Alterations and	Personal Selling	and Quality
Adjustments	Window Displays	Efficiency
Delivery	Telephone Sales	Components Effecting
Parking	STORE IMAGE	Prices:
STORE IMAGE		warehousing
		handling goods
		computerized
		controls
		STORE IMAGE

numerous diversity and functional steps, all of which are interdependent and must be planned in advance. Analysis of available information and evaluation of trends and relationships among various factors and indicators enable the decision makers to predict. Thus, they perceive current and future problems from a future perspective (Lazer and Kelly 1961). At this planning level, plans for controlling the effectiveness of implementation are also made.

Upon the completion of plans, attempts are made to obtain as much information as possible on the specifics of the retail segment to which the store is aiming. Thus, plans are further scaled down or are more sharply focused. At this stage, it is more feasible to program the total retailing effort. For instance, Woodward and Lothrop of Washington, D.C., on the basis of analysis and predictions, expects the black segment of the apparel market to grow substantially. Hence, it has made plans to enter this particular market segment. Once this decision has been made, it becomes possible to program the retail effort effectively.

The most important aspect of programming, the retailing effort, is to develop the retailing mix. As illustrated in Exhibit I.3, this mix has three major components: goods and services, communications, and pricing.

The goods and services mix is the reason for existence in retailing. Without the proper merchandise and service combination, the firm does not have a chance to cater to particular market segments or to assume the position to which it aspires.

The effectiveness of the goods and services mix depends on numerous conditions. These conditions are expressed as questions:

1. How does the product and service mix fit the communications mix?

2. How does the product and service mix fit the physical distribution mix?

3. Is the product and service mix appropriate for the market segment at which the firm is aiming?

4. Do we have appropriate controls and feedback to update the product and service mix?

5. Are the goods and services that are offered in the total mix compatible?

6. Is the product and service mix different from that of the competitors so that the firm will have comparative advantage?

7. Is the product and service mix compatible with the image the retail establishment is projecting?

COMMUNICATIONS MIX

Since the retailer is separated from the consumer in terms of time and space, the retailer must overcome these barriers. This task is performed by the communications mix (Lazer and Kelly 1961). The retailer attempts to overcome the barriers, first, by obtaining information about the market, second, by communicating with the market, and, third, by providing information. Many components of the communications mix are utilized in these communication and information activities. Various components in the promotional mix are presented in Exhibit I.3. This is not an exhaustive list, but it presents some of the most important factors.

PRICING MIX

The pricing mix also has three major components. The *efficiency component* implies the firm's efficiencies in running the retail establishment which are passed onto the customers through lower prices. The *competitive component* implies the retail establishment's use of the pricing mix as a major competitive tool. Discount stores, bargain basements, and similar retail operations use prices for that purpose. Finally, the *image component* implies utilization of prices in order to enhance a specific image. The store's image as a reasonable place with some exceptional buys cannot be implemented without carefully planned pricing strategy.

All three of the mixes, as seen in Exhibit I.3, include a store image factor: all the factors of the three mixes are either image-building variables or depend on the already existing image. In either case they are interdependent with image.

The optimization of the retailing mix involves an integration of all three submixes. For the retail establishment to be successful, the submixes must interact effectively with each other. Furthermore, the integrated retailing mix must be completely congruent with the image the retail store is attempting to project. Lack of congruence in this respect implies that, even though the submixes are integrated, they are not aiming at the intended market segment.

MANAGEMENT OF STORE IMAGE

Store image is important because, first, it represents all the aspects of communication that the store performs which are geared to a specific marketplace. Second, it is the most significant retail marketing management feedback that provides decision makers with specific strategic alternatives. Furthermore, it guides management in making the adjustments needed to fulfill specific goals.

Store image management is therefore the crux of retail marketing management, and as such it helps the total marketing strategy to be formulated, implemented, tested for effectiveness, and adjusted for better congruity between the image and the market segment. Image as a whole is synergistic. Although it has numerous components such as appearance of the store, attitude of the salespeople, quality of the merchandise, internal layout, and many others, the image involves more than the sum total of all of these elements. It is the unity and congruence among these elements that determine the nature of image.

Image is a help in formulating and implementing strategy. If, for instance, the store is aiming at the older well-to-do segment, a dynamic youthful image is not likely to be successful. Consider the following example:

The Glo-wood Restaurant was located adjacent to a major metropolitan university. It was open for 24 hours and catered primarily to students and unskilled blue collar workers employed in the immediate area. A good atmosphere of communication and relaxation prevailed. Food was cheap and waitresses were friendly. The place was very successful. When the owners were ready to retire they sold the restaurant. The new owner wanted to make the restaurant an elegant, high class place. He changed the interior, the menu, and the appearance of the restaurant. In less than six months he was out of business. The elegant image he created was not acceptable to the existing segment, and he failed to attract other people from other market segments because of competition and the socio-economic makeup of the community.

Thus, developing a retail marketing strategy without paying attention to image is most likely to end in failure. The firm must first establish its goals in terms of positioning and market segment and then must decide what kind of image needs to be projected in order to fulfill the objectives. Image management cannot be successful, however, unless the image intended is the same as the image perceived.

A bank in the midwest considered itself to be catering strictly to the upper middle class in the community. All of its promotional activity, its services, and its layout were designed to that end. Research pointed out that it was catering primarily to the lower middle class, and the customers did not really care for all the frills that the bank offered.

If the image intended is not the same as the image received, the establishment is likely to be wasting its resources and creating customer dissatisfaction. Consumer satisfaction depends on the completeness of the overlap between intended

Exhibit I.4
Extremes in Retail Image Management

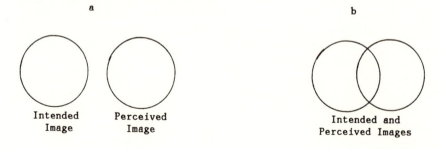

image and perceived image. Exhibit I.4 illustrates this point. While ''a'' displays a situation of failure in image management and therefore unsuccessful marketing strategy, at the other extreme ''b'' indicates nearly complete success in the overlap and therefore a successful case of image management and a successful marketing strategy. Most cases lie between these two extremes, but there are many variations between these two extremes. Perceived image is closely tied in with the customer's self-perception.

CONSUMER SELF-PERCEPTION

Every individual has self-perception that reflects a self-image. The self-image may have been formed by the individual's psyche through the environment. The environment includes membership in large groups, for example, socioeconomic class, subculture, or ethnic group as well as small groups, such as the family, reference group, or peer group. It also includes the educational institutions and many other direct and indirect variables. All of these environmental factors make an impact on the individual's psyche which forms and perceives a self-image.

Only within the constraints of this perceived self-image can the store image be realistically measured and assessed. For instance, the individual may perceive himself or herself as youthful, dynamic, and open to new ideas and new products. If the same person perceives a store to be static, stuffy, and too conservative, then the individual either will not patronize the store or will be very uncomfortable during visits to that store. When the perceived store image is congruent with the consumer self-perception, consumer satisfaction is considered to be very high.

The planned retail marketing strategy therefore aims at a perfect self-image store image congruence. Without such a congruence, a retail establishment cannot survive, let alone be successful. More will be said about this concept in conjunction with differential congruence.

CONSUMER SATISFACTION

In the final analysis, only if the store can satisfy consumer needs will it be able to survive and prosper. Prosperity is generated by the positive profit picture which is the market's reward to the store for a job that is being well done. Thus, it is of the utmost importance that the retail establishment make sure that it provides satisfaction to its customers. Customer satisfaction has to be determined periodically to avoid a negative profit picture. Short of periodically asking the store customers for their degree of satisfaction, the retail store's aims to determine congruence between the projected and perceived images are likely to be futile. If the store begins to lose money or to show decreasing profits, the retail establishment will have to reexamine its image and its market segment so that customer self-perception and perceived image will coincide. If the image and self-perception of the market segment are not congruent, then major decisions must be made. One of the firm's key options is to change its goals regarding segmentation and positioning. The firm can then explore various components of its marketing mix and make minor or major changes. Finally, a combination of these options may be employed in changing the retail marketing strategy.

The final concept in Exhibit I.2 is the feedback. Although provisions for feedback must be made at every decision-making stage, a general feedback as to the store's overall success must be obtained at the end of all retail marketing efforts. Throughout this book customer satisfaction is considered to be a function of ''differential congruence.'' This concept is discussed later in this chapter.

FEEDBACK

Examining the degree of customer satisfaction is a necessity and must be done regularly. Regular research in this area provides direction for retail marketing planning and control. Effective changes in the marketing strategy can come about only through effective feedback. Without proper research information this feedback cannot materialize. Thus, it is rather easy to make a case for periodic retail market research studies that provide the basis for feedback (Gentile and Gentile 1978: 55–58).

Planning and control work almost simultaneously. As part of the planning process, certain control criteria can be established. These criteria could be financial parameters, market store, percentage increase or decrease in sales and expenditures, and many others. Thus, as feedback facilitates planning by providing direction, controls keep the implementation effective.

THEORY OF DIFFERENTIAL CONGRUENCE

The retail establishment has numerous strategic alternatives. As it uses the retailing mix it planned, it will invariably appeal to a specific segment in the market. In implementing the strategic plans by using its retailing mix, the retail

Exhibit I.5

The Key Sequential Aspects of Retail Marketing Strategy Development

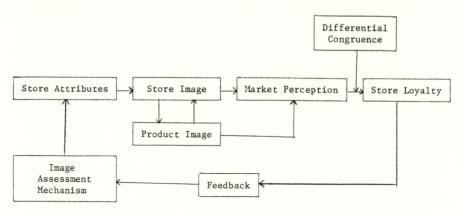

establishment is managing and manipulating a store image. This particular image management, by definition, makes an impact on the particular market segment to which the store has been appealing. The individuals in that segment have a self-image which they nurture. If this self-image and store image overlap and show a positive congruence, consumer satisfaction is achieved. As the customers are satisfied and kept satisfied, they become loyal to the store. A store that has a loyal following has achieved what Wroe Alderson calls ''differential advantage.'' Behind this advantage is the most important force in retailing: differential congruence. As the retail store manages to appeal to its market segment by its image and as that image becomes congruent with the self-image of its customers, the retail establishment achieves differential congruence. The reward for this achievement in the market is survival, growth, and profit for the retailer. Exhibit I.5 illustrates this point. Differential congruence begets store loyalty, which in turn begets success in retail management. Thus, retail marketing management revolves around developing and maintaining positive differential congruence.

SUMMARY

Exhibit I.5 summarizes the chief aspects of the total retail marketing strategy development process. As illustrated there, all retail stores have some special attributes. Whether or not these are the desirable ones and how they should be manipulated will determine the direction of retail marketing strategy. Store attributes are reflected in store image, which is perceived by the market. If this image and market characteristics are in harmony, differential congruence takes place. Differential congruence creates store loyalty which reflects customer satisfaction. Feedback provides information to readjust the whole system if the results are not desirable.

This introductory chapter presents the general plan of this book. Retail marketing management commences with the establishment of retail objectives and positioning. Planning, based on analysis evaluation and prediction, follows the goals stage. In the planning stage, the market segment is decided on and the total retailing effort is programmed. This program, by definition, includes the development of a retailing mix. The mix consists of three submixes: the goods and services mix, the communications mix, and the pricing mix. The mixes create the store image. Store image is so critical that it calls for special management. In managing the store image, it is necessary that it be congruent with the self-perception of store customers. Only then would it be possible for the store to successfully satisfy consumer needs and be profitable. Finally, determining the degree of effectiveness through research is used as feedback to modify, change completely, or retain the existing marketing strategy.

REFERENCES

Alderson, Wroe. *Marketing Behavior and Executive Action*, Homewood, Ill.: Richard D. Irwin, 1957.

Gentile, Richard J., and Anne Gentile. *Retailing Strategy*. New York: Labhas-Friedman Books, 1978.

Kerin, Roger, and Richard Miller. "Diversity of Retail Operations and Financial Performance," in Kenneth Bernhardt et al., eds., *The Changing Marketing Environment*. Chicago: American Marketing Association, 1981, pp. 24–26.

Lazer, William, and Eugene J. Kelly. "The Retailing Mix Planning and Management." *Journal of Retailing* (Spring 1961): 32–44.

Macke, Kenneth A. "Managing Change: How Dayton Hudson Meets the Challenge." *Journal of Business Strategy* (Summer 1983): 78–81.

Mason, Barry J., and Morris L. Mayer. *Modern Retailing*. 3rd ed. Plano, Tex.: Business Publications, 1984.

———, Morris Mayer, and Anthony Koh. "Functional Marketing Plan Development in Department Store Retailing." *Journal of the Academy of Marketing Science* (Summer 1985): 161–82.

May, Eleanor G., et al. "Marketing—in Concept and in Practice." In R.L. King, ed., *Retailing: Theory and Practice for the 21st Century*. Academy of Marketing Science and the American Collegiate Retailing Association, 1986, pp. 31–35.

Miller, Richard. "Pathways to Growth in Retailing." *Journal of Business Strategy* 3 (1981): 25–35.

Whalen, Bernie. "People Oriented Marketing Delivers Lots of Dough for Domino's." *Marketing News*, March 16, 1984, Section 2, pp. 4–5.

1 A Theory of Retail Competition

Retailing is more competitive than most other aspects of marketing because at the retail level multidimensional competition exists. Multidimensionality can be attributed to the presence of various levels, as well as different factors in each level. Exhibit 1.1 illustrates this multidimensionality concept. Five levels of retail competition are identified in the diagram. Although level 5 indicates the broadest level, level 1 deals with the most specific aspects of retail competition. A successful retail establishment must understand the varying nature of retail competition at each level, and it must cope with this competition at each level according to that level's competition patterns.

THE SEARCH FOR DIFFERENTIAL ADVANTAGE

The total retail competition can be described with one statement: the search for the differential advantage. Differential advantage implies that a retailer has managed to be different from its competitors. This difference is recognized and appreciated by its customers. Hence, the individual retail establishment has developed a certain degree of monopoly power that facilitates its survival and prosperity.

As was discussed in the Introduction, the differential advantage is achieved by differential congruence. This congruence implies the positive balance between the store's image and the individual's self-image. Successful retail management, therefore, implies achieving differential congruence by coping with and overcoming competition. It may be stated that Sears customers know what to expect from that store and they feel comfortable shopping there. All of the existing indicators reveal that differential congruence exists here. The same can be claimed for customers of Gucci on the higher end of the socioeconomic spectrum and Woolworth's at the lower end of the socioeconomic spectrum. This issue is discussed in subsequent chapters as well as in the following section.

FROM DIFFERENTIAL ADVANTAGE TO DIFFERENTIAL CONGRUENCE

The movement from perfect competition to monopolistic competition (Chamberlain 1973) made a significant impact on the theory and practice of retail competition. Retailers (at least those that have been successful) understood that they were (and are) all unique and that their well-being was associated with the market's appreciation of this uniqueness. Wroe Alderson (1957) subsequently suggested that all marketers strive for differential advantage, which implies that the retailer can manage his or her uniqueness which is understood and appreciated by the market. If successful, the retailer will achieve differential advantage. Achieving differential advantage is made possible primarily by differential congruence.

The meaning of differential congruence is illustrated in Exhibits 1.2 and 1.5. In its attempts to successfully differentiate itself from its competitors, a retail establishment can create a congruence between the store's perceived image and the customer's self-image. To the extent that this congruence is strong and positive, the retailer enjoys the customer's loyalty to the store. Customers of Neiman-Marcus or Gucci are considered to be quite loyal. They come back again and again because they identify themselves with the store and their needs are satisfied in these stores. Similarly, a small boutique can also command a high degree of loyalty because its customers are pleased with that store. The degree of this loyalty indicates the intensity of differential advantage and hence the profitability of the retail establishment.

The search for differential congruence is necessitated by the very nature of the milieu within which the firm survives and functions. The milieu is the particular corner of the market in which the firm is trying to establish a niche. It has a lot of competition, and market segments have unique idiosyncrasies. The firm must be successful in providing unique goods and services that satisfy these segments. Thus, at the broadest level the very nature of the market system launches the quest for competitive advantage.

FROM PERFECT COMPETITION TO MONOPOLISTIC COMPETITION

The retail market can be described as the typical example of monopolistic competition. Here each establishment has certain unique features; no two establishments are exactly alike. Hence, each establishment has a certain degree of monopoly power. It may be unique in terms of its merchandise mix, its location, its prices, its store layout, or some other special feature.

To the extent that a particular feature is appealing to the specific target market,

Exhibit 1.1
Multidimensionality of Retail Competition

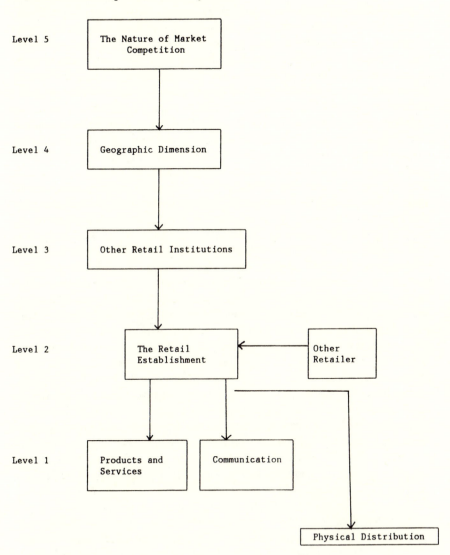

the establishment claims monopoly power. Basically, monopoly power implies a certain degree of store loyalty whereby the customer remains particularly attached to the store without having an immediate tendency to switch stores even if the prices of that store go up. Unlike the textbook case of perfect competition where no single enterprise has distinguishing features and hence monopoly power, which is highly unlikely in practice, monopolistic competition forces the retail establishment to strive for differential congruence.

Since less than perfect competition is the realistic way of describing the milieu of retailing, every retailer has an opportunity to develop certain specific features that will create differential congruence which will give the firm advantage over its competitors. Through the ability to use the opportunity to create differential advantage, the retailer establishes his or her monopoly power. That, in turn, insures survival and profitability. The ability to use the opportunity to create competitive advantage is indicative of good management. By using the remaining four of the five levels in Figure 1.1, this particular ability can create differential congruence for a retail establishment. The retailing sector is full of examples of good competitive managerial skills and imagination.

The conditions that monopolistic competition imposes on the retail establishments are (1) relative ease of entry; (2) relative ease of exit; (3) less than perfectly elastic demand function; (4) less than perfect information for individual enterprise; (5) possibility of acquiring additional information; and (6) consumers less than rational, some of them, however, being more informed and closer to being rational than others. Under these given conditions which reflect the reality of monopolistic competition, the individual firm establishes differential congruence. The conditions of this differential congruence do not have to be purely factual. For instance, Sears claims it has the best battery values for the given price. This claim may not be factual, but special skills in advertising and promoting this notion make it possible for Sears to establish an advantage over its competitors.

Thus, in less than perfect competition, differential advantage may be based on real or make-believe features that the retailers either have or claim to have. Even if the make-believe features are claimed and are not factual, if the retailer can do an effective job of convincing its market targets, it can be very successful. This implies the ability to create differential congruence and therefore advantage over competitors. The skills to achieve such competitive advantage are not equal or proportionately distributed among retail enterprises according to some concrete criterion. Exhibit 1.2 illustrates how the individual retailer enjoys the benefits of differential congruence. Firm A has a limited differential advantage reflected in its demand, which has a limited slope. Firm B, on the other hand, has a substantially greater differential advantage, which again, is reflected by the very steep demand curve. As can be seen, all things being equal, Firm B has a substantially more favorable profit picture. In both cases, the firms are selling the same amount, OM = OM' However, L'N'P'Q' area is greater than LNPQ which reflect the total profit picture for firm B. The slope of the demand curve for B is the measure of its monopoly power, which is created by its ability to

Exhibit 1.2
The Payoff of Competitive Advantage

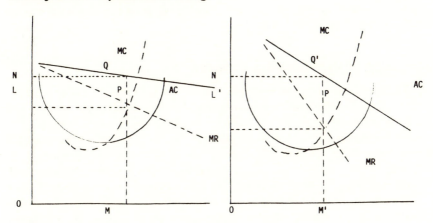

generate differential congruence and therefore to gain advantage over competitors.

This type of economic advantage or competitive superiority over competition is the outcome of successful retail marketing strategy. Although a small women's clothing chain may position itself as an upscale specialty store, emphasizing high fashions and charging relatively high prices, a discount chain such as Wal-Mart can prosper strictly by locating in small rural communities which other merchants or major chains have basically avoided (*Wall Street Journal*, July 2, 1984; Berman and Evans 1986). In both cases retail strategy has paid off handsomely.

GEOGRAPHIC DIMENSION

The fourth level of retail competition as shown earlier in Exhibit 1.1 is the geographic dimension. Spatial dimension can easily be used as a key contributor to the total differential congruence mix. The advantages of spatial dimension can be analyzed at three distinct levels: location of town, location of the shopping complex, and location of the store.

Location of Town

Elsewhere in this book, outshopping patterns are discussed. On the basis of outshopping patterns, a retail establishment could be in an advantageous position. If, for instance, satisfaction with local shopping facilities is so great that outshopping is not a widespread occurrence, then any and all retail establishments in that community have a built-in differential congruence over the stores outside of that community. This is so because residents in that community are loyal to shopping facilities in that area. Similarly, of course, people may be quite unhappy with the choice, service, prices, and so on, of the retail establishments located in town. Thus, they may go out of town to shop.

Location of the Shopping Complex

The spatial advantage is more pronounced when a clear-cut patronage preference is exhibited toward a given shopping complex regardless of whether it is a local shopping center, a local cluster, a mall, or a downtown. If people, for whatever reason, like going to the stores in that complex and are loyal to that complex, this loyalty will spill over to any specific store that happens to be located in that particular area where the preferred shopping complex is located. Thus, a retail establishment may have an advantage over its competition. In such circumstances, it is almost a forgone conclusion that the retail establishment will prefer locating in such a complex. Location in itself could provide a substantial degree of market superiority through the guise of differential congruence.

The retail location options are multiple and variable. Not only are there spectra regarding the general location such as county or central city, but also there are options regarding being in a planned or unplanned retail facility or being in a solo location. A systematic diagram of location options is presented in Exhibit 1.3. The illustration is quite comprehensive and self-explanatory. Needless to say, no single most ideal location option exists. The degree of differential advantage afforded by location depends on how adequate the location decision was regarding the capabilities, needs, basic functions, and intended image of the proposed store. The strengths and weaknesses of each alternative in Exhibit 1.3 can be found in any basic retailing book (Mason and Mayer 1984; Berman and Evans 1986, etc.). Perhaps the most important aspect of Exhibit 1.3 is the existence of numerous location options for the retailer. It must be emphasized that a retail store has these options not only at the beginning but also throughout its life. Whereas one type of location is appropriate at the beginning, the store may need a different location later. The retailer must assess the situation and periodically make location decisions as to whether to move to another location or stay in the same place.

Location of the Store

In addition to the town and the shopping complex, the specific location of the store can generate competitive advantage. A neighborhood drug store or an ice cream parlor are typical examples. Precisely because of their favorable location, these stores, even though they may have no other distinguishing characteristics, may yield substantial profits. Any store in retailing whose location satisfies its target markets is bound to develop a competitive advantage.

Exhibit 1.3
Major Location Options in Retailing

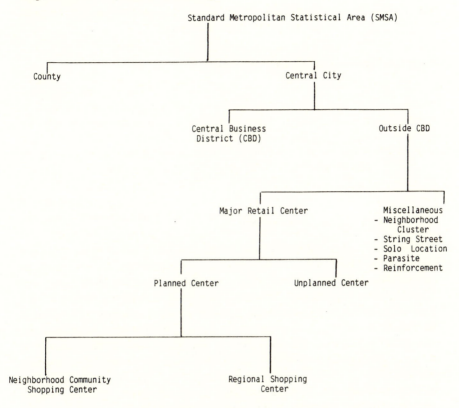

Source: Adapted and revised from Mason and Mayer 1984.

Thus, the spatial dimension of retailing could yield differential congruence in a trickle-down manner from general to specific or from the town or city to the specific site. It is almost impossible to dissect this trickle effect and to analyze or measure each factor as a separate entity. Therefore, as can be seen, the differential advantage leading to a differential congruence that is created by the spatial dimension is in itself a multiple factor phenomenon.

Ability to locate wisely can be a very critical factor in overall retailing strategy and an important explanation of success. Many major retail chains, for example, Kroger's, Sears, or International House of Pancakes, follow specific location formulas. Holiday Inns are very successful in locating their hotels in good locations. It has been stated that Econo-Travels or Econo-Lodges just follow Holiday Inns and whenever possible locate next door to them.

Exhibit 1.4
Retail Strategy Mixes of Food Retailers[a]

Type of Retailer	Location	Product	Service	Promotion	Price
Convenience Store	+	-	-	-	-
Supermarket	+	+	-	+	+
Combination Store	-	+	-	+	+
Superstore	-	+	-	+	+
Box (Limited Line) Store	+	-	-	-	++
Warehouse Store	-	-	-	-	++

[a](+) indicates special strengths and points of emphasis in retail strategy mixes. (−) indicates neutrality or even a liability in the retail strategy mixes. However, these negative signs also imply substantial cost savings, part of which (or all of which) can be passed on to the consumer.

OTHER RETAIL INSTITUTIONS

Interinstitutional competition, and hence changes in retail population, are discussed elsewhere in this book. Suffice it to say here that as other types of new retail establishments emerge, they create keen competition for existing retail establishments. Five specific theories of change in institutional structure have been identified in retailing literature: (1) the wheel of retailing, (2) the retail accordion, (3) the dialectic process, (4) the adaptive behavior model (natural selection), and (5) retail life cycle (Mason and Mayer 1984). Although there is no one universal theory of change in retailing institutional structure, no doubt the new retail institutions create a substantial degree of competition, which in turn forces the existing institutions to attempt to acquire more differential advantage. Exhibit 1.4 illustrates various types of food retailers. As can be seen, their varying and unique characteristics function as differential advantage. Needless to say, conventional supermarkets and superettes must retaliate somehow if they are to maintain their relative market position. The retaliation may be in terms of their performing more of the same functions and better.

INTRAINSTITUTIONAL COMPETITION

Level 2 in Exhibit 1.1 is related to competition among retail institutions at the same level. At a given time, in any medium- or large-size town or city, many retail establishments are quite similar. K-Mart and Woolworth's or Sears and Montgomery Ward are quite similar retail institutions. While Sears and Ward's are department stores, K-Mart and Woolworth's are discount department stores.

Department stores compete among themselves and strive for competitive advantage. Intrainstitutional competition takes four distinctly different patterns: imitation, deviation, complementation, and innovation.

Imitation

Many retail establishments consider, first and foremost, carrying basic inventories similar to those of their immediate competitors. If one were to analyze the depth and breadth of inventories carried by, say, Woolworth's and K-Mart, there would likely be no significant difference. In retailing competition, a "basic" inventory that will appeal to the "core" market is essential. Naturally, especially for larger retailers, these core markets are similar; hence, the overlap in merchandise and service mixes becomes logical.

Many small retailers are also engaged in competition through imitation. In this case, imitation is more readily related to lack of segmentation or lack of information regarding relative target markets to which individual retailers are catering. In either case, it is easier and "may" feel safer to imitate and compete in that way rather than by using other measures of competition.

Deviation

Even those who are competing primarily through imitation at the fringe (as opposed to the core which is taken care of by imitation) of the market will deviate from each other. Most retail stores in the similar areas dealing with similar markets deviate somewhat either in their product–service–price mixes or in their total image-building efforts. Although Sears and Ward's may overlap in 80 percent of their total efforts, media mixes, and product-service-price mixes, at least that 20 percent distinguishes the two. In fact, that is how they manage to have their own particular clientele.

Complementation

Certain consumer goods are sold most readily as greater choice is offered to the consumer. This principle is particularly applicable to shopping goods. Consumers have greater alternatives inasmuch as the choice is greater; thus, they will be attracted to shop more readily. As a result, if shopping goods are located near each other they will attract more demand. In this particular process, some retailers may consider using complementation. A "Tie Rack" store may be located adjacent to a store that sells shirts and ties. But the store offers a greater choice of ties and hence complements the other store's tie offering. Complementary competition also sets in as they compete and complement shirts as a special competitive line.

Innovation

Retail establishments compete with immediate competitors, not only by being similar to or different from them but also by being innovative in generating differential advantage. In addition to new ways of handling merchandise or serving customers, retail establishments through unique image management efforts compete more effectively. Pizza Hut's pan pizza or McDonald's Eggs McMuffin are examples of innovative competition. This kind of competition may be costlier than the other three types discussed thus far. Even so, it can also be more effective than the others in generating differential advantage.

COMPETITION THROUGH RETAILING MIX

In the Introduction, Exhibit I.3 illustrates three types of mixes: goods and services, communications, and pricing. The exhibit also illustrates the key elements of each of these three mixes. Most retail stores compete through any and all of these mixes and their components. Competition of this type leading to differential advantage is considered to be competition at level 1 which is the grass-roots level. Here the competition is specific, and differential advantage is detailed. If a retail store wants to develop differential advantage by using the goods and services mix, it will have to offer specific goods and services that are to be known by the market and well received. These goods and services will generate differential advantage in the direction of generating differential congruence and distinguishing the store from the rest.

TWO STRUCTURAL THEORIES

In order to understand retail competition, it is necessary to develop a structural construct of retail establishments. Two distinct and important attempts are discussed here: (1) Gist's margin–turnover classification and (2) Hirschman's principle of natural dominance. These two approaches attempt to explain retail structure, which in turn further explains the retail competitive picture.

Gist's Margin–Turnover Classification

Ronald Gist (1968) introduced a general framework to examine the retail structure so that its competitive nature could be better understood and utilized for strategy formulation. Gist defined margin as a percentage markup which the investor in a store is sold, and turnover as the number of times the average inventory is sold in a given year. On the basis of margin–turnover relationships, retail establishments can be divided into four distinct categories: high margin–high turnover stores, high margin–low turnover stores, low margin–high turnover stores, and low margin–low turnover stores.

All retail stores fall into one of these four categories. As a retail outlet is placed in its proper quadrant in Exhibit 1.5, it can be described in regards to retail strategies at the store level which must be followed in serving the store's particular market. As can be seen, the strategies depend on the quadrant in which the retail store is most likely to be located. The major retail strategies at the store level are discussed in Exhibit 1.6. The retail strategies at the store level

Exhibit 1.5
Margin–Turnover Classification

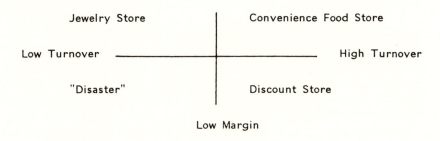

High Margin

Jewelry Store	Convenience Food Store
Low Turnover	High Turnover
"Disaster"	Discount Store

Low Margin

Source: Mason and Mayer 1984:42.

Exhibit 1.6
Store-Level Strategic Characteristics of the Two Extreme Margin–Turnover Classification Stores

Store Level Strategy Element	Low Margin–High Turnover Stores	High Margin–Low Turnover Stores
Merchandise	Mostly pre-sold or self-sold	Sold in store
Services Offered	Few or "optional charge"	Many services
Location	Isolated	Cluster or Shopping Center
Organizational Character	Simple	Complex
Assortment	Large	Smaller
Prices	Small	Larger
	Below the Market	Above the Market
Promotion	Emphasizing Price	Institutional or Merchandise Oriented

Source: Partially adapted from Mason and Mayer 1984.

are based on merchandise sold, varieties and assortments offered, services provided, price level, type of personal selling, type of promotion, complexity of organizational structure, and locational requirements (Mason and Mayer 1984; Gist 1968). Retail strategies are contrasted as follows.

The low margin/high turnover retail establishment implies customers' buying in the store, whereas the high margin/low turnover store customers are presold. Thus, in the low margin/high turnover store low prices are the most important patronage determinant. In the high margin/low turnover counterpart, on the other hand, services, distinctive merchandise, and skills as well as the personalities of the salespeople are the most important patronage factors (Mason and Mayer 1984; Gist 1968).

Hirschman's Natural Dominance Theory

Elizabeth Hirschman's concept of retail structure, natural dominance, provides further insight into explaining retail competition. The primary characteristics of this theory are discussed in the sections below (Hirschman 1979; Hirschman 1978–1979; Mason and Mayer 1984). The theory is based on the premise that general merchandise retailers can be grouped into three different categories: (1) traditional reputable department stores such as Marshall Field's; (2) national chain department stores such as Montgomery Ward's; and (3) full-line discount department stores, such as K-Mart or Woolworth's. These types of stores are present in all major competitive markets (see Hirschman 1979). Traditionally, the stores in the first group cater to local markets. They are rather independent or regional chains (e.g., J. L. Hudson's); as such, they are flexible and respond very quickly to changing conditions in the environment. They thrive on extensive customer service, store credit, and quality brand merchandise.

The second group of stores, on the other hand, is mostly controlled centrally. Their marketing programs are developed and administered on a national basis. Hence, they are not very flexible at the local level. They emphasize store brands heavily, and their promotional activity is heavily dependent on the use of national media.

The third group of stores is designed to facilitate customer self-service. They are built and laid out inexpensively, and most of the time they have ample parking. Typically, they are free-standing institutions; as such, they are built in lower price land areas and do not have many stores around them. Their merchandise is primarily national brands. They minimize customer services.

The crux of Hirschman's theory is that these three types of department stores can be put on a price/quality continuum (Exhibit 1.7). In the consumer's eye, these store offerings have distinguished themselves in terms of different levels of quality and price. Stores in each group offer ''concentrated variety'' in the multiple merchandise lines they carry. This concentrated variety is seen as the primary advantage of department stores over specialty stores such as Charles Jourdan or Thom McAn.

Specialty stores, on the other hand, offer classification dominance in one merchandise category. Hirschman maintains that specialty stores are also placed on the same price-quality continuum as department stores. As seen in Exhibit 1.8, specialty stores are placed on the price-quality continuum in terms of three levels. This three-retail structural mix is a stable retail system. If Cartier's, Charles Jourdan, or Tiffany's were to be located adjacent to K-Mart or if K-Mart in addition to its regular lines were to carry the lines typically carried by these stores, there would be a structural inconsistency and therefore instability.

According to this theory, in addition to *concentrated variety* across a number of merchandise lines, each of the three department store types achieves a *unique classification dominance* through a smaller set of merchandise. Thus, the three types of department stores form the ''locus of merchandise control'' in any

Exhibit 1.7
The Price-Quality Continuum

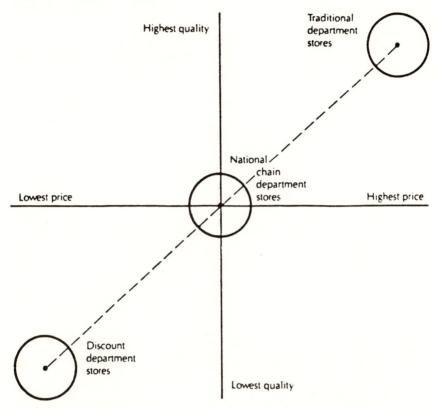

Source: Hirschman 1979: 401.

market because they simultaneously present both concentrated variety and classification dominance. The classification dominance by the department stores is based primarily on consumer perception of economic and social risks in their respective merchandise classification. This merchandise line control based on merchandise classification of each group of department stores is shown in Exhibit 1.9.

The perceived risk and the price–sensitive or quality–conscious nature of consumers will create an intensive competition concentrated within the three levels of the price–quality continuum. The competition will be substantially less intense along the continuum. The intensive intralevel competition gives each type of department store a certain type of demand-generated monopoly with given price points, quality levels, and merchandise lines. Hirschman (1979) terms the formation of this particular monopoly the principle of natural dominance. Thus, each of the three types of department stores is more supportive of

Exhibit 1.8
Retail Market Structure

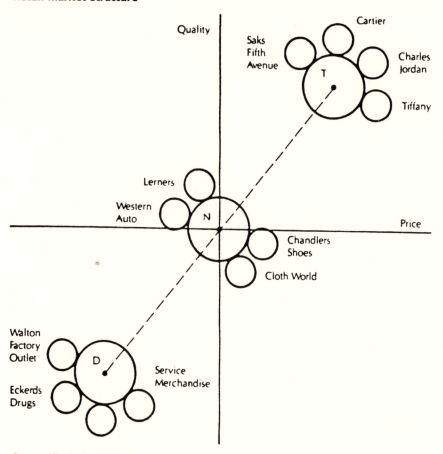

Source: Hirschman 1979: 401.

and complementary with other types than competitive, inasmuch as their sphere of dominance is in noncompeting merchandise lines, and they are differentiated on the basis of price and quality. Thus, it appears that K-Mart is competing with Woolworth's, but it is not necessarily creating a competition for, say, Bullocks or J. L. Hudson's. Hirschman's theory has additional far-reaching implications for retail competition. It is not only the department store that creates natural dominance, but also the types of specialty stores they attract. K-Mart, for example, is likely to attract Eckerds Drugs, Pic 'n' Pay Shoes, and perhaps Lowe's Foods. Thus, the natural dominance based on classification dominance and concentrated variety is likely to be the total offering of a shopping complex. However, as was mentioned earlier, if Cartier's, Charles Jourdan, or Tiffany's were

Exhibit 1.9
Perceived Risk Influence on Merchandise Line Classification Dominance

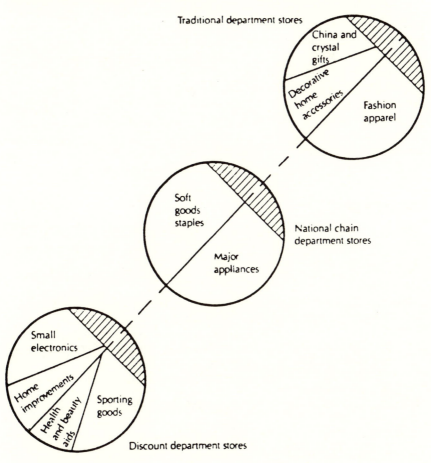

Source: Hirschman 1979: 403.

to be located in the same shopping cluster along with K-Mart or Woolworth's, then the natural dominance would be overshadowed by the diminished classification dominance and concentrated variety. The results are likely to be rather detrimental.

The natural dominance theory, therefore, presents not only an interesting picture of retail competition, but also some key location decision principles. If the natural dominance cannot be preserved or the classification dominance is not likely to be enhanced, the specialty store may not locate in the proposed site next to one of the three types of department stores.

SUMMARY

This chapter presents a theory of retail competition. The crux of retail competition is the search for and achievement of differential congruence, which begins with differential advantage. Differential advantage is achieved by being a more competitive retailer. Retail competition is a multidimensional and multilayered phenomenon.

Five specific layers and various dimensions within layers are identified and discussed. After a discussion of five specific layers—(1) nature of market competition, (2) geographic dimension, (3) other retail institutions, (4) retail establishment, and (5) components of retail mix, the chapter deals with structural theories of retail competition. The first theory is Gist's margin–turnover classification, and the second is Hirschman's principle of natural dominance.

REFERENCES

Alderson, Wroe. *Dynamic Marketing Behavior*. Homewood, Ill.: Richard D. Irwin, 1965.
———. *Marketing Behavior and Executive Action*. Homewood, Ill.: Richard D. Irwin, 1957.
Berman, Berry, and Joel R. Evans. *Retail Management*. 3rd ed. New York: Macmillan, 1986.
Chamberlain, Ed. *Monopolistic Competition*. Boston: Harvard University Press, 1973.
Gist, Ronald R. *Retailing*. New York: John Wiley, 1968.
Hirschman, Elizabeth C. "Retail Competitive Structure: Present and Potential." In Neil Beckwith et al., eds., *1970 Educators Conference Proceedings*. Chicago: American Marketing Association, 1979, pp. 401–405.
———. "A Descriptive Theory of Retail Market Structure." *Journal of Retailing* (Winter 1978–1979): 29–48.
Mason, J. Barry, and Morris Mayer. *Modern Retailing*. Plains, Tex.: Business Publications, 1984.
"Rural Retailing Chains Prosper by Combining Service and Sophistication." *Wall Street Journal* (July 2, 1984): 1, 12.

2 Major Trends in Retail Population

The retailing sector is very dynamic. There are rapid changes not only in the institutional makeup of retail establishments, but also in their actual characteristics in terms of their size and number, as well as entries and exits. This chapter first discusses the trends in this sector in terms of numbers, sizes, and efficiency factors, and second, examines the factors that influence or cause these trends.

Perhaps the most spectacular development in retailing has been in its numbers vis-à-vis the total population. Exhibit 2.1 shows that from 1929 to 1977 the number of retail establishments per 1,000 population fell from 12.13 to 8.70. This number declined further in 1982. As can be seen, the decrease has been steady and there is no evidence that it will stop at its 1982 level. Later in this chapter we show that as the retail establishments are growing and multiunits are taking up a larger proportion of total retail sales, small independent retailers are disappearing. Therefore, the number of retail establishments is expected to decline further in terms of stores per 1,000 population.

This decline is not in terms of total numbers, however. Since 1963 there has been a net increase of 222,100 retail establishments. The retail establishments that existed as of 1982, on the average, are larger than those that existed in 1963 (Exhibit 2.2). Whereas, on the average, a retail establishment sold $143,000 worth of merchandise in 1963, the same retail establishment sold $554,000 worth in 1980. Thus, average size of retail establishments based on sales volume has increased steadily.

Similarly, sales per capita have also gone up—from 1,290.69 in 1963 to 3,391.81 in 1977. This growth has continued. This figure was substantially higher in 1984 than in 1977 (Exhibit 2.3). The decrease of retail establishments per 1,000 population does not imply the retailing sector's service to the populace.

Exhibit 2.1
Retail Establishments per 1,000 Population

Year	Est. Per 1,000
1929	12.13
1948	12.11
1958	10.36
1963	9.31
1972	8.72
1977	8.70
1982	8.29

Source: Computed from U.S. Bureau of the Census data.

Exhibit 2.2
Sales per Establishment

Year	Establishment	Sales	Sales/Establishment
1963	1,707,900	$ 244,200,000,000	$ 142,982
1967	1,763,000	310,214,000,000	175,958
1972	1,780,000	457,400,000,000	256,970
1977	1,855,068	723,134,221,000	389,815
1982	1,923,000	1,065,900,000,000	554,290

Source: Computed from U.S. Bureau of the Census data.

Perhaps a case can also be made that, by becoming somewhat larger, retail establishments have also become more efficient, which also implies an improvement in the service provided for consumers.

The portion of retailing that is attributable to the efforts of corporate entities has also grown substantially. While the share of corporations accounted for 61.9 percent of the total in 1963, this figure went up to 79.8 percent in 1977 (Exhibit 2.4). This portion continued growing, reaching 84.6 percent in 1982. During the same period, the number of corporate entities as a percentage of the total number of retailing institutions also went up. Whereas 22.3 percent of all retailers were corporate entities in 1963, in 1977 this number was 37.5 percent (Exhibit 2.5). This growth trend continued and reached 42.7 percent in 1982.

Until the early 1960s multiunit retail establishments had been gaining larger proportions of total retail sales volume. By 1972 multiunits accounted for 44

Exhibit 2.3
Per Capita Sales

Year	Population	Sales	Sales/Capita
1963	189,200,000	$ 244,200,000,000	$ 1,290
1967	198,700,000	310,214,000,000	1,561
1972	204,056,000	459,040,000,000	2,249
1977	213,180,000	723,134,221,000	3,391
1982	232,100,000	1,037,727,788,000	4,471
1983	234,000,000	1,174,300,000,000	5,018
1984	336,200,000	1,297,000,000,000	5,491

Source: Computed from data presented in different issues of U.S. Statistical Abstracts.

Exhibit 2.4
Corporate Sales

Year	Total Sales	Corporate Sales	As % of Total
1963	$244,200,000,000	$ 130,732,800,000	61.9%
1967	310,214,000,000	211,780,240,000	67.4%
1972	457,400,000,000	350,706,560,000	76.4%
1977	723,134,221,000	576,853,514,000	79.8%
1982	1,037,727,788,000	901,987,375,000	84.6%

Source: Different issues of U.S. Statistical Abstracts.

percent of all retail sales. Their share went up to 47 percent in 1977 and to 53 percent in 1982 (Exhibit 2.6). The sales volume per establishment for single units showed a slow but steady increase from $100,000 in 1963 to $317,877 in 1982 (Exhibit 2.7). It appears that single units maintained a steady increase in sales per store by letting the number of stores decrease substantially. By 1982 a net loss of more than 100,000 single retail establishments was experienced (Exhibit 2.7). Exhibit 2.8 illustrates how the number of single unit retailers has gone down while the number of multiunits increased.

The trends indicate that the retail giants have grown even larger during recent years. Companies with sales of over $1 billion per year accounted for 51.6 percent of total retail sales in 1975. This share went up to 55 percent in 1978

Exhibit 2.5
Corporate Establishments

Year	Total Establishments	Corporate Establishments	% of Total
1963	1,707,900	380,860	22.3%
1967	1,763,000	451,050	25.6%
1972	1,913,000	565,970	29.6%
1977	1,855,068	695,440	37.5%
1982	1,923,000	820,538	42.7%

Source: Computed from different issues of Census of Retailing.

Exhibit 2.6
Multiunits

Year	Multi-Units Total Establishments	Multi-Unit Sales	Sales per Est.
1963	220,000	$ 90,000,000,000	409,000
1967	220,000	123,000,000,000	557,000
1972	291,000	201,000,000,000	690,000
1977	331,697	340,650,130,000	1,027,013
1982	415,000	567,000,000,000	1,366,300

Source: Computed from U.S. Bureau of the Census data.

and reached 59 percent in 1982. Discount stores showed a remarkable growth pattern in terms of their average size. Their sales volume reached 7 million in 1984. The average store size also increased (Exhibit 2.9).

The relative share of department store sales of total retail sales volume remained steady at around 10 percent between 1967 and 1982. However, the growth in the sales volume of department stores increased at a decreasing rate until 1976 (Exhibit 2.10). This trend reversed itself after that date. In 1982 a 62-percent increase was reported over the previous period. The growth rate of department store sales during 1976–1982 was more than twice the 1967–1976 rate.

Department stores also showed a relatively steady picture of employment. In 1963 they accounted for around 13 percent of total retail employment. Considering the increasing sales volume of the total retailing sector as well as department

Exhibit 2.7
Single Units

Year	Single-Units Total Establishments	Single-Unit Sales	Sales per Est.
1963	1,488,000	$ 149,946,000,000	$ 100,000
1967	1,543,000	187,000,000,000	122,000
1972	1,622,000	256,600,000,000	158,200
1977	1,523,000	369,314,983,000	242,432
1982	1,508,159	479,409,585,000	317,877

Source: Different issues of Census of Retailing.

Exhibit 2.8
Percentage Changes in Number of Establishments

Years	Multi-Units	Single-Units	Total Est.
1963 to 1967	0.0%	3.7%	3.2%
1967 to 1972	32.3%	5.1%	8.5%
1972 to 1977	13.7%	-6.5%	-3.1%
1977 to 1982	14.0%	-5.4%	.4%

Source: U.S. Statistical Abstracts, 1987.

Exhibit 2.9
Average Size and Sales Volume of Discounters

	Sales (000)	Aver. Size
1981	5,752,598	63,176 sq. ft.
1982	5,862,056	63,118 sq. ft.
1983	6,533,521	64,651 sq. ft.
1984	7,118,771	64,874 sq. ft.

Source: Discount Merchandiser, May 1985, p. 58.

Exhibit 2.10
Department Store Sales

Year	Department Store Sales	As percent of Total Retail Sales	Percent Growth Over Previous Time Period
1967	$ 32,344,000,000	10.42	
1972	46,302,000,000	10.08	43.15
1974	55,855,000,000	10.78	20.63
1976	66,200,000,000	11.02	18.52
1982	107,082,582,000	10.32	61.76
1983	116,600,000,000	9.96	
1984	129,300,000,000	9.95	

Sales growth from 1967 to 1976......................... 104.67

Sales growth from 1976 to 1982......................... 231.07

Sales growth from 1982 to 1983......................... 8.89

Sales growth from 1983 to 1984......................... 10.89

Source: Computed from different issues of Census of Retailing and U.S. Statistical Abstracts.

stores, this may indicate that efficiency measured by sales per employee has increased (Exhibit 2.11).

Discount stores' relative share of the total number of retail establishments as well as total retail sales volume has gone up substantially. This indicates a trend toward the strengthening position of discount stores (Exhibit 2.12).

Many retail establishments deal with services which is one aspect of retailing. Of all the service establishments, perhaps eating and drinking establishments are the most important. Thus, we present some information here on the performance of this sector.

During the 1963–1982 period, eating and drinking places increased in absolute numbers as well as in terms of relative share of total retail establishments. From a total of 231,591 eating and drinking establishments reported in 1963, an increase to 368,066 was reported in 1977 (Exhibit 2.13). This number declined slightly in 1982. Nonetheless, eating and drinking places captured a larger portion of total retail establishments in 1982 (Exhibit 2.13). Not only did their numbers increase, but also their sales volume increased more than threefold during the same period (Exhibit 2.14). With the increased leisure time and pressures from having two-paycheck families, eating out activity has increased substantially faster than other aspects of retailing.

Exhibit 2.11
Department Store Employment

Year	Total Retail Trade Employment	Department Store Employment	As % of Total
1967	10,081,000	1,324,000	13.13%
1972	11,705,000	1,594,000	13.62%
1974	12,751,000	1,769,000	13.87%
1976	12,834,000	1,658,000	12,91%
1977	12,968,000	1,519,000	11.71%
1982	14,468,000	1,515,000	10.47%

Exhibit 2.12
Discount Store Sales

Year	Total Establishments	Sales
1964	2,951	$10.8 bill.
1968	4,280	19.4
1972	5,928	29.0
1974	6,295	31.4
1976	6,827	36.1
1978	7,707	44.3
1984	8,738	62.2

Source: *Discount Merchandiser*, various issues.

KEY FACTORS BEHIND THE TRENDS

Many important factors underlie the trends and patterns in the retailing sector. These factors are responsible for shaping not only the trends thus far, but also the future of the whole retailing sector. These factors can be divided into two categories: external and internal (Exhibit 2.15).

External Factors

The five factors identified here are prime movers of retailing patterns and practices. They are: (1) changing competition, (2) changing consumer needs, (3) sociological factors, (4) economic conditions, and (5) political considerations.

Exhibit 2.13
Eating and Drinking Establishments as a Percentage of Total Retail Establishments

Year	Total Retail Establishments	Eating and Drinking Establishments	% of Total
1963	1,707,900	231,591	13.56%
1967	1,763,000	206,740	14.79%
1972	1,780,000	329,230	18.50%
1977	1,855,068	368,066	19.84%
1982	1,923,000	318,765	16.58%

Source: Calculated from data presented in various issues of U.S. Statistical Abstracts.

Exhibit 2.14
Eating and Drinking Establishment Sales

Year	Number of Establishments	Sales	Sales per Establishment
1963	231,591	$ 20,291,000,000	$ 87,615
1967	260,740	23,843,000,000	91,443
1972	329,230	33,891,000,000	102,940
1977	368,066	63,275,673,000	174,912
1982	318,765	104,400,000,000	328,300
1984	375,170	124,100,000,000	330,780

Source: Computed from data presented in various issues of U.S. Statistical Abstracts.

Changing Competition

Retail competition has been changing along many dimensions, three of which are spatial, institutional, and functional.

Spatial dimensions of retailing competition imply primarily that retailing has to follow population. As people move from urban to suburban areas or from countryside to the city, retailing must also be able to do so. The most specific aspect of spatial retail competition has been in the area of downtown versus suburban shopping centers. This important topic is discussed in greater detail in Chapter 3. This competition has had a far-reaching impact on retailing structure and practice.

Institutional dimensions of retail competition are depicted in numerous ways, some of which are discussed earlier in this chapter. Large enterprises have pushed

Exhibit 2.15
Factors Influencing Retail Population Changes and Theories of Retail Institutional Changes

External Factors

1. Changing Competition
2. Changing Consumer Needs-changing Lifestyles
3. Sociological Factors
4. Economic Conditions
5. Political Considerations
    a. Taxation
    b. Small Business Assistance
    c. Antibusiness Sentiment

Internal Factors

1. Undercapitalization
2. Poor Management
3. Inadequate Marketing Strategy
4. Inadequate Information
5. Poor Location

Theories of Institutional Changes

1. The Wheel of Retailing
2. Natural Selection
3. The General Specific General Cycle
4. The Dialectic Process
5. The Retail Life Cycle
6. The Markin-Duncan Adaptation Theory

small retailers out of existence or have forced them to find new ways of functioning so that they could survive. The corporate entity appeared to be stronger in terms of ability to survive; it appeared to force other retailers out of existence. For a long while Multiunit establishments captured larger proportions of total retail business at the expense of single-unit firms.

For many years, department stores carried a larger portion of total retail business. This situation continued until discount stores emerged. Strong competition has arisen between these two, and the expected outcome is to serve the consumer better.

The third dimension of retail competition—the functional dimension—has taken two distinct paths. The first is nonprice competition, and the second is price competition. Nonprice competition has led retailing to develop multitudinous functional practices that have made it easier and more pleasant to shop and buy in retail establishments. Among these are special customer services, store layout and proper signs for making shopping easier, background music, wall-to-wall carpeting, special displays, special emphasis on certain brands, air conditioning, store's own brands, and product line and merchandise mix. All of these are components of the store image which in turn provides the competitive advantage the retail store is seeking. Price competition, on the other hand, implies that, rather than other features, the store tries to establish its competitive advantage by offering better prices than those of the competitors.

Changing Consumer Needs

Changing consumer needs are reflected in changing consumption patterns. There are several reasons why consumption patterns have changed, including economic conditions, education, lifestyles, leisure-time activities, and changing values.

During the past decade or so, economic conditions have had a significant impact on consumption patterns. First, because of inflation, consumers' discretionary income shrank. As a result, some of the necessities were emphasized in purchases, for example, food, medicine, and basic apparel. There has been some decline in gift items, entertainment, eating, and other selected services. Thus, some retail businesses have suffered either losses or nonincreases in their sales. Second, because of high unemployment levels among the segments of our society where income became relatively low, retailing concentrated even more specifically on basics.

The average education in the United States has increased. Today more people have a college education than ever before, and with more education consumption patterns have changed. Studies have shown that higher levels of education have brought emphasis on housing, entertainment, and food rather than on automobiles and apparel. Similarly, higher education means higher personal income, which also would have direct impact on consumption patterns.

Lifestyles in terms of activities, interests, and opinions (AIO) are changing and are reflecting changes in consumption patterns. Cosmopolitans or jet-setters reflect specific consumption patterns that specify certain needs.

Americans have more leisure than ever before, and as their leisure time has increased, demand for certain types of leisure time and entertainment activities has also increased. Expenditures on sporting goods, hobby-related products, and other recreation-related activities have made a significant dent in the changing consumption patterns.

Finally, in time values change. When American values changed during the past quarter of a century, significant changes in consumption patterns were observed. During that time Americans became more aware of body weight, and became more do-it-yourself types, more informal, more time conscious, and, hence, perhaps more efficient and less work-oriented. As a result of these changes in values, too-fattening products lost their market position, and more products hit the market which could be assembled at home such as automobiles and TV sets. Similarly, linen table cloths, cloth napkins, and other formal products faced a substantial decline in demand. Finally, more efficient products became more popular, for example, jet planes as opposed to propeller planes.

All of these changes in consumer needs have led to changing consumption patterns. Needless to say, as consumption patterns changed, some aspects of retailing gained power at the expense of others.

Sociological Factors

Sociological factors may be categorized as the movement of people and the characteristics of people.

Americans are almost always on the move. It has been estimated that one-fifth of all Americans move every year. The movement has been from rural to urban and from urban to suburban areas. Similarly, the population center has been moving westward. Another trend is from north to south. In all of these cases, if retailing does not or cannot follow the population movement it cannot succeed. In the past, studies have indicated a high correlation between the number of enterprises and population. Although no recent data are available in this particular area, it would be easy to claim that there would be no significant difference between the past and present relationships.

Economic Conditions

Economic conditions affect retail population in at least two ways. The first is through business cycle development, and the second is through the cost of doing business based on specific economic requirements.

Business cycle development has profound impact on business failures and business discontinuances (Samli 1964). Most of the business failures and business discontinuances are retailers. Therefore, the same relationships prevail between business cycles and the retail sector. Research has shown that business failures increase during recessions and decrease during booms. In a less than perfectly competitive economic system, since it is not possible to guarantee that those who fail are inefficient, the increased failure rate does not imply any improvement in the efficiency of the retail sector. However, regardless of the efficiency factor, retail establishments fail or discontinue at substantial rates. Thus, many retailers disappear, and others appear as the economy experiences ups and downs.

Retailers' cost of doing business has gone up steadily and sharply. Much of this increase can be attributed to a number of economic factors, including rental costs, labor costs, minimum wages, costs of larger inventories necessary for modern-day competition, and costs of developing and maintaining a modern store. Modern retailers find themselves obligated to run stores in good locations with all the modern features that appeal to certain appropriate market segments. Many retailers, particularly small retailers, do not own their building and their land. Much of the land and buildings is owned by absentee owners who seldom care about the retailer's well-being. Thus, rental costs have been going up steadily.

As retailing has become more sophisticated and demanding, its labor costs have also risen. Unionization of retail employees has proven especially costly to the retail sector.

Almost by definition modern retailers have to carry larger inventories with greater depth and breadth than ever before. One reason why inventories have expanded is that the average consumer is utilizing a greater variety of products.

Finally, modern retailers are being forced to offer various services as well as making sure that their stores have certain specific features. Modern retailers provide services such as liberal return policy, credit, free delivery, packaging, and free information. In addition, many of them have to develop an elaborate internal layout so that customers can find their way around the store. Air conditioning, background music, modern displays, and show windows are part of the total image building process.

Political Considerations

The political climate is an important determinant of retail population. Three considerations touching on political climate are taxation, small business assistance, and the general sentiment toward business.

Taxation and related practices such as licensing or fees charged to practice are all significant in terms of encouraging businesses to enter the market. A substantial increase in fees to practice downtown, for instance, may determine whether a retail establishment remains in the same location, relocates, or discontinues. In addition, some administrations in the past have used tax credit incentives to stimulate business. Such practices would encourage many small businesses and particularly small retailers to enter or to remain in the market.

Small business assistance could also have a strong effect on the shape and size of the retail population. Small business assistance could be government instigated, government operated, or privately encouraged. Typically, all three processes may take place simultaneously. When funds advice, and guidance are available for small businesses, the number of these businesses increases and their share of the market does not decline as quickly as it would otherwise.

Finally, antibusiness sentiment, in addition to taxation and assistance, could cause a hardship on business in general and on retailing in particular. Antibusiness sentiment could lead to anything from antibusiness legislation (including excessive regulation) to loss of good managerial talent to nonbusiness sectors.

It is not possible to isolate the impact of any one of the five external factors discussed thus far. Many of them function simultaneously and/or in conjunction with others. It must be reiterated that the aforementioned factors do not represent an exhaustive list. Certainly other factors could have a significant bearing on retail population. It has been stated, for instance, that when New York's dock workers went on a prolonged strike many businesses in Hawaii ceased to exist.

Internal Factors

In addition to external factors, certain internal factors may cause discontinuances or failures. Again, five factors will be discussed in this category: undercapitalization, poor management, poor marketing strategy, inadequate information, and poor location.

Undercapitalization is a common problem in retailing, particularly among small and medium retail establishments. Less than adequate capital typically leads to failure because, perhaps more than in other types of business, in retailing, if large profits are to be made, large sums of money need to be spent. Many small marginal retail operations fall in this category. Because of lack of capital, they are located in undesirable sites, and they have less than adequate stocks. They barely use promotion, and their stores lack necessary internal attractiveness or appeal.

Poor management also leads to disaster rather quickly. One of the major reasons for poor management is the freedom of entry. In conjunction with the "American dream" of being one's own boss, the retailing sector is perhaps the easiest to enter. As a result, freedom of exit also comes into play, and inexperienced and underprepared owner-managers mismanage and eventually fail.

Poor marketing strategy may also refer to nonexisting marketing strategy. Regardless of its size and kind, the retail establishment has to have an effective marketing strategy first for survival and then for growth and prosperity. Without a strategy, survival is a matter of chance. However, with a strategy, survival is not guaranteed. Only when the firm has a good marketing strategy is it in a position to insure survival.

Inadequate information on retailing, particularly in small retailing, has been a proverbial problem. The retailer, especially the small retailer, makes decisions on the basis of experience and hunches. Proper information based on research is almost nonexistent. Even when information is available, small retailers typically do not know how to use it. As a result, small retail decisions relating to marketing strategy are not based on factual information which increases the probability of making poor decisions.

Finally, poor location has an irreversible, negative impact on the well-being of the retail establishment. Since traffic is the backbone of retailing, a location that does not have the necessary traffic does not provide the retail establishment with a high probability of success. In addition, some locations are poor from the beginning, and others can become poor locations in time. For instance, the downtown becomes old and dilapidated, and some locations that were fashionable and popular at one time become quite undesirable as well. This process naturally causes many business failures and is eventually reflected in retail population patterns.

THEORIES OF RETAIL INSTITUTIONAL CHANGE

This chapter first singles out and discusses the factors that influence retail population changes; and second, examines the specific trends that have taken place during the past three decades or so. At a higher plateau, six theories have attempted to explain retail institutional changes (Gist 1968; Markin and Duncan

1981). These may also be called working hypotheses. In this context, the working hypothesis concept of course implies that it must be explored further. After being tested and retested, a working hypothesis becomes part of the theory and as such explains the retail institutional change. If this general explanation of such an important phenomenon were to be developed, then individual retail entrepreneurs or the managements of major retail establishments might consider their relative positions vis-à-vis the institutional change theories. They could decide that some major changes might have to take place if their respective retail establishments were to survive and prosper. Six working hypotheses of retail institutional change (Gist 1968) can be identified and further tested, namely, (1) the wheel of retailing, (2) natural selection in retail institutions, (3) the general–specific–general cycle, (4) the dialectic process, (5) the retail life cycle, and (6) the Markin-Duncan adaptation theory.

The Wheel of Retailing

Many years ago Stanley C. Hollander (1960) popularized the wheel of retailing concept which was originally conceived by M. P. McNaire (1958). This concept explains institutional changes in the retailing structure and, hence, indirectly explains some of the changes in the retail population. The wheel maintains that as new retail establishments emerge, they are characterized by low prices, low markup, few services, austere surroundings, and low status. These characteristics can be attributed to some new procedure or system for lowering or eliminating operating expenditures. As time passes, their competition increases, they start feeling the pressure to differentiate, and they trade up their goods and services. They become characterized by high prices, high markup, multiservice, expensive surroundings, and high status. This transition makes them quite vulnerable to new retail institutions. The history of retailing in our country indicates four such cycles. The first was marked by the demise of the general store with the entry of department stores (1880–1910); the second began with the entry of discount stores; the third with new types of discounters such as "buying services"; and finally, the fourth with the entry of super stores which are ongoing at the present time. Exhibit 2.16 portrays the wheel of American retailing. Studies indicate that parallels to the American experience may be found in other countries as well.

From the point of view of retail population, the wheel implies that regardless of external and internal factors the retail population will always undergo change. These changes are mainly due to the life cycle of retail institutions which implies that in time some retail institutions will become old and obsolete and new ones will emerge.

As Rom. J. Markin and Calvin P. Duncan (1981) suggest, three arguments in support of the wheel of retailing are (1) leadership senility, (2) excess capacity, and (3) market structure.

Leadership senility implies eroding leadership or competence. It indicates that

Exhibit 2.16
Wheel of Retailing in the United States

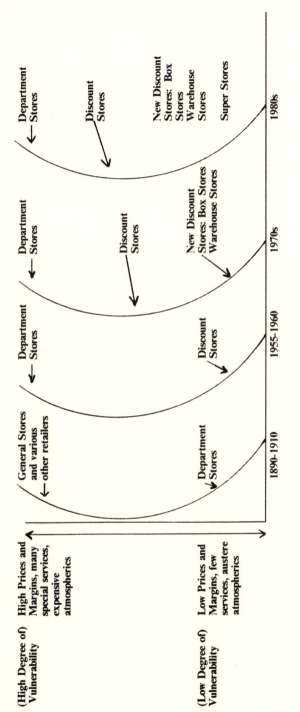

as new retail institutions emerge, they are led by cost-conscious, aggressive, and hard-working entrepreneurs who are motivated by profit maximization. They do not believe in unprofitable frills. As the new firms start entering the market, thinking changes. The original leaders relax their tight control over cost as they become richer and older. The new wave of leaders is less competent and aggressive (Markin and Duncan 1981).

The excess capacity concept is related to the ability to use plant capacity in early-growth years. As competition increases, this advantage gradually dissipates (McNair 1958). This condition can be considered to be an extension of the first condition of leadership incompetence. However, there has not been enough research in support of either condition.

Market structure is related to the fact that retailing reflects the market structure of monopolistic competition (Chamberlin 1977). In these markets the competitive emphasis is on nonprice activity. This nonprice competition forces operating expenses to rise and gross margins to increase further.

Natural Selection in Retailing

Charles Darwin's theory of natural selection has been widely recognized as the survival of the fittest. In retailing, according to this working hypothesis, retail institutions lose their relative position or disappear. The dilemma of the central business districts, or the relative decline of department stores or the disappearance of ''ma and pa'' stores, are all a function of shifting environmental conditions. The working hypothesis purports that no retail institution is sacred, that it cannot be affected by environmental changes, or it cannot disappear (Duncan 1965). The opposite of the working hypothesis also provides merit for the hypothesis itself. As Gist (1968) stated:

Clearly, those retail institutions that are keenly aware of their operating environment and which can also react without undue delay can both avoid the unfriendly elements in their environment and realize disproportionate gains from changes in the friendly elements in their environment (p. 87).

He continued:

All of this suggests that the successful retail operation should (a) hold all elements of the environment under regular scrutiny, and (b) embody the capability of quick reaction of both ''unfriendly'' environmental changes as well as ''friendly'' opportunities (p. 88).

The General–Specific–General Cycle (Gist 1968)

This working hypothesis maintains that American retailing vacillates from general to specific and to general again. For a period of time, consumers are predominantly served by general stores. Following that period, they are served by specialty stores and then again by the general. This sequence of events continues. Thus, the American retail system has undergone an era of an extremely wide variety of offerings by retailers. This era was followed by a period of great specialization and then a return to a wide variety of offerings (Hollander 1966). Gist (1968) states that a number of forces are stimulating the generalization end of the cycle. These are joining complementary lines (such as meat, grocery, and produce); creaming, which means taking "sure" merchandise from other stores; scrambling, which implies taking risky merchandise from other stores and adding full lines borrowed from other institutions; and, finally, the growth of shopping centers. However, with the rehabilitation of downtowns, the increasing energy crunch, and the growing emphasis on convenience, the specific end of the cycle may be recurring in the near future. The validity of this working hypothesis has not been tested further. However, with the emergence of boutiques and other highly specialized stores, the theory may be said to be supportable.

The Dialectic Process

The fourth working hypothesis is based on the Hegelian philosophy of dialectic logic, reinforced by Karl Marx's dialectical materialism. According to this philosophy, there are three sequences of events. First, a thesis develops (this may be a new retail institution); second, in time a position opposed to the thesis develops; and finally, there is a certain blending of the thesis and antithesis. The process does not stop with the synthesis. The synthesis of one phase becomes the thesis of a second phase and the process continues. According to this hypothesis, in retailing the process may be detected in the institutional makeup. When department stores emerged and got established (thesis), discount stores came into existence (antithesis). A few years later, discount stores began to resemble department stores and hence discount department stores emerged (synthesis).

These four working hypotheses are not mutually exclusive. All four may function under given circumstances. Much needs to be done in terms of quantifying and testing this working hypothesis.

The Retail Life Cycle

The fifth hypothesis is the retail life cycle concept (Davidson, Bates, and Bass 1976; Markin and Duncan 1981). The theory describes four stages. The first stage indicates the emergence of a new retail institution. This may be a sharp departure from existing retailing practices. The new institution may be able to increase efficiency or provide better customer satisfaction.

The second stage reflects the experience with high rates of growth in both sales volumes and profits. This stage is marked by widespread expansion into new markets, and many new entrants are attracted to different geographic areas. Toward the end of this stage, the favorable factors tend to be counterbalanced owing to increasing cost pressures because of the needed larger staff, more complex store management, more management controls, and other diseconomies of scale that emerge with size and greater number of stores.

In the third stage maturity sets in. Market shares decline and managers experience difficulties in managing and controlling their larger organizations. Managers lose the vitality and excitement of their organizations during the first two stages. They do not have the skills necessary to direct their large organizations (Davidson, Bates, and Bass 1976). By this time they have developed too much capacity, and they are vulnerable to new establishments which are efficient and lean.

The final stage is decline and death. The market share shrinks rapidly, profits dissipate, and the institution is on its way to extinction. According to some authors, executives cannot do anything to stop or to reverse this life cycle process.

Although the thesis of retail life cycle has quite a bit of merit, particularly in terms of changing strategic needs, it is a somewhat questionable theory of institutional change (Markin and Duncan 1981). Some authors think of it as a phenomenon that cannot be counteracted (Davidson, Bates, and Bass 1976), but others consider it to be a dependent variable of managerial action (Dhalla and Yuspeh 1976).

The Markin-Duncan Adaptation Theory

Markin and Duncan (1981) have adopted a Darwinian approach to the transformation of retailing institutions, maintaining that retail institutions survive through adaptation. This approach posits the doctrine that functional processes or their transformation gain value only through survival (Vanderpool 1973). Thus, Markin and Duncan maintain that the retail institution emerges, adapts, survives, or declines and disappears depending on how well it serves the market's needs. Thus, it becomes clear that retail institutions that cannot adapt to the pressures of changing environments are replaced by those that are more adaptable. They further posit that this adaptation and accommodation point of view is the real explanation of the extreme diversity of the retailing sector. For this reason, there is wide variation among retail institutions and establishments. Markin and Duncan further assert that this point of view not only is a Darwinian stance, but also satisfies classical economic theory. They theorize that the institution's functions are determined by its structure, which in turn is conditioned by market forces (Stigler 1951). When market forces change, institutions are pressured to accommodate and adapt or discontinue.

When changes by individual retail establishments resulting from changes in market forces become widely initiated or are followed by a large number of firms, then the order or structure in the retail sector is likely to become modified, which itself represents an institutional change. For example, a series of social, technological, and economic forces caused the emergence of supermarkets in food retailing. As supermarkets entered the food retailing market with their cash-

and-carry, high-turnover, low-price, and self-service practices, they caused a radical change in the appearance, location, and management of retail food marketing.

Thus, according to the biological theory of adaptation, what survives is fit at least in the present time. This fitness implies that the retailers' functions and services are deemed valuable by the marketing environment (Markin and Duncan 1981). The retailers' managerial ignorance and capital rationing can cause retail institutions that are fit today not to remain fit tomorrow. As early as 1959, Bob R. Holdren maintained that many small retailers operate under severe capital shortages; they suffer from inertia and ignorance; and they are typically too small and are afraid of large establishments. Certainly, this attitude in the face of the changing retailing environment made many retail establishments and some retail institutions extremely vulnerable. This pattern can be compared to Norbert Wiener's theory of the entropic nature of things. He posited that there is a statistical tendency for things that are left alone to run down, to deteriorate, and to change. Thus, retail management's chief responsibility is to control or forestall entropic tendencies in their institutions as their markets change. Markin and Duncan contend that retail institutions can achieve this objective first, by being able to meet institutional requirements imposed by the market, and second, by displaying some tolerance to minimum and maximum conditions in their respective ecosystems. They further maintain that these two features, that is, requirements and tolerance, are complementary but not totally proportionate. A retail establishment can fail to meet the market requirement and still show a high degree of tolerance or vice versa.

The retailing sector is composed of a very large variety of establishments, and so no one single type of retailing institution encounters optimum conditions or functions in a given habitat. Those that meet the requirements and show a high degree of tolerance can and do survive. But meeting the requirements and possessing tolerance are not unique to one type of retail institution in any given habitat. However, in time, some of these institutions experience entropic tendencies and die.

SUMMARY

This chapter discusses retail population trends. After a brief exploration of retail population trends in terms of numbers, sales volume, and types of store, the reasons behind the retail population trends are examined.

In order to explore retail population trends, external and internal factors are discussed. External factors include changing competition, changing lifestyles, sociological factors, economic conditions, and political considerations. Internal factors include undercapitalization, poor management, inadequate marketing strategy, inadequate information, and poor location. Finally, this chapter discusses six theories of retail institutional change: the wheel of retailing, natural selection in retail institutions, the general–specific–general cycle, the dialectic process, the retail life cycle, and, finally, the Markin-Duncan adaptation theory. The retail manager must understand the trends and patterns in the marketplace and hence be able to take precautionary action, if necessary, to protect himself or herself and capitalize on new opportunities.

REFERENCES

Chamberlin, E. *Monopolistic Competition*, Boston: Harvard University Press, 1977.

Davidson, William R., Albert D. Bates, and Stephen J. Bass. "The Retail Life Cycle." *Harvard Business Review* (November-December 1976): 89–96.

Dhalla, Nariman K., and Sonia Yuspeh. "Forget the Product of Life Cycle." *Harvard Business Review* (January-February 1976): 102–22.

Duncan, Delbert J. "Responses of Selected Retail Institutions to Their Changing Environment in Marketing and Economic Development." *Proceedings from the Conference of the American Marketing Association.* (1965): 583–602.

Gist, Ronald R. *Retailing: Concepts and Decisions*. New York: John Wiley, 1968, pp. 81–113.

Holdren, Bob R. *The Structure of a Retail Market and the Market Behavior of Retail Units*. Englewood Cliffs, N.J.: Prentice-Hall, 1959.

Hollander, Stanley C. "The Wheel of Retailing." *Journal of Marketing* (July 1960): 37–42.

——— "Notes on the Retail Accordion." *Journal of Retailing* (Summer 1966): 38–47.

McNair, M. P. "Significant Trends and Developments in the Postwar Period." In A. B. Smith, ed., *Competitive Distribution in a Free High-Level Economy and Its Implications for the University*. Pittsburgh, Pa.: University of Pittsburgh Press, 1958.

Markin, Rom. J., and Calvin P. Duncan. "The Transformation of Retailing Institutions: Beyond the Wheel of Retailing and Life Cycle Theories." *Journal of Macro Marketing* (Spring 1981): 58–65.

Samli, A. Coskun. "Role of Business Failures in the Economy." *University of Washington Business Review* (February, 1964): 53–63.

Stigler, George J. "The Division of Labor Is Limited by the Extent of the Market." *Journal of Political Economy* (June 1951): 185–93.

Vanderpool, Harold Y. *Darwin and Darwinism*. Lexington, Mass.: D. C. Heath, 1973.

Wiener, Norbert. *The Human Use of Human Beings*. New York: Avon Books, 1967.

3 Intermarket Shopping Patterns

The concept of spatial dimension was aptly articulated by Wroe Alderson (1957) when he said that "to create place utility is to offer the goods close at hand so as to cut down the distance consumers have to travel in searching for them." About a decade later Jac Goldstucker (1965) stated that "a firm's location is a significant ingredient for generating sales." He went on to say that there were no principles that have been developed "which can be universally applied in the analyses of trading areas."

In the case of retailing, location is the life blood of business. However, what makes the retailer's location "good" or "bad" is the movement of consumers from one shopping facility to another. Many consumers travel from one urban complex to another—in other words, they go out of town to shop. Thus, intermarket shopping behavior is a most significant factor in retail location. It, therefore, presents an important base to study the spatial dimension of marketing (Samli 1979).

Specific forces underlie this intermarket shopping behavior. It is important to understand these forces so that the intermarket shopping process can be stopped or perhaps even reversed if needed. The main premise in this chapter is that a better understanding of intermarket purchase behavior will allow us to approach retail location issues more rationally and hence more efficiently. Thus, this chapter presents a construct or a general model of outshopping behavior based on an analysis and synthesis of recent studies on this subject. The chapter starts with a macro approach to intermarket purchase behavior and scales the analyses down to a micro level.

Successful retailers have a good understanding of outshopping patterns and competition from outside a community. Such understanding could help develop successful retail strategies to counteract the outshopping activity.

THE CONCEPT OF RETAIL GRAVITATION

Retail gravitation models are perhaps the oldest models of intermarket shopping behavior, but they do not explain the reasons behind intermarket shopping. The law of retail gravitation had its beginning in J.W. Reilly's analysis of retail trade in 1927. Later, in 1949, P. D. Converse attempted to refine Reilly's findings so that the movement of retail trade among cities could be measured. The original law developed by Reilly (1931) stated:

Two cities attract retail trade from any intermediate city, or town in the vicinity of the breaking point approximately in direct proportion to the population of the two cities and in inverse proportion to the square of the distances from these two cities to the intermediate town.

Formulas for this law and numeric illustration are presented in Chapter 5.

Converse revised Reilly's formula in order to determine the breaking point. The breaking point between any two cities is the intermediate community that divides its shopping goods trade equally between the two cities. Converse contended that his formula could be used to determine the boundaries of a town's normal trading area without doing field research (1949). Numerous subsequent studies have not provided sufficient evidence to reject the law of retail gravitation. However, the law has not been very effective in providing direction for communities to understand and reverse outshopping behavior. Nor has it been very useful in enabling local merchants or Chambers of Commerce to plan more effectively for this trade area by delineating it accurately. The law of retail gravitation could be used to explain the dynamics of intermarket purchase behavior only in a very broad sense. The models that were generated after the law were particularly important as planning aids in the problem of regional shopping center location (Schwartz 1963). However, these macro models did not consider some of the most important factors of consumer characteristics and values. Questions about issues such as the relationship between cosmopolitanism and outshopping, type of people most likely to be engaged in intermarket shopping, and types of products preferred by outshoppers need to be raised. The factors behind these issues are the qualifiers for Reilly's law in delineating trading areas or in determining intermarket leakages, and hence in shedding more light on these aspects of the spatial dimension in a more micro market. Subsequent studies on outshopping have examined some of these factors.

INTERMARKET LEAKAGES

The concept of intermarket leakage emerged when a number of authors explored outshopping. The definition of outshoppers used in earlier research efforts had depended on the reported frequency of going out of town to shop. John R. Thompson (1971) used a frequency of at least one purchase per year out of town.

Robert D. Herrmann and Leland L. Beik (1968) also used a frequency figure but stipulated that the shopping trip must be outside a five-mile radius of the downtown shopping area. Fred D. Reynolds and William R. Darden (1972) increased the frequency to at least 12 out-of-town shopping trips per year. A. Coskun Samli and Ernest B. Uhr (1974) maintained that the relevant dimension of outshopping was the proportion of total dollar purchases made out of town rather than the frequency or the distance of such trips. They divided shoppers into four groups: heavy outshoppers who buy 75 percent or more of their purchases out of town; outshoppers who buy 50 to 74 percent of their purchases out of town; inshoppers who buy 51 to 75 percent of their purchases in town; and finally loyal inshoppers who buy 76 to 100 percent of their purchases in town (Samli and Uhr 1974).

Earlier studies indicated that inshoppers and outshoppers could differ significantly with regard to age, income, and education (Reynolds and Darden 1972). Other research studies showed conflicting results as to the makeup of the people who engage in intermarket shopping more than others. In addition to demographics, psychometrics were utilized in these efforts. However, the results have been indecisive.

THE NATURE OF POPULATION

Earlier studies overemphasized the premise that, typically, populations are not homogeneous. Furthermore, they attributed outshopping to the existence of different groups within populations. For instance, they maintained that groups that are highly educated, more sophisticated, and have higher incomes are more prone to engage in intermarket shopping. This approach does not explain the outshopping phenomenon in small communities where everyone, to some degree, is an outshopper. In these communities, the population is usually much more homogeneous than that in large metropolitan areas, college, and/or industrial communities. Exhibit 3.1 presents the picture in such small communities where actual retail sales are less than the estimated potential. In eight metropolitan areas the picture is reversed, indicating that people come to these areas from out of town for outshopping purposes.

The exhibit indicates that the outshopping phenomenon is rather common in small communities. Thus, the earlier explanations are less than sufficient in explaining this widespread phenomenon. In order to understand intermarket purchase behavior better, it is necessary to develop a general model.

INTERMARKET PURCHASING: A GENERAL MODEL

A general intermarket purchasing model is based on the finer points of consumer behavior and store patronage principles. Its starting point is where the need for goods and services is at the retail level. Two key modifiers of this need are lifestyle characteristics and background. Lifestyle characteristics have been

Exhibit 3.1
Estimates of Outshopping in Selected Governmental Units

Governmental Unit	State	Population (000)	A Potential (000)	B Retail Sales (000)	C Difference (000)
**Brantly	GA	8.1	17,166	8,874	-8,299
**Appling	GA	15.6	39,238	36,802	-2,436
**Clark	MO	8.4	22,888	22,350	- 538
**Iron	NO	10.6	29,428	27,408	-2,020
**Perry	NO	16.2	44,143	42,031	-2,112
**Rush	IN	21.1	62,127	44,763	-17,364
**Decatur	IN	24.2	76,841	67,445	-9,396
**Fayette	IN	27.3	94,825	81,595	-13,230
**Harrison	OH	18.2	94,008	44,265	-49,743
**Noble	OH	12.1	31,881	31,011	870
**Vinton	OH	11.0	23,706	13,869	-9,837
**Wyandot	OH	22.3	69,484	66,563	-2,921
**Alexander	IL	12.8	36,785	40,843	4,058
**Brown	IL	6.2	17,984	10,463	-7,521
**Cumberland	IL	10.4	38,421	22,049	-16,372
**Gallatin	IL	7.3	22,889	16,273	-6,616
**Putnam	IL	5.7	20,436	11,500	-8,936
*Columbus	OH	1,105.3	4,340,720	4,524,460	183,740
*San Diego	CA	1,783.0	6,974,581	7,243,673	269,092
*Seattle/Everet	WA	1,474.8	6,500,453	6,957,085	456,632
*Denver/Boulder	CO	1,520.2	6,202,897	6,441,438	238,541
*Milwaukee	WI	1,414.1	5,732,039	5,778,582	46,543
*Indianapolis	IN	1,162.8	4,727,380	5,108,772	381,392
*Louisville	KY	894.2	3,494,648	3,509,978	15,330
*Atlanta	GA	1,874.9	7,504,296	7,825,140	320,844

*Metropolitan Area.

**County.

The data for the analysis were derived from *Sales and Marketing Management*, July 1979.

Potential (A) was calculated by the following formula:

$$A = Y \times Z$$

where

Y is total U.S. retail sales.

Z is governmental unit's buying power index.

Difference (C) was calculated by subtracting potential (A) from retail sales: (B) for governmental unit. Therefore, a minus value in Column C denotes shopping activity.

Source: Samli, Riecken and Yavas 1983.

Exhibit 3.2
Tenure in the Community and Outshopping

Tenure	75% Out of Town	50-74% Out of Town	51-75% Intown	76-100% Intown
Less than two years	30.3	20.2	17.5	17.5
Two to five years	21.2	25.8	21.5	14.9
Five to ten years	33.3	16.9	26.0	18.0
More than ten years	15.2	37.1	35.0	49.5

Source: Samli and Uhr 1974: 77.

explored as determinants of outshopping behavior (Reynolds and Darden 1972; Herrmann and Beik 1968; Darden and Perrault 1976). Because of lifestyle configurations and typologies, the individual may have a special need to patronize certain types of retail facilities. If, for instance, the individual's lifestyle is that of a "jetsetter," then that person is not likely to patronize a discount department store. Similarly, the individual's brand preference may be formed by lifestyle, which is likely to be crucial in the store selection process. If, for instance, a woman is attached to the Austin brand of apparel, she will go to an apparel shop that carries this brand. These situations could easily be considered the underlying factors of outshopping.

The background of individuals, which may also be considered to be part of lifestyle conditions, is another important determinant of outshopping behavior. Being accustomed to shopping in large shopping centers or regional malls and being able to choose from a large variety of options is related to background. Whether or not people grew up in large or small communities, for example, is particularly important to outshopping considerations. Those who are used to patronizing large shopping facilities are likely to seek out the same kind of facilities if they happen to live in small communities (Samli 1977). If, for instance, a professional were transferred from Los Angeles to Murphysboro, Illinois, he or she would seek out the nearest large shopping center to shop even if it was 30 or 40 miles out of town. Such an individual might go as far as St. Louis, which is about 100 miles away. Only in this way could the individual approximate the conditions to which he or she had grown accustomed. This person may not be engaged in as much intermarket purchase behavior one or two years later. Exhibit 3.2 illustrates this concept. As can be seen in the exhibit, more than 30 percent of those who lived in town not more than two years bought more than 75 percent of their purchases out of town. Similarly, more than 49 percent of those who lived in town more than ten years made 76 to 100 percent of their purchases in town.

Lifestyles and background imply the presence of a nonhomogeneous population, which further indicates that only certain groups of people are interested in outshopping. As was discussed earlier, thus far most research efforts have been geared to exploring this particular aspect of intermarket purchase behavior. However, as we also discussed earlier, there are thousands of small homogeneous communities in the United States in which virtually everyone outshops. In such cases, intermarket purchase behavior is, at least partially, promulgated by the degree of satisfaction or dissatisfaction with the existing shopping facilities in town.

Two circumstances may modify this aspect of outshopping: (1) the proximity of other shopping facilities and (2) the attractiveness of other shopping facilities. Even though the people are not very satisfied with the home shopping facilities, without major shopping complexes in the region, it would be difficult for them to be engaged in outshopping. Closely related to the attractiveness of other shopping complexes is the proximity to the complexes. If other complexes are not within reach, then in the minds of consumers, these facilities do not exist as viable alternatives to the home shopping complexes.

Exhibit 3.3 illustrates the general conceptual framework. To the extent that this model explains the intermarket purchasing phenomenon, this aspect of the spatial dimension of retailing is explained by the micro model. It is considered a micro model because it explores individual lifestyles, likes, and dislikes. With this exception of degree of satisfaction with local retail facilities, research has at least partially explored most of the components presented in the model. The rest of this chapter explores the impact of the degree of satisfaction or dissatisfaction with local retail facilities as an underlying factor of intermarket shopping behavior. Obviously, such an attempt would primarily explain the situation depicted in Exhibit 3.1.

Two large-scale studies in a small university town were conducted in 1970 and 1977, respectively (Samli 1970, 1977). The sampling methodology was the same for both studies. After the first study findings were publicized, a new mall was built in 1974. In addition, most merchants had access to the first study results which pointed out the chief consumer likes and dislikes. Therefore, the first study may well have had some impact on the merchants' dealings with their customers. In other words, when they realized that consumers did not like the quality of their services and were going out of town to shop, they decided to improve their performance.

Exhibit 3.4 illustrates changes in attitude toward the local shopping facilities during the seven-year period. The percentage figures in the table are calculated by subtracting ''poor'' and ''very poor'' from ''good'' and ''very good'' points on a five-point scale. Thus, the responses are the net results of the attitude calculations. In 1970 a net response of 67.8 percent indicated that quality of goods in the local shopping facilities was either good or very good; however, in 1977 the response was 69.0 percent. At both points in time, prices and selection did not seem to be very satisfactory. The most significant positive change in attitude was related primarily to the parking factor. Since the new mall had plenty

Exhibit 3.3
A General Model of Intermarket Purchase Behavior

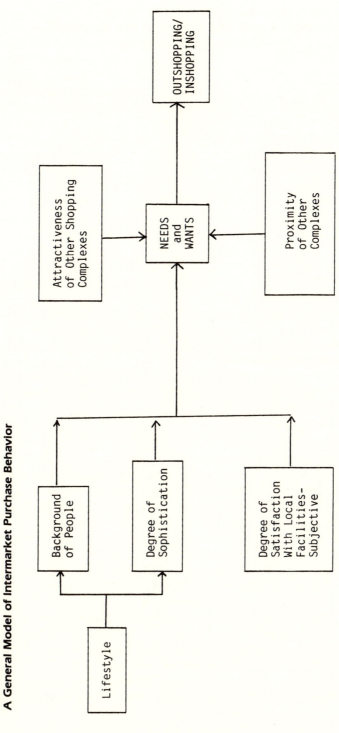

Exhibit 3.4
Attitude Toward Local Shopping Facility,[a] 1970 and 1977[b]

	1977 %	1970 %
Quality of goods	69.0	67.8
Selection	9.8	-14.8
Prices	- 2.0	-13.3
Product Knowledge	40.5	25.7
Ease of Shopping	72.8	59.3
Ease of Parking	31.7	-16.8
Service	53.3	44.8
Appearance of Stores	58.3	48.0
Store Hours	62.7	51.7

[a]Figures are calculated by subtracting "poor" and "very poor" from "good" and "very good" on a five-point scale.

[b]The 1977 study was based on a random sample of 435 households, and the 1970 study was based on a random sample of 260 households.

Source: A. Coskun Samli, "Some Observations on the Intermarket Shopping Behavior as It Relates to the Spatial Dimension," in AMA *Educators Conference Proceedings* (Chicago: American Marketing Association, 1979), p.40.

of parking facilities, the shoppers' parking problem was at least partially solved. In all nine factors the net consumer attitude has become more positive, thus indicating an overall improved sentiment toward the total shopping facilities. All nine variables shown in Exhibit 3.4 were shown to be significant in outshopping (Samli and Uhr 1974).

It is important to calculate outshopping volume in contrast with improving sentiment toward the local shopping facilities. Exhibit 3.5 depicts the intermarket shopping volume for the two study periods. The figures are calculated on the basis of the survey results. Both surveys used exactly the same methodology, and both were based on large random samples.

Exhibit 3.5 indicates a substantial decline in the estimated proportion of shopping done out of town. While outshopping accounted for 27.79 percent of the total money spent by consumers of the town in 1970, it was reduced to 16.43 percent in 1977. Therefore, outshopping appears to be a function of satisfaction or dissatisfaction with local shopping conditions. The greater the degree of satisfaction with local retail facilities, the lesser the extent of outshopping.

Exhibit 3.5
Outshopping Volume in 1970 and 1977

	1977	1970
Amount spent in town	22,611	14,691
Amount spent out of town	3,616	4,084
Outshopping expressed as a percent of total	16.43%	27.79%

Source: Samli 1979: 41.

IMPLICATIONS OF THE MODEL

It has been stated that the spatial dimension is closely related to consumer movements. If these movements between and within markets are understood, then the retail location decision can be optimized in terms of consumer satisfaction. If the retailer can optimize the location of his or her store on the basis of consumer movements, consumers will patronize the store readily and will benefit from satisfying their needs adequately. Thus, knowledge of intermarket purchase behavior provides insight into one of the most important aspects of spatial dimension.

Although our knowledge of intermarket purchase patterns and behavior is improving, numerous unanswered questions remain. For instance, what happens if out-of-town shopping conditions improve faster than in-town shopping facilities? In other words, is outshopping an absolute or a relative phenomenon? If it is an absolute phenomenon, then, if the local shopping facilities have reached a satisfactory level, there will be only a minimal amount of outshopping. This degree of intermarket purchasing activity will not be influenced by the continuing improvement of out-of-town retail facilities.

If outshopping is a relative phenomenon, however, then regardless of how well the local retail facilities are developed, if they remain behind the out-of-town shopping facilities, the level of outshopping activity is likely to be extensive. The reversal of this pattern will depend primarily on how the local shopping facilities can be improved more than proportionately.

One of the most important questions remains unanswered; how can outshopping behavior patterns be utilized to optimize the location of retail facilities? The answer to this question will provide the bridge between outshopping and the spatial dimension. The implication here is that the retail spatial dimension may be considered to be a function of outshopping behavior patterns. Hence, optimization of retail location activity is dependent primarily on understanding intermarket purchase behavior.

Perhaps the most important conclusion of this chapter is that outshopping is, to a substantial extent, a function of the degree of satisfaction or dissatisfaction with local shopping facilities.

Outshopping patterns obviously have direct impact on the individual retailer. If, for example, the retailer deals with auto parts but people are making their purchases in a large regional shopping center located 20 miles out of town, then the individual retailer must make an in-depth analysis of his or her offerings and services vis-à-vis the out of town facility. The individual retailer must also explore what plans, if any, town merchants as well as town administration have to counteract this outshopping behavior. Similarly, knowledge of outshopping patterns is essential for every prospective retailer about to enter the market. If it is known that his or her line of product is purchased out of town, a thorough examination of whether the proposed retail store can stop and reverse this outshopping behavior will be needed.

SUMMARY

This chapter deals with outshopping, a phenomenon that is crucial to the success or failure of retail establishments. Earlier intermarket purchase studies have been primarily macro in scope. Although valuable, these studies do not explain the reasons behind outshopping behavior. Earlier micro studies tried to explain the outshopping phenomenon on the basis of differences in population. They tried to single out the characteristics of outshoppers and contended that young, highly educated professionals with relatively higher income had a greater tendency to outshop. However, in many small communities where the population is homogeneous, outshopping is widespread. In order to explain this aspect of outshopping, a model is presented in this chapter. It is maintained that particularly in situations where populations are homogeneous, outshopping is a function of dissatisfaction with in-town shopping facilities. This assertion has many practical implications, one of which is that local merchants or the town administration can keep track of consumer satisfaction/dissatisfaction with local facilities. Such information will enable local merchants to reduce dissatisfaction and therefore reduce intermarket shopping. Knowing outshopping patterns will enable both prospective and existing merchants to optimize their location options.

REFERENCES

Alderson, Wroe. *Marketing Behavior and Executive Action*, Homewood, Ill.: Richard D. Irwin, 1957.

Casparis, Jr. "Shopping Center Location and Retail Store Mix in Metropolitan Areas." *Demography* 6 (May 1969): 125–31.

Clark, W. A. V. "Consumer Travel Patterns and the Concept of Range." *Annals of the Association of American Geographers*, 58 (June 1968): 386–96.

Converse, P. D. "New Laws of Retail Gravitation." *Journal of Marketing* 14 (October 1949): 378–84.

Darden, William R., John J. Lennon, and Donna K. Darden. "Communicating with Interurban Shoppers." *Journal of Retailing* 54 (Spring 1978): 51–64.

Darden, William R. and William D. Perrault. "Identifying Interurban Shoppers." *Journal of Marketing Research* 13 (February 1976): 81–88.

Getis, Arthur. "The Determination of Location of Retail Activities with the Use of a Map Transformation." *Economic Geography* 38 (January 1963): 14–22.

Goldstucker, Jac. "Trading Areas." In George Schwartz (ed), *Science in Marketing*. New York: John Wiley, 1965.

Herrmann, Robert D., and Leiland L. Beik. "Shoppers' Movement Outside Their Local Retail Area." *Journal of Marketing* 32 (October 1968): 45–51.

Huff, David L. "Defining and Estimating a Trading Area." *Journal of Marketing*, 28 (July 1964): 24–29.

Lillis, Charles M., and Delbert I. Hawkins. "Retail Expenditure Flows in Continuous Trade Areas." *Journal of Retailing* 50 (Summer 1974): 30–42.

Mazze, Edward M. "Determining Shopper Movement Patterns by Cognitive Maps." *Journal of Retailing* 50 (Fall 1974): 43–48.

Reilly, J. W. *The Law of Retail Gravitation*. 1st ed. Austin: University of Texas, 1931.

Reynolds, Fred D., and William R. Darden. "Intermarket Patronage: A Psychographic Study of Consumer Outshopping." *Journal of Marketing* 36 (October 1972): 50–54.

———, and Warren S. Martin. "A Multivariate Analysis of Intermarket Patronage: Some Empirical Findings." *Journal of Business Research* 2 (April 1974): 193–199.

Samli, A. C. *A Look at Consumption Patterns in Blacksburg, Virginia 1976–1977*. Blacksburg, Va.: Virginia Polytechnic Institute and State University Extension Division, 1970 and 1977.

———. "Some Observations on the Intermarket Shopping Behavior as It Relates to the Spatial Dimension." AMA *Educators Conference Proceedings*. Chicago: AMA, 1979.

———, and Ernest B. Uhr. "The Outshopping Spectrum: Key for Analyzing Intermarket Leakages." *Journal of Retailing* 50 (Summer 1974): 70–78.

———, G. Riecken, and U. Yavas. "Intermarket Shopping Behavior and the Small Community." *Journal of Academy of Marketing Science* (Winter 1983): 43–52.

Schwartz, George. *Development of Marketing Theory*. Cincinnati: Southwestern Publishing Co., 1963

Thompson, John R. "Characteristics and Behavior of Outshopping Consumers." *Journal of Retailing*, 47 (Spring 1971): 70–80.

4 Downtown Versus Shopping Centers

Whether shopping patterns are analyzed in intermarket or intramarket situations, retailing is concentrated in two distinct locales: central business districts (CBDs) or downtowns and shopping centers. The first locale is unplanned, whereas the second is almost always planned.

With the present changes in society, consumer behavior is also changing. As new retail competition patterns are emerging, downtowns throughout the country are experiencing difficult times. Not only are they losing their relative share of total retail volume, but also many of them are beginning to look like ghost towns. Thus, CBDs are requiring carefully planned and deliberate action to compete with planned shopping centers and regain their almost totally lost vitality. This chapter examines four questions: what is happening to downtowns, what are the advantages of shopping centers, how can the revival and revitalization of CBDs be achieved and, finally, what is the impact of all of this on the retail establishment.

THE PLIGHT OF DOWNTOWNS

Downtowns or CBDs have historically been the focal point of buying and selling at the retail level. In time, they emerged as an amorphous and uncoordinated conglomeration of groups of stores. As such, no plans were ever made for the future of CBDs, their appearance, their general offerings, or their general appeal. The plight of downtowns can be analyzed in terms of four major trends: (1) population dispersion, (2) uncoordinated marketing, (3) emergence of shopping centers, and (4) increasing difficulty in accessibility.

Population Dispersion

One of the unique characteristics of the American population is its mobility: 20 percent of all Americans move every year. The movement has gone from east to west, from north to south, from urban centers to suburbia. As the population moves, it also disperses, a situation that makes it difficult for retailers to stay abreast of markets and to satisfy their needs. Retailers can consider population dispersion to represent the disintegration of existing markets. This disintegration can be a critical factor in retail failure.

Uncoordinated Marketing

Perhaps the biggest problem of downtowns is the existence of many independent and individualistic entrepreneurs who own their own stores. These people are accustomed to certain patterns of practice and find it difficult to change these patterns even if changing market conditions call for it. Thus, they are not sufficiently flexible. Furthermore, because they are very individualistic, they do not coordinate their activities with other businesses in the same area. Therefore, the possible synergistic effect of coordinated activity is neither understood nor achieved.

In addition, since downtowns are typically unplanned, the effectiveness of a balanced overall merchandise mix for the whole CBD and the effectiveness of a proper combination of goods and services are not taken advantage of.

Emergence of Shopping Centers

The shopping center is retailing's answer to changing consumer needs as well as to dispersion of the population. Planned suburban shopping centers emerged shortly after suburbia itself emerged. The phenomenon began during the early 1950s. Unlike the downtowns, shopping centers enjoyed four features that made them superior to downtowns: (1) accessibility, (2) modern and well-planned facilities, (3) plentiful parking, and (4) coordinated merchandising and promotion.

Shopping centers are accessible on several counts. They are conveniently located since they follow the population dispersion. They invariably are located in the newly emerging population centers and are adjacent to superhighways and bypasses. Hence, they avoid traffic bottlenecks in the middle of the city and provide all the advantages of fast vehicular traffic on superhighways. In many cases shopping centers are easier to get to than downtowns. They can be reached easily by bypassing the busy city streets and by using superhighways without serious traffic problems.

Shopping centers are modern and well planned. Unlike a typical downtown, shopping centers have architectural unity and a theme. They can be ultramodern, Mexican, early American, and so on. The architectural theme provides an overall attraction and an image that is usually appealing to the public. Being modern is also related to well-designed layout of the total shopping facility. The entrances and exits are strategically located; traffic patterns in the facility are carefully planned; and parking facilities are strategically located.

In addition to planning the location and layout of shopping facilities, the total offering of shopping centers is also carefully planned. Thus, shopping centers provide a more balanced offering of goods and services than downtowns. The balance implies a stronger drawing power for the total shopping facility.

Plentiful parking is perhaps the most important strength of shopping centers. Many downtowns were not planned for heavy traffic; hence, when traffic is heavy or during busy shopping periods, downtowns do not provide good conditions for shoppers. Although downtown underground parking ramps or pedestrian malls are partial solutions to the problem, they have not been successful in many communities. First, the pedestrian malls have not been well conceptualized and hence do not have widespread appeal. Second, ramps present only a concentrated parking facility and force many people to walk long distances to shop in different parts of downtown.

Coordinated merchandising and promotion are another unique strength of shopping centers. All businesses in a specific shopping center participate in the organized promotional activity for that shopping center. There are coordination and cooperation in such endeavors. Each merchant not only participates but also performs the specific tasks involved in the total effort. A merchant may be asked to give door prizes, another to display wares on sidewalks, and a third to prepare special signs. In addition to this type of coordinated activity, there is regular promotion. All merchants participate in partially institutional (for the whole shopping center) and partially promotional advertising for individual merchants. Much of the public relations (PR) work is also coordinated and carefully planned.

Increasing Difficulty in Accessibility

Downtowns were not built for present-day traffic. Most downtowns in the United States emerged when people either walked to stores or utilized public transportation. As the inner city became more crowded and the traffic around it got heavier, downtowns began experiencing a serious problem of accessibility. Large numbers of people started avoiding shopping in downtown areas. This avoidance became proportionate to the distance to be traveled to come to the CBD. Many studies (Samli and Prell 1965) indicated that higher socioeconomic groups lived at the outskirts of the city and avoided going downtown much of the time. Thus, downtowns appear to have lost their upper socioeconomic markets and have become convenience shopping facilities for lower socioeconomic groups who live adjacent to the shopping complexes of downtowns.

In recent years, traffic diversion plans have emerged to enhance the accessibility of downtowns to those who do not live nearby. By moving around downtown the traffic not destined for downtown shopping, additional space is being made available for downtown shoppers. This is being achieved by separating through traffic from downtown destined traffic.

Although downtown revitalization projects (Spalding 1983; Stark 1980) run in the millions of dollars for construction in each and every case, the CBD problems have not yet been resolved. The fact that downtown projects are undertaken more as an architectural activity than as a retailing-related activity contributes to the problem rather than resolving it.

It is, therefore, necessary to undertake effective CBD studies and to determine the causes and possible alternatives. In this overall activity, it is essential that the remedy finally selected be acceptable to the consumers of the area. Consider, for instance, the following downtown remedial actions and their impact:

- In a major city, two large city streets were converted into a pedestrian mall. However, the ultramodern appearance did not make shoppers think the CBD was now a better place to shop.
- The downtown revitalization project of a small town sank a lot of money into a facelifting of the downtown. However, the existing merchandise mix was not altered, and that was less than adequate for consumers of the area.
- The CBD of a small town was altered by a downtown revitalization program. However, the change in appearance was not accompanied by changes in attitudes: The old storekeepers and owner-managers did not alter their attitudes toward their customers.

The following sections present an analysis of CBD studies. Such studies are necessary before a revitalization project can take place. The most important consideration in this case is the individual retailer's understanding of the situation and its implications for each retail establishment. Since many CBD studies have been conducted and, typically, there is at least one in each CBD, the individual retailer who can read and understand such studies can benefit substantially. These studies will enable the retailer to plan carefully for the future.

Objectives of CBD Studies

The CBD study evaluates the present and future potential of the total retail facility and develops a detailed program based on research findings in order to capitalize on prevailing potentials. Furthermore, the program may establish the basic framework of an economic expansion program which directly or indirectly would revitalize the CBD, provided some of the prevailing problems indicated by research are eliminated.

Analyzing Past Trends

CBD studies cannot be effective unless we understand past trends and patterns. For example, the changing patterns of the CBD should be detected in terms of the number and kind of retail and service establishments. By detecting the change, or the lack of it, in the merchant mix or the merchandise mix, we can diagnose some of the problem areas.

An analysis of the change in the population of the immediate surrounding area, coupled with the change in income and its distribution, forms the basic framework for determining the market potentials. Of course, these past data can be utilized effectively to develop future projections.

Patterns in the changing industrial picture must also be examined in as much as these patterns have both a direct and an indirect impact on the fate of CDBs. For instance, if the expected industrial expansion takes place in a widely dispersed manner and if residential developments follow suit, retail facilities can also be expected to be dispersed. Thus, instead of a substantial growth in the CBD, a series of local shopping centers or neighborhood clusters may be expected to emerge.

SUPPLY AND DEMAND

A basic framework to develop the CBD can be established only by analyzing supply and demand simultaneously. Behind supply, in addition to the actual physical retailing facility, are merchant mix, parking, merchandising, and basic needs and wants of the merchants, property owners and local government. Furthermore, CBD plans must cope with these groups' attitudes, plans, and willingness to change and improve.

Behind demand, on the other hand, in addition to purchasing power and population growth, are also attitudes, buying habits, needs and wants, and consumer mobility. Unless these factors are identified and analyzed, no development plan can be formulated that will provide guidance for the supply sector.

Once supply and demand are analyzed simultaneously, it becomes possible to detect the CBD's needs in regard to these two major forces. At this point, it becomes necessary to examine these needs as stated by demand and supply sectors separately. This kind of examination makes it possible to detect the common denominators. These common problem areas evidenced by the statements from both demand and supply should play the major role in development plans. If, for example, most of the merchants complain about the prevailing parking facilities, consumers claim the same, and field research confirms these statements, then it can safely be stated that parking must play an important role in the development plan.

Elements of Supply

The supply side of the CBD has a number of dimensions. Although no attempt will be made here to analyze them according to their relative degree of importance to the CBD, it is necessary to emphasize that these dimensions carry different weights in the role they play in different CBDs. In making plans for growth or rehabilitation, we should consider them according to their relative significance.

1. Merchant mix: The analysis of merchant mix provides a basis for evaluation in absolute terms. If, for instance, some of the most typical places of business are missing on the CBD, such as eating places or apparel stores, the problem is at least partially obvious. The same criterion can also be utilized when we compare it with other CBD merchant mixes. In fact, it may be hypothesized that the merchant mix of a fast growing CBD provides the diagnostic tools to identify relative weaknesses.

2. Parking facilities: Inadequate parking is one of the typical problems in CBDs. The supply of parking facilities and the extent to which they are utilized may indicate a serious inadequacy that may be detrimental.

3. Physical structure: Physical facilities, including stores, warehouses, and other industrial and commercial buildings, have a twofold impact. First, the physical structure stimulates or curbs the supply side by either encouraging expansion and innovation if the physical facilities are adequate or by discouraging the same. Second, it again stimulates or hinders the demand side. Because of the adequacy or inadequacy of the physical conditions, consumers will either utilize the CBD or stay away from it.

Attitudes Toward the Area—Interest Groups

Next to supply, attitudes appear to be the most important element. The attitudes of three major groups of people must be considered: those of business people, property owners, and local government.

The attitude of businesspersons must be assessed. Often indolence, a traditional orientation, or lack of knowledge may interfere with the growth of the CBD. The attitude of the businessperson can be assessed by

1. Analyzing their degree of commitment by examining efforts on expansion, remodeling and other changes during the past decade.

2. Determining the nature and scope of their plans for expansion in the near future.

3. Evaluating the nature of their leases on business buildings.

4. Assessing their feelings toward the CBD.

5. Examining their likes and dislikes about the buildings they occupy.

6. Ascertaining the ownership of the business buildings.

The attitude of property owners must be determined. In many CBDs absentee ownership and pursuant lack of interest in the area cause a significant deterrent to the growth of the CBD. In such cases property owners may find it more suitable to let the buildings deteriorate, causing substantial dissatisfaction among the merchants.

The attitude of the local government plays a definite role in the future of the CBD. Taxes, parking laws, zoning ordinances and other regulatory measures may hinder or stimulate growth of the CBD.

Elements of Demand

The size and scope of existing potentials for the CBD should be determined by studying the shopping patterns of people who patronize the CBD as opposed to those who do not. Hence, two main sources of information may be used: on-the-spot shoppers in the CBD and households.

Shoppers

In order to determine the socioeconomic class of typical CBD patrons, their income level, education, occupation, age, and residence must be known. Only then will it be possible to determine whether or not the CBD is capitalizing on the prevailing potentials. If, for instance, only the people in the immediate neighborhood area shop at the CBD, it may be concluded that the CBD is no more than a local convenience shopping center and, therefore, has almost no drawing power. Such knowledge can facilitate establishing future objectives in terms of developing power to draw from groups living outside the immediate residential areas.

Shopping habits, such as how often shoppers come to the CBD on the average and how much of their total spending takes place at this facility, are extremely important. Their evaluation of the shopping facility must be obtained not only in terms of availability of goods and services, but also parking, merchandising, and other marketing aspects. The knowledge of goods and services that shoppers are unable to find is an especially powerful diagnostic tool. Shoppers may be contacted on several occasions to confirm the findings. Studies of the license plate numbers of cars parked in CBDs and tracing these to their addresses provide further evaluation of the drawing power.

Since shoppers display certain biases, they either live in the vicinity or shop at the CBD regularly, and, therefore, are partial to the area. For better results, it is also necessary to contact area households.

Households

An analysis of households in the area will provide information on major strengths or weaknesses of the CBD. In this analysis, the buying behavior and attitudes of shoppers toward the CBD must be compared with the household survey. If, for instance, shoppers seem to be heavily concentrated in one or two socioeconomic classes such as lower middle with skilled blue-collar work and slightly below high school education, and if household surveys indicate that a substantial proportion of this category still does not patronize the CBD, serious problems in the shopping facility may be diagnosed. More important, the reasons why the CBD does not appeal to the upper classes can also be determined by going directly to the households.

In one study (Samli and Prell 1965), it was determined that consumers located in the immediate vicinity patronized the CBD 75 to 90 percent of the time. These people were relatively less educated, belonged to a lower income bracket, and were mainly unskilled blue-collar workers with a high degree of unemployment. They liked the stores, merchandise, service, and especially the convenience. As the sample moved away from the immediate vicinity of the CBD, higher income, skilled workers, and better education became the general characteristics of the sample. These people did patronize the CBD between 50 to 75 percent of the time and complained quite a bit about the merchant mix, merchandise, parking, and services in general. At the outskirts of the city, the upper socioeconomic class resided. This class was composed of people with high income and high education who were mostly professionals. They patronized the CBD less than 50 percent of the time. A large proportion of this group did not want anything to do with the CBD and complained bitterly about all aspects of it.

Without a survey of households, these facts would not have been uncovered. By analyzing the likes and dislikes of lower middle and higher income groups, we can determine how to attract the patronage of each of these groups.

Exhibit 4.1 illustrates the approach that can be utilized in a study to determine the likes and dislikes of different groups. Whereas the solid line indicates a high degree of approval from the lower income group, the broken line indicates the aspects of the CBD that do not meet the upper income group's approval. Further research can easily indicate what, for example, the upper income group does not like about the merchandise. In one such study, the consumers from the upper income category cited the lack of certain types of goods and services as well as the lack of known brands and specific color, size, and models.

On the demand side, the size of the upper income group and the frequency of their purchases would be a decisive factor in planning the CBD's future. If this group is sizable and is not purchasing at the CBD, we must determine how they can be attracted to the CBD.

In this kind of planning, we should establish the limits of the proposed measures of growth on the basis of administrative feasibility. In this context, the requirements of two major groups must be recognized and treated carefully: the local government and property owners.

If absentee ownership is widespread, not only is local leadership lacking, but also indolence and quite often outright resistance to change and progress are much in evidence. Many property owners, especially those in smaller cities, live in larger metropolitan areas and their property in the CBD represents only a small fraction of their total investments. Hence, they may not pay much attention to the prevailing structures and their upkeep. If the property is fully depreciated and still occupied, it may be a good reason to oppose any changes.

Local government officials may not go along with the research findings and may find the recommendations unreasonable. They may also lack the resources to implement their share of the recommendations. A recommended change in the parking facilities and regulations, for example, may be beyond the means of the local government. Because of their growth rate and tax base, areas other than the CBD and its periphery may often get more attention, and, hence, relatively less interest may prevail to implement the recommended programs.

Exhibit 4.1
Contrast Between Shoppers' and Households' Attitudes

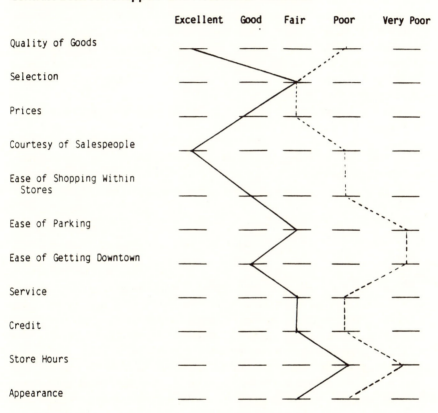

_____Shoppers
----- Households

In doing CBD research and planning, it is therefore necessary to include the attitude of the property owners and local government in the research plans. If these two groups are not willing or able to implement some of the recommendations, little can be done by the business sector alone. This type of research has given rise to specialty research centers.

Specialty Retail Centers

A new concept, the specialty retail center (SRC), has emerged during the past decade as one of the answers of downtowns to suburban shopping centers (Maronick and Stiff 1985). SRCs utilize restaurants and entertainment facilities as anchors. They take advantage of natural settings or of unifying and unique architectural designs. They make innovative use of old, well-known buildings (Maronick and Stiff 1985).

A carefully planned SRC with an entertainment image has at least four effects on downtowns (Maronick and Stiff 1985).

1. Increased consumer traffic based on the centers being perceived as a form of entertainment.
2. Strengthened drawing power, attracting people from high-income suburbs for entertainment purposes.
3. Support for nearby cultural attractions.
4. An opportunity to traditional downtown merchants to capitalize on this newly created traffic.

Based on the discussion in this chapter, the following conclusions can be made. First, CBDs are highly complex entities, and, hence, there are no simple solutions to their problems. Second, a highly feasible development or rehabilitation program requires an adequate information base. This information base reflects the supply and demand that the whole complex faces. Third, the common denominators demand and supply provide diagnostic inputs in the planning process. Fourth, in addition to demand and supply, numerous other factors must be considered; the research design adopted to develop the necessary information base must, therefore, be geared toward dealing with all the factors. Exhibit 4.2 illustrates all the factors and as such summarizes the total construct. This chapter is, of course, not the last word on this important phenomenon. Even so, it is expected to pave the way for a series of studies which will, at least partially, eliminate the acute CBD problems.

Retail Management Implications

The retailer is vitally interested in the well-being of the CBD because a healthy CBD means a healthy retail establishment. The retailer has to decide whether to locate in the CBD or elsewhere. Similarly, the retailer may be facing a

Exhibit 4.2
Key Elements of the Construct for Planning CBD Development

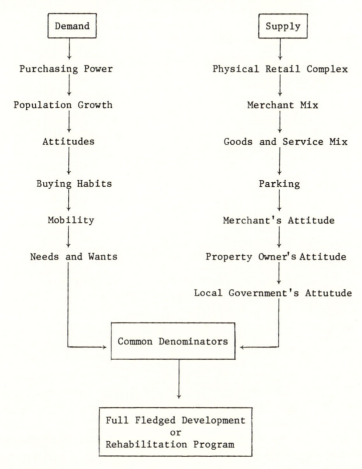

relocation decision. Quite often retailers are confronted with a decision situation in which they must decide whether or not to continue at the present CBD location or move elsewhere.

Thus, the retailer must have the analytic skills needed to assess the present and future status of the CBD and to contrast it with other general possible location sites. The retailer must understand the need to evaluate the factors discussed in this chapter, and must be able to analyze the changing conditions of demand and supply.

If the CBD is showing signs of trouble which may create suspicion about its future, the retailer must be able to receive and analyze these signs as early as possible. In this context, the retailer must ask a series of important questions and must answer them, and must also understand that this assessment process

Exhibit 4.3
A Checklist for Evaluating the Health of the CBD

		Yes	No
1.	Is the CBD making good progress?	____	____
2.	Is a healthy growth rate expected in the future?	____	____
3.	Is the general offering well balanced?	____	____
4.	Over the years, have there been significant changes in the clients of the CBD?	____	____
5.	If yes to 4, have the changes been such that the CBD clientele is now closer to the target market?	____	____
6.	Is the general image of the CBD good?	____	____
7.	What is the overall record of rents in the CBD? Is it reasonable?	____	____
8.	Are the property owners' attitude toward their property positive? (I.e., They take good care of their properties.)	____	____
9.	Is the degree of cooperation among merchants satisfactory?	____	____
10.	Do the merchants have the imagination to undertake unusual but supportive projects for the CBD?	____	____

is not a one-shot proposition. Before entry, the retailer must evaluate the CBD, and once the business is ongoing the evaluation process must continue. The retailer must be aware that the CBD's overall condition can deteriorate easily and rapidly. In such a case, early detection of the forthcoming problem will give the retailer more and better alternatives.

Exhibit 4.3 presents a checklist that retailers can use to assess the viability and vitality of the downtown that they are contemplating entering. The same instrument or a slightly revised version of it can be utilized after the entry. Retailers must keep close track of changes in the CBD so that they can enhance retail stores' viability for which they are responsible.

SUMMARY

This chapter explores the problems stemming from the conflict between the downtown and shopping centers. Since there is a wealth of literature on shopping centers and their characteristics and since the major problem lies in the future of downtowns, the discussion particularly revolves around how CBDs can be improved by undertaking special research. The key point in this overall analysis is that, unless it satisfies all interest groups, downtown revitalization projects are not adequate and are very risky.

From an individual retailer's perspective, the problem must be understood, and the effectiveness of the proposed solution and the expected impact on the individual store must be assessed. Once again, the retail manager's analytical abilities to relate his or her situation to changing economic and environmental conditions is brought to the fore.

REFERENCES

"Chicago Brings Loop Back to Life." *Engineering News-Record* (July 2, 1981):29–35.

Gobisborough, R. G. "Downtown: Good Views and Bad Views." *Advertising Age* (March 21, 1983):32–39.

"Heart of Atlanta Gets Transfusion." *Engineering News-Record*, (December 23, 1982):65–72.

Lewis, Stephen E. "Every Downtown Is Different Says Developer, but All Urban Malls Require Viable Existing Market." *The National Real Estate Investor* (May 1980):10–19.

Maronick, Thomas J., and Ronald M. Stiff. "The Impact of a Specialty Retail Center on Downtown Shopping Behavior." *Journal of the Academy of Marketing Science* (Summer 1985):292–306.

Peterson, Eric C. "Centers That Serve a Downtown Function." *Stores* (March 1983):35–39.

"St. Louis Downtown Makes Slow Comeback." *Engineering News-Record* (November 12, 1981):24–31.

Samli, A. Coskun, and Arthur E. Prell. *The Challenge to Regionalism.* Herrin, Ill.: Southern Illinois University, Business Research Bureau, 1965.

———. *The Challenge to Regionalism, Granite City Illinois.* Herrin, Ill.: Southern Illinois University, Business Research Bureau, 1966.

"Saving Downtown: Government Courts Retailers." *Chain Store Age Executive* (July 27, 1981):39–44.

Sloan, S. H. "Boston's Fasevilk Hall: A Rousing Success." *Chain Store Age* (March 1982):25–31.

Spalding, Lewis A., "Some Proof There Is Life After Death: Downtown." *Stores* (October 1983):33–38.

Stark, Morton S. "Shopping Center Future." *Stores* (March 1980).

Sutler, Gregg. "City Toils Over Seeds of Growth." *Advertising Age* (January 11, 1982):55–63.

5 Market Potentials and Feasibility

Some early studies have shown that more than 30 percent of new retail establishments survive less than six months (Churchill 1955; Sanzo, 1957). Three preliminary activities may reduce the risk of premature failure or discontinuance: assessing market potentials, evaluating the feasibility of the retail establishment, and determining the capital needs. If these three activities are performed well, the prospective retailer can determine whether or not the planned retail establishment should become a reality. Since store location is the least flexible factor in a retail strategy plan, it must be studied very carefully in advance. Once the commitment has been made to one particular location, it is difficult to make any adjustments (Ingene and Lusch 1980; Berman and Evans 1986). In order to assess market potentials, we must first define trading areas, after which the retailer can successfully locate the retail establishment. The location decision enables the retailer to determine market potential and feasibility, which in turn provides the basis for determining capital needs. This chapter presents a careful analysis of this sequential process.

TRADING AREAS

Geographical delineation of a region containing possible customers for a prospective retail firm or a conglomeration of prospective retail firms is of primary importance in retailing. Such a region is called a retail trade area (Huff 1962; Plotkin 1965; Goldstucker 1965). Ideally, a "natural" trading area minimizes the cost of contact between buyers and retailers which naturally implies the greatest access on the part of the retailers to the market with the most potential, as well as the greatest access to the best retailing facility on the part of the prospective consumers. Identification of successful trading areas leads to effective feasibility analyses and capital need determination. Such identification includes:

1. Determining the critical mass of population likely to be customers of the proposed retail store.
2. Determining what proportion of these people are located in the area. If, for instance, 55 to 70 percent of the store's customers live in that area, it is called *Primary Trading Area*. If 15 to 25 percent of the customers are located in that area, it is called *Secondary Trading Area*; and finally, the remaining proportion of the customers are located at the *Fringe Trading Area* (Chain Store Age Executive).
3. Determining what proportion of the purchases of these people will take place in the store, which implies determining the effectiveness of competing stores in the trading area.

Identifying the trading area will also lead into: (1) determining the demographic and socioeconomic characteristics of the store's customers; (2) deciding on the key aspects of advertising activity; (3) examining key location sites for a new store, a new branch, or an existing store that may be considering relocation; (4) estimating future growth or decline; and (5) examining the number of stores the area can reasonably handle (Berman and Evans 1986). Three approaches may be used to identify or delineate the trading area: (1) mathematical formulas; (2) subjective judgment, and (3) a modified approach, which combines part of the first two approaches. Mathematical formulas of retail trading areas are largely related to retail gravitation models.

RETAIL GRAVITATION MODELS

The mathematical formulation approach is depicted primarily by various approaches to retail gravitational measurement. The original versions of retail gravitation models, developed first by Reilly (1929) and later expanded by Converse (1946), were based on two variables: population and distance to be traveled. Reilly's hypothesis was that two cities attract retail trade from any intermediate point in almost direct proportion to the population of the two cities and in inverse proportion to the square of the distances from the intermediate point to either one of the two cities. Reilly's mathematical formula is as follows:

$$\frac{Ba}{Bb} = \left(\frac{Pa}{Pb}\right)\left(\frac{Db}{Da}\right)^{2}$$

Where

Ba = the proportion of the trade from the intermediate city attracted by city A;

Bb = the proportion of the trade from the intermediate city attracted by city B;

Pa = the population of city A;

Pb = the population of city B;

Da = the distance from the intermediate town to city A; and

Db = the distance from the intermediate town to city B.

Assuming that city A has a population of 100,000 and city B 300,000, and that intermediate town X is 40 miles from A and 60 miles from B, by using the above formula we can see that the percentage of the population of X attracted by A will be 75 percent.

$$\frac{Ba}{Bb} = \left(\frac{100,000}{300,000}\right)\left(\frac{60}{40}\right)^2 = 1/3 \times 9/4 = 3/4$$

City A has drawing power which is three times greater than B; the drawing power is interpreted as being 75 percent.

As an extension of the same phenomenon, the breaking point between A and B can be determined. The breaking point (or the point of indifference) is determined by the following formula (see Appendix for construction of the formula):

$$\text{As breaking point miles from B} = \frac{\text{Miles Between A and B}}{1 + \sqrt{\dfrac{\text{Population of B}}{\text{Population of A}}}}$$

Assuming the populations of cities A and B are 100,000 and 900,000, respectively, and the distance between the two cities is 80 miles, we can compute the breaking point to be 20 miles, as follows:

$$Bb = \frac{80}{1 + \sqrt{\dfrac{900,000}{100,000}}} = \frac{80}{1 + \sqrt{9}} = \frac{80}{1 + 3} = \frac{80}{4} = \text{approximately 20 miles}$$

This indicates that the breaking point between the trading areas of A and B is 20 miles. The breaking point here is also coined as the point of indifference. At this point the location is optimized because this location will attract business from both A and B without favoring one or the other.

The Curtis Publishing Company revised this approach by substituting population with the square footage of each retail center and by substituting physical distance between retail centers by travel time (Ellwood 1954; Huff 1962). On the basis of these revisions, Exhibit 5.1 and Exhibit 5.2 illustrate the delineation of trading area for a proposed shopping center. Exhibit 5.1 presents the hypothetical data used in the computations and their results in determining the potential trading area of a proposed retail facility. In recent years two developments have provided an extension of the gravity models. First, attempts have been made to

Exhibit 5.1

Hypothetical Data Used in Delineating the Trading Area of a Proposed Shopping Center

Shopping Center	Sq. footage of selling space	Travel time from A	Breaking point from shopping center to A
A	250,000	0	0
B	125,000	5	6.5
C	200,000	15	9.7
D	75,000	15	3.7
E	400,000	25	14.5

Source: Adapted and revised from Huff 1962.

develop simulation models based on the gravity concept (Crask 1979). Second, the multiple regression technique has been applied to expand versions of gravity models (Lord and Lynds 1981).

COMBINING THE GRAVITY MODEL WITH CENSUS DATA

Once a trade area map is developed based on the gravity model, it can be superimposed over a census tract map, as shown in Exhibit 5.2. Although detail is omitted, census tracts provide special information as to the number of people, housing units, income, education, and so on, of the people residing within the confines of each tract.

Based on this information, total retail potential or retail potential for a specific line can be established. If the establishment in question is one type of retail activity such as food, potential for food sales can be established as follows: assuming, for instance, tracts 1, 2, 3, and 4 have a population of 6,200, 5,320, 3,230, and 4,160, respectively, and assuming food purchases per capita in each tract are $6.41, $5.50, $7.60, and $6.05, we construct Exhibit 5.3.

At this point, an additional bit of information is needed to relate tract potentials to Supermarket X. Of the per capita expenditures in each tract, what proportion is likely to be spent at X? Past observation or surveys of typical customers in tracts 1, 2, 3, and 4 are likely to indicate how much of the total potential can be absorbed by Supermarket X.

Exhibit 5.2
Hypothetical Trading Area of a Proposed Shopping Center

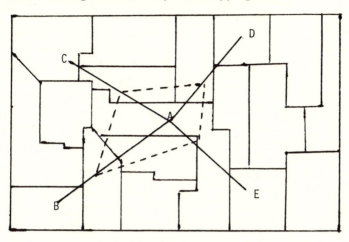

```
----- Trade Area Boundary
B-E   Competing Shopping Centers
A     Proposed Shopping Center
```

Source: Adapted and revised from Huff 1962: 10.

Exhibit 5.3
Census Tracts and Market Potential Within the Trade Area of Supermarket X

Census Tracts	Population	Per Capita Food Purchases	Potential for Tract	X's Share
1	6,200	6.41	39,742	23,845
2	5,320	5.50	29,260	11,705
3	3,230	7.60	24,548	6,137
4	4,160	6.05	25,168	3,775

On the basis of a survey, it may be found that 60, 40, 25, and 15 percent of the total food expenditures in tracts 1–4 may take place at Supermarket X. Thus, the last column in Exhibit 5.2 indicates the expected share of Supermarket X. Exhibit 5.4 presents the simple questionnaire utilized in a survey to obtain information needed for this kind of analysis. As can be seen, the questions indicate proximity to retail facility, mode of transportation, and data relating to the respondents' socioeconomic status.

Because the trading area is not homogeneous and the impact of competition varies from one part of the trading area to another, primary, secondary, and tertiary (or fringe) trading areas may be identified. Although objectively this identification may be made on the basis of distance and time (driving or walking time), subjectively it may be based on proportions of the store's total business. As stated earlier, the primary trading area may be thought of as the geographic core from which a store obtains between 55 to 70 percent of its business (Applebaum 1966). Secondary trading area is the geographic fringe from which the store gets between 15 and 25 percent of its business. The remainder of the store's business comes from territory or the fringe trading area.

An objective breakdown of the trading area may be achieved on the basis of distance: on total trade area map circles or zones with radii of 1/4, 1/2, 3/4, and 1 mile on down in an effort to establish primary, secondary, and tertiary markets.

By interviewing customers in eight supermarkets on a Thursday or Saturday, William Applebaum established value indexes by multiplying the total purchases of each interviewee on that day with the number of visits they paid to the particular store in question (Exhibit 5.5). On this basis, Exhibit 5.6 was developed. It indicates the zones and the store's customers who come from these zones. By using a population dot map, we can determine the population within each zone and sales per capita for each zone. If, for instance, 20 percent of the store's spotted customers are coming from 0–1/4 mile zones and the store's weekly volume is $30,000, $6,000 of the total volume is expected to come from this particular zone. On the basis of a population dot map, the number of people within the zone can be determined (assume 3,000 people), and hence per capita sales in this zone can be determined as $2.00 per week (Applebaum 1966).

Similarly, instead of dealing with a distance of 1, 2, 3, or 4 minutes' walking or driving, distances may be utilized to draw the circles or zones shown in Exhibit 5.6. This may be equally or more effective than the actual distance analysis.

The importance of the primary, secondary, and tertiary types of classification is obvious. Within the trading area, the store may have a more realistic picture of what kind of volume to expect and the source of that business. The answer to these questions may also determine its promotional activities in direct mail, local radio spots, and the like.

Two opposing approaches are utilized to delineate intraurban retail trade areas of proposed retail facilities: (1) subjective judgments based on observation and prior experience which lend themselves to generalizations, and (2) empirically

Exhibit 5.4
Consumer Behavior Questionnaire

1. At what SHOPPING CENTER did you LAST make a purchase of the following items?

    Clothing _____   Household Furnishings_____

    Food _____   Hardware _____

    Cosmetics/Drugs _____   Home Electronics _____

2. How many members of your household normally work in excess of four hours per day? _____

3. What type of WORK does the major income earner of your household do?

    _____Self-Employed? Yes ( )   No ( )

4. What are the APPROXIMATE AGES of those persons living within your household?

    MALE ( ) ( ) ( ) ( )   FEMALE ( ) ( ) ( ) ( )

5. How many CARS in the family? _____

6. At what shopping center do you NORMALLY MAKE THE MAJORITY of the following family purchases?

    Clothing _____   Household Furnishings_____

    Food _____   Hardware _____

    Cosmetics/Drugs _____   Home Electronics _____

7. What bracket as indicated below most closely fits your total FAMILY INCOME?

    $ 0 - 3,999 _____ $12,000 - 15,999 _____
    4,000- 7,999 _____   16,000 - 19,999 _____
    8,000-11,999 _____   20,000 - 23,999 _____

                    $24,000 and above _____

Source: Adapted and revised from Huff 1962: 39.

Exhibit 5.5
Customers' Residence and Purchases

Zone of Customer's Residence	Weekly Value Index
.00 - .25	1.00
.25 - .50	.96
.50 - .75	.93
.75 -1.00	.93

Source: Adapted from Applebaum 1966: 127.

derived mathematical formulations, which are often referred to as retail gravitation models (Goldstucker 1965). In 1972 Huff attempted to computerize his version of a gravitation model, and more recently, attempts have been made to simulate retail feasibility. Judgment approach is not discussed here. Different retailers as well as some scholars have developed simple checklists or certain subjective criteria for determining the trading area.

In recent years, a modified approach has emerged which uses not only pure and arbitrary judgment, but also judgments based on specifically defined statistical data. A modified judgment approach is presented in the following section.

A MODIFIED JUDGMENT APPROACH

This approach has four major stages: (1) defining the trading area, (2) determining the site, (3) assessing market potentials, and (4) estimating sales potentials. The trading area is important because it reflects the potential which the retailer is likely to experience. Thus, the judgment approach carries the activities from identifying a particular area to selecting tentative sites. Exhibit 5.7 illustrates specific steps in this undertaking.

The first step is to define or identify the particular geographic area (Markin 1971; Gist 1968; Rudelius et al. 1972), and, immediately afterward, to describe the area. This description should include general characteristics of the area: boundaries should be identified as established or delineated by location of population; natural and manmade boundaries such as highways, buildings, and rivers; and distances and size of the area.

The second step is to prepare a demographic description of the trading area, including age, sex, occupation, income levels, marital status, family size, education levels, and other demographic variables as deemed appropriate. Third, an environmental evaluation should be made, including the history of the area and future plans and developments that may be pending by public agencies and private businesses. The area, for instance, may be developing very rapidly and may be the fastest growing residential area. It, therefore, could be a good prospect

Exhibit 5.6
Customer Distribution of Store A

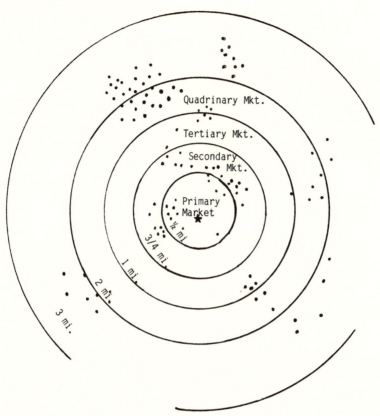

• A Customer

Source: Adapted and revised from Applebaum 1966: 130.

for further location. An evaluation of the available public and private transportation is also an essential part of this step. Finally, selecting tentative sites,
determining rent ranges in the area, and exploring the zoning patterns and zoning
laws are essential to bring all the information gathered to an operational level.
This final step can be achieved by checking with real estate agencies, established
business people, and the license bureau of local government, city, town, or
county planning offices.

SITE SELECTION

For a particular prospective business, the process of selecting a site starts from
the opposite end of Exhibit 5.8. A prospective retail establishment is already

Exhibit 5.7
Trading Area Assessment Process

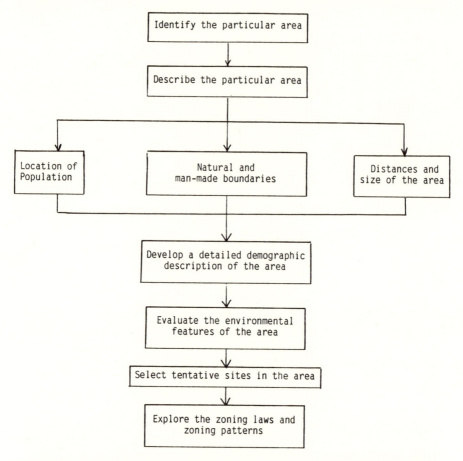

exposed to a number of proposed sites and has to start the process from this
particular perspective. It assesses the site according to its merits and then expands
its analyses to determine the trading area first and the market potentials second.

The site selection process comprises at least four steps: (1) evaluating the
traffic and history of the site (Markin 1971; Gist 1968; Rudelius et al. 1972);
(2) evaluating access to the site and parking facilities (Markin 1971; Gist 1968;
Rudelius et al. 1972); (3) determining legal aspects of the site, and (4) determining which site is to be selected.

Evaluating the Traffic and History of the Site

Evaluating the traffic is perhaps the most important activity in site selection,
for traffic is the backbone of retailing. In order to evaluate this factor, traffic

Exhibit 5.8
Major Steps in Assessing Retail Feasibility

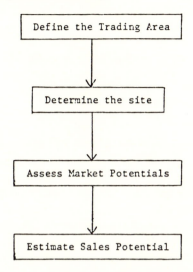

counts are conducted and are broken down into vehicular and pedestrian traffic. Of course, when a site in a mall or shopping center is assessed, then pedestrian traffic is important. However, if a location is considered for, say, a cluster of stores or for the type of store to which people would drive, then vehicular traffic becomes very important. The individual store and location must be considered according to the particulars of the case in hand.

If pedestrian traffic counts are used as part of the assessment process, then these pedestrians may also be interviewed. Similarly, prospective customer interviews are quite valuable. Finding out how far the consumers go to buy, say, groceries or apparel is another approach that will indicate whether or not the new proposed retail establishment is likely to enjoy an adequate pedestrian traffic. In either case, traffic counts combined with consumer interviews provide better and more in-depth information than only traffic counts or only consumer interviews.

Evaluating Access to the Site

Depending on whether vehicular or pedestrian traffic is primary, the site must be evaluated as to its accessibility. If the primary concern is the vehicular traffic, the following questions must be asked:

1. Is there traffic congestion? Part of the time or all of the time?
2. Do major and secondary highways connect the site with major residential areas from which customers are likely to come?

3. If the site is located in an already existing shopping center, are there enough exits so that exiting the shopping center will not be a frustrating experience?

4. Are there enough parking facilities in the immediate area so that consumers will not face the difficulties and frustration of finding a parking space?

Similarly, if the primary concern is pedestrian traffic, then these questions must be asked:

1. What features of the site attract pedestrians?
2. Is it safe for the pedestrians to walk around?
3. If they are driving from a distance, do they have ample parking facilities?
4. Are there enough prospective customers within a reasonable walking distance?

These are only a few questions. Depending on the conditions and the retailer's particular needs, many other questions may be pertinent. In addition, the questions raised here can be revised, again depending on specific needs.

It must be reiterated that as the access to the site is evaluated, the parking facilities must also be considered and assessed. One without the other is not nearly as effective as both factors.

Determining Legal Aspects of the Site

In attempting to evaluate a site, a number of factors are relevant, including zoning laws, landlord responsibilities, renter responsibilities, and rent values.

Zoning laws have direct and indirect impact on a site. If, for instance, zoning laws are rather changeable in the area where the site is being considered, then it becomes impossible to plan properly for future competition. Certain land in the immediate area could easily be changed from multifamily residential area to commercially zoned land which immediately creates a threat for the retail store that is being planned.

Indirect impact takes place if, for example, the zoning laws are tightened so as to discourage growth. If the land-use patterns are such that housing is scarce, then immigration to the area will be discouraged. Similarly, indirect impact can be experienced if zoning laws encourage the growth of other parts of the town rather than the area surrounding the proposed site.

Landlord responsibilities are an important factor in the site selection process. In most cases, the retailer is likely to lease rather than buy or build. In the case of leasing, a number of landlord responsibilities must be considered:

1. Are the landlords responsive to the retailers' needs?
2. Are the landlords concerned about keeping the buildings in good shape?
3. Are the landlords inclined to give long-term leases?
4. Are the increases in rents likely to be reasonable or exorbitant?

5. Are the landlords residents, and therefore involved in the well-being of the town, or do they live out of town and not have any interest in the well-being of the town?

In terms of renter responsibilities, how much is expected of the renter is the primary concern. If the landlords shift all the responsibilities of maintenance, remodeling, repairs, and related activities to the renter, then the site becomes substantially less desirable.

The rent value of a site is closely related to the cost/benefit ratio of that location. Every site has both advantages and disadvantages. If the disadvantages outstrip the advantages, then the site may be construed to have a negative rent value. Positive rent value, on the other hand, depends on how significantly the positive features of the site exceed the negative features.

Selecting the Site

The discussion thus far has provided the specific steps and has pointed out the necessary information for site selection. Once all the steps have been followed and all the information has been gathered, the rest is almost automatic. It will be necessary to contrast among, perhaps, a number of sites to choose the best. If each site goes through the already discussed selection process, it will be possible to decide on the best.

MARKET IDENTIFICATION AND POTENTIAL ASSESSMENT

Although trading area identification and market potential analyses often overlap or are used interchangeably, a clear distinction is made here. Trading area identification is considered before a site selection process takes place (Exhibit 5.8). Once the site is selected, it is still necessary to identify the prospective store's markets and to determine its potential. This type of analysis would lead to estimating the sales potential of the proposed store. In identifying the market and determining its potentials, we must consider (1) economic and business activity, (2) the nature and quality of competition, and (3) customer analysis.

Economic and Business Activity

The economic and business activity of the area where the site of the store is located may be analyzed from two separate perspectives: business activity and commercial structure. This distinction is necessary for the specific reason that these two perspectives explain two important dimensions of economic and business activity. If, for instance, the level of business activity is too low, the market may be less than desirable. If the estimated sales volume for groceries is less than $1.5 million and if Kroger needs an estimate of well over $2.5 million to open up a new store, the area is likely to be scratched. In order to determine

Exhibit 5.9
Blacksburg, Virginia, Buying Power Index[a]

Income[b]	.00011 x 5	=	.00066
Retail Sales[c]	.00007 x 3	=	.00021
Population[d]	.00008 x 2	=	.00016
			.00103 ÷ 10 = .00010

[a]Hypothetical figures.

[b]Income as a percentage of the national total.

[c]Retail sales as a percentage of the national total.

[d]Population as a percentage of the national total.

the level of business activity, four different approaches can be considered: (1) physical observation of the area, (2) buying power index, (3) quality and sales activity indexes, and (4) the indicator approach.

Physical observation of the area can be achieved in a number of ways, one of the most forward looking ones being to take aerial photos of the area. Such pictures show not only the population density, new construction, the highway network, and similar indicators, but also the location and extent of the competitive activity.

The buying power index is one of the most commonly used tools in determining the level of business activity in all towns and counties larger than 10,000 population. The buying power index is based on three variables: effective buying income, retail sales, and population. These variables are weighted by 5, 3, and 2, respectively. Thus, the effective buying power of a town, say Blacksburg, Virginia, is calculated as shown in Exhibit 5.9. As can be seen, Blacksburg's effective buying power is estimated to be .00009 percent of the national total. By using a national total sales figure for groceries and multiplying that figure by Blacksburg's buying power index (.00009 in this case), we can estimate the amount of groceries likely to be sold in that town.

The quality index provides an additional opportunity to evaluate the level of business activity in the area. The percentage of the U.S. population of an area divided into the buying power index would yield the quality index. Using the earlier example presented in Exhibit 5.9, if we wanted to calculate the quality index for Blacksburg we would get $0.00011 \div 0.00008 = 1.25$. Finally, an index of sales activity can be calculated by dividing the percentage of the population by the retail sales proportion. Again if we calculate this measure for Blacksburg, Virginia, it is as follows: $.00008 \div .00007 = 1.12$.

The indicator approach is related to tying the local level business activity to one or more indicators. If a certain type of consumption or purchase activity is being explored, calculations can be tied in with per capita or per household figures. Naturally, the population or the number of households in the area must be known. Exhibit 5.10 illustrates such an approach. In order to determine the

Exhibit 5.10

District in Montgomery County, Virginia, and National Distribution of Expenditures and Household Furnishings and Equipment

Income per Household	Percentage of All Households	Total Percentage of Expenditures on Household Furnishings & Equipment in U.S.[a]
$10,000 - 14,999	19.0	3.3
$15,000 - 24,999	30.8	3.2
$25,000 - 49,999	18.2	2.6
$50,000 & Over	1.8	1.6

Total number of households was 22,100 as of December 31, 1981.

[a]Figure derived by dividing average expenditure by average income before taxes.

Source: *Sales & Marketing Management*, July 26, 1982, C-201 and C-203. Percentage of total figures is from *Consumer Expenditure Survey Series: Interview Survey, 1972-73*, BLS Bulletin 1985, U.S. Department of Labor, 1978, pp. 2-3, 11-12.

Exhibit 5.11

Estimated Total Personal Income, Number of Households in Each Income Category, and Estimated Expenditures on Household Furnishings and Equipment, Montgomery County, Virginia

Income Per Household	Number of Units (a)	Total Est. Income (b)	Total Est. Expend. on Furnishings & Household Appliances (c)
10,000 - 14,999	4199	52,487,500	1,732,088
15,000 - 24,999	6807	136,140,000	4,356,480
25,000 - 49,999	4022	150,825,000	3,921,450
50,000 & Over	398	31,840,000	509,440
			10,519,458

[a]Estimated by multiplying household percentages in Exhabit 5.11 by the total number of households of 22,100.

[b]Midpoint of Income per Household was multiplied by the number of units with the exception of the last category, for which the estimated average income of $80,000 was used.

[c]Figures were arrived at by multiplying the total income figures by the Total Percentage of Expenditure figures in Exhibit 5.10.

market potential, the income distribution and the number of households in each income category are determined.

After the total income in each income category is determined the consumption patterns in each category are examined. Exhibits 5.10 and 5.11 show that consumption patterns in each income category vary. However, the national averages are considered to be homogeneous throughout the country. In order to determine the market potential for furniture in Hoboken, New Jersey, or Pocatello, Idaho, we use the same procedure.

Exhibit 5.12

A Procedure to Establish a Market Potential for a New Service Station*

1. Number of automobiles in Blacksburg area (estimation) 20,000

2. Number of service stations in Blacksburg area   30

3. Average market share per service station

   $= \dfrac{\text{Number of autos}}{\text{Number of service stations}} = \dfrac{20,000}{30} = 667$ autos per station

4. Costs associated with auto maintenance and operation (including gas, oil, service)

   A = cost of driving one mile = 12.5¢[a]

   B = average mileage driven per year = 12,000 miles

   A (multiplied by) B = average amount spent per year

   12.5 (12,000) = $1,500.00 per year in automotive service

5. Estimate of the business available for each service station

   Number of autos (multiplied by) average amount spent per year

   667 ($1,500) = $1,000,500

   A million dollar business per service station

*All estimates are subjective, based on facts and intuition.

---

[a]Automotive Magazine.

Exhibit 5.12 presents another example of using indicators. In order to determine the market activity level for gasoline stations, we utilize the number of cars, number of miles, and cost per mile as indicators of market activity.

Depending on the retail business, various indicators can be useful. In all cases, per capita expenditures or per household expenditures relating to the product in question (say apparel or food) are very basic and most commonly used indicators.

The second aspect of economic and business activity is related to commercial structure evaluation. Commercial structure evaluation has two significant phases: evaluating the degree of store saturation and determining the adequate number of establishments for a given area. Store saturation is measured by

$$S = \frac{C \times RE}{RF}$$

where

C = number of customers.
RE = average expenditures.
RF = retail facilities.
S = store saturation.

As can be seen, as the number of stores increases more than proportionately or as RE or C decreases, S goes down, which means that the area is no longer attractive to retailers. In some cases, S here is referred to as the saturation index.

Determining the adequate number of establishments in a given area can effectively indicate whether or not there is room for the proposed retail establishment. The commercial structure model for an area is determined by a series of three equations. In the first equation (1), the total expenditures for current consumption by the area residents is determined:

(1) $E = (C)(I)(a)(b)$

where

E = expenditures for current consumption.
C = consumption units (families a nd unrelated individuals).
I = median family income (before taxes).
a = tax ratio.
b = expenditures ratio.

The second equation allocates the total expenditures for current consumption on the basis of shopping behavior data. It therefore facilitates the calculation of estimated annual expenditures in retail and service establishments in the market area.

(2) $T = (d)(E)(e)(f)$

where

T = expenditures in retail and service establishments in the market area.
d = percentage allocation of expenditures for current consumption (E) by type of store.
e = shopping pattern ratio.
f = trade flow ratio.

The recommended number of retail establishments for each line of product and service trade is then determined in equation (3).

(3) $S = \dfrac{T}{gh}$

where

  S = recommended number of establishments for each line of retail and service trade.

  g = dollar sales per square foot for each line of trade.

  h = recommended average establishment size in square feet for each line of trade.

The three equations combined provide information about existing opportunities or lack thereof.

The Nature and Quality of Competition

Once economic and business activity is established, the quality of the competition must be delineated so that the proposed retail establishment can determine its opportunities fully. The evaluation process can be achieved through (1) consumer surveys and (2) observation of existing stores.

Consumer surveys indicate where people shop and intend to shop. If consumers appear to be very loyal to existing competition and if the competition appears to be strong, then the proposed retail establishment may not find the existing opportunities very enticing. The same observations are true for an existing store.

Exhibit 5.13 illustrates a single, small grocery store which we call Pixie Market. It is located in a residential section of a major city. The three concentric areas indicate walking distances of 1 1/2, 1 1/2 to 3 minutes, and 3 to 4 1/2 minutes. Area A represents 2 percent of four census tracts, whereas B and C each represent 4 percent.

Consider the following example: Assume that a survey was conducted to determine to what extent the residents bought their groceries at the Pixie Market. (See Exhibit 5.14). It became clear that the Pixie Market was dealing with a $382,955 market potential. A fraction of the population was purchasing all of their groceries in the Pixie Market (Exhibit 5.15).

If the Pixie Market were to go on sale, major food chains would not consider it because of its potential. A Seven Eleven type of convenience grocery store, on the other hand, might find it very attractive. If a prospective grocery store were to consider locating near the Pixie Market, there would be $615,545 worth of market potential not tapped by Pixie Market. If the proposed store could capture a large proportion of this part of the market, it would then be quite attractive for a competing convenience grocery chain. However, there would still be insufficient potential for a major supermarket.

Systematic observation of existing stores can reveal valuable information about the existing competition. In this context, observation may be divided into internal and external observation. Internal observation may include factors such as size

Exhibit 5.13
Pixie Market

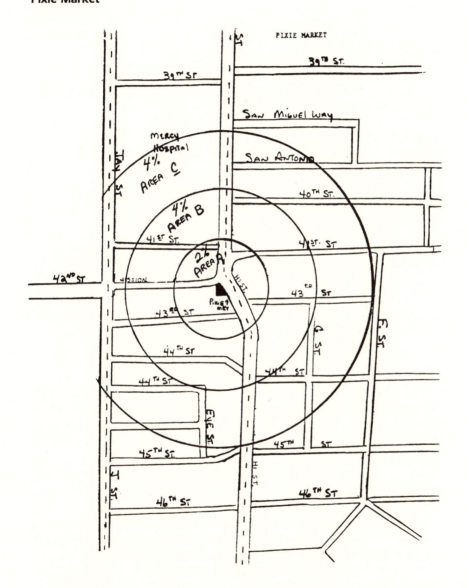

Exhibit 5.14
Information about Areas A, B, and C[a]

Areas	Estimated No. of Families	Average Income	Proportion Spent on Food	Total Grocery Dollars
A	50	$25,000	23.0%	$287,500
B	40	20,000	27.0%	216,000
C	110	15,000	30.0%	495,000

[a]Hypothetical data. Could be estimated from Census Tract data and Bureau of Labor Statistics consumer spending data.

Exhibit 5.15
Proportion of Groceries That Local Customers Bought at the Pixie Market

Proportional Groceries Purchased	Area A	Area B	Area C
All (100%)	20%	13%	00%
Part (50%)	55%	40%	40%
A Fraction (25%)	27%	20%	40%
None (0%)	00%	27%	20%
TOTAL	100%	100%	100%

of the store, internal layout, merchandise depth and breadth, prices, quality, customer in-store movements, and many other important bits of information. External observation may include factors such as the drawing power (based on parking patterns and license plate numbers of parked cars), location evaluation, traffic patterns, store exteriors, and related important information. See Exhibits 5.14, 5.15, and 5.16.

Customer Analysis

Finally, in further identifying the market and its strengths, customer analysis is utilized. Two major approaches can be employed in customer analysis: (1) evaluating demographic data and income levels and (2) determining attitudes and habits through consumer surveys. Both approaches have merits and are complementary rather than substitutes for one another.

Evaluation of demographic data has already been mentioned in this chapter. Secondary data relating to the trading area of the market need to be analyzed so

Exhibit 5.16
Dollar Amount of Groceries That Local Customers Bought at the Pixie Market[a]

Proportional Groceries Purchased	Area A	Area B	Area C
All (100%)	57,500	28,080	-
Part (50%)	77,625	43,200	90,000
Fraction (25%)	17,250	10,800	49,500
None (0%)	-	-	-
TOTAL	152,375	82,080	139,500

[a]Exhibit 5.12 is based on the percentages presented in Exhibit 5.14 and the total figures presented in Exhibit 5.15.

that the extent of the trading area and the total potential of the defined market can be realistically assessed. Not only market potentials but also the socioeconomic makeup of the market and, therefore, its suitability for the proposed retail establishment, can be determined through the evaluation of demographic data.

Sales Potential Estimates

Although market potential analyses approximate the possible sales volume of a retail establishment, they do not give specific sales volume estimates. Thus, the final step in market potential and feasibility analysis is the sales potential estimates.

Estimating the sales volume (Rudelius et al. 1972) activity can be illustrated by the following example based on the annual revenue estimates of a supermarket located in a specific Census Tract located in the store's retail trading area. Four separate factors are included in the method as illustrated in Exhibit 5.17. These are (1) number of households, (2) median income, (3) proportion of annual income, and (4) amount of money on each product line. These four factors make it possible to determine the estimated annual revenue for the proposed store. Exhibit 5.18 illustrates the calculation for this estimated revenue figure. Assuming, for instance, that a new supermarket is being considered in the given trading area and assuming that the minimum acceptable potential sales volume is about $1,000,000, we find that the proposed area is not acceptable for the grocery store in question.

FROM MARKET POTENTIALS TO FEASIBILITY AND CAPITAL NEEDS

To this point, this chapter has focused on market potentials and trading areas. However, market potentials, trading area identification, and location decisions

Exhibit 5.17
Calculating Estimated Sales Volume

FACTOR:

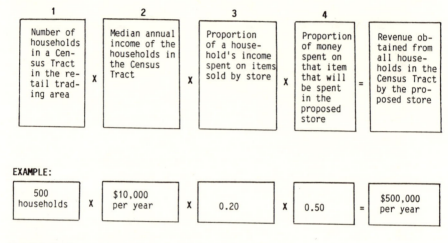

EXAMPLE:

| 500 households | X | $10,000 per year | X | 0.20 | X | 0.50 | = | $500,000 per year |

Exhibit 5.18
Operating Expenditures for Proposed Store[a]

	%
Net Sales	100.0
Cost of Merchandise Sold	61.64
Gross Margin on Sales	38.36
Gross Income	43.71
Operating Expenses	38.77
Net Profit (before tax)	3.41
Net Profit (after tax)	1.93

[a]This type of information is typically available at the Small Business Administration, Washington, D.C., or in National Cash Register publications on retail expenditures, operating expenses, cost of inventory, and preopening expenses.

are only means to an end, establishing the feasibility for a specific retail establishment and determining its capital needs.

Although the specific potential for a store has been dealt with in Exhibit 5.18, this topic needs further exploration. It must be emphasized that numerous approaches can be used to determine market potential in general and for a proposed retail establishment in particular.

A Specific Example

Assume that you are contemplating opening a furniture store in Montgomery County, Virginia.

As we saw earlier, Exhibits 5.10 and 5.11 illustrate what can be done simply by using secondary data. Sales and marketing management data provide income distribution figures, and the Bureau of Labor Statistics supplies the proportion of income spent on different product categories. Exhibit 5.10 illustrates these data. Exhibit 5.11 is based on the data presented in Exhibit 5.10. As can be seen, the total potential for furniture and related products in that county is estimated to be more than $10 million. If it is known that the total furniture and related product sales are about $9 million, then there is a potential of over $1 million. The question here is, could the proposed store survive with that potential volume if it were to capture most of it? More specifically, what may be expected in terms of return on investments and in terms of capital for a store of this size? Exhibit 5.18 provides data on this issue: If this store were to have sales of about $1 million, it would have a net profit of 1.93 percent or $19,300. The question here is, just how much capital is needed to get this business started? The needed capital can be classified as (1) operating expenses, (2) inventory costs, and (3) preopening expenses.

Using the above example, we see that monthly sales volume, on a simple average basis, is 83,000. Since total operating expenses account for 38.77 percent of the net sales volume, $32,300 per month has to be set aside for monthly operating expenses. This is assuming a very slow start of one month of almost no business at the beginning. The average stock turnover is 2.97 or 3; $1 million sales volume is $616,000 expressed at cost; one-third of $616,000 is $205,300, which is the average inventory. A six-month revolving credit brings the investment on inventory down to $205,300 \div 6 = \$34,200$. The first three months are not likely to bring in large profits. Conservatively, at least two months' expenses should be met at the beginning of the business venture, a sum equal to $64,600. Preopening expenses are not usually excessive because the land is likely to provide the support to make the site operational. Perhaps anywhere between 10 to 50 percent of the monthly expenses can be allotted for exterior and internal fixtures. Assuming in this case approximately 30 percent of the monthly expenses as the preopening capital requirement, we find that approximately $10,000 will be necessary. By combining the three components, $10,000 + 32,300 + 64,600 = 106,900$. The total capital needs appear to be $106,900. If half of this sum were to be raised internally, it would be possible to borrow at least on a one-to-one basis. Thus, conservatively, $106,900 \div 2 = 54,450$. With $53,450 it may be possible to start a business that will yield $19,000 net profit/annum. Thus, the investment will yield approximately 36.0 percent over and beyond all the expenses.

SIMULATION MODELS

Earlier in this chapter, simulation models are mentioned as a recent version of the retail gravity concept. However, simulation as a management information support technique has not quite yet been developed in retailing. An attempt is made to introduce one such simulation effort into the retailing field. Graphic

Evaluation Review Technique Simulation (GERTS) is not new in business literature, but it is not utilized effectively in the retailing decision areas. The uniqueness of GERTS is its flexibility. It combines decision tree and PERT (Program Evaluation and Review Technique) models into a probabilistic simulation technique. At the end of this chapter two GERTS episodes are presented. The first attempts to determine the best location for the retail establishment, and the second illustrates the simulation results in an effort to determine the feasibility of adding a new department to a retail store. Significantly more efforts of this type will be made in the retailing literature in the foreseeable future.

SUMMARY

This chapter deals with the all-important topic of market potentials and retail feasibility. Market potential analysis begins with the trading area delineation. There are basically three approaches to delineating trading areas: subjective judgment, mathematical formulation, and the modified approach. Mathematical formulas are related to retail gravitation models. The modified judgment approach has four major stages: (1) defining the trading area, (2) determining the site, (3) assessing market potentials, and (4) estimating sales potentials. The trading area is defined by identifying the area, describing it demographically, and evaluating it environmentally. Site selection involves evaluating the traffic and history, assessing parking facilities, and determining the legal aspects of the site. Assessing market potentials begins with studying the level of business activity. Next, the commercial structure is analyzed. Identification and evaluation of the quality of competition are the next steps. Finally, customer analysis is performed to determine market potentials. Sales potential estimate is the last step in the overall market potential and feasibility analyses. It is necessary to reduce the analysis to the point where the retail establishment's sales volume can be estimated. This chapter presents a specific model to accomplish this task.

Once the sales volume is estimated, it is necessary to establish the capital needs to operationalize the proposed store. Only then will it be possible to determine the true feasibility of the proposed store. Different techniques are available to determine the expected sales volume of the proposed store. Perhaps it is necessary to use more than one technique and to establish a range rather than just one figure.

REFERENCES

Applebaum, William. "Methods of Determining Store Trade Areas, Market Penetration, and Potential Sales." *Journal of Marketing Research* (May 1966): 128–134.

Berman, Barry, and Joel B. Evans. *Retail Management.* 3rd ed. New York: Macmillan, 1986.

Converse, P. D. *Retail Trade Areas in Illinois.* Business Study No. 4, Urbana: University of Illinois, 1946.

Crask, Melvin. "A Simulation Model of Patronage Behavior Within Shopping Centers." *Decision Sciences* (January 1979): 37–47.

Ellwood, L. W. "Estimating Potential Volume of Proposed Shopping Centers." *The Appraisal Journal* (October 1954): 581–589.

Expenses in Retail Business. Dayton, Ohio: National Cash Register Co.

Gist, Ronald R. *Retailing Concepts and Decisions*. New York; John Wiley, 1968.

Goldstucker, Jac. "Trading Areas." In George Schwartz, ed., *Science in Marketing*. New York: John Wiley, 1965.

Huff, David L. *Determination of Intra-Urban Retail Trade Areas*. Real Estate Research Program, University of California at Los Angeles, 1962.

———. "A Probabilistic Analysis of Consumer Spatial Behavior." In W. S. Deckes, ed., *Emerging Concepts in Marketing*. Chicago: American Marketing Association, 1972, 443–461.

Ingene, Charles A., and Robert F. Lusch. "Market Selection Decisions for Department Stores." *Journal of Retailing* (Fall 1980): 20–30.

Kaplan, A. D. H. *Small Business*. New York: McGraw-Hill, 1948.

Lord, Dennis J., and Charles O. Lynds. "The Use of Regression Models in Store Location Research." *Akron Business and Economic Review* (Summer 1981): 13–19.

Markin, Rom. J. *Retailing Management*. 2nd ed. New York: Macmillan, 1971.

Plotkin, Manuel D. "The Use of Credit Accounts and Computers in Determining Store Trading Area." In Frederick Webster, ed., *New Directions in Marketing*. Chicago: American Marketing Association, 1965, pp. 270–275.

Reilly, William J. *Method for the Study of Retail Relationships*. Research Monograph No. 4, University of Texas Press, 1929.

Rudelius, William, Robert F. Hoel, and Roger Kerin. "Assessing Retail Opportunities in Low-Income Areas." *Journal of Retailing* (Fall 1972): 99–108.

Sanzo, Richard. "What Is Behind the Rise in Business Failures." *Dun's Review* (December 1957): 40–43.

APPENDIX: THE USE OF SIMULATION IN RETAIL FEASIBILITY ASSESSMENT: A GERT EXAMPLE

A. C. Samli and Thomas D. Daley

ABSTRACT

Although feasibility analysis is one of the chief determinants of the success or failure of a retail store, the techniques that have been used in this area have been based primarily on research-generated hard data. These techniques are quite useful and the data quite valid. However, much of the time the database is not broad enough. Thus, a broader database generated by various simulation techniques could be used to remedy the situation. This appendix is based on one such example. Although its implications are not completely known, GERT simulation is shown to be quite appropriate in this context.

INTRODUCTION

As stated in this chapter, the lifeblood of retailing is traffic. Adequate traffic substantially enhances the viability of a retail establishment. In order to assure this adequate level, site selection is perhaps the primary factor to be considered. Studies have shown that more than 30 percent of new retail establishments survive less than six months. One of the prime contributors to this attrition rate is the inability to choose an appropriate site. The process of selecting a suitable site is often time consuming and expensive, however.

A number of logical, descriptive, and analytic treatments of site selection problems are available. Various techniques, most of them based on research-generated hard data, have proven quite useful. In most cases, generating hard data for such studies is also costly and time consuming. A broader database generated by various simulation techniques could remedy this problem, but there have not been many computer-based site selection models, particularly those using simulation techniques. This appendix attempts to illustrate how a management science tool, the Graphic Evaluation and Review Technique (GERT), can be used in retail feasibility analysis.

Two major objectives are pursued here: first, to distinguish the major characteristics of GERT simulation, and second, to illustrate the use of GERT as a planning and control tool in retail feasibility assessment projects.

GERT: AN INTRODUCTION

GERT combines flowgraph theory, moment-generating functions, and, as suggested by its name, PERT (Elmaghraby 1966; Pritsker and Happ 1966; Pritsker and Whitehouse 1966; Moore and Clayton 1976). It is used primarily to solve networks that contain multiparameter stochastic branches and nodes with ''or'' and ''and'' properties. In complete networks, such a computer-based analytic system functions rapidly and effectively. In addition to its features of solving network problems, GERT also lends itself to simulation. Both the GERT technique and the GERT simulator are briefly discussed here.

GERT overcomes many PERT deficiencies (Elmaghraby 1966; Pritsker and Happ 1966). In PERT, for instance, branching from a node is deterministic, since every branch (activity) must be completed at some time. However, GERT allows probabilistic branching, and, therefore, a given activity may not be taken under certain conditions or with a certain probability. Individual activities are assigned a probability of occurrence, a parameter set for time and cost, and a distribution type. The type of distribution selected by the user determines the time information they must supply. For example, the normal distribution requires a parameter set that contains the mean, standard deviation, and minimum and maximum time, whereas the constant distribution requires only the constant time. GERT provides more flexibility than PERT in the realization of nodes (events). Unlike PERT, the GERT user specifies the number of activities needed to realize the node the first time and the number needed to realize the same node the next time it is encountered in the simulation run. Another feature of GERT is looping, because an activity may be repeated. If there is uncertainty in a project, that is, if outcomes of certain activities are probabilistic, then a failure may lead to a recycling or repeating of some previous event.

Another unique feature of GERT is that the realization of more than a single event can terminate the network. This feature, multiple sink nodes, is useful for collecting statistics for numerous possible terminal events. Statistics, other than those at terminal events, can also be collected at specified critical points throughout the network.

Each of the GERT features outlined above makes it a more powerful analytic tool than PERT. Networks of activities and events can be constructed to more closely represent real-life situations and provide the user with more meaningful information.

FEASIBILITY ASSESSMENT: A MODEL

Numerous attempts have been made to develop feasibility models for retail establishments. Although there may not be a perfect model for the process that is involved in feasibility analysis, certain generally accepted sequential steps are common to all models. An attempt is made here to develop one such model. The model has basically four stages: (1) defining the trading area, (2) determining the site, (3) assessing market potentials, and (4) estimating sales potentials.

Defining the Trading Area

Geographical delineation of a region containing the possible customers for a prospective retail firm or a group of prospective retail firms is of primary importance in retailing (Huff 1962). Ideally, a natural trading area delineation minimizes the cost of contact between buyers and retailers (Goldstucker 1965). This implies providing the greatest access to the retailer to reach the markets with the greatest potential. Typically, three criteria are utilized in delineating trading areas. Population dispersion is the first consideration. In trading area analysis, the dynamics of population dispersion are analyzed within a given natural geographic area (Goldstucker et al. 1978). The second consideration is geographic distance. Analyzing population density within a given geographic area makes it possible to evaluate what might be considered the logical trading area for a retail establishment. Earlier examples of retail gravitational models attempted to do just that (Reilly 1931; Converse 1946; Huff 1962). The third consideration relates to natural barriers which by definition would depict the physical trading area in terms of accessibility.

Determining the Site

Although there is a rich literature on determining the site (Mason and Mayer 1987; Goldstucker et al. 1978; Applebaum 1966; Eisenpreis 1965; Dalrymple and Thompson 1969), feasibility assessment usually takes place after the site is decided on. Four groups of approaches are used for site selection. These approaches will only be named in this discussion: (1) the checklist method, (2) the analogue method, (3) the gravity model, and (4) the advanced mathematical model (Goldstucker et al. 1978). Although many entrepreneurs will undertake the site selection activity themselves, larger companies and particularly national chains work with consultants.

Assessing Market Potentials

In identifying the market and determining its potentials, three considerations are paramount: (1) economic and business activity, (2) the nature and quality of competition, and (3) customer analysis. Economic and business activity in the area where the site is located is analyzed from two separate perspectives— business activity and commercial structure. In order to determine business activity, a number of techniques have been developed by different marketing scholars. Among these are physical observation of the area, buying power index (BPI) analysis, and quantity and sales activity indexes (Mason and Mayer 1981; Goldstucker et al. 1978). With regard to commercial structure, two points should be considered: (1) evaluating the degree of store saturation and (2) determining the adequate number of establishments for the given area (Gist 1968; Goldstucker et al. 1978). A number of formulas have been developed to accomplish these two objectives (Goldstucker 1978; Amato and Anderson 1972; Dalrymple and Thompson 1969). Finally, customer analysis implies a thorough evaluation of socioeconomic data and consumption patterns within each socioeconomic class. Some authors will go as far as exploring the psychological and attitudinal makeup of the prospective consumers (Forbes 1968; Moore and Mason 1970–1971; and Enis and Cox 1968).

Estimating Sales Potentials

Estimating the sales volume activity can be based on objective and subjective data. Objective data include the number of households in the given area, the median annual income in that area, and the proportion of the household income spent on the items sold by the stores. Subjective data involve the proportion of these households likely to patronize the store and the attitude of the households in terms of their inclination to patronize the store.

It is assumed that some or all of the technical aspects of this model will be taken care of either by consultants or by the prospective retailers themselves. Hence, in the following simulation model only the choice between whether the company will use its own expertise or that of a consultant is considered to be problematical.

FEASIBILITY ASSESSMENT: AN EXAMPLE

Apparell Unlimited, Inc. (fictitious name), a small women's apparel store chain, has been considering opening up a new store in a small southeastern university town. The management needs to know approximately how long it would take to do a complete feasibility study and, if the feasibility analysis is positive, to actually begin operations. Similarly, the management would like to know how much it would cost to operationalize these goals. In order to facilitate this research undertaking, Appendix Exhibit 1 was developed. It is the logical flowchart describing the questions to be asked and steps taken in sequential order. Assuming some degree of previous experience in this particular area, the researcher can easily develop such a flowchart which depicts the total model and its constraints, to be subsequently utilized for simulation purposes. Although the details of the present project were not known to the management, they know, for instance, that either they themselves or a local consultant could provide the approximate time and cost estimates. On this basis, Appendix Exhibit 2 lists all of the activities required in the course of developing the complete feasibility analysis.

For each activity, a probability estimate was given for optimistic, pessimistic, and most likely outcome measured in days (beta fitted to three parameters) and a one-point estimate for approximate costs. Thus, a certain degree of sophistication and knowledge in feasibility assessment in general is a prerequisite to the utilization of GERT in this particular project. GERT, as applied here, is based on the principle that typical feasibility analysis of this type can be broken down into a number of standard components.

Appendix Exhibit 3 is the GERT network for the proposed feasibility study. It transforms the logic of the flowchart presented in Exhibit 1 into the format required for simulation. The relationship between the flowchart elements and those of the network, however, are not one to one. An activity described in a flowchart box becomes an arrow in the network. However, the questions in the flowchart are decided on by the realization of decision nodes.

THE SIMULATION

A simulation of 1,000 runs used the data in Appendix Exhibit 2 and the relationships depicted in Appendix Exhibit 3. Program output appears in Exhibits 4, 5, and 6. Node 31 represents successful completion of the feasibility study and subsequent commencement of retail operations. As can be seen in Appendix Exhibit 4, this particular outcome can be achieved only 7 percent of the time. If successful, the total process will take 91 to 278 days with a mean period of 135 days. The same exhibit illustrates that the project is terminated at the level

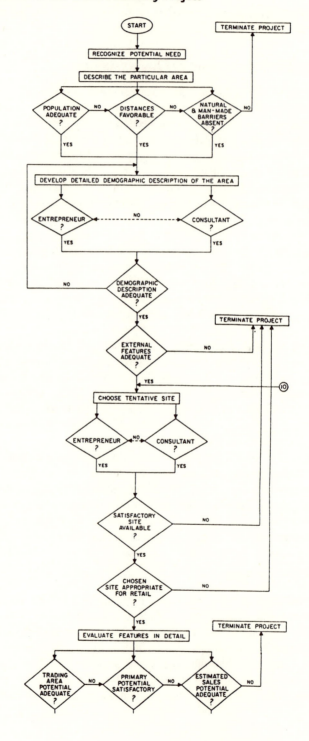

Appendix Exhibit 1 Continued

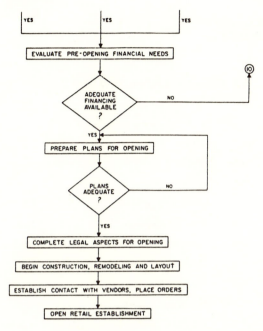

of node 8 because of either insufficient population, unfavorable barriers, or unfavorable distances. This is likely to be the case almost 30 percent of the time. The simulation implies that management would know somewhere between 3 to 16 days that the whole project was not feasible. Some other critical points are also depicted in Appendix Exhibits 4 and 5. These particular nodes illustrate the versatility of the simulation program regarding its ability to accumulate information at any prescribed node.

Appendix Exhibit 5 presents the same general type of information on the basis of cost. According to the cost analysis, the average completion cost of the study for the same given degree of success (i.e., 7 percent) is estimated to be $37,000, with the range of possible value from $30,000 to $89,000. This illustration, as can be seen, provides cost information for the same critical nodes presented in Appendix Exhibit 4.

Although the GERT user cannot associate any given time with any given cost because of the unparalleled time and cost options, it is still necessary to think about a scheduled completion time. From Appendix Exhibit 6, the management can be sure that the project has an 81 percent probability of completion in 140 days or less. If this probability needs to be increased to 100 percent the completion time expands significantly more than proportionately.

The same pattern is observed regarding the cost picture. An 89 percent probability indicates that the project can be completed with a cost of $46,000 or less.

Appendix Exhibit 2
Activity Description

Activity	Nodes	Descriptions	Probability	Days a	b	c
1	2-3	recognize potential of the area				
2	3-4	consultant describes the area	.35	3	7	10
3	3-4	entrepreneur describes the area	.65	3	7	10
4	4-5	dummy	1.00			
5	4-6	dummy	1.00			
6	4-7	dummy	1.00			
7	5-8	insufficient population	.50			
8	5-9	sufficient population	.50			
9	6-8	unfavorable natural and man made barriers	.30			
10	6-9	no problem barriers	.70			
11	7-8	distances too far	.35			
12	7-9	favorable distances	.65			
13	9-10	consultant develops demographic description	.65	1	3	
14	9-10	entrepreneur develops demographic description	.35	3	5	
15	10-11	evaluate demographic description	1.00			
16	11-10	demographic description inadequate	.40			
17	11-12	demographic description adequate	.60			
18	12-32	external features inadequate	.25			
19	12-13	external features adequate	.75			
20	13-14	consultant picks tentative site	.60	1	3	5
21	13-14	entrepreneur picks tentative site	.40	3	6	10
22	14-33	no satisfactory site available	.20			
23	14-15	satisfactory sites available	.80			
24	15-16	consultant chooses best site	.60	1	1.5	2
25	15-16	entrepreneur choose best site	.40	300		
26	16-34	chosen site appropriate for retail	.20			
27	16-17	chosen site inappropriate for retail	.80			
28	17-18	evaluate features in detail	1.00	5	10	20

Appendix Exhibit 2 (Continued)

Activity	Nodes	Descriptions	Probability	Days		
29	18-19	dummy	1.00			
30	18-20	dummy	1.00			
31	18-21	dummy	1.00			
32	19-35	trading area potential inadequate	.40			
33	19-22	trading area potential adequate	.60			
34	20-36	primary potential unsatisfactory	.30			
35	20-22	primary market satisfactory	.75			
36	21-37	est. sales potential unsatisfactory	.30			
37	21-22	est. sales potential satisfactory	.70			
38	22-23	evaluate preopening financial needs	1.00	7	15	20
39	23-13	adequate financing not available	.35			
40	23-24	adequate financing available	.65			
41	24-25	prepare plans for opening	1.00	7	15	20
42	25-24	plans inadequate	.15			
43	25-26	plans adequate	.85			
44	26-27	complete legal aspects for opening	1.00	3	6	9
45	27-28	begin construction and remodeling	1.00	30	60	90
46	27-29	estab. contact with vendors, place orders	1.00			
47	28-30	dummy	1.00			
48	29-30	dummy	1.00			
49	30-24	progress unsatisfactory	.10			
50	30-31	open retail establishment	.90			

Appendix Exhibit 3
GERT Diagram for the Feasibility Simulation

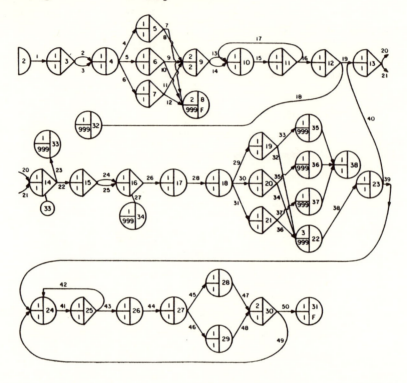

Again, if 100 percent probability is required, the cost figure goes up to $89,000. The management in this case can use Appendix Exhibit 6 for two additional purposes. First, the management may wish to keep its cost below $35,000 but might not be very happy with the 51 percent probability. They can go back to Appendix Exhibit 4 and analyze critical nodes to determine whether or not there are some ways of reducing the costs. For example, they may decide that the cost of completing node 24 is too high (mean cost $12,000). It can be reduced by revising the financial requirements and the financial sources that are to be considered appropriate. After simulating a few similar revisions, the management may be able to put together a feasibility and preopening program for the proposed store which has an 80 percent or 90 percent probability of successful completion at a cost of $35,000. Project plans can thus be revised by readjusting the network parameters.

The second use of Appendix Exhibit 6 is related to the alternative approaches of establishing feasibility and planning the commencement of the store. If the management has three distinct alternatives in determining feasibility, it can run a simulation for each and therefore develop three sets of data. This type of "what

Appendix Exhibit 4
Time Statistics

NODE	PROBABILITY (%)	MEAN TIME (Days)	STANDARD DEVIATION (Days)	MINIMUM	MAXIMUM
8	29.90	7.82	2.49	3.37	16.26
12	70.10	12.19	3.09	5.93	23.50
17	32.80	21.40	9.51	10.63	79.49
24	7.20	54.15	31.12	32.20	202.99
26	7.20	68.64	31.65	44.71	211.95
31	7.20	135.19	32.12	91.29	278.74
32	19.10	12.35	3.19	5.99	21.27
33	12.00	18.45	9.81	9.15	66.50
34	7.60	21.05	10.40	10.69	73.88
35	14.10	33.17	10.83	20.73	91.90
36	9.00	31.53	8.30	20.73	64.72
37	10.40	32.70	9.79	20.24	65.53
38	24.20	32.67	10.07	20.24	91.90

NODE	ACTIVITY DESCRIPTION
8	Project terminated due to occurrence of 2 of following three conditions (1) insufficient population; (2) unfavorable natural or man-made barriers; (3) unfavorable distances
12	Develop adequate demographic description
17	Chosen site determined suitable for retail
24	Adequate sources of financing available
26	Opening plans adequate
31	Open retail establishment
32	External features deemed inadequate, project terminated
33	Project terminated, no satisfactory sites available
34	Project terminated, chosen site inappropriate for retail establishment
35	Project terminated, trading area potential inadequate
36	Project terminated, primary potential inadequate
37	Project terminated, estimated sales potential inadequate
38	Average of nodes 35, 36, 37

Appendix Exhibit 5
Cost Statistics

Node	Mean (in 000's of Dollars)	Standard Deviation	Minimum	Maximum
8	1.86	2.22	.30	5.00
12	2.17	2.23	.50	5.40
17	4.66	3.26	.80	20.10
24	12.23	10.24	4.80	63.70
26	16.22	10.45	8.80	67.70
31	37.63	10.58	30.30	89.20
32	2.12	2.21	.50	5.40
33	4.83	3.49	.80	22.50
34	4.68	3.21	.80	17.80
35	6.83	3.54	2.80	22.10
36	6.46	2.87	2.80	17.70
37	6.45	3.16	2.80	17.40
38	6.64	3.32	2.80	22.10

Appendix Exhibit 6
Cumulative Probabilities for Successful Project Completion

Time in Weeks	Probability of Project Completion	Cost $1.000's	Probability of Project Cost
95	1.0	32	25.0
100	3.0	34	51.0
105	4.0	36	62.0
110	10.0	38	78.0
115	22.0	40	85.0
120	36.0	42	87.0
125	47.0	44	87.0
130	64.0	46	89.0
135	68.0		
140	81.0		
279	100.0	89.2	100.0

if'' program modification is generally referred to as sensitivity analysis. The outcome of such an activity will enable the management to choose the best cost probability and time probability combination and hence the most appropriate course of action.

CONTROL FUNCTION

In developing a GERT simulation, critical points can be singled out, and probabilities related to time and cost can be determined. These critical points can be carefully monitored, and the progress of the project can be checked step by step. If probabilities established for the critical points are realistically fulfilled, the credibility of the total simulation for this project is likely to be enhanced. Some of these critical nodes are identified in Appendix Exhibits 4 and 5. If, for instance, node 8 is achieved in 20 days at a cost of $5,000, there is a reasonable doubt that the whole project will be completed in 279 days at a cost of $89,000.

One of the hypothetical preliminary figures can be replaced with the actual figures as the sequential activities occur. Then the situation can be reevaluated on the basis of the new probabilities and time parameters. The impact of the occurrences on certain critical branchings and expected subsequent activities can be assessed by a series of simulations in which the effects of the new activities on completion time and cost are noted. If the expected probability of taking a branch is 50 percent but the probability of 60 percent would cause a substantial decrease in completion time or cost, then emphasis can be placed on raising the expected probability by only 10 percent and making sure it will not decline. Thus, a marginal change in probability may have a significant effect on time and/or cost.

CONCLUSIONS

For the sophisticated retail manager who does not know the expected outcome of a proposed feasibility and a new store opening project but is very familiar with the standardized inputs required, GERT can be a phenomenal tool regarding the critical go or no go decision before the project really gets underway. Thus, GERT eliminates much intuition in such retailing projects. In all areas of feasibility analysis and preopening plans where there are horizon dates and significant cost constraints, GERT is likely to become a very important technique of planning and control.

REFERENCES

Amato, Henry N., and Evan E. Anderson. "The Location of Retail Activity." Working Paper Series, No. 75. New Orleans, Graduate School of Administration, Tulane University, July 1972.

Applebaum, William. "Guidelines for a Store-Location Strategy." *Journal of Marketing Research*, (October 1966): 128–134.

Converse, P.D. *Retail Trade Areas in Illinois*. Business Study No 4, Urbana: University of Illinois, 1946.

Dalrymple, Douglas J., and Donald L. Thompson. *Retailing*. New York: Free Press, 1969.

Eisenpreis, Alfred. "An Evaluation of Current Store Location." Presented at the National Conference of the American Marketing Association, Chicago, 1965.

Elmaghraby, Salah F. "On Generalized Activity Networks." *Industrial Engineering*, 18 (November 1966): 75–86.

Enis, Ben M., and Keith R. Cox. "Demographic Analysis of Store Patterns." In Robert L. King, ed., *Marketing and the New Science of Planning*. Chicago: American Marketing Association, 1968.

Forbes, J. D. "Consumer Patronage Behavior." In Robert L. King, ed., *Marketing and the New Science of Planning*. Chicago: American Marketing Association, 1968.

Gist, Ronald R., *Retailing: Concepts and Decision Making*. New York: John Wiley and Sons, 1968.

Goldstucker, Jac L. "Trading Areas." In George Schwartz, ed., *Science in Marketing*. New York: John Wiley, 1965.

———, Danny N. Bellenger, and Thomas J. Stanley. "New Developments in Retail Trading Area Analysis and Site Selection." Georgia State University, 1978.

Huff, David L. "Determination of Inter-Urban Retail Trade Areas." Real Estate Research Program, University of California, 1962.

Mason, Joseph, and Morris Mayer. "Modern Retailing." Dallas: Business Publications, 1987.

Moore, Charles T., and Joseph B. Mason. "Empirical Behavioristic Assumptions in Trading Area Studies." *Journal of Retailing*. (1970–1971): 31–37.

Moore, Lawrence J., and Edward R. Clayton. "GERT Modeling and Simulation." *New York Periodical* (1976).

Pritsker, A. Alan B. *Modeling and Analysis Using Q-GERT Networks*. New York: John Wiley, 1979.

———, and William W. Happ. "GERT: Graphic Evaluation and Review Technique, Part I Fundamentals." *Journal of Industrial Engineering*, 17 (June 1966).

———, and C. Elliott Segal. *Management Decision Making*. Englewood Cliffs, N.J.: Prentice-Hall, 1983.

———, and Gary E. Whitehouse. "GERT: Graphic Evaluation and Review Technique, Part II Probabilistic and Engineering Applications." *Journal of Industrial Engineering* 17 (June 1966).

Reilly, William J. *The Law of Retail Gravitation*. New York: McGraw-Hill, 1931.

6 Consumer Behavior and Retail Marketing Strategy Development

In order to increase the probability of success, the retailer must also understand consumer behavior. Consumer behavior may be defined as the process that underlies an individual's decision of what, when, where, how, and from whom to purchase goods and services (Walters 1978). This chapter presents a consumer behavior model as it applies to retailing. An eclectic approach is used to construct the theory presented here. The model draws from numerous consumer behavior theories and research efforts in an attempt to make it applicable and beneficial to the retailer.

The focal point in the model is extracting behavioral principles in the store selection and store patronage processes that are so important for the retailer. In this context, some socio-economic and racial differences have been assumed, along with lifestyle characteristics and education and numerous other external factors that influence behavior.

THE NEED FOR A MODEL

Consumer behavior models and research that either support these models or contribute to their construction have enjoyed much popularity during the past fifteen years. Increased emphasis on the marketing concept and simultaneously the increasing voice of dissident consumers have helped accelerate consumer-related research. However, this research was only partially extended into retailing and retailing-related areas. Thus, retailing has been deprived of the ever accumulating knowledge about consumer behavior.

Purchase behavior at the retail level is a complex phenomenon with multiple phases and dimensions. Any attempt to systematize and organize information relating to purchase behavior is desirable for retailers, allowing them to adjust retail marketing strategies in favor of the consumer. By providing proper goods and services through effective marketing strategy, retailers will improve not only consumer satisfaction, but also the store's profit picture.

In order to use existing consumer-related information, the retailer needs a model to put this information into a systematic and organized format. The information will thereby be effective for the retail marketing strategist during the retail decision-making process. Such a model has not ever been attempted. This chapter therefore represents a special effort in developing a comprehensive consumer behavior model based on basic consumer behavior information available in the current literature.

The model consists of three phases—pre-purchase, purchase, and post purchase—and five components: (1) shopping motivation, (2) shopper characteristics, (3) planned versus unplanned purchase, (4) specific purchase behavior model, and (5) post-purchase activities (Exhibit 6.1). In the purchase phase, specific aspects of the consumer behavior model pertinent to retailing are offered. This model is the crux of this chapter and is expected to bring together the theory of consumer behavior and practice of retailing. The model attempts to distinguish shopping motivation from shopper characteristics. It is assumed that shopping motivation is external and further conditioned by external stimuli. Shopper characteristics are internal, but they further modify shopping motivation. One aspect of buying behavior, whether the shopping is planned or unplanned, is kept separate. In retailing this particular aspect of shopping is believed to carry special weight.

The specific consumer behavior model is extremely intricate and intertwined with store choice as well as brand and/or product choice. It is particularly important for the retailer to understand these relationships in developing an effective marketing strategy. This strategy must take into account factors such as specific target market behavior, the influence of product image, and the role of store image.

The last phase of the general model, post-purchase behavior, is discussed in conjunction with the specific model. Even more than in product management, in retailing this phase should be included in overall retail marketing process. Since the retail establishment has innumerable products, Festinger's (1957) so-called "cognitive dissonance," or post-purchase second thoughts, could be devastating, because cognitive dissonance toward the products could eventually spill over to the whole store.

SHOPPING MOTIVATION

As every retailer knows, people shop for different reasons. In dealing with shopper behavior, it is necessary to distinguish between "why people shop where they do," which in essence means store selection, and "why do people shop," which is basic shopping motivation (Assael 1981). Of these, answering the second question first will also lead to answering the first question. Why people

Exhibit 6.1
Consumer Behavior and Strategic Retailing

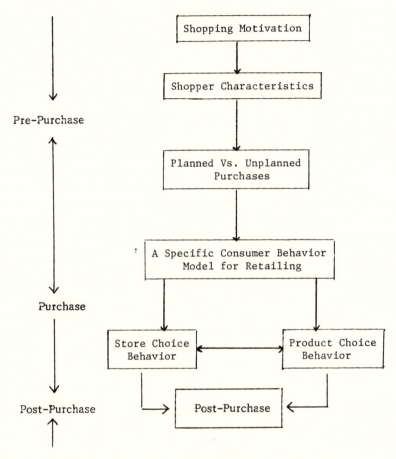

shop or their basic motivation to shop has been studied by Tauber (1972). His in-depth interviews reveal seven shopping motives:

1. Diversion—the need to get away from daily routines.

2. Self-gratification—the expected boost to the psyche produced by the shopping process itself.

3. Learning About New Trends—learning about new products and services by visiting stores.

4. Physical Activity—exercise by walking around and shopping in large shopping complexes.

5. Sensory Stimulation—using the perception system by handling merchandise, trying it on, or trying it out.

6. Social Experiences Outside the Home—having the opportunity to run into friends, meet salespersons, and see other people.

7. Pleasure of Bargaining—opportunity to compare, contrast, haggle over the price, and have the satisfaction of making a wise purchase (Tauber 1972).

Pre-purchase shopping behavior is determined by shopping motives. If the consumer is seeking diversion, he or she may consider going to a very elegant or an unusual store. Similarly, each of the seven shopping motives will force the consumer to consider certain types of stores before the purchase process begins.

Other motives that could be added to the above typology would be need satisfaction most effectively or need satisfaction in a faster manner. Perceived need by the consumer is likely to determine pre-purchase behavior. If the consumer needs to buy a certain product, he or she may go to the specialty store that provides the best quality of that product line. Or the individual may go to a nearby discount department store and hence satisfy the need in a fast manner.

No single motive can be said to be the most important force behind shopping behavior. The seven motives are not necessarily mutually exclusive: multiple factors may simultaneously affect pre-purchase behavior. The existence of different shopping motives reflects the existence of various shopper types. Thus, various shopping behaviors based on shopping motives may be classified into various typologies to explain pre-purchase behavior. Some of the attempts to profile consumers and classify them into various typologies are discussed in the following section.

SHOPPER CHARACTERISTICS

If consumers could be classified according to some aspects of shopping profiles, retailers would be able to develop marketing strategies and tactics that would be more satisfactory for their customers and more profitable for them. One of the earliest and most widely used typologies, the one developed by Nystrom (1929), was replicated and researched by Stone (1954). Stone classified shoppers into four categories:

Economic consumers: people who are primarily inclined to achieve efficiency in shopping. They judge a store on the basis of objective criteria such as price, quality, and merchandise assortment as opposed to store personality or convenience. Economic consumers are likely to be motivated by learning about new trends, need satisfaction effectively, and need satisfaction in a faster manner.

Personalizing consumers: people who need social contact. They form very strong personal attachments to store employees, and as a result, prefer stores that are more intimate. These consumers are motivated by social experience, diversion, and self-gratification motives, among others.

Ethical consumers: people who are motivated by normative criteria regarding taking care of local small businesses. They shop to help local merchants, particularly the "little guy." These consumers may be motivated by social experience and self-gratification motives, among others.

Apathetic consumers: people who do not like to shop. Consequently, they do not like to establish personal relations with store personnel. They like to minimize the trouble of shopping by favoring convenience. These consumers may be motivated by need satisfaction effectively and need satisfaction in a faster manner, and particularly need satisfaction with minimum amount of interaction with store personnel.

Stone maintained that consumers in higher socioeconomic groups belong in the ethical category and lower socioeconomic groups in the apathetic category. Darden and Reynolds (1971) further validated Stone's findings. Further attempts by Darden and Ashton (1974–1975) revealed the existence of other categories of consumers. They extended Stone's typology to seven groups and discovered that there could be different groups based on the phenomenon being researched. For instance, an examination of shopping in supermarkets revealed the existence of special groups. Groups such as stamp collectors, stamp haters, and convenient location shoppers were all part of the total clientele of these stores (Darden and Ashton 1974–1975).

Another classification is offered by George P. Mochis (1976) who in a study of the purchase behavior of cosmetics customers specified the following consumer groups: (1) special sales shoppers, (2) brand loyal, (3) store loyal, (4) problem solving, (5) socializing, and (6) name conscious. Of these six groups, the first four are self-explanatory, the fourth implying a group of consumers who cannot make up their minds regarding the purchase of cosmetic products. Socializing consumers buy cosmetics for peer group reasons. Finally, name-conscious consumers judge cosmetics by the store that sells them. If Neiman-Marcus decides to introduce a new line of cosmetics, the name-conscious loyal customers will buy them.

Bert McCammon and his colleagues (1987) also have developed a new classification of consumers. They identify five consumer groups: (1) transitional shoppers, (2) impacted shoppers, (3) dedicated shoppers, (4) contemporary shoppers, and (5) social shoppers.

Transitional shoppers represent 7.6 percent of the population. Although they are well educated and have high career aspirations, at the moment they are price conscious. They will move up soon. Impacted shoppers account for 26.8 percent of the population. These people have been affected by economic changes and are cautious in shopping; they therefore collect information and compare prices. Dedicated shoppers, 24.8 percent of the population, shop more departments than stores. Contemporary shoppers, who represent 25.4 percent of the population, are upper class in terms of education, income, and lifestyle. Price is their least concern. Finally, social shoppers, representing 15.4 percent of the population, consider shopping an extension of their social life. As can be seen, many such classifications can be generated. These classifications may have significant benefits for individual retailers as well as the retailing sector as a whole.

The purchase behavior of each group can be identified and specified. For instance, the information needs of each group may differ significantly. Brand loyalty and/or store name-conscious shoppers (or contemporary shoppers) pay most attention to advertising (Darden and Ashton 1974–1975). Similar information about product preferences, need perception, brand and store loyalty, and other consumer behavior areas can be found by the retailer and used to evaluate pre-purchase behavior and to plan for certain purchase behavior patterns.

One vital question, however, remains to be answered: Are there general or universal buyer typologies that are based on more than one dimension (unlike Mochis' typology which is based on a communications aspect or Darden and Ashton's which is based on supermarket shopping), and applicable to all retail situations? Of the various classifications, at least two appear to be applicable to all retail situations: store-loyal and brand-loyal shoppers. Either store loyalty or brand loyalty (or both) would enter in any kind of retail shopping and purchase situation. These two forces would work against each other if the store did not carry certain brands. Similarly, these forces could reinforce each other if the store carried the specific brand. If, for instance, the consumer is loyal to Sears and wants to buy a Sony turntable, a conflict of loyalty will occur if Sears does not carry Sony products. Then it becomes a contest between attachment to Sears and attachment to Sony, a contest that will decide where and what product is likely to be purchased. If Sears carries Sony products, this decision will of course be simple. Because the two loyalties impinge one on the other, the shopper plans to go to Sears in advance.

Thus, particularly during the pre-purchase phase, a crucial concept comes into play—loyalty. There are two distinct types of loyalties: product or brand loyalty and store loyalty. The particular product and the particular store where it may be purchased are the two key components of planning a purchase. The following section focuses on the planning aspect of the pre-purchase phase.

PLANNED VERSUS UNPLANNED PURCHASE

Shopping behavior is generally influenced by learning processes and information sources (Bettman 1973). Consumers learn to plan for the purchase, that is, they decide where to or what to buy, or both, in advance. If and when consumers plan a purchase, they will plan where this product is to be purchased and what brand or make it is going to be. On this basis, it may be maintained that the least planning at the retail level is done when the consumer does not know which product and where. Similarly, it is maintained that most planning is done when the consumer knows exactly what product and where it is going to be purchased. Thus, four pre-purchase planning points can be identified on a purchase planning spectrum and are identified in terms of four situations (Exhibit 6.2):

Exhibit 6.2
Planned-Unplanned Shopping Spectrum

Unplanned Shopping	Product Planned Shopping[a]	Store Planned Shopping[b]	Planned Shopping[c]
Product Purchase Unplanned	Product Purchase Planned	Product Purchase Unplanned	Product Purchase Planned
Store Selection Unplanned	Store Selection Planned	Store Selection Unplanned	Store Selection Planned

[a]The likelihood of brand loyalty.

[b]The likelihood of store loyalty.

[c]The likelihood of both brand and store loyalty.

1. The consumer realizes the existence of a shopping problem but has not decided on the store or the brand and product. This could have been a spur of the moment situation with intended purchase of a new product such as a videotape player or a situation that would take much longer to plan, such as a washer-dryer combination.
2. The consumer realizes the existence of a shopping problem and has decided on the product and brand but has not yet decided where the product will be purchased. Since the consumer has not decided on the store, there will be a search of the stores that carry that product. For instance, the consumer has decided to buy a new TV and that it will be a Zenith Console. He or she explores the stores that carry that particular product and brand before actual purchase takes place.
3. The consumer realizes the existence of a shopping problem and has decided on the store but has not yet decided on the product and brand. The person needs a new suit for an important business meeting. He is likely to go to the apparel shop where he is known and where he knows everybody. He has not yet decided what kind of outfit he wishes to purchase.
4. The consumer realizes the existence of a shopping problem and has decided on both the store and the product and brand. The family has decided to purchase a new car, and as a change from the past, decides on a medium-sized Japanese car. Further analyses indicate that a Honda Accord will be the product. After searching a number of Honda dealers, they decide on one. By the time they are ready to purchase, they know exactly what car they want and where it will be purchased.

Thus, the pre-purchase phase is conditioned by the consumer's particular shopping motivation, by his or her particular characteristics as a shopper, and by the extent to which some planning was done for the purchase. At this point, it is important to explore the total consumer behavior leading to the closing of the purchase process. In this context, the details of a consumer behavior model are extremely useful for the retailer to develop effective marketing strategy, policy, and tactics that will simultaneously satisfy customers' needs as they provide better opportunity for higher profits.

Exhibit 6.3
A Consumer Behavior Model for Retailers

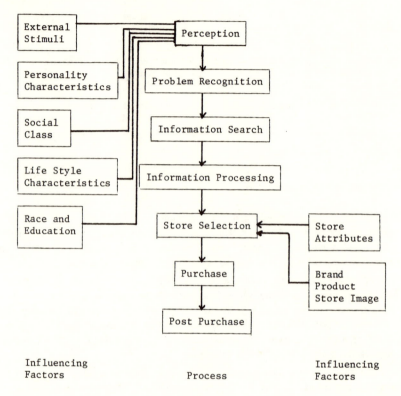

```
┌──────────────┐                    ┌──────────────────┐
│ External     │─────────────────── │   Perception     │
│ Stimuli      │                    └──────────────────┘
└──────────────┘                             │
                                             ▼
┌──────────────┐                    ┌──────────────────────┐
│ Personality  │                    │ Problem Recognition  │
│ Characteristics│                  └──────────────────────┘
└──────────────┘                             │
                                             ▼
┌──────────────┐                    ┌──────────────────────┐
│ Social       │                    │ Information Search   │
│ Class        │                    └──────────────────────┘
└──────────────┘                             │
                                             ▼
┌──────────────┐                    ┌──────────────────────┐
│ Life Style   │                    │ Information Processing│
│ Characteristics│                  └──────────────────────┘
└──────────────┘                             │
                                             ▼
┌──────────────┐          ┌──────────────────┐    ┌──────────────┐
│ Race and     │          │ Store Selection  │◄───│ Store        │
│ Education    │          └──────────────────┘    │ Attributes   │
└──────────────┘                   │              └──────────────┘
                                   ▼
                          ┌──────────────┐         ┌──────────────┐
                          │ Purchase     │         │ Brand        │
                          └──────────────┘         │ Product      │
                                   │               │ Store Image  │
                                   ▼               └──────────────┘
                          ┌──────────────┐
                          │ Post Purchase│
                          └──────────────┘
```

Influencing   Process   Influencing
Factors   Factors

A SPECIFIC PURCHASE BEHAVIOR MODEL FOR PARTICULAR USE IN RETAILING

Having established the conditions surrounding the retailing-related consumer behavior model, we are now ready for the specific purchase behavior model itself.

Exhibit 6.3 illustrates a slanted consumer behavior model that is appropriate for retailing. Regardless of the buyer motivation and shopper characteristics discussed earlier in this chapter, a general consumer behavior pattern is applicable to all retailers. As the illustration shows, in addition to the process itself, a series of modifiers (or influencing factors) affect the outcome of the total behavior pattern even among individuals and groups. Even though everyone may undergo the same behavior process because of these modifiers, the end results are different and varied. The retailer must first understand the consumer behavior process and its modifiers, so that this process can be used for the mutual benefit of retailers and consumers.

Exhibit 6.4
Most Important Sources of Retail Information According to Respondent's Tenure[a] in Town

Tenure in Town	TV	Radio	News Papers	Neigh- bors	Acquaint- ances in social organi- zations	Professional and job Associates	Relative
less than a year	15.4	42.3	69.2	38.5	26.9	19.2	0
1- 2 years	18.2	40.9	86.4	40.9	36.4	31.8	4.5
3- 5 years	18.4	40.8	65.3	34.7	20.4	18.4	6.1
6-10 years	7.7	30.8	80.8	46.2	11.5	26.9	0
11-15 years	17.4	17.4	82.6	60.9	8.7	13.0	4.3
Over 16 years	21.9	26.6	82.8	34.4	20.3	21.9	26.6

[a]Percentages are based on number of respondents in the tenure category. Since some respondents considered two or more information sources to be equally important, percentages will not total 100.0.

Source: A. C. Samli, "A Look at Consumption Patterns in Blacksburg, Virginia," Blacksburg, Virginia: Virginia Tech, College of Business.

The Retail Buyer Behavior Process

As illustrated in Exhibit 6.3, the process starts with perception which here implies exposure to the mass media and other types of information (Lambert 1970; Enis and Stafford 1969; Bettman 1973). The perceptual encoding process (Bettman) indicates a personal interpretation of a stimulus. The stimulus can either enhance a purchase need recognition or a store patronizing need recognition, or perhaps both. The stimulus can be at the conscious or the subconscious level (Cohen 1978). At the conscious level, the stimulus may either establish or enhance an image for a product or a store. This depends on whether the stimulus penetrates the absolute threshold, in which case it is likely to establish an image for a product or a store. However, if it penetrates the differential threshold, the stimulus is more likely to enhance the image for a product or a store. Finally, subliminal perception is a questionable way of providing stimuli for the retail buyer (Cohen). Because there are many legal implications and because this type of stimulus is not used in retailing, this topic is not discussed here.

Since the *perception* process begins with some information, it is important to explore the question of where shoppers at the retail level get their general information. The availability of water beds in the community could be the first bit of information triggering the whole process in Exhibit 6.3. Exhibit 6.4 depicts the relative importance of different sources of information regarding local retail shopping. The table indicates that, among other factors, the individual's period of residence in a community has a bearing on the relative importance of the sources of information. For example, friends and relatives play a more important role as a source of information among those who have lived in the area 20 years than those who have lived in the area two years.

Problem recognition is the second step in the process. The intensity of the recognized problem is related to the perception process itself as it filters through a host of modifiers. The intensity of the recognized problem is likely to determine the success in retailing. The problem must be sufficiently intense that the consumer feels that it is necessary, for instance, to buy a video recorder. In retailing, along with the intensity of the problem, the intensity of the make (brand) and particularly intensity of the store (image) must be sorted out in the consumer's mind. If the problem recognition is not strong enough for the consumer to desire the purchase of the product, then the make and store intensities of the problem are nonexistent. Thus, recognition of the problem would either automatically lead to the make of the product and the store where it might be purchased, or to an information search designed to solve the problem.

In addition to a host of modifiers that will be discussed later in this chapter, problem recognition is also related to shopping motives. The individual who, for instance, is in great need of diversion or self-gratification is likely to exaggerate the perceived message and to recognize the problem as an extremely acute one.

Information search is the third step. Consciously or unconsciously, all buyers search for some information. Shopping behavior is mainly a learned behavior, which means that all shoppers experience a basic learning process. This process conditions the individual to buy groceries at Krogers, appliances at Sears, and shoes at Florsheim's. In order for learning to take place, information is needed. Before learning, therefore, an individual searches for information. The intensity of the search process depends on the seriousness of the purchase problem and the temperament of the shopper. If the purchase is going to take a large chunk of the shopper's budget and/or if it is a complicated and particularly important product, the search for information is likely to be intensified.

As Henry Assael states:

The amount of search for information for a given product is contingent on the nature of the product (high risk or high price will generate more search), the situation (an involving situation will generate more search), the consumer's past experience and characteristics (less experience will generate more search), brand attitudes (weakly held attitudes will generate more search), and group influences (products important to the group will result in more search) (p. 493).

Although Assael's statement is related primarily to products, the information search can be related to both the product and store. As discussed in Exhibit 6.3, particularly in situations where store selection is likely to be planned, the information search for the store will exceed the information search for the product. The process is illustrated in Exhibit 6.5. As the illustration shows, the same process is used in the search for information for both the product and store.

Exhibit 6.5
Consumer Information Search Process

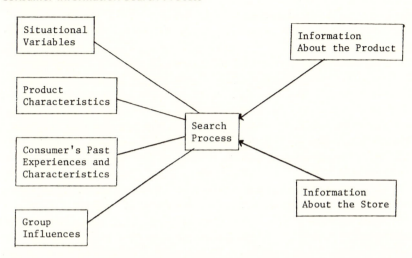

The information search process involves screening multiple sources and gathering information from these sources. Some authors (for example, Bettman 1973) maintain that information acquisition is different from the information search process inasmuch as acquisition can occur without searching. This point is particularly important for the retailer. Although many retail shoppers may search for information, the others can acquire information without searching. The retailer must, of course, plan for both.

Whether it is information search or information acquisition, information pertaining to retailing is gathered on two topics in particular: product and store (Exhibit 6.5). Since no one knows exactly which of these two types of information is more important, the retailer has to make sure that both are made amply available.

Consumers search information internally as well as externally (Bettman 1973; Lusch 1982). *Internal search* implies a mental recall or a review of what an individual has previously learned about a store, a product, or both. The internal search is often the result of a previous external search. If a substantial amount of external search has taken place, then *linear learning* has already occurred and external search is cut short. Linear learning is based on the *linear learning theory* which holds that the pattern of store selection probabilities is conditioned by the knowledge of past decisions as to store choice (Kuehn 1962). The theory maintains that "A consumer's store selection to purchase a product is not completely random. The consumer exhibits bias in the choice of a store. The more recent the purchase experience in a particular store, and the more frequent the visits to the store, the more likely the consumer is to repurchase the product in that store."

Exhibit 6.6
Consumer Information Processing

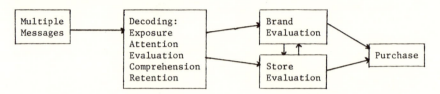

A. Kuehn formulated the linear learning theory in conjunction with the product-brand choice process. As D. Jones Aaker has stated, Tanniru has applied Kuehn's theories to the store selection process and, hence, has provided evidence of the linear learning hypothesis. *External search* is the actual process of seeking information from various sources (Exhibit 6.4) including friends (group influences), packages in store displays, and advertisements (situational variables). Unfortunately, there is little if any information on the relative importance of internal search versus external search for the retailer. Furthermore, it is not really known precisely which information source is more important for the retailer; much research is needed in these particular areas.

Information processing is the fourth step in the specific consumer behavior model. The retailer's message is encoded and transmitted through various media. The consumer receives and processes this message. In order for the message to be processed, it has to be decoded. Once again the literature about decoding the retailer's message is rather weak. It is maintained here that the process is not any different than decoding product-related messages. In fact, the retailer's message may often be partially, mostly, and sometimes even exclusively product related. The total decoding process involves at least five stages: exposure, attention, evaluation, comprehension, and retention (Exhibit 6.6). According to some authors evaluation may mean either evaluating the source or evaluating the message itself. Studies have concluded that the perceived credibility of the source is closely related to the acceptability of the message. The more credible the source, the greater the acceptability (Watts and McGuire 1964; Miller and Basehart 1969). The retail store must make sure that its credibility will not be questioned. (This point is discussed further in Chapter 12.)

Other studies indicate that source credibility is related to message acceptance only for low-involvement products. In greater involvement situations, when the consumer does not agree with the message, it will be rejected even if the credibility of the source is not being questioned (Cohen and McCann 1978). Thus, it must be reiterated that, although there is not enough research evidence, retailers will increase the believability of their message by enhancing their credibility in low-involvement cases. For high-involvement situations, in addition to source credibility more attention must be paid to message credibility. In retailing, message credibility is closely related to the believability of the message itself and to the degree of realism within the message. For more information on this point, see Chapter 14.

As illustrated in Exhibit 6.6, the consumer receives multiple messages from different stores; if the messages achieve exposure and attention, then the evaluation process takes place. Comprehension and retention follow suit. The outcome of this process is brand and/or store evaluation which might lead to purchase in that particular store. Thus, Sears hopes that middle-class Americans will have exposure to its advertisements. If these advertisements communicate well, consumers will pay attention to them and this attention will lead to evaluating Sears' brands and products. Subsequently, Sears' image will be evaluated. If all is positive, people will shop at Sears.

The evaluation process described here is based on the use of evaluative criteria which are expressed in the form of attributes or characteristics used to compare existing alternatives. Through the use of evaluative criteria, consumers will process the information that will ultimately make them purchase at a certain store.

Store selection is the fifth phase and is itself an extremely important topic. Therefore, it will be treated in greater detail than the other stages of the total model.

According to the existing literature, two paths lead to store selection: "attribute orientation" and "activity orientation" (Monroe and Guiltinan 1975; Samli, Tozier, and Harps 1980). *Attribute orientation* implies a greater role for store characteristics in the store selection process. Store attributes such as neatness, reputation, sales clerks, displays, special sales brands, and special buyer information may play a decisive role in the consumers' store selection process (Exhibit 6.7). On the other hand, activity orientation may be equally or even more important under special circumstances. *Activity orientation* implies preoccupation with the selection process itself before specific store attributes are considered. It further implies somewhat more intensive pre-store selection planning. Therefore, activity orientation puts the emphasis on planning the budgeting, product, and brand aspects of the selection process. In activity orientation, all of these bits of information are being sorted and processed before the decision is made regarding the store to be patronized. Although the literature is not totally clear on this point, one might be led to believe that attribute orientation has a more positive predisposition to store image as the decisive criterion in the store selection process. On the other hand, activity orientation implies that the total store selection process is to be based on information processing before entering the store as well as in the store. Exhibit 6.7 contrasts the major elements of these two orientations. Two studies dealing with the store selection process indirectly implied that perhaps activity orientation was more prominent among white women and that attribute orientation was more widespread among black women (Samli, Tozier, and Harps 1980; Monroe and Guiltinan 1975).

The next stage in the general model is *purchase* and follows store selection.

Exhibit 6.7
Store Selection

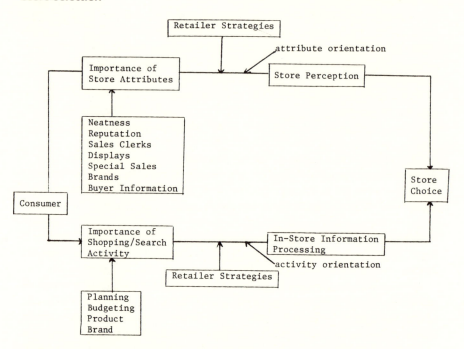

Here we examine the details of exchanging money (or credit) for promised satisfaction of the problem.

In the purchase process, the individual customer may display behavior patterns that may be categorized as autonomous, semiautonomous, and dependent decisions. Autonomous purchase may be considered to be a continuation of activity orientation. Since careful plans have been prepared in advance through information search and information processing, the consumer can purchase in a retail store without needing any help from retail sales clerks and other internal stimuli. At the other extreme of the spectrum, purchase behavior for those who have attribute orientation involves dependent purchase decisions. The salesclerk's help and advice are part of the store attributes that make the purchase process possible (Samli, Tozier and Harps 1980). Semiautonomous purchase behavior implies the partial adoption of attribute orientation and activity orientation. Although there is no research evidence, it is posited here that, with the exception of extreme cases, most people are likely to use a combination approach. For instance, a middle-class consumer with reasonable education and financial means may use a combination approach. He or she may use an attribute orientation in purchasing clothing or small appliances, but an activity orientation in shopping for a more expensive product, such as an automobile, a video recorder, or a home computer.

Purchase behavior relating to different retail stores may also take different

Exhibit 6.8
An Exploration of Post-Purchase Policy Effectiveness

Store	Store's Customers %	Those Who Plan to Come Back to Shop %	Those Who Would Recommend the Store to Friends %
A	100.00	85.00	75.00
B	100.00	52.00	49.00

forms. For example, Bloomingdale's in New York may thrive on attribute orientation leading to dependent purchase decision with the proper inputs of the salespeople. Purchase behavior relating to Woolworth or K-Mart can very well be the opposite. A study contrasting information search and knowledge behavior of specialty stores and department stores indicates that specialty store customers have more product knowledge, more experience with the product, and greater exposure to mass media and that they seek advice and/or information (Dash et al. 1976). Starting with activity orientation could lead to an autonomous or semiautonomous purchase decision. An ideal situation for a store is to have store attributes established in such a way that attribute orientation will be natural. However, those who have activity orientation will also shop at the same store because once the individual consumer searches and processes the information he or she will also shop at the same store. However, this may not be very practical.

POST-PURCHASE ACTIVITIES

Post-purchase is the last stage in the total behavior model. Leon Festinger (1957) has formulated the theory of *cognitive dissonance* which, as noted earlier, relates to having second thoughts about a transaction after the fact. In a retail situation, the buyer's development of second thoughts about shopping in store A or about the merchandise he or she has purchased reflects some serious problems. The problem may stem from pressure selling at the store, less than adequate treatment of the customer, or finding special displeasing features about the merchandise purchased. Regardless of the cause, if cognitive dissonance is present, the store's post-purchase policies must be deficient (see Exhibit 6.8). Store A is likely to lose some customers because there appears to be a 15 percent attrition rate with only 85 percent planning to return to the store. In other words, the post-purchase *attrition quotient* is 15 percent. Additional potential attrition is based on whether or not the respondents would recommend the store to friends. It appears that the *attrition quotient* measured this way goes up to 25 percent.

Store B, on the other hand, demonstrates a substantially more severe case of

Exhibit 6.9
The Cognitive Dissonance Spectrum

No Dissonance	Dissonance with the product	Dissonance with the store	Dissonance with both product/store
No likelihood of attrition	Partial attrition	Partial attrition	Heavy attrition

post-purchase problems. The attrition quotient measured by shoppers' expectations to return appears to be 48 percent. The same measure based on whether or not the shoppers would recommend the store to friends appears to be 52 percent.

Post-purchase satisfaction or dissatisfaction leading to the *attrition quotient* appears in the form of a spectrum (Exhibit 6.9). On one end of the spectrum there is no dissonance and hence no expected attrition. The second stage shows that the consumer has dissonance about the product, although he or she is satisfied with the store. The next stage shows dissatisfaction with the store, even though the product is satisfactory. The other extreme of the spectrum indicates dissonance about both store and product. The attrition role is likely to be excessive at this stage (Lusch 1982).

The retailer must assess the *attrition quotient* in advance and if it is excessive, then policies and tactics must be initiated to counteract the possible attrition. The retailer who does an effective job of selling and satisfying its customers is not very likely to experience an excessive attrition quotient. However, conditions in retailing could change quickly and unexpectedly. Therefore, the retailer should make sure that (1) customers are satisfied after they have left the store, (2) if customers have second thoughts about the purchase, they can bring the merchandise back, (3) periodic attempts are made to determine the attrition quotient, (4) customers have recourse in terms of not only returning the merchandise but also complaining and seeing that their complaints are listened to and acted on.

INFLUENCING FACTORS

The consumer behavior process is influenced and modified by a number of factors, especially personality characteristics, social class, lifestyle characteristics, and race and education.

Personality Characteristics: Personality characteristics are deep-seated and reflect consistent, enduring patterns of behavior, and as such influence consumer behavior in retailing. Based on Allen L. Edwards' (1957) analyses, Assael has identified 14 specific personality traits that are likely to play an important role in retail buying behavior. These traits include personality items such as achievement, compliance, and order. Not enough research has been done to define the specific impact of each of these traits. The retail store that has carefully trained salespeople may particularly appeal to those who may be considered dependent personalities. On the other hand, retail stores that emphasize self-service and self-help may particularly appeal to those who have autonomous personalities.

Social Class: Social classes are based on income, education, occupation, housing, and the like, and so use purchasing power differently from each other. Retail purchase behavior also varies. The lower classes, for instance, are considered to have less than adequate information and little, if any, discretionary income. They are more attached to local, "friendly retailers." Middle-class consumers likely do a lot of information search and shop out of the neighborhood or even the shop. Upper class consumers use information imparted by special media, and they frequent prestige stores (Berman and Evans 1986).

Lifestyle Characteristics: An individual's lifestyle affects that individual's consumption patterns. Lifestyle may be defined as the way an individual chooses and uses possessions. Thus, consumers with different lifestyles also display different chasing behaviors and consumption patterns. In examining lifestyles, activities, interests, and opinions (AIO) are utilized as indicators, and a series of questions are typically asked of individuals in each of these three areas. The answers are correlated with behavior regarding store or brand preference, store selection, and the like. The value of activity interest opinion research is enhanced when related to demographics. In that way, numbers can be attached to behavior in terms of market size or potential demand.

If an AIO survey is being conducted in the activities area, for example, topics such as memberships, hobbies, travel, shopping, entertainment, sports, and work are considered. In exploring interests, involvement in the home and the family are considered. Finally, opinions involve such issues as feelings about politics, advertising, or economics. Unfortunately, AIO has had little, if any, use and application in retailing.

Race and Education: Race and education are considered together here because the racial factor has not been identified as the primary factor in the behavior differentials between blacks and whites. Although there appear to be some differences in the way black and white consumers select stores, no systematic, definitive research work has pointed out these differences. Along with differences, there are also specific similarities. Linda Edmunds (1979) found more similarities than differences between black and white professional females. It is not clear whether the similarities or differences are more important for the retailer. Obviously, the retailer should become familiar with both aspects of the behavior patterns. However, for some retailers, the similarities may be more important. The retailer, for instance, who is seeking to satisfy both black and white women may emphasize the similarities, whereas the retailer who is emphasizing blacks or whites exclusively may focus on the differences. The Edmunds study also showed that, instead of blackness or whiteness per se, racial identity along with a certain educational level made a difference. Whites with a higher educational

Exhibit 6.10
Possible Corresponding Shopping Motives and Retail Policies

Shopping Motives	Retail Policies
1. Diversion	Making shopping interesting.
2. Self-gratification	Helping the consumer to buy good products by making good logical decisions.
3. Learning about New Trends	Carrying some new, revolutionary products and information about these and others.
4. Physical Activity	Providing opportunity for the consumer to walk around, try products, and let off steam.
5. Sensory Stimulation	Not only stimulating consumers in terms of attractive arrangements and appearance, but also providing opportunity for the consumer to try products on or to try them out.
6. Social Experiences	Having outgoing salespeople and other store personnel, as well as try to maintain a high level of traffic in the store.
7. Pleasure of Bargaining	Giving an opportunity to the consumer to discuss the merits and de-merits of the products and the negotiate nominally price or the service attached to the product.

level were found to have distinguishing behavioral patterns compared with blacks with a lower educational level.

RETAIL STRATEGIC MARKETING IMPLICATIONS

A model such as the one presented in this chapter provides ample opportunity for the retailer to plan marketing strategies accordingly. Therefore, the retailer not only must understand the model and its finer points, but also must be able to interpret the model and its specifics into retailing action.

In dealing with shopping motivation, the retailer may have difficulty if the store is projecting an image as the convenient neighborhood store and is trying to be a major disseminator of new products or to be a major trend setter. However, the store can easily be projecting an image as an up-to-date and ultramodern establishment, as well as being a place where some well-known people work or where the merchandise is rather revolutionary. Exhibit 6.10 illustrates some possible retail marketing policies related to a specific shopping motive. Much research is needed to determine which of the shopping motives is more dominant and whether or not some of them are particularly predominant among different groups of retail shoppers.

As we move from shopping motives to shopper characteristics, a new set of information becomes available to the retailer. It is clear that retailers can use shopper profiles to develop guidelines about advertising, other types of promotion, some aspects of merchandising, and other related marketing decision areas. Tactical implications of buyer typologies are almost self-evident. The retail establishment should be in a position to decide whether it is capable of attracting, say, economic consumers and, if so, whether it can put together a series of marketing policies and tactics to satisfy this market.

The planned versus unplanned purchase spectrum has additional implications for the retailer. Lower and medium-price range department stores (or discount department stores) may rely on good-name brands being sold at reasonable prices. Hence, they may be emphasizing brand satisfaction rather than store satisfaction. In such cases, stores promote brand satisfaction as part of their marketing strategy.

Similarly, good-name department stores and specialty stores emphasize the store name rather than the merchandise. In such cases, convenience goods such as men's underwear with a common brand name, say Fruit of the Loom, can be treated as a specialty good. This is a desirable situation for the manufacturer, since his or her products will receive a higher value than they otherwise would receive, or will enjoy a greater degree of monopoly power.

The most desirable situation occurs when brand and store loyalties overlap. Most exclusive women's apparel stores, for examples, carry most exclusive brands. The practice here is consistent with the theory constructed earlier in this book: if specialty stores emphasize specialty goods, they have reinforced monopoly power. That is the strongest position to be in when the firm's viability, longevity, and profitability are being considered. Most reputable apparel stores, for instance, carry most reputable apparel brands, which illustrates the implementation of the above policy.

STRATEGIC TRICKLE-DOWN DECISION PROCESS

Strategy has to do with the overall orientation and activities needed to fulfill the general objectives of an establishment. *Policies*, on the other hand, are more specific and short-term, and have a clear-cut and more limited purpose. *Tactics* are even more limited and shorter lived. It is quite possible, for example, to develop specific customer tactics based on shopper classification categories. If, for instance, economic consumers are being considered, it would be tactically sound for the retail establishment to emphasize price–product related information in promotional efforts as well as in personal selling activity.

If we were to try to put all three concepts together at three different levels, that is, strategy, policy, and tactics, it might be as follows: assume the retail establishment wants to position a middle-class apparel shop in a given town that has no such shop (Exhibit 6.11). It may adopt the policy of making sure that the customer will feel that he or she will make a wise purchase by buying in this store, as well as the policy of taking care of customers rapidly and satis-

Exhibit 6.11

Strategic Trickle-Down Decision Process in Retail Marketing

The Level of Decision Activity	Scope of Decision Activity	Impact at the Consumer Level
General Marketing Strategy	Far-Reaching Store-Wide Relatively Long Range	Appealing to one or more large groups
Store Policy	Limited Store Wide Relatively Shorter Range	Concentrating on Specific Purchase Motives
Specific Customer Tactics	Very Limited Store-Wide Short-Range	Using Specific Practices to Satisfy Special Consumer Characteristics

factorily. Tactically, the store may have to emphasize the product–price–quality combination in store selling as well as in its advertising. Thus, the interrelationship among strategies, policies, and tactics is called the strategic trickle down. Retail establishments that are market and consumer oriented will have to seek congruence among these concepts at three separate layers of the decision-making process.

An example of trickle down is as follows: XYZ Company is an elegant women's apparel store. As such, it appeals to middle-aged professional or well-to-do married women who are slim and enjoy dressing in the latest fashions. It provides for "learning about new trends," "sensory stimulation" and "social experiences" by carrying most up-to-date fashion merchandise, good color combinations, and very desirable in-store decor. The store is visited by a steady stream of upper-middle-class women who know each other reasonably well. The store makes every effort to take care of "personalizing consumers."

The consumer behavior model presented in this chapter provides the basis for developing an almost step-by-step marketing program. The seven phases of the process, perception, problem recognition, information search, information processing, store selection, purchase, and post-purchase, are all part of the picture. The retailer who understands the usefulness of such a model can develop the specifics of the marketing program accordingly. The model provides the basis for advertising, promoting merchandising, pricing, and all other features of a retail store. The most important point that the model brings about is that all of the components of the model and the related retail decisions have to be consistent, and all must hold together if the retail establishment is to perform effectively and profitably.

SUMMARY

This chapter reviews some of the knowledge about consumer behavior in conjunction with retail marketing strategy development. The basic model consists of five specific areas: shopping motivation, shopper characteristics, planned versus unplanned purchases, consumer behavior in retailing, and post-purchase activities.

Shopping motivation is a strong guide for retail marketing strategy. Various shopping-purchase motives can be used for specific retail policies as well as general retail strategy. In addition to specific shopping motives, consumers can be classified according to certain characteristics, groupings that imply certain consumer behavior patterns. These behavior patterns can be interpreted in terms of retail strategy, policy, and tactics.

The consumer behavior model used in this chapter is composed of a seven-layer sequential process: (1) perception, (2) problem recognition, (3) information search, (4) information processing, (5) store selection, (6) purchase, and (7) post-purchase. The process is modified by external stimuli, personality characteristics, social class, lifestyle characteristics, and race and education.

Use of the model provides the basis for sound marketing programs for retailers.

REFERENCES

Aaker, D. Jones. "Modeling Store Choice Behavior." *Journal of Marketing Research* 8 (1971).

Assael, Henry. *Consumer Behavior and Marketing Action.* Boston: Kent Publishing, 1981.

Berman, Berry, and Joel R. Evans. *Retail Management.* New York: Macmillan Co., 1986.

Bettman, James R. "Perceived Risk and Its Components: A Model and Empirical Test." *Journal of Marketing Research* 10 (May 1973): 184–90.

Cohen, Samuel Craig, and John M. McCann. "Assessing Communication Effects on Energy Conservation." *Journal of Consumer Research* 5 (September 1978): 82–88.

Darden, William R. and Dub Ashton. "Psychographic Profiles of Patronage Preference Groups." *Journal of Retailing* 50 (Winter 1974–1975): 99–112.

Darden, William R. and Fred D. Reynolds. "Shopping Orientations and Product Usage Rates." *Journal of Marketing Research* (November 1971): 505–508.

Dash, Joseph F., Leon G. Schiffman, and Conrad Berenson. "Information Search and Store Choice." *Journal of Advertising Research* (June 1976): 35–39.

Edmunds, Linda. "Clothing Buying Practices and Life Style Differentials Between Employed Black and White Women." Ph.D. diss., Virginia Polytechnic Institute and State University, 1979.

Edwards, Allen L. *Edwards Personal Preference Schedule Manual,* New York: Psychological Corp., 1957.

Enis, Ben M., and James E. Stafford. "Consumer's Perception of Product Quality as a

Function of Various Informational Inputs." In Phillip R. McDonald, ed., *Marketing Involvement in Society and the Economy*. Proceedings, American Marketing Association, 1969, pp. 340–44.

Festinger, Leon. *A Theory of Cognitive Dissonance*. Stanford, Calif.: Stanford University Press, 1957.

Kuehn, A. "Consumer Brand Choice as a Learning Process." *Journal of Advertising Research* 210 (1962).

Lambert, Zarrell V. "Product Perception: An Important Variable in Pricing Strategy." *Journal of Marketing* (October 1970): 68–71.

Lusch, Robert F. *Management of Retail Enterprises*. Boston: Kent Publishing, 1982.

McCammon, Bert C., Jr., Deborah S. Coykendall, and Mary B. Whitfield. "Structure and Strategy in Retailing." A special presentation at the AMA Faculty Consortium in Retailing, University of Alabama, July 1987.

Miller, G., and J. Basehart. "Source Trustworthiness, Opinionated Statements and Response to Persuasive Communication." *Speech Monographs* 36 (1969): 1–7.

Mizerski, Richard W., James M. Hunt, and Charles Petri. "The Effects of Advertising Credibility on Consumer Reactions to an Advertisement." In Subhash C. Jain, ed., Proceedings of the American Marketing Association Educators' Conference, Series 43 (1978), pp. 164–68.

Mochis, George P. "Shopping Orientations and Consumer Uses of Information." *Journal of Retailing* (Summer 1976): 61–70.

Monroe, Kent B., and Joseph B. Guiltinan. "A Path-Analytic Exploration of Retail Patronage Influences." *Journal of Consumer Research* 2 (June 1975).

Nystrom, Paul H. *Economics of Consumption*. New York: McGraw-Hill, 1929.

———. *Economic Principles of Consumption*. New York: Ronald Press, 1929.

Samli, A. Coskun, Enid Tozier, and Yuette Harps. "Social Class Differences in the Store Selection Process of Black Professional Women." *Journal of the Academy of Marketing Science* (Winter-Spring 1980): 138–152.

Stone, Gregory P. "City and Urban Identification: Observations on the Social Psychology of City Life." *American Journal of Sociology* 60 (July 1954): 36–45.

Tauber, Edward M. "Why Do People Shop?" *Journal of Marketing* 36 (October 1972): 46–49.

Walters, C. Glenn. *Consumer Behavior*. Homewood, Ill.: Richard D. Irwin, 1978.

7 Heterogeneity of Markets and Segmentation in Retailing

Segmentation, the most prevalent retail strategy, has unique aspects that are not fully covered in regular segmentation literature in marketing. This chapter emphasizes that retail markets are extremely heterogeneous and that retailers have to learn to function, in heterogeneous markets that is, be able to segment.

As many retailers realize, no one store can cater to all segments of the market simultaneously and be completely successful. A market, whether it be for automobiles, appliances, or carpeting, is not homogeneous; it is composed of many different groups with different incomes, tasks, values, and motives. These segments are identifiable, measurable, accessible, and significant (Kotler 1984).

In a competitive market system, retail establishments that understand their markets and try to satisfy the prevalent needs and wants of these markets have a better chance of success. Coping with heterogeneous markets represents the retailer's greatest challenge. Those who succeed are rewarded by the market system by gaining a store image and store loyalty, all of which lead to favorable market share and, ultimately, to profits (Samli 1968, 1969, 1975).

The segments of a market can be identified on the basis of different sets of criteria. A component or a segment is any subsection of a total market that is worth cultivating (Roberts 1961; Samli 1966). Different behavior patterns prevail in various segments of the consumer market. Marketing practitioners identify their own market segments on the basis of existing possibilities of stratification of the market. A marketing strategy of segmentation, which is simply dealing

Most of this chapter is based on and updated from three articles by A. C. Samli: "Interrelationships between the Market Behavior and the Buyer Behavior," in David Rahman, ed., *Readings in Retailing*; "Segmentation and Covering a Niche in the Marketplace," *Journal of Retailing* (Summer 1968); "Use of Segmentation Index to Measure Store Loyalty," *Journal of Retailing* (Spring 1975).

with different components of the market differently (Smith 1956), enables practitioners to be selective and to concentrate on more feasible segments. As early as 1965, however, some scholars expressed skepticism about segmentation (Reynolds 1965). They argued that appealing to mass markets with a broad product line may be better. However, since then segmentation has become a most widely accepted marketing strategy.

Instead of answering questions relating to segmenting or not segmenting directly, this chapter presents an inductive approach involving (1) a detailed discussion of a series of studies that have attempted to identify different market segments to which separate retail establishments have been catering; (2) the construction of what is termed a segmentation index; and (3) an analysis of a uniflow model as a guideline for developing a segmentation index. We use an "after the fact" orientation, which means that analyzing the market segments to which a retail store appeals can be achieved more effectively by analyzing a retail store's existing clientele.

Most of this chapter is devoted to a detailed examination of empirical studies. Also included are a brief discussion of the criteria that can be used for segmentation, the findings of a field study, and, finally, an attempt to measure the segments on the basis of an index and to focus on the role of segmentation in the struggle for survival.

BASIS FOR SEGMENTATION

Although Joan Robinson and Edward Chamberlain made important contributions in bringing imperfect market systems into focus as more realistic models for study, it was sociologists like Lloyd Warner who provided a workable path for marketing practitioners. Warner and his associates analyzed the heterogeneous markets in terms of Index of Status Characteristics (ISC) and divided them into five socioeconomic categories. Following this pattern, students of marketing like Pierre Martineau (1958) have delved into the specific consumption behavior of each category. Such analyses paved the way for what has come to be known as market segmentation. Perhaps because they were more tangible and easy to identify, earlier attempts to segment the market were based on demographic characteristics. In addition to ISCs, age, sex, income distribution, geographic location, educational and occupational background, and stage in the life cycle, all are utilized as the basis for segmentation. Indeed, any one of these variables, or a combination thereof, has been very useful in many marketing decisions.

Numerous researchers have asserted that demographics are not the best way of looking at markets. Rather, markets should be scrutinized, as Daniel Yankelovich (1964, p. 84) in a classical article, contended, "for important differences in buyer attitudes, motivations, values, usage patterns, aesthetic preferences, or degree of susceptibility." This is necessary, as he further asserted, because "we are not dealing with different types of people, but with differences in people's values." Morris J. Gottlieb (1958), among others, examined concepts such as compulsiveness or punitiveness as factors to segment the market for antacids-analgesics. He asserted that it follows that a man who drives an expensive car may prefer cheap whiskey, or a woman who shops at Woolworth's may wish to have dinner occasionally at the Brown Derby.

Other scholars have tried to analyze market segments on the basis of demand elasticities attributable to different groups. The reaction of different consumer groups to changes in prices may be used to group them into distinguishable segments. John G. Myers (1967) used price quality relationships in segmenting the market for a group of private brands.

In recent years, more creative and perhaps functional techniques of segmentation have emerged, and among these, benefit segmentation stands out. Proponents of this technique maintain that different groups of consumers derive different benefits from the use of a product, service, or store. Thus, the degree of benefit becomes the key criterion by which different segments in the market can be identified (Bahn and Granzin 1985).

If the consumers of certain products or customers of certain retail establishments are to be analyzed and categorized *after the fact,* segmentation will be more realistic. Exhibit 7.1 illustrates some of the most important bases for retail segmentation and gives examples for each segmentation criterion. Six criteria are distinguished for segmentation: (1) demographics, (2) sociological considerations, (3) behavioral characteristics, (4) store loyalty, (5) benefit, and (6) geography. The examples presented in the illustration make these criteria rather self-explanatory. A rich store of writings is available on all of these criteria, some of which are presented in the bibliography. Much effort has been made to segment the market on the basis of similar criteria. These efforts reflect a ''before the fact'' attempt to segment the market on the basis of one of these criteria, which makes the effort arbitrary and unidimensional. It is *arbitrary* because it is before the fact, and it is not clear whether a retail store that is segmenting its market on the basis of age is succeeding. It is *unidimensional* because age-based segmentation reflects only one dimension, and it is possible that the store's customers can be grouped in terms of age, sex, behavior, benefit, and perhaps other bases simultaneously.

Users or consumers of certain products share certain characteristics. To the extent that these characteristics can be detected and measured, segmentation is achieved. If, for instance, it is found that, on the average, Porsche owners are between the ages of 35 and 55 and belong to the upper socioeconomic category and are achievers, it may be possible to develop, change, or continue the marketing strategy for Porches accordingly. All aspects of market potential, pricing, promotion, product characteristics, and distribution can be planned along similar lines.

In the case of retailing, especially for specialty stores, the demographic and behavioral characteristics of the immediate market appear to be of great significance since they are determinable and somewhat quantifiable. Although some degree of heterogeneity always exists in its markets, a high-status apparel spe-

Exhibit 7.1
Basis for Retail Segmentation

Criteria	Examples
Demographics	
Age	Teenage market, elderly market
Income	High-income market, low-income market
Education and Occupation	Highly educated sophisticates
Sex	Male or female consumers
Sociological	
Subcultures	Yuppies, wasps
Racial differences	Blacks, orientals
Behavioral	
Psychographics	Extraverted yuppies or narcissistic jocks
Life cycle	Empty-nesters, young married couples
Lifestyles	Jet setters
Innovativeness	People who try products early
Store loyalty	
Heavy users	Those people who buy products often
Regulars	Those who come to the store regularly
Benefit	
Direct benefit	Satisfaction from the store or products directly
Indirect benefit	Satisfaction delayed as in gifts, health foods
Greater versus lesser benefit	Those who experience greatly improved health from attending a health spa
Geography	
Distances	Those who live nearby versus those who live far away
Reputation of the location	Fashionable area
Urban versus rural	Those who live in inner-city versus those who live in the country

cialty store such as I. Magnin's appeals primarily to an identifiable and quantifiable market. This quantification lends itself more readily to demographic and behavioral criteria. In such cases, it is more important to determine the segments that patronize the retail outlet rather than to identify the market segments most suitable for that retail outlet. On this premise, an attempt was made to combine a number of variables under the title of *segmentation index*.

PRELIMINARY CONSIDERATIONS AND METHOD USED

Consumers make three basic decisions when shopping for carpeting: the style they like best—the color and texture best suited for the home; the best quality; and the price that can best be afforded.

In a market in which specialty stores are competitively pressured by department

Exhibit 7.2
Income Level Distribution[a]

Income	Store A Percent Respondents	Store B Percent Respondents	Store C Percent Respondents	Store D Percent Respondents
Under 20,000	6.2	---	2.8	2.4
20,000-27,999	6.2	4.2	2.8	---
28,000-34,999	8.6	4.2	8.3	7.1
35,000-41,999	11.1	4.2	---	4.8
42,000-48,999	16.0	8.3	11.1	19.0
49,000-55,999	28.3	29.1	30.6	28.6
56,000-62,999	22.1	41.6	36.1	26.2
Over 63,000	1.2	8.3	8.0	11.9

[a]Adjusted to current values of $.

and discount stores, the specialty carpet store has to convince the prospective consumer that its store is the place where all three of these basic decisions can be made effectively. Discount carpeting stores, on the other hand, emphasize price and bargain aspects, which they expect to be of prime importance to buyers. Both approaches are designed to appeal to different consumer groups and, hence, to enable the stores to survive and prosper.

The data for this study were obtained through a survey of 294 families in a large western metropolitan area. The sample was drawn from random lists of customers of a discount carpeting specialty store and an exclusive carpeting specialty store, as well as from lists of recently completed homes in the area, telephone solicitations for prospective respondents, and door-to-door canvassing for families that had purchased carpeting in the past two years.

Four retail stores were involved in the study: Store A, a discount specialty carpeting store; Store B, a high-status specialty carpeting store; Store C, a high-status department store; and Store D, a middle-class department store.

SOCIOECONOMIC ANALYSIS

An analysis of the respondents by income distribution indicated significant differences among the clients of the four stores. As shown in Exhibit 7.2, Store A had the smallest percentage of customers in the top three income categories ($49–55,999, $56–62,999, and over $63,000). Store A was the lowest in the highest income category.

Exhibit 7.3 depicts the educational background of the respondents according to stores patronized and shows that Store A customers have had relatively less education than customers of other stores. The highest level of education was found among the customers of Store B (the high-status specialty carpeting store).

The occupational characteristics of the customers were consistent with their educational and income characteristics. As indicated in Exhibit 7.4, Store A

Exhibit 7.3
Education of the Respondents[a]

Income	Store A Percent Respondents	Store B Percent Respondents	Store C Percent Respondents	Store D Percent Respondents
Less than eight years	4.9	---	---	2.4
Eight to twelve years	49.2	29.1	41.7	31.7
Some college	32.0	41.6	38.9	43.9
Bachelor's degree	8.6	16.6	16.6	14.6
Beyond bachelor's	2.5	8.3	2.8	5.0
Master's degree	2.5	4.2	---	2.4

[a]Head of the household only.

Exhibit 7.4
Occupation of the Respondents[a]

Occupation	Store A Percent Respondents	Store B Percent Respondents	Store C Percent Respondents	Store D Percent Respondents
Supervisory	8.6	14.3	20.0	12.0
Clerical	2.5	---	5.7	---
Other white collar	13.5	33.3	20.0	12.0
Professional	11.1	14.3	11.4	24.0
Skilled workers	24.6	4.8	14.3	14.4
Unskilled workers	7.4	4.8	---	7.2
Government employees	17.2	4.8	8.6	12.0
Self-employed	7.4	14.3	5.7	4.8
Retired-unemployed	7.4	9.5	14.3	7.2

[a]Man of the house only.

customers were more heavily composed of skilled workers and government employees, as opposed to a substantially greater concentration of white-collar, supervisory, and professional workers for Store B. Store C also showed a significant deviation from Store A in the occupational makeup of its customers.

The monthly payments of the Store A customers for their homes also show a slight tendency to be lower (see Exhibit 7.5). The average monthly payment for this group was $636 as opposed to $672 for Store B and $684 for Store D customers. Home ownership also indicated that the payments of Store A customers were less than those of Stores B and C.

Survey findings indicated that Store A customers lived in homes that were, on the average, nine and one-half years old, and they had lived in them a little over five years. In contrast, Store B customers lived in newer homes (about six and one-half years old) and had lived in them about four years. The size of the home and the number of rooms with wall-to-wall carpeting were not significantly different among consumers of the various stores.

Exhibit 7.5
Monthly House Payments of the Respondents[a]

Monthly Payments	Store A Percent Respondents	Store B Percent Respondents	Store C Percent Respondents	Store D Percent Respondents
Below $360	8.2	---	---	2.4
$361-479	14.1	7.1	13.9	14.3
$480-599	16.5	21.4	30.6	23.8
$600-719	24.7	35.8	13.9	23.8
$720-839	21.2	17.9	19.4	9.5
$840-959	4.7	7.1	13.9	9.5
Over $960	4.7	3.6	---	14.3
House paid for	5.9	7.1	8.3	2.4

[a]Adjusted to current values.

Exhibit 7.6
Ownership of Various Luxury Items[a]

Item	Store A Percent Respondents	Store B Percent Respondents	Store C Percent Respondents	Store D Percent Respondents
Color television	9.3	21.4	11.1	9.5
Stereo	54.1	70.4	55.5	66.7
Boat	14.0	25.0	14.9	11.9
Air conditioning	61.9	75.0	63.9	66.7

[a]The items in this exhibit were luxury products when the study was undertaken.

Ownership of luxuries is another indicator of socioeconomic class. For the purpose of this study, four products were singled out as luxury items: color television, stereo phonographs, boats, and air conditioning. Exhibit 7.6 shows that relatively fewer Store A customers owned these luxuries.

Finally, a few comments can be made about car ownership by the respondents as an indication of socioeconomic class. Store A customers owned more cars than other carpet buyers—13.2 percent had three cars as opposed to about 4 percent in other groups. This finding is consistent with the fact that more wives in this group worked (26 percent in contrast with 21 percent for Store B), and thus more cars were needed. An analysis of cars according to price range shows that Store A customers owned relatively lower priced cars (Exhibit 7.7).

SEGMENTATION INDEX

By using weights for each category, it was possible to develop an index indicating segmentation, called the Segmentation Index (SI). Exhibit 7.8 displays total points for each of the four stores for each socioeconomic category as well

Exhibit 7.7
Car Ownership by Price Range

Price Range	Store A Percent Respondents	Store B Percent Respondents	Other Percent Respondents
High	3.5	12.5	1.3
Medium	28.3	37.5	36.2
Low	68.0	50.0	57.6

Exhibit 7.8
Segmentation Index[a]

Socioeconomic Criteria	Store A	Store B	Store C	Store D
Income level distribution	502.9	611.5	589.1	588.1
Education of respondents	261.2	216.1	280.5	295.3
Occupation of respondents	151.3	200.1	182.8	177.6
Monthly house payment of respondent	351.8	378.9	355.6	399.8
Ownership of luxury items	393.3	571.8	413.5	431.0
Car ownership by price ranges	170.4	225.0	202.7	202.7[b]
Total	1,830.9	2,303.4	2,024.2	2,094.5

[a]Points are arrived at by multiplying the assigned weights for each category with the percent distribution figures presented in Exhibits 7.2–7.7

[b]Since Stores B and D are somewhat closer, the same figure was used for this category because the available data were for both of these stores combined.

as the total points. As can be seen, in all but one, Store A had the lowest and Store B had the highest totals. If the SI for Store A is assumed to be 100, then the SIs of Stores B, C, and D are 125.8, 110.5, and 114.4, respectively. As evidenced by these figures, significant differences in SIs prevailed, especially between Stores A and B.

Thus, it can be seen that the customers of the discount specialty store belonged primarily to a relatively lower socioeconomic group. The buying behavior of this group should be analyzed in order to determine the merchandising, pricing, and advertising policies that would improve the image of this store. In addition, the services rendered by this company should be examined to improve the image of its marketing performance.

To this point, the analysis has shown that the SI works. In this study the index was composed of six objective criteria. In subsequent studies, subjective factors such as hobbies by cost, membership in civic and professional groups, and

Exhibit 7.9
Occasion on Which Respondents Bought Carpeting

Occasion	Store A Percent Respondents	Store B Percent Respondents	Store C Percent Respondents	Store D Percent Respondents
Moving	15.3	50.0	25.0	38.1
Remodeling	14.1	17.9	8.3	7.1
Refurnishing	27.1	17.9	19.4	28.6
Family event	1.2	---	5.6	---
Purchasing new furniture	1.2	3.6	2.8	2.4
Deciding to buy carpet	14.1	---	8.3	9.5
Replacing old carpet	12.9	10.7	13.9	4.8
Other	14.1	---	16.7	9.5

ownership of credit cards were considered. Analyses indicated that similar results could be obtained by using subjective or objective criteria (Samli 1975). However, researchers of a retail establishment should experiment with numerous subjective and objective variables and then concentrate on those that would help merchants to identify their market segment more readily. Within this context, certain objective criteria may be very appropriate in different communities.

THE BUYING BEHAVIOR OF STORE A CUSTOMERS

The following analyses of the buying behavior of the Store A group also indicate what could be done with the customer groups of Stores B, C, or D if one were interested in their marketing performance as well.

In analyzing the occasions that prompted the purchase of carpeting, the total survey results showed that refurnishing and moving were the most important, although, in the case of Store A, refurnishing was by far the most important of these two (27.1 percent). As shown in Exhibit 7.9, the customers of Store B, on the other hand, stated that the major occasion was moving (50.0 percent). As shown in the exhibit, most of the carpeting sold by the discount specialty store is of the replacement type rather than that purchased for the first time for a new home. Shopping before the purchases was not very common among Store A customers. Overall, the largest proportion of the respondents in this group did the least shopping (see Exhibit 7.10). Either they considered the choice of stores rather limited, or they had made up their minds before shopping; further evidence shows that the second assertion is correct.

The survey established that advertising plays an important role in communicating the name of Store A to the market. A great majority of its customers (63.0 percent) reported that they first heard of this store through newspaper advertisements (Exhibit 7.11). On the other hand, for Stores B and C, word-of-

555

5555

Exhibit 7.10
Shopping Before the Purchase

Customers of	Did not shop around	Shopped one store	Shopped two stores	Shopped three stores
Store A	54.1%	12.9%	17.6%	16.4%
Store C	55.6	5.6	16.7	22.2
Store B	32.1	14.2	21.4	32.1
Store D	52.0	20.0	28.0	---
Total survey results	44.8%	14.0%	21.4%	19.8%

Exhibit 7.11
Where Respondents First Heard about Store

Sources	Store A Percent Respondents	Store B Percent Respondents	Store C Percent Respondents	Store D Percent Respondents
Recommendation-friends	11.3	30.4	40.0	9.1
Recommendation-relative	3.8	4.4	---	9.1
New store	1.3	---	---	---
Saw the store	13.8	26.0	20.0	27.3
Newspaper advertisement	63.0	17.4	40.0	27.3
Friend worked there	6.0	---	---	---
Radio	---	4.3	---	---
Other	3.8	2.5	---	27.3

mouth advertising or reputation played a more important role: 30.4 percent and 40.0 percent of their respective customer respondents indicated that the store was recommended by friends.

Another important aspect of buying behavior involves the reasons for preferring a store. Significant differences were detected when the reasons customers bought at one particular store were analyzed (Exhibit 7.12).

Although price orientation can easily be detected among the customers of the discount specialty store, the customers of the exclusive specialty store paid more attention to selection, reputation, and word-of-mouth advertising, as indicated by heavy emphasis on the recommendation of friends.

The method of buying also differed among the customers of different stores. For example, a greater percentage of Store A clients visited the store than did the clients of Store B (Exhibit 7.13). Evidently, the lower socioeconomic class customers preferred to go to the store personally rather than ask the salesperson to visit them at home.

Customer purchase satisfaction was determined by asking the respondents whether or not they would recommend the store to others. Exhibit 7.14 shows that the high-status department store (Store C) had the greatest popularity in this

Exhibit 7.12
Factors That Made Customers Decide to Buy at One Particular Location[a]

Factors	Store A Percent Respondents' Preference	Store B Percent Respondents' Preference	Store C Percent Respondents' Preference	Store D Percent Respondents' Preference
Reasonable price	8	5	7	6
Good selection	3	1	3	4
Close to home	7	6	9	7
Newspaper advertising	5	11	9	10
Advertising	9	6	9	10
Right price	2	6	7	2
Best buy avaiable	4	6	2	4
Recommendation of friend	6	2	9	7
Recommendation of relative	9	6	9	10
Sales	1	11	5	1
Good guarantee	12	11	5	10
Good reputation	9	3	1	2
Better service	12	4	4	7

[a]Same numbers indicate similar weights in rating.

Exhibit 7.13
Customers' Method of Purchase

Method of Buying	Store A Percent Respondents	Store B Percent Respondents	Store C Percent Respondents	Store D Percent Respondents
Visited the store	83.0	65.8	75.0	64.7
Had salesman come to home	11.0	23.7	13.9	20.5
Both	6.0	10.5	11.1	7.3

Exhibit 7.14
Would the Respondents Recommend the Store?

Store	Percentage
Store A	88.1
Store B	92.9
Store C	94.4
Store D	83.3

Exhibit 7.15
Would the Respondents Go to the Same Store Again?

Store	Percentage
Store A	46.5
Store B	53.5
Store C	63.9
Store D	29.3

Exhibit 7.16
Where Would the Respondents Shop?

Customers	Store A Percent Respondents	Store B Percent Respondents	Store C Percent Respondents	Store D Percent Respondents
Store A	---	6.7	22.2	16.1
Store E	---	13.3	5.6	---
Store C	50.0	60.0	---	61.0
Store D	4.3	6.7	11.1	10.5
Store F	4.3	---	---	---
Store G	8.7	---	5.6	---
Store B	2.2	---	22.2	---
Store H	2.2	6.7	11.1	---
Store I	6.5	---	---	---
Others	21.7	6.7	22.2	16.1

Note: Stores F through I are other stores in the region which were identified by respondents as alternative competing stores.

respect. Store loyalty can also be tested by learning whether or not the respondents would go back to the same store. Exhibit 7.15 shows these survey findings. Once again, loyalty was the highest toward Store C, for a greater percentage of its customer respondents said they would go back to the same store again.

Although the customers of the specialty discount store did not shop around much, when they were asked where they would choose to shop, the exclusive specialty store was the most popular place, as indicated in Exhibit 7.16.

According to analyses of buying behavior in relation to socioeconomic classifications, different motives and different points of emphasis prevail in buying carpeting. As a result, consumers patronize retail establishments that are distinctly identifiable.

The typical customer of Store A belonged to a relatively lower socioeconomic group, but his or her buying behavior seemed to be consistent with the socioeconomic status. This group of respondents was more price-oriented; they did not shop around very much before the purchase; they went to the store to buy rather than have the salesperson come to their home; they paid more attention

Exhibit 7.17
Segmentation Index Expressed by Loyalty

Stores	All Customers	Loyal Customers	Less Loyal Customers
A	110.8	130.6	104.7
B	104.2	112.8	104.2
C	100.0	100.0	100.0

Source: Samli 1975: 59.

to advertisements than to reputation or word-of-mouth advertising; and they were economy-minded, practical people who made up their minds and then acted accordingly.

SEGMENTATION INDEX AND LOYAL CUSTOMERS

Loyal customers can be considered to be the core of a retail store's market. If SI is not significantly different at this level, *it cannot possibly* be at the fringe, that is, transient buyers who buy only occasionally.

Store loyalty is a very important topic for both researchers and retailers. Loyal customers of a store can be identified in a number of ways, one of which is to find out how much customers shop around before they buy in the specific store. A second method is that customers report loyalty to the store where they do most of their shopping (Cunningham 1962). Still another is the number of times within a given period of time one might shop at a specific store (Samli 1975). By using this third method, it has been shown that if there are differences in the general SIs of stores, these differences are accentuated by distinguishing customers as loyal and nonloyal (Samli 1975). Exhibit 7.17 reports the findings of a study other than the one featured in this chapter. As can be seen, at the core, SI can discriminate between or among stores much better than the fringe.

CONSIDERATIONS FOR POLICY DECISIONS

After studying the socioeconomic groups and buying behavior, we can conclude that Store A is a successful concern in terms of identifying its segment on the basis of socioeconomic criteria and dealing with that segment effectively. As a discount specialty carpeting store, it emphasizes price and variety rather than trying to establish a status image. It utilizes mainly factual and promotional advertising, with heavy emphasis on price and sales, and there is virtually no emphasis on institutional appeal.

This type of approach evidently appealed to the store's current market. Its customers, being more price- and economy-minded, were attracted mainly by newspaper advertising. They purchased primarily wall-to-wall carpeting for re-decoration of the house; hence, price and economy appeals were stronger to them than high status, image, and reputation.

The fact that customers of the store were hesitant to go back to it or to recommend it to friends and relatives indicates a need for a change in emphasis. Some institutional appeal could be useful in advertising to create a better name for the store. Another danger that exists is that an overall company policy of treating the present sales as a one-shot proposition can promote an inadequate image. In this case, the possibility of future repeat sales is not considered to be an important goal. A change in this attitude means emphasizing the fact that, within a few years, these customers will come back either for replacement or, more important, for additional carpeting for the rest of the home. Most important, word-of-mouth advertising is still one of the cheapest and most effective types of promotion. Even though the sales to customer A may be a one-shot proposition, if A is not satisfied, he or she may influence the thinking of B, C, and D who otherwise would be potential customers for Store A.

In developing a strategy for the future, Store A has basically three alternatives. First, it may try to appeal to a slightly higher socioeconomic group without endangering its present business. This approach is desirable because a slight upgrading in the image will allow the store to gain further esteem with the present clientele, and they will start a word-of-mouth campaign. In addition, some higher socioeconomic customers may start patronizing the store. Some effort in slightly more institutionalized advertising as opposed to exclusively promotional adver-tising may, at least partially, fulfill this objective. Second, Store A may attempt to maintain the status quo. Although the store has been successful, this is no assurance for the future; lack of loyalty may become a significant bottleneck in later years. The third—and least feasible—alternative is to change the image completely and try to appeal totally to a higher socioeconomic group. This will mean direct competition with Stores B and C.

The success of Store A depends on meeting the needs of its well-defined market. The discount specialty store managed to carve a niche in the market by identifying a socioeconomic group and by satisfying its desires effectively. Its success in the future will also depend on the continuation of the present situation (Smith 1956).

CONDITIONS FOR GENERAL APPLICABILITY

Although only one major product line has been analyzed in this chapter, the method used and results are applicable to a wide variety of products and retail stores. In fact, subsequent studies have indicated this to be the case (Samli 1975). Quite likely, only in shopping goods will an SI be significant and shopper behavior readily identifiable. Although a store's image is identifiable and sig-nificantly different in retail establishments dealing primarily with convenience goods, for example, grocery stores or drug stores, buyer behavior is not substantially different from that of customers of shopping goods. In this study, the relative status of all four stores was known beforehand. Otherwise, it would have been necessary to determine the image of the store in question. Once the image is known, it is appropriate to consider a change in the strategy in terms of appealing to the same segment or changing it.

Upon establishing the image, an SI must be developed. The method discussed here for the construction of such a tool is by no means fixed. Factors used in the index, as well as their relative weights, can be changed. The construction of an index sensitive enough to distinguish one store from stores of competitors is the important point. Proper use of this index requires knowledge of consumer purchase behavior. A sensitive SI is not important where buyer behavior and segments cannot be related to each other.

In matching market segments and buyer behavior, it must be realized that this match applies only to the business in question. Therefore, we are concerned about the purchase behavior of customers of, say, Store A who as a group also have distinguishing characteristics that help to identify them. These characteristics might be lost if we were to study the wall-to-wall carpeting buying habits of a large subsector in the economy, for example, senior citizens. Thus, by matching the segment and buyer behavior the firm can carve its niche in the marketplace.

Exhibit 7.18 illustrates a logical flowchart for the firm's segmentation efforts. It is applicable to manufacturers as well as to retail stores. Many of the details of what the factors are and how the SI is developed are omitted. Two steps are distinguished: questions and necessary actions. Proper sequencing provides a logical order for the strategy development. Such models can also be used in computer simulator studies.

The model here implies the existence of a going concern. It then makes provisions for a logical exploration of the prevailing strategy. Similar models can be developed for different product lines as well as different establishments. For a beginning firm or a new product line, a somewhat different model is likely to be utilized. In such cases, since the image of the firm or the product is not known, activities will be geared to a special market segment somewhat arbitrarily. However, in time as it becomes possible to establish and change the firm's appeal in the marketplace, the proposed model is likely to become necessary for survival and success.

STRATEGY FOR SURVIVAL

The data presented in this chapter show that marketing practitioners can learn to identify their markets. Such identification is necessitated by the lack of homogeneous demand caused by different customs, by desire for variety or desire for exclusiveness, or by basic differences in user needs, that is, by socioeconomic differences. This identification of the immediate market enables merchants to understand their customers better. Hence, they are able to formulate more ef-

Exhibit 7.18
A Logical Flowchart of Segmentation Activity of a Retail Establishment

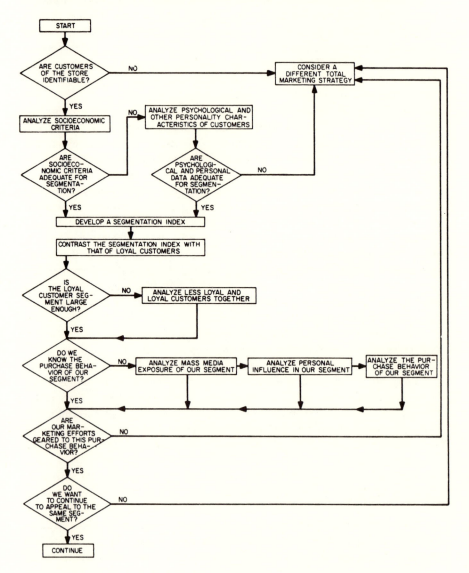

fective policies by matching their segmentation efforts and the buyer behavior in their segments. The result of this endeavor is satisfaction for both the marketing practitioner and his or her market.

This practice of identifying the market and catering to it adequately is the process of carving a niche in the market. The impact on the economy as a whole is the minimization of waste, resources, and marketing effort and stimulation of welfare. These can be considered to be the basic goals of the market economy.

Just like individuals or species, a firm survives because there is a place for it in the existing external structure. As our research shows, existing conditions in the environment offer an opportunity which, if explored properly, enable the firm to survive and prosper. It is not the total environment as much as one of its well-defined components that is crucial to the firm's survival.

This well-defined slice, which can be called a segment, niche, foothold, or footing (Alderson 1957), can be analyzed effectively according to its socioeconomic characteristics. Once the segment is identified, its characteristics may be further analyzed on the basis of nonsocioeconomic criteria. Identification of the segment for a going concern, particularly for specialty stores, appears to be especially possible on the basis of these criteria. The identification and careful definition of this phenomenon can at least guide the firm partially to establish the right pattern of behavior. The rest of this right pattern of behavior depends on considerations other than the characteristics of the segment. The objectives of the firm and its ability to utilize the tools it has in its possession, such as advertising, product, price, and capital, are among these considerations. They enable the firm to carve either a deep and well-defined niche or a superficial and blurred one. Dealing with a well-defined market segment and capitalizing on it by carving a niche, however, is not the only way to survive. It is one of many different ways of surviving and prospering (Alderson 1957), but it is a very important one.

SUMMARY

Segmentation is less clearcut for retailers than for producers of specific products for specific markets such as children's toys, baby food, or tonics for the elderly. As a result, in order to understand the degree of segmentation that a retailer has been able to accomplish, a concept segmentation index (SI) is introduced in this chapter. SI is necessary to determine and distinguish the *core* market from the *fringe* market in retailing. If the core market is not large enough, the store may have to emphasize the fringe markets. This may necessitate certain changes in the marketing strategy. Similarly, if both core and fringe markets indicated by SI are not adequate or are shrinking, the retail establishment might consider aiming at other segments. SI and related research efforts would indicate what kind of changes have to take place in the store's marketing strategy for it to appeal to other segments.

REFERENCES

"A & P Looks Like Tengelmann's Vietnam." *Business Week*, No. 2724, February 1, 1982.

Alderson, Wroe. *Marketing Behavior and Executive Action*. Homewood, Ill.: Richard D. Irwin, 1957, p.55.

Bahn, Kenneth D. and Kent L. Granzin. "Benefit Segmentation in the Restaurant Industry." *Journal of Academy of Marketing Science* (Summer 1985): 226–247.

Bass, Frank M., Douglas J. Tigert, and Ronald T. Lonsdale. "Market Segmentation: Group Versus Individual Behavior." *Journal of Marketing Research* (August 1968): 264–276.

Berkowitz, Eric N., Roger A. Kerin, and William Rudelius. *Marketing*. St. Louis: Times/Mirror Mosby, 1986.

Berman, Barry, and Joel R. Evans, *Retail Management*. New York: Macmillan Co., 1986.

Bucklin, Louis. "Retail Strategy and the Classification of Consumer Goods." *Journal of Marketing* (February 27, 1973): 45–54.

Cunningham, R. "Customer Loyalty to Store and Brand." *Harvard Business Review* (December 1962): 127–137.

Davidson, William R., Albert D. Bates, and Stephen Bass. "The Retail Life Cycle." *Harvard Business Review* 54, no. 6 (November-December 1976): 89–96.

Frank, Ronald E., and William F. Massy. "Market Segmentation and the Effectiveness of a Brand's Price and Dealing Policies." *Journal of Business* (April 1965): 186–200.

Gottlieb, Morris J. "Segmentation by Personality Types." In Lynn H. Stockman, ed., *Advancing of Marketing Efficiency*. Chicago: American Marketing Association, 1958, pp. 148–158.

Green, Norma. "Furniture Makers Adjust Marketing to Hit Less Home Oriented Life Styles." *Advertising Age*, January 17, 1977, p. 3.

Joyce, Mary, and Joseph B. Guiltinan, "The Professional Woman: A Potential Market Segment for Retailers." *Journal of Retailing* (Summer 1978): 59–70.

Kotler, Philip. *Marketing Management Analysis, Planning and Control*. 5th ed. Englewood Cliffs, N.J.: Prentice-Hall, 1984.

Lincoln, Douglas, and A. Coskun Samli. "Evolution in Retail Marketing Strategies." *Academy of Marketing Science Conference Proceedings* (1981).

McCarthy, E. Jerome, and William Perreault. *Marketing Management*. Homewood, Ill.: Richard D. Irwin, 1987.

Martineau, Pierre. "Social Class and Spending Behavior." *Journal of Marketing* (October 1958): 121–130.

Mochis, George P., Roy L. Moore, and Lawndes F. Stephens. "Purchasing Patterns of Adolescent Consumers." *Journal of Retailing* (Spring 1977): 17–28.

Myers, John G. "Determinants of Private Brand Attitude." *Journal of Marketing Research* (February 1967): 73–81.

Ohmae, Kenichi. *The Mind of the Strategist*. New York, Penguin Books, 1982.

Porter, Michael. *The Competitive Edge*. New York: Random House, 1985.

Reynolds, William. "More Sense About Market Segmentation." *Harvard Business Review* (September-October 1965): 107–114.

Roberts, Alan A. "Applying the Strategy of Market Segmentation." *Business Horizons* (Fall 1961): 65.

Samli, A. Coskun. "Marketing Segments—A Key to Marketing Strategy Development." *Business Perspectives* (Winter 1966): 21–26.

———. "Segmentation and Carving a Niche in the Market Place." *Journal of Retailing* (Summer 1968): 35–49.

———. "Segmentation Index and Store Image in Retail and Service Establishments." Proceedings of ESOMAR Seminar XXIX on Research That Works for Today's Marketing Problems, 1976. From talk delivered before the X ESOMAR Seminar at Lucerne, November 2–5, 1969.

———. "Use of Segmentation Index to Measure Store Loyalty." *Journal of Retailing* (Spring 1975): 51–60.

———, and Douglas Lincoln. "Comparative Advertising and Evolution in Retailing." Paper presented at Southwest Marketing Association meetings, 1981.

Satow, Kay. "Some Comments on Changing Life Styles Among Single Young Adults." In William Perreault, ed., *Advances in Consumer Research*, Vol. 4, Chicago: Association for Consumer Research, 1977, pp. 333–37.

Smith, Wendell R. "Product Differentiation and Market Segmentation as Alternative Marketing Strategies." *Journal of Marketing* (July 1956): 3–8.

Sweeney, Daniel J. and Richard C. Reizenstein. "Developing a Retail Market Segmentation Strategy for a Women's Specialty Store, Using Multiple Discriminant Analysis." Combined Proceedings, American Marketing Association, 1972.

Yankelovich, Daniel. "New Criteria for Market Segmentation." *Harvard Business Review* (March-April 1964): 83–90.

Zikmund, William. "A Taxonomy of Black Shopping Behavior." *Journal of Retailing* (Spring 1977): 61–72.

8 Alternative Retail Marketing Strategies

This chapter explores the development of retail marketing strategy from three different perspectives: from an evolutionary point of view; on the basis of the retail establishment's stage of the life cycle; and in terms of developing congruence between the product classification and retail store classification. The chapter does not attempt to establish priorities, norms, or parameters. It gives all three dimensions the same emphasis and importance. The evolutionary process is given more space in the chapter because, in order to understand the importance of changing retail marketing strategy in time, it is necessary first to examine the evolution in manufacturers' marketing strategies. This is because manufacturers' marketing strategies have been paralleled to specific advertising programs and both evolved in a similar manner. The same analyses need to be applied to retailing. In order to fulfill its objectives and to develop a competitive edge, the retail establishment should pursue any one of these three dimensions (Ohmae 1982; Porter 1985). These dimensions are not mutually exclusive, however. Thus, in pursuit of a strategy, the retailer may use one, two, or all three of these dimensions.

THE EVOLUTION OF MANUFACTURER MARKETING STRATEGIES

A marketing strategy is the "plan of action" or the "game plan" used by the manufacturer's marketing department to achieve determined ends. These ends are normally referred to as the firm's basic objectives or goals (Ohmae 1982). It can be shown that there has been an evolution of the marketing strategy in the last 50 years and that an evolution in advertising strategy has occurred simultaneously. Exhibit 8.1 depicts this evolution (Lincoln and Samli 1981).

Exhibit 8.1
Evolution of Marketing and Advertising Strategies

Name of Marketing Strategy	Advertising Strategy	Approximate Date of Initial Appearance
Market Aggregation	Omnibus	Pre 1930's
Product Differentiation	Competitive	1930's
Market Segmentation	Rifle	1950's
Positioning	Comparative	1970's

Early production-oriented firms used the market aggregation strategy, treating their entire market as a single, undifferentiated, homogeneous unit. Managers of these firms developed one product, and one marketing program was designed to reach as many customers as possible (Berkowitz et al. 1986). The market aggregation strategy called for an advertising approach that could be termed "omnibus." The omnibus approach was to use one message for the entire market. The appeal of advertisements was broad, more or less stressing to the customer that the one product was capable of serving several different needs.

The move away from the market aggregation strategy occurred as competition stiffened and as supply began to catch up with demand. In order to prevent price cutting and its associated lowering of profits, the firm attempted to differentiate its product from those of its competitors. Economically speaking, the firm moved within the theoretical framework of monopolistic competition and tried to command slightly higher prices and/or sustain buyer loyalty. Although the product differentiation strategy often incorporated product feature changes or additions (new sizes, new flavors, new colors, etc.) the strategy tended to be characterized by the heavy use of advertising and was classified as a promotional strategy approach to marketing (Smith 1956). Advertising attempted to convey information about the new features, but at the same time to create a product image that was more favorable than that of competing products. Thus, advertising used in the product differentiation strategy could be termed "competitive." This is an appropriate term since the purpose of this advertising was to set the product off from the competitors' product offerings.

Manufacturers next recognized that the total market for products was too heterogeneous to rely solely on the product differentiation strategy. As a result, a new strategy emerged called market segmentation. This was the process of taking the total, heterogeneous market for a product and dividing it into several submarkets or segments, each of which tends to be homogeneous in all significant aspects (Stanton 1982). As with the earlier marketing strategies, advertising played a crucial role in determining the effectiveness of a market segmentation strategy. The advertising strategist needed to know consumer media habits, levels of education, degrees of audience involvement, and several other variables about the segment(s) to be reached. The advertising programs for a multiproduct firm with multimarkets must aim carefully at each market. Because advertising within the framework of the market segmentation must be very accurate, it could be termed "rifle" advertising.

Before discussing the most recent marketing strategy, two observations on product differentiation and market segmentation are in order. First, these strategies have been shown to be important to a firm attempting to establish a "differential advantage" (Alderson 1965). Second, the two strategies can be, and often are, used simultaneously. Wendell Smith (1956) noted this second fact.

In 1972 Jack Trout and Al Ries heralded the coming of a new era in marketing strategy which they called the "Era of Positioning." They stated that:

Positioning has its roots in the packaged goods field where the concept was called product positioning. It literally meant the product's form, package size and price as compared to its competition . . . today we are entering an era that recognizes the importance of both the product and company image, but more than anything else, stresses the need to create a position in the prospect's mind (Trout and Ries 1972).

Since Trout and Ries' original writings, interest in the concept of positioning has increased. Positioning is viewed as an extension of product differentiation and basically calls for a promotional differentiation among competitors and brands within previously established market segments (Brown and Sims 1977).

The positioning strategy appears to be especially attractive to those firms whose products are in the mature stage of their product life cycle. Since these products have limited opportunities for market expansion (via the segmentation and differentiation strategies), positioning may be the only major alternative left for the firm and its product. This would be accomplished by carefully spelling out similarities and/or differences between the product and its competing products. The "mature" product may be limited to deriving its additional sales volume from competitors (Sims 1970).

In developing a positioning strategy, the following steps should be followed:

1. Determine the wants and needs of selected market segments.
2. Analyze the benefits your product offers compared to those offered by other organizations serving those market segments.
3. Determine which benefits are most important to the markets desired and which are least important.
4. Study what benefits are being offered by competing organizations and how the market views the total offer.

5. Adjust your product offer so that the groups of benefits you offer better meet the needs of a particular market segment.

6. Promote your product to create the image that you want the market to see and understand (Nickels 1978: 99).

Notice that step six calls for an effective promotional program in carrying out the positioning strategy.

An approach to advertising that has been recently popularized by the need to position products is called *comparative advertising*. This approach is defined as advertising that (1) compares two or more specifically named or recognizably presented products/services of the same generic class and (2) makes such a comparison in terms of one or more specific product/service attributes (Wilkie and Farris 1975). Manufacturers apparently feel that comparative advertising is the promotional technique best suited to effective positioning. Trout and Ries (1972: 52) offer the following support: ''in the positioning era . . . to establish a position you must often name competitive names . . . the prospect already knows the benefits of using the product . . . to climb on his (consumer's product ladder you must relate your brand to the brands already there.'' Because the positioning strategy is closely tied to what competitors are doing, comparative advertising has become the manufacturers' preferred promotional approach.

As the basic marketing strategy has become more sophisticated and complex, so has the need for more sophisticated advertising approaches. Accordingly, manufacturer-sponsored advertising strategies have undergone an evolution that coincides with the marketing strategy evolution. The current stages of both evolutions are product positioning and comparative advertising.

THE EVOLUTION OF RETAIL MARKETING STRATEGIES

Has retail marketing strategy development followed the same evolutionary process as that for manufacturers? If so, is the evolution chronologically identical? A review of the literature and field observations reveals that the evolution of the retail marketing strategy lags behind that of the manufacturers. Four retail strategies have evolved over time: mass retailing, differentiating, segmenting, and positioning. Exhibit 8.2 points out the starting points and goals of each strategy. It must be stated at the outset that these four strategies are not mutually exclusive. They could and do coexist at any given time at any market, and all of them are practiced in today's retailing. However, segmenting and positioning are more recent strategies than the other two.

Mass Retailing

Retailers, much as manufacturers, have exploited the market aggregation strategy. The mass retailers start basically similar marketing mixes as their competitors. They assume that the market is large enough and that they could capture

Exhibit 8.2
Retail Marketing Strategy Alternatives

	Starting Point	Goals
Positioner	Starts with a specific market position aiming at a specific competitor	Attempts to take away a good share of the market from a well-established competitor
Segmenter	Starts with market segmentation	Attempts more precise adjustment of supply to heterogeneous demand
Differentiator	Starts with marketing mix differentials	Tries to develop better mixes for the measurement
Mass Retailer	Starts with basically similar marketing mix as the competitor's appeals through convenience or ease of shopping	Tries to capture a part of the market by not doing anything different than competitors

a portion of it by imitating others. They thrive on convenience and ease of shopping. Examples of this group include the general trading stores of the 1800's and early department stores. These retailers attempted to serve the total market by making a wide assortment of products available. For them, advertising played an informative role by emphasizing store location, variety of products carried, and similar variables. Advertising messages were the same for all segments as the retailer attacked the total market. All customers are viewed as basically alike. In such cases achieving differential congruence is not a concern. The retailer is basically imitating. The retail store is not developing any unique characteristics.

Differentiating

As retailers faced increased competition such as chain store operations and declining profits (which stemmed from price cutting as well as large-scale, more efficient retail operations), they began using the product differentiation strategy. This strategy starts with marketing mix differentials (Exhibit 8.2). Its goal is to develop better mixes for the mass market and hence to develop competitive advantage. This strategy is practiced in the department store. In striving for monopolistic competition in their retail trade areas, the department store frequently added such features as credit, gift wrapping, delivery, expanded store hours, and restaurants with fashion shows, and used advertising in the form of these new features. Most important, their advertising programs attempted to create and promote the store image that distinguished it from its competitors. Differentiating does *not* necessarily provide differential congruence. Typically, a differentiator may not think of matching the store's unique features with the target market's self-image.

Segmenting

In time, retailers realized that neither their customers nor their trade areas were homogeneous. Further realizing that their trade areas were comprised of several heterogeneous submarkets within which there was homogeneity of needs, motives, and so on, some retailers attempted to employ the market segmentation strategy (Samli 1966, 1968, 1975, 1976). Retail marketing evolved considerably later than that of the manufacturers; this is illustrated by the way the literature concerning these topics developed. Generally, the pace of retail store market segmentation research has tended to be somewhat slower and less sophisticated than that for product/market segmentation (Sweeney and Reizenstein 1972). To this day, market segmentation is a "new" strategy to several retailers.

As for manufacturers, advertising plays a key role in determining the effectiveness of a retail segmentation strategy. Advertising programs are directed at specific market segments with unique needs, which means that retailers have to be cautious about media selection and scheduling as well as message construction.

Segmenters begin by identifying variable segments. Their goal is to adjust the supply to heterogeneous demand (Exhibit 8.2). They view the market as one of varied customers, and they try to offer a select market mix to satisfy specific needs. Many of the specialty stores can be shown to be examples of segmentation in retailing. I. Magnin's, Thom McAn's, and Robert Hall's are all examples of specialty retail chains that appeal to carefully defined market segments. Some department stores also have segmentation; Bloomingdale's, Marshall Field's, and K-Mart are examples. While Bloomingdale's may be aiming at the upper class, Marshall Field's may be aiming at upper middle class and K-Mart at the lower middle class. Although the companies may not have planned it that way, they still appeal primarily to these segments.

At best, the evolution of marketing strategy development for retailing is still in the segmentation stage. Accordingly, the most significant contrast between the manufacturers' and retailers' evolution exists at the positioning stage. It is here that we see that the retail evolution is incomplete. The literature concerning manufacturer (product) positioning first appeared in the early 1970s, and it was not until 1977 that similar recognition was given to the concept of retail positioning (Doyle and Sharma 1977). Because segmentation is still the major practice and research area, it was treated in greater detail in the previous chapter. Although segmentation is necessary for differential congruence, it is not sufficient. Segmentation must produce congruence between the store image and the consumer's self-image.

Positioning

The positioner in retailing starts with a specific position aiming at a specific competitor: it attempts to take away a good share of the market from a well-established competitor. In a specific well-defined market, a new retailer may position itself so that it will take advantage of the best market with the least competition.

The positioner views the market as if there were some crucial differences between his or her loyal customers and the immediate competitor's loyal customers. He or she segments the market and differentiates the marketing mix. However, the mix is not only different but also better for the segment which the retailer is aiming to take away from the key competitor. Exhibit 8.3 distinguishes the four different retail marketing strategies and presents a comparative summary. Positioning, like segmentation, is necessary for differential congruence but is not sufficient. Successful positioning implies successful segmentation and successful congruence between the store image and customer's self-image.

A TIME FOR RETAIL POSITIONING?

The current need to apply the positioning strategy in the retail situation is very real. During the late 1970s, sharp changes in the retailing environment brought about a need to move beyond the market segmentation strategy. The "historical" position occupied by already established retailers may erode as those changes take place. Among these changes are the following:

1. *New demographics*—A continuation of shifts of population to the southeast, southwest, far west, and Rocky Mountain states, changing age distribution with great increases in the 25- to 44-year-old age bracket, and a declining birth rate.

2. *New values*—Examples include growing concern with environmentalism, consumerism, energy conservation, women's liberation, and "use" versus ownership of products.

3. *New economic realities*—Forecasters predict a slower rate of growth in GNP as well as continued inflation, which is especially harmful to retailers since they tend to be labor intensive.

4. *Continued competition*—Increasing intra- and intertype competition and innovations in retailing situations, e.g., catalog showrooms, nonstore retailing, superstores, and so on (Bogard 1973; Bates 1976; Doyle and Sharma 1977; Berry and Wilson 1977).

In order to move with these changes and still achieve basic objectives, retailers may find it necessary to utilize the positioning strategy. The key to effective retail positioning is selecting a segment of the market that is not particularly well served in terms of its specific requirements and then designing a total offering to fulfill these requirements. Berry and Wilson also note that more and more

Exhibit 8.3
How Different Retail Strategists Compete Over Time

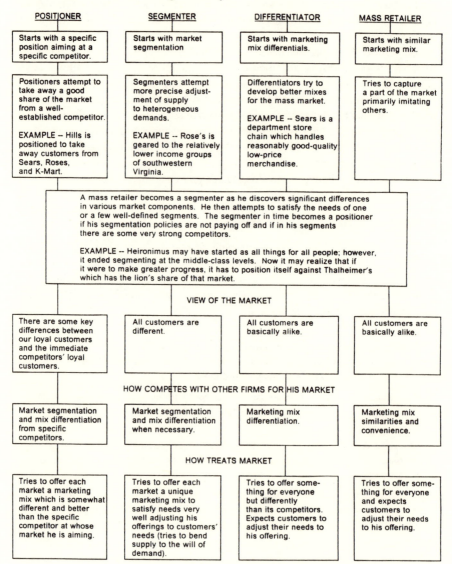

	POSITIONER	SEGMENTER	DIFFERENTIATOR	MASS RETAILER
	Starts with a specific position aiming at a specific competitor.	Starts with market segmentation	Starts with marketing mix differentials.	Starts with similar marketing mix.
	Positioners attempt to take away a good share of the market from a well-established competitor. EXAMPLE -- Hills is positioned to take away customers from Sears, Roses, and K-Mart.	Segmenters attempt more precise adjustment of supply to heterogeneous demands. EXAMPLE -- Rose's is geared to the relatively lower income groups of southwestern Virginia.	Differentiators try to develop better mixes for the mass market. EXAMPLE -- Sears is a department store chain which handles reasonably good-quality low-price merchandise.	Tries to capture a part of the market primarily imitating others.

A mass retailer becomes a segmenter as he discovers significant differences in various market components. He then attempts to satisfy the needs of one or a few well-defined segments. The segmenter in time becomes a positioner if his segmentation policies are not paying off and if in his segments there are some very strong competitors.

EXAMPLE -- Heironimus may have started as all things for all people; however, it ended segmenting at the middle-class levels. Now it may realize that if it were to make greater progress, it has to position itself against Thalheimer's which has the lion's share of that market.

VIEW OF THE MARKET

There are some key differences between our loyal customers and the immediate competitors' loyal customers.	All customers are different.	All customers are basically alike.	All customers are basically alike.

HOW COMPETES WITH OTHER FIRMS FOR HIS MARKET

Market segmentation and mix differentiation from specific competitors.	Market segmentation and mix differentiation when necessary.	Marketing mix differentiation.	Marketing mix similarities and convenience.

HOW TREATS MARKET

Tries to offer each market a marketing mix which is somewhat different and better than the specific competitor at whose market he is aiming.	Tries to offer each market a unique marketing mix to satisfy needs very well adjusting his offerings to customers' needs (tries to bend supply to the will of demand).	Tries to offer something for everyone but differently than its competitors. Expects customers to adjust their needs to his offering.	Tries to offer something for everyone and expects customers to adjust their needs to his offering.

retailers will turn to the positioning strategy as competitive pressures mount (Berry and Wilson 1977).

As with manufacturers, retail positioning may be most appropriate for those retailers located in the maturity stage of the retail life cycle (Davidson, Bates, and Bass 1976). One retail institution that is believed to occupy this stage is the department store. Today's department stores face new forms of competition and must reassess their market position. Positioning may be pivotal to the department store's profitability because it can be considered to be the main determinant of both the shopper's choice of store (the revenue function) and the way management allocates resources (the cost function). Shoppers choose among competing stores on the basis of how those stores are perceived to perform along dimensions that the shoppers deem important (Doyle and Fenwick 1975–1976). An effective positioning strategy employs a marketing approach that profitably distinguishes the department store from its competitors along these dimensions (Doyle and Sharma 1977). It has been said that the W. T. Grant department store chain failed because of improper positioning (Mason and Mayer 1987). W. T. Grant Company maintained its activities and its practices as they were for years. In the meantime, society kept on changing, and the retail competition continued quite different and more rigorous than before. Thus, changes in the retailing environment necessitate consideration of the strategy which manufacturers are currently popularizing.

Although the retail positioning strategy is theoretically attractive, effective retail positioning appears to be possible only if certain required conditions exist. The retailer who does not meet these requirements is likely to fail in the positioning attempt.

Necessary Conditions for Effective Retail Positioning

Five conditions are necessary for effective retail positioning. First, positioning is considered an attractive strategy for the nondominant firm. For the nondominant retailer, just as for the nondominant manufacturer, it is best as a viable alternative to the leader. The leading retailer in a given market has little to gain from positioning against the second or third place entrants and at the same time may have a great deal to lose. On the other hand, a second or third place retailer has much to gain and little to lose relative to the number one retailer (Brown and Sims 1977).

Second, the positioning firm must be aware of market opportunities. The retailer should audit its current position and ask itself how favorably consumers view that position and whether that position is likely to be effective in the future. Understanding market opportunities requires the forecasting of shopping and competitive trends in market segments relative to the store's present position and future objectives. Because of this condition, positioning cannot be effectively performed without some form of marketing research.

Third, the positioning retailer must be able to assess his or her position relative to that of the competition. The retailer's primary concern is how its own products and services are viewed vis-à-vis those of its competitors. Perhaps the most accurate assessment of the retailer's position comes from identifying what image consumers have of that store and competing stores. Retailers should not have difficulty in meeting this condition since considerable literature has been developed concerning the retail store image.

The fourth necessary condition states that the positioning retailer must have the resources needed to perform the strategy. These resources might include personnel, dollars, store location, and quality and assortment of merchandise. The retailer can only make claims that are within the ''comparison boundaries'' possessed by the consumer. For example, some years ago, the Ford Motor Company was partially successful in upgrading the image of the Granada automobile by making comparisons with the Mercedes-Benz automobile. However, it seems unreasonable for K-Mart to attempt the same type of positioning strategy by comparing its stores to Neiman-Marcus. A retailer cannot position itself as being something it is not.

The last necessary condition for effective positioning requires that retailers be able to effectively communicate with their markets. Retailers' positioning strategy will be ineffective unless they plan and execute a promotional campaign that accurately conveys the desired position. The promotional effort must clearly show the consumer what the retailer has to offer relative to the competition. The advertising program, therefore, is crucial as it actually establishes the retailer's position in the consumer's mind.

COMPARATIVE ADVERTISING AND RETAIL POSITIONING

At this point, it has been maintained that (1) retailers lag behind manufacturers in the knowledge and application of the positioning strategy, (2) retailers need to apply the positioning strategy in order to adjust to significant environmental changes, (3) advertising plays a critical role in determining the effectiveness of the positioning strategy, and (4) manufacturers use comparative advertising in executing their positioning strategies.

It is now contended that retailers can also perform effective positioning strategies if they use comparative advertising to promote their ''position'' relative to that of their competitors. Comparative advertising could be used for retail repositioning. For example, W. T. Grant might have improved its position by informing consumers how they compared to Sears, Roebuck and Company. However, one must still remember that the positioning firm must meet a total of five necessary conditions (e.g., W. T. Grant would not advertise higher quality products than Sears if it did not possess this attribute). A retailer just entering the market might also employ comparative advertising as potentially useful to existing retailers. However, this retailer might also employ comparative advertising to let the consumer know how that product "fits in" with those retailers already in the market.

Clearly then, comparative advertising presents great promise for many retailers. It is through this form of communication that a retailer can tell consumers exactly how it differs from or is similar to the competition.

Although the evolution of strategies is one way of looking at retail strategy options, the retail life cycle is also an important dimension. In fact, it may be difficult to establish one of the evolutionary options unless we understand the stage of the retail establishment in its life cycle.

RETAIL MARKETING STRATEGY IN DIFFERENT STAGES OF THE RETAIL LIFE CYCLE

Just as the product has a life cycle, retail establishments are also considered to have a life cycle (Davidson et al. 1976; Alderson 1965). Davidson et al. have considered four distinct stages: innovation, accelerated development, maturity, and decline. A clear-cut marketing strategy is appropriate for the retail establishment in each of the four stages.

Innovation

It is in this stage that the retail establishment makes its first appearance. The establishment may not have too many competitors. Although its growth rate may be very rapid, its productivity is likely to be low to moderate. The stage may last anywhere between three and five years. Since the risks are rather high, investments are minimized; central management is likely to search and experiment; only a minimal amount of management control techniques is used; the management style is entrepreneurial; rather extensive use of informative advertising is made; many of the prices are low and introductory; and both product depth and breadth are low owing (1) to efforts to limit already too high risks and (2) to rather limited resources at the beginning of the venture.

Accelerated Development

This second stage is characterized by increasing competition. Sales grow at a rapid rate, and the profit level progresses from low to high. Innovative retailers expand their geographic basis of operation, and companies that were not innovators enter the new field. For instance, after discount department stores became an undeniable power in retailing, mature companies such as Federated, Kresge, and Woolworth's made major commitments to their own discount operations.

During the early part of this stage, increasing sales volume results in high levels of economies of scale, which in turn cause higher levels of profit. However, toward the end of the period these favorable factors tend to be affected by cost pressures that arise from the need for larger staff, a more complex inventory system, and more extensive controls. Near the end of the period, both market share and profits approach their maximum level.

Emphasis on advertising continues during this period. Prices are likely to be somewhat higher since the establishment is now established. Product strategy at this stage revolves around breadth. Even though there may not be enough depth, a wider variety of products will be offered at this point.

Maturity

The third and most significant stage of development leads to a slippage in the retailer's market share. A number of factors come together to create the adverse conditions.

First, entrepreneurial managers begin to face difficulties in controlling their large and complex organizations. Although they were very proficient in maintaining the vitality and excitement of their organizations in the first two stages, they often lack the management skills necessary to direct organizations in stable markets. Thus, the overall quality of operations begins to decline.

Second, too much capacity becomes a problem. Retailers expand beyond the levels justified by the size of the total market, and in doing so they increase the level of total square footage to unprofitable levels.

Third, management finds itself facing direct competition from new forms of retail distribution. The challengers manage to capture some of the sales volume and hence create profit reductions for the established retail institutions.

Thus, this stage is characterized by strong competition and by moderate to slow growth. The retail management needs to employ extensive management control techniques so that numerous operational problems can be dealt with successfully. In this stage specially trained professional management is not a luxury but a necessity.

Since the store is rather well known, at this stage advertising efforts are likely to be eased off. Prices are likely to be high, so that the adverse impact of excess capacity and declining profits can be offset. (Note: this is not recommended; rather, this is how it is practiced.) Finally, high depth and high breadth in the product mix may simultaneously be considered an advantage and a weakness. It is an advantage because the broader the offering, the greater the drawing power of the retail establishment—at least up to a certain point. At the same time, broad offering implies increased costs of maintaining excessive amounts of inventories.

Decline

The final stage in the life cycle process is decline. It is often avoided, or at least temporarily postponed, by repositioning. By modifying its marketing strategy, management attempts to prolong maturity and avoid decline. However, it is not always possible to succeed in this demanding and risky undertaking. Hence, many retail establishments fail.

When decline takes place, major losses of market share occur, profits are marginal, and a fatal inability to compete in the marketplace becomes obvious to investors and competitors. For example, A & P has been in the decline stage for more than a decade. Saddled with old and poorly located stores, inefficient distribution, and often stodgy management, it has been struggling for years to stem mounting losses and to fight its way back to health. It has shut down a number of stores during the past few years. Under a new chief executive, the company tried to halt the closings, but with no indication that the situation will be reversed, more stores are now being closed. Many marketing specialists are beginning to doubt that A & P will make it in the increasingly competitive grocery business (A & P, 1982).

Thus, in the decline stage, the rate of sales growth is slow or negative, and profitability is again very low or negative. Retail establishments refrain from reinvesting capital in the venture. Central management is involved in "run-out" strategies. Control techniques are no longer used extensively, primarily because of administrative layoffs. The management style can be described as caretaking, which implies just trying to continue what the company already has. Advertising is used only moderately. Some prices are likely to be reduced, but all in all they are still high. High depth and high breadth in merchandising continue as in the previous stage. These stages are shown in detail in Exhibit 8.4.

Marketing strategies therefore, vary on the basis of the stage in the retail life cycle. The strategies discussed are not construed to be ideal—in fact, far from it. The retail establishment, after the peak point in the development stage, is likely to emphasize the wrong aspects of overall strategy, for example, cutting down expenses or employing totally wrong marketing strategies. The fact remains, however, that unfortunately, many retailers behave this way. Correct or incorrect behavior notwithstanding, all retail establishments go through a life cycle, and at each stage of this cycle retail marketing strategy components must be evaluated and changed so that the general strategy will facilitate coping with the changing external and internal conditions.

RETAIL MARKETING STRATEGY BASED ON PRODUCT AND STORE CLASSIFICATIONS

Consumer products are generally classified into three categories: convenience goods, shopping goods, and specialty goods (Kotler 1980). Similarly, authors in retailing have attempted to classify retail establishments and have come up with convenience stores, shopping stores, and specialty stores (Bucklin 1973). Since these classifications are basic, no attempt is made here to describe or define them. The reader can refer to any basic marketing and retailing book for these definitions; see, for example, McCarthy and Perreault 1987, and Berman and Evans 1986.

Exhibit 8.4
Activities in the Life Cycle

	Area of Subject of concern	Stage of Life Cycle Development			
		1. Innovation	2. Accelerated Development	3. Maturity	4. Decline
Market Characteristics	Number of competitors	Very few	Moderate	Many direct competitors. Moderate indirect competition	Moderate direct competition. Many indirect competitors
	Rate of sales growth	Very Rapid	Rapid	Moderate to slow	Slow or negative
	Level of Profits	Low to moderate	High	Moderate	Very low
	Duration of new innovations	3 to 5 years	5 to 6 years	Indefinite	Indefinite
Appropriate Retailer Actions	Investment/risk decisions	Investment minimization – high risks accepted	High levels of investment to sustain growth. Second use space.	Tightly controlled growth in untapped mkts. Secondary mkts. Institutional markets. Growth in services and service retailing. Acquisitions	Minimal capital expenditures and only when essential.
	Central Management Concerns	Concept refinement through adjustment and experimentation	Establishing a preemptive mkt. position.	Prolonging maturity and revising the retail concept. Attract new customers. Emphasize research. Life-style retailing	Harvesting

Exhibit 8.4 (Continued)

Area of Subject of concern		Stage of Life Cycle Development			
		1. Innovation	2. Accelerated Development	3. Maturity	4. Decline
	Use of management control techniques	Minimal	Moderate	Extensive	Moderate
	Most successful management style	Entrepreneurial	Centralized	Professional	Caretaker
Analytical Competitive Dimensions	Product Position	Innovative	New features added to the product.	Look for new market segments for the product. Stimulate increased usage. Reposition the product. Narrow product lines with depth	Withdraw product.
	Pricing Strategy	Low	High	High to Competitive	Low
	Promotion Techniques	High Promotion Product awareness	Shift promotion to acceptance and purchase	Increase promotional budget	Reduce Budget
	Place	New Area Underveloped	Maintain Place	Look for secondary use space	Bargain Barn, etc.

169

Since there are three types of stores and three product categories, there are nine distinct strategies (See Exhibit 8.5). It is difficult to decide which of the nine strategies or which combination of strategies must be preferred by the retail establishment. Obviously, Tiffany's is a combination of specialty store and specialty product, whereas typically the corner drug store is a combination of convenience goods and convenience store. All the rest lie somewhere between these two extremes.

Although there are no clear-cut rules or quick formulas as to which combination is the best for a given store, there are a few dos and don'ts as to which of these strategies should be adopted.

1. Two degrees removed combinations may be rather ineffective.
2. If the firm is going to adopt more than one of the nine strategies, two strategies that are adjacent are better than others.
3. The choice of strategy is likely to be related to the general positioning of the store.

Two degrees removed combinations imply a convenience store with primarily specialty goods or a specialty store emphasizing primarily convenience goods. Although some combinations are likely to be acceptable, for Tiffany's to sell cheap custom jewelry (convenience good) would hardly be an effective retail strategy. Similarly, buyers do not go to the corner drug store to buy an expensive Omega watch.

In adopting combination strategies, a store cannot be expected to be both a convenience and a specialty store. Thus, if a specialty store is likely to carry more than just a specialty good, it may expand partially into shopping goods (adjacent strategy). Similarly, a convenience store, for example, the corner hobby shop, cannot possibly act like a specialty store and carry expensive diamonds.

Finally, in choosing the strategy as well as a combination strategy, positioning of the store must be determined. If, for instance, there is an expensive specialty apparel shop in the area which carries primarily exclusive and expensive lines, another store in the area may position itself as a specialty store carrying specialty as well as shopping goods and hence may emphasize price competition. Such a store is likely to position itself below the already existing expensive store.

Thus, retailers could develop a marketing strategy on the basis of store and product combination. Since three different groups of retail marketing strategies have been discussed in this chapter, a basic point must be emphasized. Although any one of the strategies in any one of the three groups could be and most often is used, it does not necessarily imply that these strategies are mutually exclusive. It was already implied in the first section that the retail firm could have moved from being a general merchandiser to a positioner in time. In the meantime, this establishment is likely to adjust its marketing strategy further as it moves from one to another stage of its life cycle. Furthermore, using the store–product match-up strategy may further sharpen the overall strategy. It is therefore maintained

Exhibit 8.5
Product Store Combinations as Strategic Alternatives

PATRONAGE	CONVENIENCE GOODS	SHOPPING GOODS	SPECIALTY GOODS
Convenience Store	Consumers prefer to buy the most readily available brands at the most accessible stores. No brand or store loyalty	Consumers choose to purchase from among assortment carried by the most accessible store. No brand loyalty	Consumers purchase favorite brand from the most accessible store which carries the product. Brand loyalty
Shopping Store	Consumers are indifferent to the brand or product. They shop at different stores in order to get the best service or lowest price. No brand or store loyalty	Consumers make comparisons among both stores as well as products, trying to purchase the best price and service from the best store possible. No brand or store loyalty	Consumers have strong product-brand preferences. They shop in a number of stores in order to receive the best service along with the preferred product. No store loyalty, only brand loyalty
Specialty Store	Consumers prefer to shop at a specific store. They are indifferent to the product and/or the brand. Store loyalty	Consumers prefer to shop at a certain store. They are uncertain as to which product to buy. They examine products for best purchase. Store loyalty	Consumers prefer to buy a particular product or a particular store. Both brand and store loyalty

Source: Adapted and revised from Bucklin 1973: 53–54.

that these groups of strategies could very well be complementary and be used simultaneously.

The point must be emphasized here that the individual retail store *must* monitor its efforts to develop and implement its marketing strategy. After all, it is the planning and implementation of this strategy that will achieve differential congruence. Thus, individual retail establishments must undertake periodic research efforts in order to determine the effectiveness of their strategic marketing efforts. (For discussions of such a feedback function, see Chapters 1 and 16.)

Summary

This chapter explores the development of retail marketing strategy along three separate dimensions: evolution, life cycle, and product–store mix. Through the evolutionary process, retailing has moved from being any one of general merchandiser or differentiator to a segmenter or a positioner. The retail life cycle, just as its product counterpart, has various stages. The retail marketing strategy changes noticeably as the establishment moves from one stage to the next in its life cycle.

Finally, product–store combinations provide a specific base for retail marketing strategy development. It is quite conceivable for the three groups of retail strategies to coexist and be complementary. The retail establishment must have a feedback mechanism to determine how successful it has been in developing and implementing its marketing strategy.

REFERENCES

"A&P Looks Like Tenglemann's Vietnam." *Business Week*. No. 2724, February 1, 1982.

Advertising Age. August 28, 1978.

Alderson, Wroe. *Dynamic Marketing Behavior*. Homewood, Ill.: Richard D. Irwin, 1965.

Bates, Albert D. "The Troubled Future of Retailing." *Business Horizons* (August 1976): 22–28.

Berkowitz, Eric N., Roger A Kerin, and William Rudelius. *Marketing*. St. Louis: Times/Mirror Mosby, 1986.

Berry, Leonard C. and Ian H. Wilson. "Retailing: The Next Ten Years." *Journal of Retailing* (Fall 1977): 5–28.

Bogard, Leo. "The Future of Retailing." *Harvard Business Review* (November-December 1973): 16–18.

Brown, Herbert E., and J. Taylor Sims. "Market Segmentation, Product Differentiation and Market Positioning As Alternative Marketing Strategies." Proceedings, American Marketing Association Educators' Conference, 1977, pp. 483–487.

Bucklin, Louis P. "Retail Strategy and Classification of Consumer Goods." *Journal of Marketing* (January 1973): 45–54.

Davidson, William R., Albert D. Bates, and Stephen J. Bass. "The Retail Life Cycle." *Harvard Business Review* (November-December 1976): 89–96.

Doyle, Peter, and Ian Fenwick. "Shopping Habits in Grocery Chains." *Journal of Retailing* (Winter 1975–1976): 39–52.

———, and Alok Sharma. "A Model for Strategic Positioning in Retailing." Proceedings, American Marketing Association Educators' Conference, 1977, pp. 10–14.

Kotler, Philip. *Marketing Management*, 5th ed. Englewood Cliffs, N.J.: Prentice-Hall, 1984.

Lincoln, Douglas, and A. Coskun Samli. "Evolution in Retail Marketing Strategy." Academy of Marketing Science, Conference Proceedings, 1981.

Mason, Joseph Barry, and Morris Lehman Mayer. *Modern Retailing: Theory and Practice*. Dallas: Business Publications, 1987.

McCarthy, E. Jerome and William Perreault. *Marketing Management*. Homewood, Ill.: Richard D. Irwin, 1987.

Nickels, Williams G. *Marketing Principles*. Englewood Cliffs, N.J.: Prentice-Hall, 1978.

Ohmae, Kenichi. *The Mind of the Strategist*. New York: Penguin Books, 1982.

Porter, Michael. *The Competitive Edge*. New York: Random House, 1985.

Roberts, Alan A. "Applying the Strategy of Market Segmentation." *Business Horizons* (Fall 1961): 65.

Samli, A. Coskun. "Segmentation and Carving a Niche in the Marketplace." *Journal of Retailing* (Summer 1968): 38–49.

———. "Use of Segmentation Index to Measure Store Loyalty." *Journal of Retailing* (Spring 1975): 51–60.

———. "Segmentation Index and Store Image in Retail and Service Establishments." Proceedings of ESOMAR Seminar XXIX on Research That Works for Today's Marketing Problems, 1976.

Sims, J. Taylor. "On Measuring the Long-Run Effects of Product Line Extension." Ph.D. diss., Graduate School of Business, University of Illinois at Urbana, 1970.

Smith, Wendell R. "Product Differentiation and Market Segmentation as Alternative Marketing Strategies." *Journal of Marketing*, (July 1956): 3–8.

Stanton, William J. *Fundamentals of Marketing*. New York: McGraw-Hill, 1982.

Statistical Abstract of the United States, U.S. Census Bureau, Department of Commerce, 1986.

Sweeney, Daniel J., and Richard C. Reizenstein. "Developing a Retail Market Segmentation Strategy for a Women's Specialty Store, Using Multiple Discriminate Analysis." Combined Proceedings, American Marketing Association, 1972.

Trout, Jack, and Al Ries. "Positioning Cuts Through Chaos in Marketplace." *Advertising Age*, May 1, 1972, pp. 51–53.

———. "The Positioning Era Cometh." Reprint of a three-part series in *Advertising Age*. Chicago: Craig Publications, April-May 1972.

Wilkie, William, and Paul Farris. "Comparison Advertising: Problems and Potential." *Journal of Marketing* (October 1975): 7–14.

9 Store Image Definition, Dimensions, Measurement, and Management

A regular customer of Saks Fifth Avenue who visits a factory outlet store is not likely to be pleased with the atmosphere, merchandise, service, and other store features. That person is likely to feel uncomfortable. By the same token, a regular factory outlet store goer will also feel quite uncomfortable at Saks Fifth Avenue. In these cases, not only the store images are different but also the self-images of these store goers. The retailer must learn why the first person is comfortable and satisfied in Saks Fifth Avenue and not in a factory outlet store or vice-versa.

The synergistic characteristics of the retail store illustrate the importance of the store image. A retail store is a place not only where some goals and services are purchased but also where a combination of functional and emotional stimuli is present (Oxenfeldt 1974–1975). Thus, simply stated, there is more to a store than meets the eye. The store has many personal and impersonal aspects that distinguish it from other stores and from which many tangible and intangible stimuli emanate. Thus, the synergistic characteristic of the retail store becomes obvious. The total synergism is depicted by the store image, which is the sum total of the functional qualities and psychological attributes (Martineau 1958) of a store. The image not only distinguishes the store from all other stores, but also provides the basis for competitive advantage (Alderson 1957). Since the image is very important to the well-being of the store, its management becomes a focal point in total retail management. This chapter deals with the definition, dimensions, measurement, and management of the store image.

STORE IMAGE CONCEPTS AND DEFINITIONS

Pierre Martineau made one of the earliest attempts to analyze the concept of image and to measure it. He described image as ''the way in which the store is defined in the shopper's mind,'' and in analyzing the components of image, he proposed two components: functional qualities of a store and its psychological attributes. By ''functional quality'' Martineau meant such store elements as assortment of product offerings, store layout, store location, price-value relationships, and other such qualities that the consumer can somewhat objectively compare to competitors. The second component, ''psychological attributes,'' refers to the consumer's perception of the store attributes, such as friendliness and helpfulness of store personnel, or attractiveness of decor. Both of Martineau's phrases imply the existence of multiple descriptors to which a goodness–badness rating can be attached. Although he did not discuss the interaction between the two or even a possible casual relationship, Martineau set the stage for a number of subsequent definitions of store image and numerous research attempts to measure the concept.

A study measuring the effects of television advertising on store image defined store image as ''a complex of meanings and relationships serving to characterize the store for people'' (Arons 1961, p.1). This definition implies that consumers take a complex of factors and reduce them to manageable proportions. The phrase ''meanings'' also implies dimensions and would therefore parallel Martineau's definition.

The customer's store image may depend on how well the store has met the customer's aspiration level with regard to price, quality, and service. Thus, store image is determined by comparing the perceived and desired level of store performance across these dimensions.

Alfred R. Oxenfeldt, following the functional qualities and psychological attributes dichotomy of Martineau, discussed ''a combination of factual and emotional material which constitute the image'' (p.9). This viewpoint stresses that many customers will hold factually based opinions about a store and feel certain ways toward it. Leonard Berry (1969) undertook a more systematic attempt to analyze store image. He emphasized the discriminative capability of the retail image and how this discrimination must be reinforced so that a comparative advantage can be achieved. In his words the store image is ''the discriminative stimuli for expected reinforcement, i.e. image is the total conceptualized or expected reinforcement that a person associates with a given store'' (p. 2). This reinforcement aspect provides manageability to retail management, which may mean success or failure of the retail store. Berry's position purports that store image is developed through experience. Retailers, therefore, could reinforce certain favorable image dimensions in order to create or maintain this experience on the part of the consumers.

According to Wyckham (1967, p. 333), ''store image is the summation of all the attributes of a store as perceived by the consumers through their experience with that store.'' This point was repeated by Blackwell et al. (1983), which is the perception of consumers. However, they indicated that the objective characteristics also contribute to the image.

Cox's (1974) definition of image was similar to those presented earlier. He maintained that image is "the combination of stimuli, both tangible and intangible, emanating from a variety of personal and impersonal communication sources which a person associates with a particular store." His contribution was the personal and impersonal dichotomy.

Thus, the store image is the store's personality as perceived by different publics. This personality is made up of physical attributes, character, and skill qualities. When customers enter a store they want the store's displays and departments to tell them what the store is like. The image that the store is attempting to project must be realistic enough that it will be immediately obvious. The store must therefore deliberately project an image through personal and impersonal communicators, in the form of a combination of tangible and intangible. In the simplest sense, the store image is the way that store says "this is what I am." The greater the discrepancy between the store's claims regarding its image and the consumers' perception of it, the less effective the image management activity of that store. It is also important to discuss what is meant by "different publics." All retail stores deal with different publics, including loyal customers, irregular customers, loyal customers of competitors, the rest of the community store management itself, and competing managers. Obviously, the image perceived by loyal customers is quite different from the image of those who dislike that store. The retailer must be able to project a certain image and in time to manipulate it to make the store more appealing to the intended customers or to target market segments. Thus, a very important aspect of strategic retailing is image management.

DIMENSIONS OF IMAGE

If retailers are to manipulate the store image to gain competitive advantage, they must first determine its dimensions. In managing the overall image, it will be necessary to deal with these dimensions individually. Once again, all the dimensions put together provide an overall store image that is synergistic and means more than all of the individual components put together. Roger D. Blackwell et al. (1983) acknowledge that store image definitions differ somewhat, but an essential point is that the store exists in the perception of consumers as well as in objective characteristics. Thus, store image researchers must be able to identify the chief dimensions of a store. These, when put together, compose and project the store image.

Martineau (1958) described the store image in terms of four dimensions: symbols and color, layout and architecture, advertising, and sales personnel. This was a rather limited orientation, and subsequently, many authors identified more than four dimensions.

John H. Kunkel and Leonard L. Berry (1968) compiled an image dimension list. By answering three open-ended questions, their respondents provided 3,737 statements describing their perceptions of Phoenix, Arizona, department stores; statements of dimensions they liked and disliked; and statements of why they

Exhibit 9.1
Key Store Image Dimensions

Merchandise -- The five dimensions considered here are quality, selection or assortment, styling or fashion, guarantees, and pricing. Merchandise itself is taken to mean the goods and services offered by a retail outlet.

Service -- The dimension areas are service-general, sales clerk service, presence of self-service, ease of merchandise return, delivery service and credit policies of the store.

Clientele -- Social class appeal, self-image congruency, and store personnel are included as dimensions of this factor.

Physical Facilities -- This dimension category covers the facilities available in a store to include such things as elevators, lighting, air conditioning, and washrooms. It may also be used by a customer to include store layout, aisle placement and width, carpeting, and architecture.

Convenience -- Three dimensions have been identified that fit into this classification; namely, convenience-general, locational convenience, and parking.

Promotion -- Within this summary grouping one finds sales promotions, advertising, displays, trading stamps, and symbols and colors.

Store Atmosphere -- This dimension category consists of what the author would dub atmosphere -- congeniality. This refers to customer's feeling of warmth, acceptance, or ease.

Institutional Factors -- Within this grouping is the conservative-modern projection of the store, and also the dimensions of reputation and reliability enter the picture.

Post-Transaction Satisfaction -- This classification of dimensions would include such areas as merchandise in use, returns, and adjustments. In essence, was the consumer satisfied with his purchase and with the store?

Source: Lindquist 1974–1975, pp. 31–32.

thought other people shopped in those stores. From these statements, the authors identified 12 categories derived from a total of 43 individual dimensions.

Jay D. Lindquist (1974–1975), after having reviewed and published the results of 19 studies, synthesized the store image frameworks into nine image/attribute dimension categories: merchandising, service, clientele, physical facilities, convenience, promotion, store atmosphere, institutional factors, and past transaction satisfaction. For a description of these categories, see Exhibit 9.1.

Using a ''Percent of Scholar Mentions,'' Lindquist identified what the literature considers important image dimensions. The results of these popularity measures are provided in Exhibit 9.2. Lindquist (1974, p. 30) cautions the retailer's use of his findings for the following reason:

Exhibit 9.2
Percentage of Scholar Mentions for Store Image Dimensions[a]

Category-Attribute[b]	Scholar Mentions
Merchandise-Selection or Assortment	42%
Merchandise-Quality	38%
Merchandise-Pricing	38%
Convenience-Locational	35%
Merchandise-Styling, Fashion	27%
Service-General	27%
Service-Sales Clerk	27%

[a]Percentage of Scholar Mentions was calculated by dividing the total number of times the issue was mentioned by the number of scholarly studies reviewed.

[b]Attribute is synonymous with dimension.

Note: The above seven items are combinations of Lindquist's categorical titles (nine) and specific attributes within those categories. These seven were most popular with the work of the 26 auditors recognized by Lindquist.

Source: Adapted from Lindquist 1974–1975: 29–38.

respect to consumer retail store image formulation based upon relative frequency of mention by the investigators cited is not encouraged. However, one may assert that such relative frequency of mention is a valuable indicator of potentially key attributes.

Rachman (1975) offers an even more detailed list than Lindquist. Rachman, expanding on Fisk's (1961–1962) basic dimensions, presented six basic dimensions: (1) location convenience, (2) merchandise suitability, (3) value for price, (4) sales effort and store service, (5) congeniality of store, and (6) post-transaction satisfaction. Ronald P. Stephenson offered another alternative composed of eight basic dimensions, whereas Berry proposed a 12-dimensional store image. Of all the researchers, Robert A. Hansen and Terry Deutscher (1977) presented the most detailed list with 41 elements (Exhibit 9.3). Thus, it appears that there is no universal agreement on the dimensions of store image. The only point all authors agree on is the multidimensionality of the concept.

One study attempted to identify the determinants of image factors significant in actual store choice (Schiffman et al. 1977) and found that the store image characteristics that appeared to be important in the specialty store selection were quite different from those that influenced the selection of department stores. As Roger L. Jenkins and Sandra M. Forsythe (1979) indicate, "these results suggest that consumers who purchase similar merchandise from different types of retail

Exhibit 9.3
Consumer-Based Store Image Dimensions

Number		Description
1.	Dependable Products	21. Many Friends Shop There
2.	High Quality	22. Store Is Clean
3.	High Value for Money	23. Easy to Move Through Store
4.	Wide Selection	24. Easy to Find Items You Want
5	Fully Stocked	25. Fast Checkout
6.	Numerous Brands	26. Attractive Decor
7.	Well-Known Brands	27. Company Operates Many Stores
8.	High-Fashion Items	28. Store Is Nearby
9.	Low Prices Versus Competition	29. Short Time to Reach Stores
10.	Many Specially Priced Items	30. Easy Drive to Store
11.	Layaway Available	31. Convenient to Other Stores Shopped
12.	Courteous Sales Personnel	32. Easy to Park
13.	Helpful Sales Personnel	33. Advertising Is Informative
14.	Adequate Number of Sales Personnel	34. Advertising Helps Planning
15.	Easy to Return Purchases	35. Advertising Is Appealing
16.	Easy to Get Credit	36. Advertising Is Believable
17.	Easy to Get Home Delivery	37. Friendly Store Personnel
18.	Store Is Known by Friends	38. Company Is Well Known
19.	Store Is Liked by Friends	39. Been in Community a Long Time
20.	Store Is Recommended by Friends	40. Easy to Exchange Purchases
		41. Fair on Adjustments

Source: Adapted from Hansen and Deutscher, 1977–1978: 58–72.

establishments might constitute unique image or benefit segments which should be catered to differently by each type of retailer.'' Consequently, they maintain that different stores may emphasize different image attributes as a part of their merchandising and promotional strategies.

In studying the determinant patronage store attributes, William O. Bearden (1977) pointed out the importance of seven store characteristics, four of which were significantly different for patrons of downtown versus shopping center customers. This study suggests that different marketing strategies should be directed toward various market segments.

In an investigation of the intermarket reliability of the components of store image, Elizabeth C. Hirschman et al. (1978) found that the major dimensions underlying store image varied from market to market. The retailer, therefore, has to determine the major image dimensions within each market in order to assure the positioning of the store within a given market.

Thus, it appears that images vary by store types, from one segment to another as well as from one market to another. The retailer must be able to account for these variables as well as for straight image components that must be carefully manipulated.

STORE IMAGE MEASUREMENT

Unless the store image can be measured, it cannot be subjected to effective deliberate action. If, for instance, an attempt is made to change the image, unless the old and the new images can be measured and compared, no progress can be made in this area. The new image cannot be compared with the old image unless we have successfully measured both.

Approaches to the measurement of store image are a function of the researcher's definition of store image and conception of what specific store dimensions make up the store image. Nonetheless, all store image measurement approaches can be classified as either structured or unstructured.

Unstructured approaches include word association tests, nondirective questioning, and other projective techniques. An unstructured psycholinguistic technique was used where individual consumers provide names of stores (nouns) and bases of similarity and dissimilarity (adjectives) among stores (Cardozo 1974–1975). In a more recent study, the same technique was used to measure images of men's retail clothing stores (Muse 1974–1975). In an attempt to explain why consumers left a store without making a purchase (''walkouts''), Robert Myers employed an unstructured store image measurement approach. ''Walkouts'' were asked what thoughts or concepts came to mind when they thought of the particular store they had just left (Myers 1960).

A variety of projective techniques, including cartoon tests, were employed to investigate image variation among sister units of major retail institutions in Los Angeles (Marcus 1972). G. H. G. McDougall and J. N. Fry (1974–1975) have suggested using open-ended questions as a superior alternative to other store

Exhibit 9.4
Sto ⁀ Image Measurement Techniques

<u>**Unstructured Methods**</u>

Method   Example

1. Word Association   Cardozo and Muse

2. Nondirective Questioning   Myers

3. Cartoon Tests   Marcus

4. Open-Ended Questions   McDougall & Fry

<u>**Structured Methods**</u>

Method   Example

1. Semantic Differential   Kelley and Stephenson

2. Multidimensional Scaling   Blackwell. Engel, Kollat

3. Multiattribute Models   Fishbein

4. Multivariate Techniques   Marks

image measurement techniques. However, the open-ended technique requires strong verbal skills on the part of the respondents and great interpretative skills on the part of the researcher. Most important, this technique yields little information from nonpurchasers. Exhibit 9.4 illustrates different research techniques used in measuring store image. They are classified in two main categories, unstructured and structured.

As Kunkel and Berry suggest (1968), unstructured techniques allow critical image dimensions to be determined. Thus, unstructured techniques are not necessarily totally separated from structured techniques. They can be used to develop lists and concepts of image dimensions to be employed in structured techniques which, for the most part, have special applications and advantages in analysis.

Among the structured techniques used to solve a store image measurement problem are the semantic differential, multidimensional scaling, and multiattribute attitude modeling. The semantic differential is the most popular of these approaches (Mindak 1961).

Semantic Differential

Kelley and Stephenson (1967) proposed using the semantic differential to identify the factors underlying consumer patronage decisions. The same technique was used to measure department store image (May 1974–1975; Wycham, 1967); investigate possible differences in customers' versus retailers' department store image (Arons 1961; Pathak 1972); measure the effect of television advertising on department store image (Wycham 1967); and assess the semantic differential's weaknesses relative to an open-ended question technique (Blackwell, et al. 1983). [1]

Marketing scholars have traditionally used the semantic differential approach to solve the store image measurement problem. This technique is simple to administer and tabulate, allows the presentation of qualified data in a format that is easily understood, is easy to replicate, requires minimal verbal skills on the part of the respondent, and is relatively reliable (Arons 1961; Weale 1961; Wycham 1967). Two serious problems must be overcome in using the semantic differential: (1) the researcher must determine the adjectives to be included and be sure that adjectives/phrases are actually stated in a bipolar manner (Blackwell et al. 1983); and (2) the researcher has to select a large number of attributes to be scaled. The question that then arises is, how many of these attributes are viewed as interrelated in the mind of the consumer. Furthermore, the number of attributes important to the consumer in terms of his or her overall image of a store is sometimes not considered (Marks 1974; Wycham 1967). In addition, the relative importance of each of these attributes is not considered separately. The way the semantic differential technique is applied makes their relative importance all equal.

Multidimensional Scaling

Multidimensional scaling (MDS) is also used to measure store image. This technique has been used to measure the image of several South Carolina discount department stores (Doyle and Fenwick 1974–1975), measure differences in store images held by consumers with varying degrees of store loyalty, and measure grocery store images (Doyle and Fenwick 1974–1975).

The MDS technique makes the fewest assumptions about the ability of the respondent to be precise, and it gives the respondent a chance to make minimally structured judgments (Doyle and Fenwick 1974–1975). Thus, the respondent has a chance to be more objective in a subjective, attitudinal questioning situation. The technique allows the manager to evaluate the store's image in relation to the competitor's store image. On the negative side, it is difficult to administer MDS and to analyze its data (Blackwell et al. 1983). In the analysis of the data gathered through MDS, interpreting the axis or dimensions of the perceptional map is especially difficult, and it is not possible to assess statistical significance with this procedure (Marks 1974).

---

[1] The reader who is not familiar with these techniques should refer to any basic marketing research text.

Multiattribute Models

Multtattribute models came into being primarily because of the specific deficiencies of semantic differential discussed earlier. The marketers have been applying multiattribute models for the purpose of measuring store image (Fishbein 1967). V. P. Lessig (1973) adopted a Fishbein attitude model to examine the relationship between consumer images of grocery stores and consumer loyalty to those stores. In an image study of a men's clothing store, Don James et al. (1976) concluded that a multiattribute approach was a good prediction of store image. The multiattribute approach has been employed in corporate image measurement of a department and clothing specialty store (Marks 1974), as well as to isolate different market segments for a 20-store restaurant chain (Stephenson 1969).

The multiattribute approach to measuring store image makes up for several disadvantages of the semantic differential and MDS. The multiattribute approach focuses on the importance of store attributes and performance evaluations of the same attributes. Thus, through this approach both the salience and valence of the store attributes are detected. In essence, this means that the relative and absolute significance of the variables is determined, and, hence, their relative contribution to the store image as a whole is properly assessed.

The multiattribute approach can retain the advantages of the semantic differential and, at the same time, handle the problem of differing attribute importance. Such models should be used carefully, however, since several issues of concern are involved in their application, including (1) specification of the multiattribute model, (2) attribute generation and inclusion, (3) inclusion of the importance component, (4) measurement of the importance component, (5) measurement of the belief components, (6) scoring the importance of belief components, and (7) halo effects.

Multivariate Techniques

Ronald B. Marks (1974) used two specific multivariate techniques to illustrate the potential benefits of multivariate techniques in assessing store image: factor analysis and multiple regression. In an effort to measure the image of a women's specialty clothing store, he surveyed a random sample of 139 female undergraduates. Each respondent was asked to indicate an overall attitude toward the store on a bipolar seven-point scale. Following factor analysis, 30 variables utilized in the semantic differential scale were simplified into eight, which of course then simplified the whole problem. Subsequently, the multiple regression technique was used to determine that only four of the eight factors identified by factor analysis were important to consumers' overall image of the store. It was concluded that fashionability was the most important factor in forming the image of the specialty store in the study. The other three important factors were, in order, salesmanship, outside attractiveness, and advertising. Chen (1981) illustrated that, not only in absolute but also in relative terms, this combination of factor analysis and multiple regression techniques is powerful. She used the technique in order to compare the image factors of three men's apparel shops. Although multivariate techniques have helped alleviate the problem associated with the traditional semantic differential, they have not often been used by marketing researchers (Schiffman et al. 1977).

IMAGE MANAGEMENT

If properly conducted, store image studies increase the likelihood of retailing success. Theoretically, developing and maintaining favorable images within selected market segments can lead to increased sales and profitability.

Accordingly, a retailer's repeat business is considered to be a function of the image that consumers have of that store (Marks 1974). There is also evidence that store loyalty is closely related to store image (Lessig 1973). Douglas J. Dalrymple and Donald C. Thompson (1969) maintain that the image of the store is sometimes much more important to the consumer than the image of the merchandise bought. For example, one study found carpet samples from a high prestige store to have more favorable product images than the same samples from a low prestige store (Enis and Stafford 1969). Thus, the consumer's evaluation of products purchased is influenced by knowledge of where they were purchased. Ted Roselius (1975) also found store image ranking to be high with consumers as a method of reducing risk in the product purchase situation. The implication here is that store image may be used as a surrogate indicator of product quality. Samli (1968) found that the store's reputation (or image) is very important in attracting certain market segments to the store. The store image may also be used as a surrogate indicator of a store's success. Managing the store well is managing its image successfully.

We next present a store image management model that can be used by any small, medium, or large retail store, whether it is independent or part of a chain. The paradigm presented in Exhibit 9.5 consists of five steps.

Step 1. Examine Current Store Image

Store image management begins with understanding the present image. In order to gain this understanding, the present image needs to be defined. Its salient image dimensions and their valence must also be defined. Although it is shown as the third task in step 1, store image can be measured simultaneously with the first and second tasks. The important point here is that, unless the retailer is keenly aware of the present store image and its salient characteristics, it is impossible to manipulate it. The relative weights of these salient characteristics will indicate better directions and more viable alternatives as to how the present image should be modified. If, for instance, the retailer finds out that the store layout is one of the store's strengths as indicated by semantic differential scaling and this feature carries more weight than any other factors indicated by mul-

Exhibit 9.5
Store Image Management Paradigm

Step 1	EXAMINE CURRENT STORE IMAGE

	TASKS:	1. Defining Store Image
		2. Identifying Salient Image Dimensions and Their Valence
		3. Measuring of Store Image

↓

Step 2	EXAMINE COMPETING STORE IMAGES

	TASKS:	1. Identifying Key Competitors in the Peer Group
		2. Determining Salient Image Dimensions and Their Valence
		3. Measuring Store Images
		4. Comparing Competitor's versus Owner Image

↓

Step 3	DESIGN AND IMPLEMENT IMAGE CHANGE/ENHANCEMENT PROGRAM

	TASKS:	1. Identifying Store Strengths and Weaknesses
		2. Determining Importance of Image Dimensions, within Market Segments
		3. Designing Retail Mix (Goods/Services, Communications, and Physical Distribution) Changes

↓

Step 4	ASSESS THE CHANGE IN STORE IMAGE

	TASKS:	1. Examining the Changes in Image Since Step 1
		2. Assessing the Impact of New Image Improvement Attempts
		3. Determining the Direction and Intensity of the Change

↓

Step 5	DETERMINE THE IMPACT IN TERMS OF RETAIL SUCCESS

	TASKS:	1. Measuring the Change in Sales and Market Share
		2. Determining the Store Loyalty
		3. Assessing Customer Turnover/Degree of Increase or Decrease
		4. Examining Change in Profitability

tiattribute technique, then it is rather obvious where that retailer is likely to go regarding image manipulation and management. If the retailer wants to continue appealing to the same target segment, he or she will continue doing more of what has been done previously.

Step 2. Examine Competing Store Images

Store image salience and valence cannot be assessed without a comparison with other store images. If, for example, Kresge stores want to upgrade their image and position themselves against Sears, they must understand the strengths and weaknesses of Sears' image as opposed to those of Kresge stores. Then, it becomes possible to determine where the emphasis belongs so that Kresge stores can successfully position themselves against Sears. Research may indicate that Sears has an image of good quality at reasonable prices, attractive store layouts, and good locations, among other image features. If Kresge stores find out that their image indicates low price and low quality, relatively unattractive store layouts, and somewhat questionable locations, it becomes clear where the company must put its emphasis for improvement. It is important to find out what features of image are below par for Kresge stores, and it is at least equally important for them to know the relative importance of these factors within the total image valence.

Whether at this stage or in stage five or both, dynamic comparative retail image research is a must. Unlike static studies which analyze image character- istics at a given point in time, dynamic comparative retail image studies focus on a marketing strategy change. Management attempts to change store mix variables. When such marketing changes are implemented, consumers must perceive the image change efforts exactly the way management intended. How- ever, this perception cannot be measured in isolation. It must be assessed vis- à-vis other changes and developments in the retailing environment (Downs and Flood 1979). It also has been maintained that by comparing consumers' reactions to strategy change with management's intent, a timely direct evaluation strategy success can result. Although Downs and Flood (1979) did not expand their study to include a comparison between the store and its competitors' image changes before and after efforts, the implication here is that image is a dynamic concept. Its management must undertake a comparative analysis before and after the attempts have been made to manipulate the store image.

Step 3. Design and Implement Image Change/Enhancement Program

Once the store image is assessed, it is easy to identify the store's strengths and weaknesses. Radio Shack, for instance, may be known for its product variety, quality, and reliability, but it may not be admired for its location, atmosphere, or helpful salespeople.

Next, we must consider the importance of image dimensions within the particular market segments. If, again, Radio Shack is dealing primarily with upper- and lower-middle-class markets, and if these classes emphasize price and salespeople's expertise, then Radio Shack is likely to be in trouble. Obviously, it is not emphasizing the image components that are particularly important for its target markets.

The third activity in this major step toward managing the image is designing the retail mix so that it will project the image needed for the targeted market segment. Special effort has to be expended to make sure that the intended image and the perceived image are not too far apart. The closer these two are, the more efficient the image projection efforts.

Step 4. Assess the Change in Store Image

Once the new image becomes a reality, the changes between the previous and present images must be examined, and to do so image-related research data must be obtained for the before and after situation. The data must be comparable in both cases, that is, have acceptable validity and reliability. Once the previous and present images are compared, it becomes obvious whether the image improvements are paying off. If the difference between the present and previous images is in the direction that was agreed on before the new image was developed, then efforts have been successful.

Continuing with the earlier example of Radio Shack, after having found out that the company has been dealing primarily with the upper and lower middle class and that price and salespeople expertise are less than par, let us assume they have made a concerted effort to rectify the situation. The question, of course, is not only knowing whether or not the new efforts in changing the image have been successful, but also how successful they have been. The direction and intensity of the change from the earlier image measurement must therefore be identified.

Step 5. Determine the Impact in Terms of Retail Success

In the final analysis, the image is important because it indirectly indicates the degree of success. However, the real success is in the way the market performance of the retail store has changed. Market performance indicating retail success is measured in four different ways. First, changes in sales volume and market share are measured. Second, the change (if any) in the degree of store loyalty is determined. Third, the outreach of the retail establishment, through its attempts to change its image, is assessed by examining whether or not new customers are coming to the store and whether or not they develop a certain degree of commitment to the store. Finally, the profitability of the store is examined. If, as a result of the efforts to achieve a new image the profitability of the store improves, it can be inferred that the image management efforts have been successful.

SUMMARY

Four key areas of store image are explored in this chapter: definition, dimensions, measurement, and management. Most definitions imply the perception of a combination of, first, functional characteristics and, second, psychological attributes. Thus, image is first of all perceived and second synergistic. The complex combination of all the attributes creates a sum total that is different and greater than the individual components of the concept.

There is no universal agreement regarding the dimensions of store image. Various researchers point out the existence of numerous image dimensions. Not only do image dimensions appear to be differently perceived by various researchers, but also evidence is presented that images vary by store types, by segments, and by markets.

Techniques for measuring store image can be categorized, first, as unstructured and, second, as structured. The primary measurement techniques used in the first category are word association, nondirective questioning, cartoon tests, and open-ended questions. Four specific techniques are discussed under the general category of structural methods: semantic differential, multidimensional scaling, multiattribute models, and multivariate techniques.

Finally, this chapter presents a store image management paradigm containing five steps: (1) examine current store image; (2) examine competing store images; (3) design and implement image change/enhancement program; (4) assess the change in store image; and (5) determine the impact in terms of retail success.

REFERENCES

Anderson, Thomas W., Eli P. Cox III, and David G. Fulcher. "Bank Selection and Market Segmentation." *Journal of Marketing* 40 (January 1976): 40–45.

Arnold, Stephen J., and Douglas Tigert. "Marketing Monitoring Through Attitude Research." *Journal of Retailing* 49 (Winter 1973–74): 3–22.

Arons, Leon. "Does Television Viewing Influence Store Image and Shopping Frequency?" *Journal of Retailing* 37 (Fall 1961): 1–13.

Bearden, William O. "Determinant Attributes of Store Patronage: Downtown versus Outlying Shopping Center." *Journal of Retailing* (Summer 1977): 15–22.

Bellenger, D., E. Steinberg, and W. W. Stanton. "The Congruence of Store Image and Self-Image." *Journal of Retailing* 52 (Spring 1976): 17–32.

Berkowitz, Eric N., Terry Deutscher, and Robert A. Hansen. "Retail Image Research: A Case of Significant Unrealized Potential." Proceedings, American Marketing Association Educators Conference, Chicago, 1978, p. 63.

Berry, Leonard. "The Components of Department Store Image." *Journal of Retailing* (Spring 1969): 2.

Blackwell, Roger D., James F. Engel, and David T. Kollat. *Consumer Behavior*. 4th ed. Hinsdale, Ill.: Dryden Press, 1983, p. 41.

Bucklin, Louis. "Retail Strategy and the Classification of Consumer Goods." *Journal of Marketing* (January 1963): 9.

Cardozo, Richard N. "How Images Vary by Product Class." *Journal of Retailing* (Winter 1974–1975): 2.

Cox, Charles E., Jr. "An Analysis of Infrequent Shopper Attitudes Towards Department Store Appeals." Unpublished Master's Thesis, The University of Tennessee, 1974.

Dalrymple, Douglas J., and Donald C. Thompson. *Retailing: An Economic View*. New York: Free Press, 1969, p. 12.

Downs, Phillip E. and Richard G. Flood. "Dynamic Comparative Retail Image: An Empirical Investigation." Southern Marketing Association Proceedings, 1979, 434–437.

Doyle, Peter, and Ian Fenwick. "How Store Images Affect Shopping Habits in Grocery Chains." *Journal of Retailing* 50 (Winter 1974–1975): 333.

Enis, Ben M., and James E. Stafford. "Consumer's Perception of Product Quality as a Function of Various Information Inputs." In Philip R. McDonald, ed., *Marketing Involvement in Society and the Environment*. Chicago: American Marketing Association, 1969, pp. 340–44.

Fishbein, Marin. "A Behavior Theory Approach to the Relations Between Beliefs About an Object and the Attitude Towards the Object." *Readings in Attitude Theory and Measurement*. New York: John Wiley and Sons, 1967, 256–266.

Fisk, George. "A Conceptual Model for Studying Customer Image." *Journal of Retailing* (Winter 1961–1962).

Hansen, Robert A., and Terry Deutscher. "An Empirical Investigation of Attribute Importance in Retail Store Selection." *Journal of Retailing* 53 (Winter 1977–1978): 58–72.

―――. "Measure Validation in Retail Research Image Research." Proceedings of the 1977 Conference of the Southern Marketing Association, pp. 152–55.

Hirschman, Elizabeth C., Barnett Greenberg, and Dan H. Robertson. "The Intermarket Reliability of Retail Image Research: An Empirical Examination." *Journal of Retailing* (Spring 1978).

Hollander, Stanley C., and Delbert J. Duncan. *Modern Retailing Management*. Homewood, Ill.: Richard D. Irwin, 1983, p. 444.

James, Don L., Richard M. Durand, and Robert A. Drewes. "The Use of a Multi Attribute Model in a Store Image Study." *Journal of Retailing* (Summer 1976): 23–32.

Jenkins, Roger L., and Sandra M. Forsythe. "Retail Image Research: State of the Art Review with Implications for Retailing Strategy."

Kelley, R. G., and R. Stephenson. "The Semantic Differential: An Information Source for Designing Retail Patronage Appeals." *Journal of Marketing* (December 1967): 43–47.

Kunkel, John H., and Leonard L. Berry. "A Behavioral Adaptation of Retail Image." *Journal of Marketing* (October 1968): 21–27.

Lazer, William, and Eugene J. Kelley. "The Retailing Mix: Planning and Management." *Journal of Retailing* 37 (Spring 1961): 34–41.

Lessig, V. P., "Consumer Store Images and Store Loyalties." *Journal of Marketing* 38 (October 1973): 72–74.

Lindquist, Jay D. "Meaning of Image." *Journal of Retailing* 50 (Winter 1974–1975): 29–38.

McDougall G. H. G., and J. N. Fry. "Combining Two Methods of Image Measurement." *Journal of Retailing* (Winter 1974–1975): 53–61.

Marcus, Burton H. "Image Variation and the Multi-Unit Retail Establishment." *Journal of Retailing* (Summer 1972): 29–43.

Marks, Ronald B. "A Multi-attribute Approach to the Store Imagery Problem." Ph.D. diss., University of Missouri, Columbia, 1974.

Martineau, Pierre. *Motivation in Advertising*. New York: McGraw-Hill, 1957, p. 175.

———. "The Personality of the Retail Store." *Harvard Business Review* (January-February 1958): 48.

Mason, Joseph Barry, and Morris Lehman Mayer. *Modern Retailing Theory and Practice*. Dallas: Business Publications, 1987, p. 445.

May, Elenor G. "Practical Applications of Recent Retail Image Research." *Journal of Retailing* (Winter 1974–1975): 15–20.

Mindak, W. A. "Fitting the Semantic Differential to the Marketing Problem." *Journal of Marketing* (April 1961): 28–34.

Muse, William A. "Using Word Association Tests to Develop a Retail Store Image." *Journal of Retailing* (Winter 1974–1975): 35–42.

Myers, Robert H. "Sharpening Your Store Image." *Journal of Retailing* (Fall 1960): 129–137.

Oxenfeldt, Alfred R. "Developing a Favorable Price-Quality Image." *Journal of Retailing* 50 (Winter 1974–1975): 8–14.

Pathak, D. S. "A Study of Department Store's Images Held By Customers and Management." Doctoral thesis, Michigan State University, E. Lansing, 1972.

Rachman, David J. *Retail Strategy and Structure*. Englewood Cliffs, N.J.: Prentice-Hall, 1975.

Roselius, Ted. "Consumer Rankings of Risk Reduction Methods." *Journal of Marketing* 35 (January 1975): 56–66.

Schiffman, Leon F., Joseph F. Dash, and William K. Dillon. "The Contribution of Store Image Characteristics to Store Type Choice." *Journal of Retailing* (Summer 1977): 3–44.

Semenik, Richard J., and Robert A. Hansen. "Low Income vs. Non-Low-Income Consumer Preference Data as Input to Socially Responsive and Economically Profitable Decision-Making." Proceedings of the 1976 American Marketing Association Educators Conference, pp. 205–208.

Soldner, Helmut. "Conceptual Models for Retail Strategy Formulation." *Journal of Retailing* 52 (Fall 1976):49–56.

Stephenson, Ronald P. "Identifying Determinants of Retail Patronage." *Journal of Marketing* 33 (July 1969): 57–60.

Stern, Bruce L., Ronald F. Bush, and Joseph H. Hair, Jr. "The Self-Image/Store Image Matching Process: An Empirical Test." *Journal of Business* 50 (January, 1977): 63–69.

Weale, Bruce W. "Measuring the Customer's Image of the Department Store." *Journal of Retailing* (Summer 1961): 40–48.

Wyckham, R. G. "Aggregate Department Store Image: Social and Experimental Factors." Proceedings of the American Marketing Association Conference. Chicago: American Marketing Association (1967): 333–337.

10 Management Versus Customer Perception of Image

A. Coskun Samli and Douglas Lincoln

The image perceived by the market does not reflect the total picture. That image must be contrasted with that perceived by the management itself. As opposed to semantic differential, multiattribute models are more realistic in the development of image studies. This chapter discusses the usefulness of multiattribute techniques in assessing the differences between the customer's perceived image and management's self-perceptions as a diagnostic tool.

The differential congruence, as discussed earlier in this book, implies a positive match between the store image and the customer's self-image. Since store image is all the impressions perceived by different publics, this concept needs careful scrutiny. The concept of different publics implies the presence of various groups with which the retail establishment is involved both directly and indirectly. Directly, the most important involvement is with the loyal customers of the store. The loyalty factor is discussed elsewhere in this book. Other publics with which the retail establishment is involved are less loyal customers, noncustomers, and the retail management itself.

Since differential congruence is achieved by a positive balance between the store image and the customer's self-image, the question that must be raised here is, what is the store image? Ideally, the store should have one image, that is, all publics perceive the store as the store's loyal customer perceives it. In a practical sense, this is a near impossibility. Different publics do perceive the store's features, characteristics, and personality quite differently. In this chapter one very important aspect is discussed: management's perception versus the store customer's perception of the image. If there are important differences between the two, then the management in its attempts to manipulate the store image is involved in putting wrong resources in the wrong areas. In short, it is not managing the store optimally. If, for instance, customers think that the store layout is desirable but the management thinks the layout is the prime weakness of the store, then the management will unnecessarily put a lot of resources into changing the store layout. Thus, the management's perception of the store image must be very close to the customers' perception. If a study illustrates how the differences between the two perceived images are related, then such an approach can be used to improve management's effectiveness. The discrepancy between the customer's and management's image can be an important diagnostic base and, as such, represents a critical feedback factor in retail management leading to effective control.

REVIEW OF IMAGE RESEARCH

A review of the literature on retail image leads to a series of important conclusions: first, that the store image is an extremely complex phenomenon (Martineau 1958, Boulding 1959, Arons 1961); second, that it consists of tangible and nontangible factors (Kunkel 1968, Wycham 1969); and third, that the image of the store is a function of attitudes held toward the various image dimensions (Alpert 1971).

Image researchers should, therefore, strive to elicit those store attributes that make up the image. Most important, an attempt must be made to find those attributes that are most critical in formulating the total image. These attributes lead to the choice of that store (Alpert 1971).

The most extensively used technique in determining store image is semantic differential (Osgood et al. 1957, Osgood 1952, Howard and Sheth 1969, Kelly and Stephenson 1967, Dornoff 1972, Weale 1961, May 1971, Rich and Portis 1964). This technique is easy to apply, reliable, and simple in that it eliminates problems such as ambiguity which is inherent in question phrasing (Mindak 1961). Despite its popularity, among others, the semantic differential has one main shortcoming (Berry 1969, Kunkel and Berry 1968, Fry and McDougall 1975, Muse 1975): it does not isolate those dimensions which store customers may hold salient. The approach, therefore, does not allow a weighting of responses according to their relevance for the customer (Doyle and Fenwick 1975, Ehrenberk 1972).

In addition to using mostly semantic differential and not distinguishing among the components of the image, the state of the art thus far has barely gone beyond the consumer's perception of the image. Perhaps the most significant contribution of image studies would lie in attempts to contrast management and consumer perceptions of the image (Pathak 1972, Crissy et al. 1975, McClure and Ryans 1968). The significant discrepancies or conflicts between the image perceived by management and by customers would indicate most vulnerable aspects of the business. If these weak areas can be ranked according to their importance, then obviously management has a clear-cut picture of the business's present position in terms of its effectiveness in catering to its market segment.

This chapter is based on a preliminary study that sought (1) to establish the congruence or conflict in the management and customer images; and (2) to determine the relative importance of the image components from the customer's point of view and, therefore, to determine the relative seriousness of the management–market discrepancies.

METHODOLOGY AND THE DATA

The multiattribute model was used in this study (Fishbein 1967, Rosenberg 1956, Doyle and Fenwick 1975, Wilkie and Pessemier 1973, Oxenfeldt 1975). This technique allows store attributes to be differently weighted. The revised Fishbein model is still one of the most popular multiattribute models, as indicated by its appearance in recent consumer behavior literature. This new model is also called the "adequacy-importance" model. It is algebraically expressed as follows:

$$A = \sum_{i=1}^{n} P_i D_i$$

where

A = an individual's attitude toward an object.

P = importance of attribute i for the individual.

D = the individual's evaluation of object with respect to the attribute i.

n = number of attributes.

It has been concluded that the "adequacy" model may predict consumer attitudes more accurately and therefore may be most useful for developing attitude change strategies (Maris et al. 1975, Lindquist 1975, Greyser 1973, Isaacson 1964, May 1971).

The retail store selected for the study is a small gift shop located in the downtown area of a small university town in southwest Virginia. Data were gathered by handing out questionnaires to shoppers systematically when they had made a purchase and were preparing to leave the store. Respondents returned the questionnaires by mail. Of 100 questionnaires distributed, 70 were returned. Three employees and one owner-manager also completed the questionnaire. Since the respondents had already gone through a purchasing decision in the store, they had recently considered price–value–image relationships. Thus, they represent the main source of information in the marketplace.

The questionnaire had four parts: (1) demographic information, (2) a measure of store attribute importance (salience), (3) a measure of store performance of those attributes (valence), and (4) a measure of the shopper's attitude toward shopping. The store attributes that were investigated included general characteristics, product selection, price ranges, personnel, services, advertising, and physical characteristics. The questionnaire was designed so that topical components were intermixed. In measuring valence, positive and negative components were also intermixed in order to avoid bias.

Salience (attribute, importance) was measured by using a one-dimensional preference scale. Respondents were asked to rate the importance of 43 attributes when considering a gift shop (where 1 = most important and 5 = not important). Valence was measured by using a semantic differential scale with seven intervals across all 43 attributes (May 1971).

To arrive at an overall attitude toward the store attributes and, thus, the store itself, image scores for salience and valence were first multiplied and then summed for each responding individual. In order to make the expected contribution to attitude equal to the actual contribution, salience and valence were compatibly scaled. Salience components (given to respondents as 1 through 5) were scaled as $+2$, $+1$, 0, -1, -2. Valence components ranging from "extremely" to "extremely" were scaled as $+3$, $+2$, $+1$, 0, -1, -2, -3. Thus, the bipolarity pattern was assumed for both valence and salience measures (Bonfield and Ryan 1975).

FINDINGS AND DISCUSSION

Exhibit 10.1 presents four sets of data. Both special strengths and weaknesses are displayed by the direct semantic differential data for both customers and management. Among the strengths the following are prominent: enjoyable place to shop, has been in the community a long time, is modern, commands a reasonable degree of customer loyalty shown by the statement of "would recommend to friends," has interesting merchandise, is good for gifts, offers freedom to browse, has fast checkout service, has good window displays and merchandise displays, offers convenient location of merchandise in store, is easy to move about in, and offers good decor and cleanliness. It is extremely important to note that, in most of these cases, management's perception of the image is substantially more favorable than the customer's perception. These are potential problem areas.

Again, on the basis of semantic differential, the clear weaknesses of the store involve parking, value for money spent, markup level, special ordering of merchandise, telephone ordering, advertising frequency, and advertising information. The last two imply not advertising enough and not providing enough information in the ads.

The second half of Exhibit 10.1 illustrates what happens to both of the images when salience is added. First, the following strengths are deemed relatively unimportant to the consumer: how long the store has been in the community, how modern the store is, window displays, and merchandise displays. Thus, an advertisement stressing "we have been serving this community for 40 years" is likely to be wasteful. Again, of the weaknesses, only two appeared to be significant after the salience was added: value for money spent and size of

Exhibit 10.1
Store Image as Perceived by Customers and by the Management

Extremely Quite Slightly Neither Slightly Quite Extremely

<u>General Characteristics of Store</u>

Short time required to reach store from work		Long time required to reach store from work
Store is progressive		Store is conservative
All types of people shop in this store		Only a few types of people shop in this store
This store is well-known		Store is unknown
This store is an enjoyable place to shop		Store is unenjoyable place to shop
Convenient store hours		Inconvenient store hours
Store has been in community a long time		Store has been in community a short time
Short time required to reach store from home		Long time required to reach store from home
Store is modern		Store is old-fashioned
Easy to find parking place for auto		Difficult to find parking place for auto
Near to other stores you shop		Long ways from other stores you shop
Store that you would recommend to friends		Store you would not recommend to your friends

Exhibit 10.1 (Continued)

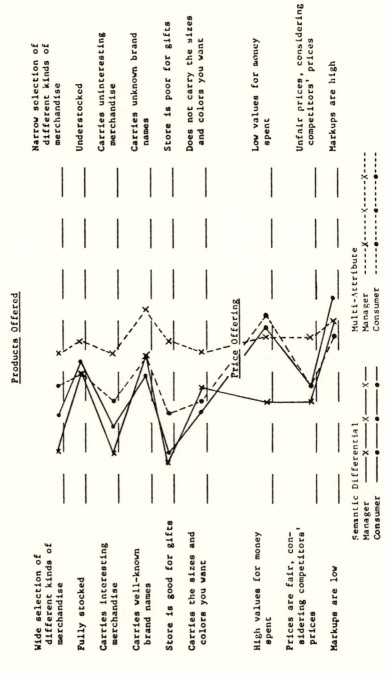

Exhibit 10.1 (Continued)

Extremely Quite Slightly Neither Slightly Quite Extremely

Advertising

		Ads never seen or heard by you
Ads frequently seen or heard by you		Ads are uninformative
Ads are informative		

Physical Characteristics

Store is uncluttered with merchandise		Store is too cluttered with merchandise
Music in this store is enjoyable to listen to		Music is unenjoyable to listen to
Attractive window display		Unattractive window display
Store is exciting		Store is dull
Merchandise is displayed in attractive manner		Merchandise is displayed in an unattractive manner
Easy to find location of merchandise in store		Difficult to find location of merchandise in store
Easy to move about in		Difficult to move about in
Has attractive decor		Has unattractive decor
Store is clean		Store is dirty

Exhibit 10.1 (Continued)

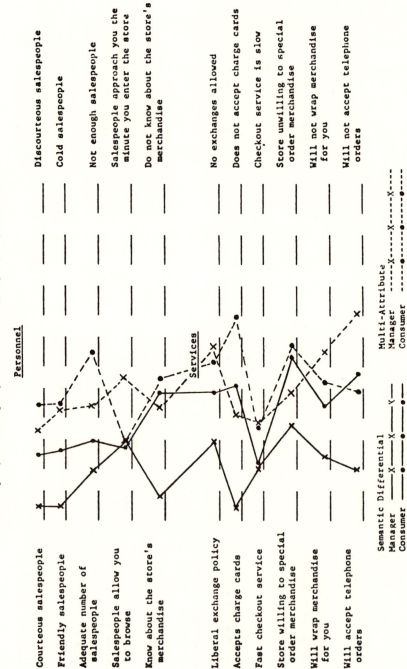

Exhibit 10.2
Special Problem Areas Depicted by the Multiattribute Model[a]

	Management	Consumers
How long the store has been in the community	.1	-1.5
How modern the store is	.8	- .2
Availability of parking space	-2.0	- .9
Availability of gifts in the store	.1	1.5
Has sizes and colors you want	.3	1.3
Fair prices in relation to competition	.0	1.0
Number of salespeople available	1.0	.0
Freedom to "browse" in store	.5	1.7
Ability to charge purchases	1.2	- .7
How easy it is to move about in the store	- .5	1.3
Accepts credit cards	1.4	- .8
Accepts telephone orders	- .5	.6

[a]Combined average of multiattribute scores depicting the product of salience and valence characteristics of each attribute. Minus scores indicate negativeness of the attribute, whereas zero means neutral. Scores range from $+3$ to -3.

markup. It would, therefore, be foolish for the retailer to promote telephone ordering since most consumers consider it to be unimportant.

On the other hand, a new weakness, prices in relation to competition, emerged as a result of salience analysis.

One of the most significant contributions of salience scores is to reduce management's unrealistic perception of the store image. While according to valence ratings 29 of the 43 attributes were overrated, once the salience scores are introduced, the number of overrated attributes went down to 16.

The multiattribute data, if used for diagnostic purposes, indicate that there are some 12 problem areas (See Exhibit 10.2). The problems stem from the discrepancy between management's perception and the customer's perception of certain attributes expressed as the product of salience and valence. Of the chief problem areas, four are especially important from the consumer's point of view. First, unlike management, consumers do not think the store is modern; second, unlike management, consumers do not think that parking is very bad; third, unlike management, consumers think that their ability to charge purchases is rather poor; and finally, in consumers' opinions the number of salespeople available is not nearly as adequate as the management thinks.

On the other hand, management's perception gap could cause serious problems. Management's perception, for example, of the availability of gifts and size and color selection is much more pessimistic than that of the consumers. Similarly, management has a more pessimistic view of the parking facilities and the store layout. It can be speculated that, given the options, management may try to change the store layout rather than add more salespeople or improve the existing credit system. Exhibit 10.2 shows that this is likely to be an unfortunate move in terms of utilizing the store's resources and enhancing its marketing effectiveness.

A DIAGNOSTIC SEQUENCE

Diagnosis of problem areas centers on understanding the discrepancy between management and customer perceptions of the store image. It must be reiterated that the basic objective here is twofold: First, the two images must be as close to each other as possible; and second, both of the images must be on the positive side as shown in Exhibit 10.1. Thus, once the critical gaps between the two images have been pinpointed, management's major marketing tasks should be in the direction of narrowing and eventually eliminating these gaps.

If there are multiple gaps, management should prioritize the gaps according to their relative importance and their relationship to the store's profit picture and then establish corrective measures. For example, management might realize that there is a gap between its own and customers' perceptions of the merchandise mix, and that without the proper merchandise mix, no matter how adequate the internal decor, the store is not likely to be very profitable.

After management takes corrective action on as many gaps as possible, given the firm's financial resources, time, and know-how, the consumer-perceived store image must be reassessed (Exhibit 10.3). This assessment process should be used as feedback for management to reorient its marketing activities to further both of the images.

Based on these research findings, it can be concluded that management and consumer perceptions of the store image are not likely to be perfectly congruent. The greater this discrepancy, the more serious are management's problems. A diagnostic tool must be used to measure the discrepancy. Multiattribute models are effective in depicting the problem areas because they combine salience and valence. Since management's resources are limited, if these are put to use in the areas that are not considered important by the consumers, then the outcome is one of suboptimization. The store will not be able to take advantage of the market opportunities, nor will it be able to establish its competitive advantage by segmenting the market efficiently. Instead, it will emphasize the factors that are deemed important by management and unimportant by consumers.

Much remains to be done in regards to isolating the attributes that are more meaningful in management decision processes. Similarly, the question remains as to whether or not it is more desirable to determine the consumer image as

Exhibit 10.3
Utilization of Diagnosis

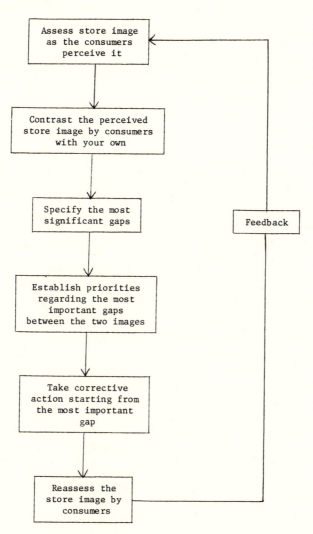

perceived by the store customers or by the nonpurchasing public. It is clear, however, that multiattribute models can be effective diagnostic tools.

SUMMARY

This chapter explores an important issue in retail marketing management— different perceptions of store image by different publics. In order to illustrate the issue, study findings are reported. It is found that management and customer perceptions of image differ significantly.

It is posited that the key managerial problems stem from this discrepancy. The greater the difference between the two images, the more critical are the problems. The chapter proposes a systematic approach to detecting this problem so that corrective measures can be taken.

REFERENCES

Alpert, Mark I. "Identification of Determinant Attributes: A Comparison of Methods." *Journal of Marketing Research* 8 (May 1971): 184–191.

Arons, Leon. "Does TV Viewing Influence Store Image and Shopping Frequency?" *Journal of Retailing* 37 (Fall 1961).

Berry, Leonard L. "The Components of Department Store Image: A Theoretical and Empirical Analysis." *Journal of Retailing* 45 (Spring 1969): 3–20.

Bonfield, E. H., and Michael T. Ryan. "The Fishbein Extended Model and Consumer Behavior." *Journal of Consumer Research* 2 (September 1975): 118–36.

Boulding, Kenneth E. *The Image*. Ann Arbor: University of Michigan Press, 1959

Cohen, Joel B., Martin Fishbein, and Olli T. Ahtola. "The Nature and Uses of Expectancy-Value Models in Consumer Attitude Research." *Journal of Marketing Research* 9 (November 1972): 456–60.

Dornoff, R. J., and R. C. Tatham. "Congruence Between Personal Image and Store Image." *Journal of the Market Research Society* 14 (1972): 45–52.

Doyle, Peter, and Ian Fenwick. "How Store Image Affects Shopping Habits in Grocery Chains." *Journal of Retailing* 50 (Winter 1974–1975).

Ehrenberk, A. S. C. "Multivariate Analysis in Marketing." Annual Conference of the Market Research Society, Brighton, 1972.

Fishbein, Martin. "A Consideration of Beliefs and Their Role in Attitude Measurement," and "A Behavior Theory Approach to the Relations Between Beliefs About an Object and the Attitude Toward the Object." In *Readings in Attitude Theory and Measurement*. New York: John Wiley, 1967, pp. 256–66 and 389–400.

Fry, J. N., and G. H. G. McDougall. "Combining Two Methods of Image Measurement." *Journal of Retailing* 50 (Winter 1974–1975): 53–61.

Greyser, Stephen A. "Making Image Research Work for You." A speech presented at the National Retail Merchants Association Conference, January 1973.

Howard, J. A., and J. H. Sheth. *The Theory of Buyer Behavior*. New York: John Wiley, 1969.

Isaacson, Lawrence H. "Store Choice." DBA diss., Harvard University, 1964.

Kelly, Robert F., and Ronald Stephenson. "The Semantic Differential: An Information

Source for Designing Retail Patronage Appeals." *Journal of Marketing* 31 (October 1967): 43.

Kunkel, John H., and Leonard L. Berry. "A Behavioral Concept of Retail Image." *Journal of Marketing* 32 (October 1968): 21–27.

Lindquist, Jay D. "Meaning of Image—A Survey of Empirical and Hypothetical Evidence." *Journal of Retailing* 50 (Winter 1974–1975): 29–38.

McClure, Peter J., and John K. Ryans. "Differences Between Retailers and Consumers' Perceptions." *Journal of Marketing Research* 5 (February 1968): 35–40.

Maris, Michael B., Olli T. Ahtola, and Eugene R. Klippel. "A Comparison of Four Multi-Attribute Models in the Prediction of Consumer Attitudes." *Journal of Consumer Research* 2 (June 1975): 38–52.

Martineau, Pierre. "The Personality of the Retail Store." *Harvard Business Review* 36 (January-February 1958): 47–55.

May, Eleanor G. "Image Evaluation of a Department Store: Techniques for Conducting the Study." Working paper, Marketing Science Institute, October 1971.

Mindak, William A. "Fitting the Semantic Differential to the Marketing Problem." *Journal of Marketing* 25 (April 1961): 28–33.

Muse, William T. "Using Word-Association Tests to Develop Retail Store Image." *Journal of Retailing* (Winter 1974–1975).

Osgood, Charles E. "The Nature and Measurement of Meaning." *Psychological Bulletin* 49 (May 1952): 197–237.

———, George J. Suci, and Percy H. Tannerbaum, *The Measurement of Meaning*. Urbana: University of Illinois Free Press, 1957.

Oxenfeldt, Alfred R. "Developing a Favorable Price-Quality Image." *Journal of Retailing* 50 (Winter 1974–1975): 8–14.

Pathak, Devendron S. "A Study of Department Store Images Held by Customers and Management." Ph.D. diss., Michigan State University, 1972.

———, William J. E. Crissy, and Robert W. Sweitzer. "Customer Image Versus the Retailer's Anticipated Image." *Journal of Retailing* 50 (Winter 1974–1975).

Rich, S. U., and B. D. Portis. "The Imageries of Department Store." *Journal of Marketing* 28 (April 1964): 10–15.

Rosenberg, Milton J. "Cognitive Structure and Attitudinal Affect." *Journal of Abnormal and Social Psychology*, 53 (November 1956): 367–72.

Weale, W. B., "Measuring the Customer's Image of a Department Store." *Journal of Retailing* 37 (Summer 1961): 40–48.

Wilkie, William L., and Edgar A. Pessemier. "Issues in Marketing Use of Multi-Attribute Attitude Models." *Journal of Marketing Research*, 10 (November 1973): 428–41.

Wyckham, Robert G., "Aggregate Department Stores Images: Special Experimental Factors." Ph.D. diss., Michigan State University 1969.

11 Congruence Between Store Image and Self-Image

M. Joseph Sirgy, A. Coskun Samli, Kenneth Bahn, and Theofanis G. Varvoglis

Differential congruence gives life to a retail establishment. It is achieved by finding a positive balance between the store image and individual customer's self-image. The congruence between these two images takes different forms, four of which are identified here: self-congruity, ideal congruity, social congruity, and ideal social congruity. These concepts are discussed in the context of store patronage and store loyalty, and subsequently, a model is presented which integrates these concepts and evaluates the four market segments for a retail establishment. These market segments need to be distinguished by the retail management and treated quite differently from each other if the retail establishment is to allocate its resources effectively for better results.

SELF-CONCEPT AND RETAILING STRATEGY

Ever since the concept of market segmentation was first introduced (Smith 1956), marketers have searched for new methods of segmentation to give them a differential advantage in the marketplace. In retailing, marketers have traditionally segmented the market on the basis of store image involving consumer perceptions of store attributes such as prices, quality of merchandise, store personnel, and store location (Jenkins and Forsythe 1980; Lessig 1973; Lincoln and Samli 1979). Although it may be implied, none of these segmentation methods deals, explicitly with symbolic store image attributes. The role of symbolic (personality-related) store image attributes has not yet been considered seriously in retail segmentation.

This chapter posits a construct as to how self-concept store image congruence emerges in retailing (involving the interaction of symbolic store image with consumer self-concept). It also explores how this congruence concept may be

Exhibit 11.1
Various Single Self-Image/Store Image Congruity Constructs

Match Between Self-Concept and Store Image	Self-Image/Store-Image Congruity
Actual Self-Image and Symbolic Store Image	Self-Congruity
Ideal Self-Image and Symbolic Store Image	Ideal Congruity
Social Self-Image and Symbolic Store Image	Social Congruity
Ideal Social Self and Symbolic Store Image	Ideal Social Congruity

used as a means of segmenting retail markets and devising retail strategy. Consider, for instance, a consumer who patronizes Sears because of the perception that the company appeals to solid middle-class America. The consumer also perceives him or herself that way. This congruence enhances that individual's satisfaction, increasing that person's loyalty to Sears.

STORE IMAGE AND SELF-CONCEPT

The symbolic (value-expressive) store image as used here refers to the stereotypic personality image which shoppers have of a specific retail store (Samli and Sirgy 1981; Sirgy 1982; Varvoglis and Sirgy 1984). Examples of stereotypic personality images which people may have of a particular store include traditional versus modern, classy versus folksy, sexy versus plain, friendly versus formal, and high status versus low status (cf. Birdwell 1968; Dolich 1969; Grubb and Grathwohl 1967; Levy 1959; Ross 1971).

Generally, self-concept may be defined as the "totality of the individual's thoughts and feelings having reference to himself as an object" (Rosenberg 1979: 7). Traditionally, in consumer behavior self-concept has been considered to be comprised of different self-perspectives such as actual self-image, ideal self-image, social self-image, and ideal social self-image (Sirgy 1982). The actual self-image refers to how the individual sees himself or herself along a specific personality attribute; the ideal self-image refers to how the individual likes to see himself or herself along a specific attribute. The social self-image is defined in terms of how the individual believes others see him or her along a specific attribute. Finally, the ideal social self-image is how the individual believes significant others like him or her are seen in a particular personality attribute (Sirgy 1982) (see Exhibit 11.1).

Self-image/store image congruity refers to the match or mismatch of one or more self-perspectives (i.e., actual self-image, ideal self-image, social self-image, or ideal social self-image) with corresponding personality images of the designated store. The match between actual self-image and store image has been referred to as "ideal congruity," that between social self-image and store image as "social congruity," and that between ideal social self-image and store image as "ideal social congruity" (see Sirgy 1982, 1984a).

SINGLE CONGRUITY VERSUS MULTIPLE CONGRUITIES

The issue of whether store image interacts with one or more self-perspectives such as the actual self-image, the ideal self-image, the social self-image, or the ideal social self-image has been addressed by Sirgy (1982, 1984a, 1984b). Many studies (e.g. Bellenger, Steinberg, and Stanton, 1976) have treated self-image/ store image congruity only and exclusively in terms of a single congruity effect, namely, self-congruity (i.e., involving only the actual self-image). These studies provide support for the relationship between self-congruity and patronage behavior. Other studies have been found to assess the independent effects of ideal self-image versus actual self-image (or ideal congruity versus self-congruity) on patronage behavior (Dornoff and Tatham 1972; Samli and Sirgy 1981; Stern, Bush, and Hair 1977). It is assumed however, that, if there are different levels of self-image, store image/self-image congruities also take place at different levels.

In the following section, a self-image/store image congruence model is developed based on the concepts of self-congruity and ideal congruity in a retail setting. Thus, it is posited that a retail store that can achieve multiple congruities may be significantly more successful than those competitors that can achieve only single congruity. These concepts have already been empirically supported by a few studies in both product and retail settings. (For a literature review, see Sirgy 1982 and 1984a). This chapter focuses on integrating these concepts and applying them in retail management.

AN INTEGRATED SELF-CONCEPT MODEL

As previously stated, a match between a store image and a customer's actual self-image can be identified as self-congruity. In contrast, a match between a store image and a person's ideal self-image has been referred to as ideal congruity. What happens when a customer experiences different levels of both self-congruity and ideal congruity? Exhibit 11.2 shows the result of combining the effects of both self-congruity and ideal congruity on store loyalty.

The underlying assumption in the model, as shown in Exhibit 11.2, is that the effects of self-congruity and ideal congruity on store loyalty are additive, that is, not interactive. A study conducted in the product sector testing this assumption (Sirgy 1984b) provides support for the addivity notion. In other words, if the store can achieve self-congruity and ideal congruity simultaneously, it will satisfy its customers more effectively than if it were to achieve only one

Exhibit 11.2
Integrating the Effects of Self-Congruity and Ideal Congruity

Self-Congruity	Ideal Congruity	Congruity Segment	Self-Esteem Motivation	Self-Consistency Motivation	Store Patronage/ Loyalty
High	High	Positive Self-Congruity	High	High	High
Low	High	Positive Self-Incongruity	High	Low	Moderate
High	Low	Negative Self-Congruity	Low	High	Moderate
Low	Low	Negative Self-Incongruity	Low	Low	Low

of these congruities. Customer-enhanced satisfaction is instrumental in enhancing customer loyalty to the store.

As shown in Exhibit 11.2, the interrelationship of self-congruity and ideal congruity results in at least four discrete conditions: high self-congruity/high ideal congruity (labeled positive self-congruity in the illustration), high self-congruity/low ideal congruity (negative self-congruity), low self-congruity/high ideal congruity (positive self-incongruity), and low self-congruity/low ideal congruity (negative self-incongruity).

Self-congruity affects store loyalty through the activation and operation of the *self-consistency* motive (Sirgy 1982, 1983, 1984a, 1984b). In contrast, ideal congruity affects store loyalty through the mediation of the *self-esteem* motive. The self-consistency motive refers to an individual's need to act in ways that are consistent with his or her self-perceptions. To do otherwise would cause dissonance, a psychological discomfort threatening to invalidate his or her beliefs about him or herself. A number of researchers have repeatedly addressed the psychological dynamics of this motive (e.g., Lecky, 1969). Earlier studies by W. Lloyd Warner (1949) and Pierre Martineau (1958) have indicated that the upper-middle-class family shopped at specialty stores for their public appearance clothes, and hence its members were motivated by self-consistency motives. If the members of the family were to shop exclusively, say, in second-hand stores, they would all be quite frustrated knowing and feeling they were not in their element.

The self-esteem motive, on the other hand, refers to an individual's need to act in ways that are instrumental in achieving goals that maintain and/or increase positive self-regard. This motive is extremely important and occupies a central focus in clinical psychology. Many personality-clinical psychologists have elaborated on the dynamics of this motive (e.g., Rogers 1951).

As shown in Exhibit 11.2, in the positive self-congruity condition, the consumer would be motivated to approach a store that would satisfy both self-esteem and self-consistency needs. For example, "this store seems to have an image of high social class" (store image) can match the consumer's self-image as "a classy person" (high self-congruity). If these personality attributes are ideally valued by the individual then there is high ideal congruity. By patronizing that store, this consumer would be able to maintain his or her ideal self-image (satisfaction of his or her self-esteem needs) and simultaneously reinforce his or her self-consistency needs (high level of store loyalty). We maintain here that the crux of retail marketing strategy is to achieve high self and ideal congruities. This is called positive self-congruity, which implies *differential congruence*. This concept goes beyond Wroe Alderson's "differential advantage" (1959) in the sense that through congruence it implies a state of equilibrium between the store and its particular segment, with the optimum amount of satisfaction accruing for both.

Under the negative self-congruity condition, consumers would experience a conflict state regarding the store since the patronage of the store would in one way frustrate their self-esteem need and in another way satisfy their self-consistency need.

An example of the negative self-congruity condition is: "I believe that the people who typically patronize this store are conservative" (store image). This condition is matched by "I am conservative" (high self-congruity) but "I don't like being conservative" (low ideal congruity). Here the person would not be motivated to maintain a state that he or she views in a negative light, since by doing so self-esteem would decrease; however, this person would be acting consistently with his or her conservative actual self-image to satisfy the self-consistency need. The result is a motivational state reflecting conflict (moderate level of store loyalty).

Under a positive self-incongruity condition, the situation is reversed, but the motivational outcome remains the same. Here, the consumer will also experience a conflict between the self-esteem and self-consistency motives. On the one hand, patronage of that store would satisfy the self-esteem need but would frustrate the self-consistency need. An example of this situation is as follows: A store with a "preppy" image may match the consumer's ideal self-image ("I like to be preppy"), causing high ideal congruity. However, the consumer might not presently see himself or herself that way ("I am not preppy")—low self-congruity. Patronizing that store would therefore help the consumer attain the ideal self-image of being "preppy" (satisfying the self-esteem motive), but doing so would threaten that person's self-image as "not the preppy type" (frustrate the self-consistency motive). Store loyalty reflects this conflict toward the store (moderate level of store loyalty).

Finally, under the negative self-incongruity condition, the consumer would optimally be motivated to avoid that store, since the patronage of the store would frustrate both his or her self-esteem and self-consistency needs. An example may be the consumer who perceives the customers of a particular store as "conservative and old-fashioned" (store image). Such a consumer does not have a "conservative or old-fashioned" self-image (low self-congruity), nor does he or she like to be "conservative or old-fashioned" (low ideal congruity). In this case the consumer would avoid patronizing the store (low level of store loyalty).

RETAIL STRATEGY IMPLICATIONS

As can be seen from the integrated model, consumers who experience positive self-congruity with a particular store would be most motivated to patronize that store, assuming other factors are constant. Hence, the retail manager should be able to identify and segment the market into the four different congruity groups: (1) a positive self-congruity group, (2) a positive self-incongruity group, (3) a negative self-congruity group, and (4) a negative self-incongruity group. The positive self-congruity group should be considered the retailer's primary target market, since it leads to the highest level of store loyalty.

Two kinds of retailing strategies can be pursued by retailers in an attempt to market their merchandise to the positive self-congruity target market: (1) the passive approach and (2) the active approach.

The Passive Approach

The passive approach to retail strategy involving the integrated self-concept model entails segmenting the customer population into the various congruity segments (positive self-congruity, positive self-incongruity, etc.) and positioning the elements of the retailing mix to appeal to the positive self-congruity target market.

The passive approach suggested here is recommended only for existing stores in mature markets. Conversely, the active approach is recommended for new stores in growing markets. This is because once the store is established the retailer can take advantage of the situation as it exists and optimize it by focusing attention on the positive self-congruity market. However, given that the store is not established (i.e., most customers are not familiar with the store), the retailer does have the option of thinking in terms of the preferred target market for his or her store and of formulating retail strategy to appeal to that market directly.

The recommended steps for formulating a retailing strategy based on the passive approach are as follows:

1. The retailer should conduct a perceptual test identifying the symbolic store image attributes associated with a given store. This can be done through a variety of research techniques such as focus groups, free elicitation methods, and/or personal in-depth interviews. Using one or more of these methods, retailers can identify their stores' stereotypic image profile in terms of personality or symbolic image attributes such as "classy," "modern," "old fashioned," and "young."

2. Using these symbolic store image attributes as identified by the aforementioned research methods, retailers should then measure the sample respondents' actual and ideal self-images along the same set of attributes (e.g., "classy," "modern"). This can be done through a variety of self-report measures (e.g., Likert-type scales, rating scales, semantic differential scales, to name a few). The same self-report scale should be used to measure the symbolic store image along the same set of attributes.

3. In order to obtain self-congruity scores, the retailer should use a distance index such as the absolute difference between the store image score and the consumer actual self-image score for each symbolic image attribute. The sum of the absolute difference scores across all symbolic image attributes can be used as an indicator of self-congruity for that respondent. A similar procedure should be conducted to obtain an ideal congruity score for each sample respondent. Since the absolute difference distance model is used to measure self and ideal congruity, a *high* score means *low* self (or ideal) congruity and vice versa. A respondent who ends up with a low self-congruity score and a low ideal congruity score is then classified as belonging to the positive self-congruity group; a high self-congruity score and a low ideal congruity score are classified in the positive

Retail Marketing Strategy

Exhibit 11.3
Deviation of Congruity Scores

Ideal Congruity

$$\sum_{i=1}^{n} |SI_i - ISI_i|$$

		Low Level Congruity (High Score)	High Ideal Congruity (Low Score)
Self-Congruity $\sum_{i=1}^{n} |SI_i - ASI_i|$	High Self-Congruity (Low score)	Negative Self-Congruity	Positive Self-Congruity
	Low Self-Congruity (High Score)	Negative Self-Incongruity	Positive Self-Incongruity

NOTE: SI_i = Symbolic Store-Image Attribute, i = 1, 2, . . n

ASI_i = Actual Self-Image Along Attribute i.

ISI_i = Ideal Self-Image Along Attribute i.

self-incongruity group; a low self-congruity score and a high ideal congruity are classified in the negative self-congruity group; and, finally, a high self-congruity score and a high ideal congruity score are classified in the negative self-incongruity group (see Exhibit 11.3).

In other words, the market population should be segmented into those who may experience positive self-congruity, positive self-incongruity, negative self-congruity, and negative self-incongruity along those symbolic store image attributes. For example, given that the symbolic store image was found to be "classy," then those who see themselves as "classy" (actual self-image) and like to see themselves as "classy" (ideal self-image) are to be classified in the positive self-congruity group, and so on.

4. Retailers should focus on the positive self-congruity group. In doing so, they should identify the demographics, psychographics, geographics, shopping habits, media habits, and the evaluation of utilitarian store image attributes (including prices, product assortment, product quality, personnel, atmosphere, and advertising, to name a few) of the positive self-congruity market. The demographic, psychographic, and geographic information about that target market may help the retailer assemble a merchandising mix that is more suitable to that market. The shopping habits may help the retailer make optimal location/place decisions. The information on media habits would allow the retailer to develop media plans that are efficient in reaching that market. The information pertaining to the target market's evaluation of the utilitarian store image attributes may help the retailer make changes in the store image (utilitarian, not symbolic attributes) that would be favorably evaluated by the positive self-congruity target market. For an application of the usage of utilitarian store image attributes as

they relate to symbolic store image attributes, the reader is referred to a study conducted by Theofanis Varvoglis and M. Joseph Sirgy (1984).

5. With respect to promotion, the retailer should reinforce or maintain the positive store image (to maintain high ideal congruity) and provide instrumentalities for those shoppers to further enhance themselves by maintaining their actual self-image (high self-congruity). For example, a specific store, such as Bloomingdale's, may project an image of high status, affluence, and prestige. The shoppers who perceive themselves as having high status and prestige (high self-congruity) and who like to be thought of as such (high ideal congruity) will experience a positive self-congruity state with that store. This positive self-congruity state, according to the integrated self-concept model presented here, should increase those shoppers' store loyalty to that store.

The Active Approach

In contrast to the passive approach, under the active approach the retailer elects to appeal to a specific target market that has specific actual and ideal self-images. In other words, the retailer may choose to appeal to a specific set of customers such as the "classy customers," the "modern customers," the "preppy customers," the "old-fashioned customers," and so on. Having made that decision, the retailer should develop the retail mix in a way that facilitates the creation of a symbolic store image that results in a *positive self-congruity* state in the *selected* target population (i.e., cause a match between the store's symbolic image and those customers who have this image and who idealize it).

The steps involved in the active approach are as follows: 1. The retailer should first identify the symbolic images of the existing competition. With respect to these symbolic image attributes, the retailer then examines the extent to which each of the competition's clientele usually experiences positive self-congruity, positive self-incongruity, negative self-congruity, or negative self-incongruity (see Exhibit 11.4).

If a substantial segment of a competition's clientele experiences a congruity state *other than* positive self-congruity (i.e., positive self-incongruity, negative self-congruity, and/or negative self-incongruity), this situation may be identified as a strategic gap for one or more new stores in that market. That is, there may be a potential market that can be served by one or more stores that position themselves using symbolic store image attributes compatible with the actual and ideal self-images of these customers. For example, Exhibit 11.4 shows that 25 percent of Store A's clientele experience a negative self-incongruity state, and Store A has the largest clientele segment. That these customers shop at Store A, even though they do not find the store image compatible with their actual and ideal self-image, may indicate that patronage to that store may be determined by utilitarian store image attributes. Consequently, in establishing a new store, the retailer can focus on these customers and treat them as potential customers for a new store that has a symbolic image compatible with these customers. That

Exhibit 11.4
An Example of Identifying Strategic Gaps Using a Self-Image/Store Image Congruity Framework

Retail Competition

	Store A is Mostly Perceived as "Traditional"	Store B is Mostly Perceived as "Modern"	Store C is Mostly Perceived as "Thrifty"	Store D is Mostly Perceived as "High Class"
Positive Self-Congruity	70%	50%	45%	60%
Positive Self-Incongruity	2%	20%	20%	15%
Negative Self-Congruity	3%	10%	20%	20%
Negative Self-Incongruity	25%	20%	15%	5%
	100% N_A=20,000	100% N_B=15,000	100% N_C=10,000	100% N_D=17,000

Note: Classification of respondents into the various congruity conditions can be undertaken using a similar procedure that was described under the passive approach.

N = Number of people indicating that they "usually" patronize specified store as estimated through market survey.

e.g., the % figure in Store A/positive self-congruity condition represents 70% of the 20,000 customers patronizing Store A experience a positive self-congruity condition with that store.

is, the retailer has to "dig" further to know more about these customers and identify the positive self-images (actual and ideal self-image attributes) of these customers. The retailer also has to *position* the new store with a store image that may effect a positive self-congruity experience with regards to these customers. For example, suppose that through market research the retailer of a new store finds out that the designated 25 percent of Store A customers positively view themselves as "college students who can't afford to spend much because of their transition stage." They patronize Store A for utilitarian attributes such as convenient location. A new store can therefore be established, positioning itself as a store for "college students who can't afford to spend much." Consequently, it is very likely that 25 percent of the Store A customers would switch to the new store, given that the new store would maintain the same attractive utilitarian attributes provided by Store A (which attracted these customers to Store A to begin with).

Therefore, in establishing the new store, the retailer must maintain the utilitarian characteristics of the store which involve those customers viewed as "potential switchers." The new store will appeal to those "potential switchers" by satisfying their self-esteem and self-consistency needs *in addition* to their utilitarian needs.

2. The retailer should then identify the demographics, psychographics, geographics, shopping habits, media habits, and ideal utilitarian store image attributes of these potential customers.

3. Based on this information bank, the retailer can effectively position his or her store to appeal to those customers who experience a positive self-congruity state with those stores and consequently develop a high degree of store loyalty to them.

4. Since store patrons contribute to the formation of the symbolic store image, the retailer should monitor the strength of that image. Weakening of the symbolic store image may be attributed to the fact that customers of the new store are experiencing congruity states other than positive self-congruity. In other words, the store's clientele may involve more patrons that are not in the primary target market (e.g., positive self-incongruity). Take for an example a nightclub that is positioned to appeal to "affluent married couples," but instead many of its patrons are "single and swinging types." Since store patrons contribute to the strengthening or weakening of the symbolic store image, this situation may be a cause for concern. This may sound counterintuitive at first glance, since most retailers think that attracting nontarget as well as target customers increases the store's profitability. This may be true in the short run but in the long run, those nontarget customers deter the unique positioning aspect of the store. Hence, the retailer is advised to maintain the unique and distinct symbolic store image even by marketing efforts designed to deter nontarget customers.

SUMMARY

The role of store symbolism in patronage behavior is a new concept that has been discovered lately. Retailers are beginning to realize that consumers react to affect-laden symbolic (value-expressive) store image attributes as well as affect-free functional (utilitarian) store image attributes. This is an enormously rich area for retailers to exploit. On the other hand, lack of awareness concerning how these symbolic image attributes interact with the self-concept of the consuming population can be very costly when a retail establishment fails to understand and therefore control those store images.

The self-concept principles presented in this chapter enable retail management to accomplish three major tasks. First, it becomes possible to establish specific goals, for example, to attain a specific desired level of positive self-congruity in a target market. Second, the retailer, based on this concept, can segment the market along symbolic dimensions into a positive self-congruity segment, a positive self-incongruity segment, a negative self-congruity segment, and a negative self-incongruity segment. This segmentation helps the retailer to target his or her marketing efforts to the positive self-congruity segment, that is, treat it as the primary target market.

If the primary target market (i.e., positive self-congruity segment) is small, instead of expanding to one or more of the other congruity segments, the retailer may be well served by keeping the store small and perhaps open another one directed to the same positive self-congruity target market in a different location. Many successful retail chains knowingly or unknowingly have followed this strategy. It is quite likely that if a retail store were to attempt to appeal to more than one of these four segments, it would end up not satisfying any of them.

Finally, the model presented in this chapter provides a control mechanism that can be used in performance assessment of the retail establishment. Periodic research by the retailer would indicate the relative proportion of a positive self-congruity target market in the specific market niche in which the store is operating. If, for instance, the relative share of the positive self-congruity market of the retailer is shrinking, then a strategic plan needs to be reformulated based on the integrated self-concept model as presented here.

The positive self-congruity as discussed in this chapter is termed differential congruence in this book. The retail marketing strategies are aimed at achieving this special state of affairs, which implies a high degree of equilibrium and mutual satisfaction for the market segments and the store.

REFERENCE

Alderson, Wroe. *Marketing Management and Executive Action,* Homewood, Ill.: Richard D. Irwin, 1959.

Bellenger, D., E. Steinberg, and W. W. Stanton. "The Congruence of Store Image and Self Image." *Journal of Retailing* 52 (1976): 17–32.

Birdwell, A. "A Study of Influence of Image Congruence on Consumer Choice." *Journal of Business* 41 (1968): 76–88.

Dolich, I. J. "Congruence Relationship Between Self-Images and Product Brands." *Journal of Marketing Research* 6 (1969): 80–84.

Dornoff, R. J. and R. L. Tatham. "Congruence Between Personal Image and Store Image." *Journal of Market Research Society* 14 (1972): 45–52.

Grubb, E. L. and H. L. Grathwohl. "Consumer Self-Concept, Symbolism, and Market Behavior: A Theoretical Approach." *Journal of Marketing* 31 (1967): 22–27.

Jenkins, R. L., and S. M. Forsythe. "Retail Image Research: State of the Art Review with Implications for Retail Strategy." In V. V. Bellur and B. G. Gnaudi, eds., *Developments in Marketing Science,* Vol. 3. Academy of Marketing Science, 1980, pp. 189–196.

Lecky, P. *Self-Consistency: A Theory of Personality.* New York: Island Press, 1969.

Lessig, Y. P. "Consumer Store Image and Store Loyalties." *Journal of Marketing* (October 1973): 72–74.

Levy, S. J. "Symbols for Sale." *Harvard Business Review* 37 (1959): 117–24.

Lincoln, D., and A. C. Samli. "Retail Store Image: Definitions and Measurement." *Proceedings of the Southern Marketing Association,* 1979.

Martineau, Pierre. "Social Classes and Spending Behavior." *Journal of Marketing* (October 1958): 121–130.

Rogers, Carl. *Client-Centered Therapy: Its Current Practices, Implications, and Theory.* Boston: Houghton Mifflin, 1951.

Rosenberg, M. *Conceiving the Self.* New York: Basic Books, 1979.

Ross, I. "Self-Concept and Brand Preference." *Journal of Business of the University of Chicago* 44 (1971): 38–50.

Samli, A. C., and M. Joseph Sirgy. "A Multi-Dimensional Approach to Analyzing Store Loyalty: A Predictive Model." In Ken Bernhardt and Bill Kehoe, eds., *The Changing Marketing Environment: New Theories and Applications.* Chicago: American Marketing Association, 1981.

Sirgy, M. Joseph. "Self-Concept in Consumer Behavior: A Critical Review." *Journal of Consumer Research* 9 (December 1982): 287–300.

———. *Social Cognition and Consumer Behavior.* New York: Praeger Publishers, 1983.

———. "Self-Image/Product-Image Congruity and Consumer Decision Making." *International Journal of Management* 2 (December 1985): 19–63.

———. "Using Self-Congruity and Ideal Congruity to Predict Purchase Behavior." *Journal of Business Research* 13 (June 1985): 195–206.

Smith, W. R. "Product Differentiation and Market Segmentation as Alternate Market Strategies." *Journal of Marketing* 20 (1956): 3–8.

Stern, B. L., R. F. Bush, and J. F. Hair, Jr. "The Self-Image/Store Image Matching Process: An Empirical Test." *Journal of Business* 50 (1977): 63–69.

Varvoglis, Theofanis, and M. Joseph Sirgy. "The Interrelationship Between Value-Expressive and Utilitarian Store-Image Attributes." Proceedings of the Academy of the Marketing Science Annual Conference, 1984.

Warner, W. Lloyd, and Associates, *Democracy in Jonesville.* New York: Harper and Brothers, 1949.

12 Promotion and Retail Marketing Strategy

Although it is customary to talk about a promotional strategy (Larson et al. 1982; Dickson 1979; Hartley 1975), it should not be thought of as an autonomous entity. Rather, it carries out the general objectives of the overall retailing strategy. Thus, the promotional strategy is an extremely important component of the total retail marketing strategy. This chapter explores the relative role of promotion in general and its role in different retail marketing strategies in particular. In order to explore promotion or any of the marketing mix components, its planning, administration, feedback, and control have to be explored.

PROMOTION, ITS IMPORTANCE TO RETAILING

Since developing a retail marketing strategy is almost synonymous with image manipulation, the role of promotion becomes obvious. The creation and/or manipulation of retail image can only be achieved through communication. Because image basically means the sum total of impressions that different publics perceive about a retail establishment, by definition promotion communicates the image. Creation and manipulation of the appropriate image require a calculated and tightly controlled communication activity regardless of the size and nature of the retail establishment. Consider the following two examples.

In the 1960s, Sears wanted to get into some of the more expensive specialty goods such as diamonds and furs and so began to upgrade its image. It aspired to become an upper-middle-class establishment where quality and value offered by the store for the money would be particularly attractive for those in middle- and upper-middle-class America. Sears ran an elaborate, carefully planned advertising campaign backed by proper merchandising policies. Although there are no published research results on this particular point, it is generally accepted that the company did well.

A local apparel shop, on the other hand, in order to establish itself as the local fashion leader, ran a series of fashion shows supported by some carefully researched local mass media advertising and, of course, by proper merchandising. The store managed to enhance its already good image, and so this promotional activity became an annual event.

Many similar examples could be given. As can be seen, it is not the size or the nature of the retail establishment as much as proper planning that facilitates the image creation and management. If the store management wants to develop or manipulate the store's image according to overall strategic goals, it will have to manipulate the total communication of the retail establishment accordingly. A major portion of the retail store's perceived communication by the market is promotion.

PLANNING FOR PROMOTION

A retail establishment, like any other social or economic institution, communicates with its actual and potential publics regularly, both directly and indirectly. Planning this communication entails developing a promotional plan and a program.

Exhibit 12.1 outlines six components of such a plan: (1) promotional objectives, (2) components of the promotional mix, (3) promotional budget, (4) review process, (5) implementation, and (6) control.

Promotional Objectives

The retail store's promotional objectives must be consistent with the image development and image manipulation process. If the retail store wants to project an image as the fashion leader in the area and it advertises only its prices and its conservative orientation to fashion merchandising, it cannot fulfill its promotional objectives.

Exhibit 12.2 illustrates the points of emphasis in different retail marketing strategies. These points of emphasis either explicitly or implicitly identify promotional objectives. In the case of the general merchandiser for instance, mass information about all of the store's merchandise as well as the store itself needs to be promoted. This has to be done in the form of the least cost and widest amount of information dissemination.

Because strategic options have already been discussed and because the promotional emphasis part of Exhibit 12.2 is rather self-explanatory, it is unnecessary to discuss each. The reader is urged to think along the lines of a well-known retail establishment and to single out the actual versus "ideal" strategic options and then evaluate that store's promotional activities.

It is not necessary for a retail establishment to pursue only one strategy. In

Exhibit 12.1
A Retail Promotion Model

STEP

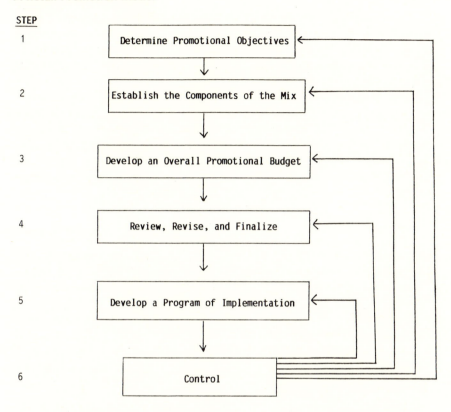

1   Determine Promotional Objectives

2   Establish the Components of the Mix

3   Develop an Overall Promotional Budget

4   Review, Revise, and Finalize

5   Develop a Program of Implementation

6   Control

fact, in most cases a combination strategy is necessary. Consider, for example, a retail establishment that is a differentiator and is at the stage of being a "fast grower." In such a case the retail store not only will be researching its differences and strengths but will also enhance these special characteristics. As a result, that store will gain further acceptance in the market segment to which it has been aiming. Thus, the two strategic objectives are likely to reinforce each other for more effective performance.

Components of the Promotional Mix

Retail and marketing promotional mix components are basically the same. However, the relative points of emphasis in retailing differ substantially from those of the marketing promotional mix. In retailing, for instance, the local nature of the business and the immediacy of advertising messages imply much heavier emphasis on local radio and local newspapers. By the same token,

Exhibit 12.2
Strategic Alternatives and Promotional Emphasis Objectives

Strategic Options	Promotional Emphasis
1. General Merchandiser	Mass information about all of the merchandise and the store.
2. Differentiator	Emphasis on surfacing differences and strengths of the store.
3. Segmenter	Emphasizing the key characteristics of the store which will satisfy the obvious needs of an identified segment.
4. Positioner	Comparative advertising to reassure capturing the position that is aimed.
5. Store-merchandise Congruence	Emphasizing the store characteristics and matching product groups to the image.
6. Beginner	High level of information dissemination to promote the store (information).
7. Fast Grower	Enhancing the store characteristics to gain stronger acceptance in view of increasing competition (persuasion).
8. Mature	Trying to maintain the successful image and the position in a changing market (reminding).
9. Declining Store - Scaling Down Revitalization Redirection	Overall decline in promotional efforts. All-out emphasis on one new feature. Renewed emphasis on features that have been somewhat neglected up to that time.
10. Specialty Store - Specialty Goods Shopping Goods Convenience Goods	Maintaining differential advantage of the store and its image by the uniqueness of its selection service and advertising.
11. Shopping Store - Specialty Goods Shopping Goods Convenience Goods	Advertising extensively the prices for even the best brands.
12. Convenience Store - Specialty Goods Shopping Goods Convenience Goods	Emphasizing the convenience and practicality of patronizing that store through widespread advertising.

because of the advance or lead time required before an ad is to be run in a magazine or on network TV (Hartley 1975), these media are relatively less desirable for the typical retail promotional mix.

Development of the retail promotional mix depends on at least seven factors:

1. Strategic objectives
2. The audience to be reached
3. The size of the trading area
4. The message or product that is going to be advertised
5. The relative cost of available media
6. The amount of lead time required before an ad is run
7. General trade practices

Strategic Objectives

As opposed to, for instance, the general merchandiser, the differentiator, segmenter, or positioner has to use selective media such as television and select magazines. If the merchandise in question is related to fashions, it becomes particularly important to use effective visual promotion such as television and some special fashion-related national or local magazines.

A speciality store that advertises primarily specialty goods will use TV or magazines for the store and newspaper or radio for the specialty goods it is promoting. In contrast, a convenience store promoting convenience products is not likely to use major mass media such as TV or magazines. It will rely heavily on its appearance and location and will use flyers and other more specialized promotional devices.

The reader should analyze the strategic options presented in Exhibit 12.2, and associate each promotional emphasis area with the specific practices of retail stores that are known to them. It becomes clear that there are some notable patterns, some of which are as follows:

1. Major discount drug stores or discount grocery stores, which are general merchandisers, mostly use newspapers and disseminate information about their merchandise in a most cost-effective manner.
2. Differentiators proceed more readily with long-lasting print media (magazines) and store appearance. They emphasize the differentiating characteristics of their store.
3. Segmenters behave basically like differentiators; however, they emphasize the differentiating characteristics of their store geared specifically to the segment to which the store is aiming. They use primarily long-lasting print media (magazines), some TV, and the store's appearance.
4. Positioners are usually engaged in comparative advertising; as a result, they rely on visuals (magazines, TV, and newspapers).
5. Store–merchandise congruence emphasizers rely heavily on the store's appearance

and on disseminating information about both the store and the merchandise. They are likely to use local print media or radio.

6. Beginning retail stores try to disseminate as much information as possible. In addition to trying to obtain public information (new items in the local newspaper), they use heavy radio and newspaper advertising as well as general store site promotion, along with direct mail.

7. Fast growers try to persuade by more long-lasting messages in local magazines, newspapers, store displays, and the store's appearance.

8. The mature establishment continues using the promotional activity that has enabled the store to reach its present position. Unlike the fast grower, it needs more immediate impact; hence, it may emphasize newspapers and radio.

9. The declining store has three alternatives: (a) if it is scaling down its activities, the major emphasis is likely to be on low-cost immediate promotion, e.g., radio, newspapers, point of purchase displays; (b) if the store is attempting to revitalize, it is almost in the same shape as the beginner and must behave similarly; and (c) if it is trying to redirect its efforts, it may be behaving like the fast grower and has to act accordingly.

10. The specialty store, regardless of the products it carries, must project the image of a specialty store. Maintaining the differential advantage of a specialty store requires at least three special arrangements: (a) Advertising in special media, prestigious magazines, special newspaper advertising on special occasions, and definitely the store's appearance; (b) if the company is national, national network TV and major magazines; and (c) if the company is very local, emphasis on its image, merchandise, and service.

11. The shopping store, regardless of the product group it emphasizes, must communicate the idea that there are gains to be made and economies to be enjoyed in this store. Thus, it has to emphasize local promotional efforts by stressing local newspapers and the radio.

12. Unless it is very large, a convenience store relies on the traffic built by the stores around it. Hence, a convenience store typically does not have the means to advertise. Unless it can get into a cooperative effort with the manufacturer who is advertising a product that the store is carrying, it can use primarily direct mail or flyers and the store atmosphere, merchandise, and service.

Audience to Be Reached

Assuming that strategic decisions have been made, that the market segments and customer profiles are known, and that promotional objectives have been decided on, we may conclude that reaching the audience implies the development of an effective media mix.

The retailer can choose from among newspapers, telephone directories, direct mail (flyers), television, magazines, outdoor billboards, and transit media found in busses or taxis. Each of these media reaches a special audience. Barry Berman and Joel R. Evans (1986) and Hoight (1976) present a detailed account of the strengths and weaknesses of each of these media. Suffice it to say here that the retailer must have a good idea about the store's market segment so that it can be reached by using the appropriate media mix. It is quite well known that the local radio stations have their own market segments (Samli 1966, 1965, 1972; Windeshausen 1977, 1980). Teenagers and senior citizens listen to different radio stations and watch different TV channels and some TV programs. Thus, the retailer must know not only the specific target markets, but also the audiences of the retail media.

Different retailers have different media mixes that are appropriate for their purposes. In order to develop an effective media mix, an intermedia selection process must take place so that different media classes are compared and analyzed and the most appropriate media mix can be developed. Here at least six critical factors come into play: (1) quintile analysis, (2) media objectives, (3) audience selectivity, (4) message tone, (5) media sense modality, and (6) geographic dispersion.

Quintile Analysis. This special market research technique indicates different socioeconomic market segments in quintiles and their media exposure (Sandage et al. 1979; Gilson and Berkman 1980).

Media Objectives. This factor deals with broadness of coverage in terms of reach or depth of the media in terms of frequency. If, for instance, the retail establishment wants to expand its market, it may emphasize reach, whereas the establishment that may be trying to penetrate a certain specified segment will emphasize frequency.

Audience Selectivity. The audience the retailer wants to reach is a significant factor in choosing one media class over another. Obviously, radio listeners and *Reader's Digest* or *Cosmopolitan* readers constitute very different groups of people. Depending on the target audience to be reached, the media classes as well as the specific medium within the media class can be selected.

Message Tone. This factor refers to the nature of the message that is going to be communicated. The message may or may not be congruent with the media. To the extent that the retail establishment is trying to project its forward-looking aspects, it should not use media which consumers may identify as conservative. In particular, the message tone may not be consistent with the editorials of a magazine or a newspaper. Similarly, the emotionality or rationale of the message calls for analyzing the media message tone carefully.

Media Sense Modality. This factor is related to the media's impact on consumer perception. The media may have a motion or video or audio effect, or a combination of the three. The retail establishment that finds motion desirable will, of course, choose TV as the medium.

Geographic Dispersion. Each medium has a different reach, which can be measured in terms of socioeconomic as well as geographic dimensions. When the retail establishment has a good idea about its target markets and trading areas, it becomes necessary to match this information against the geographic reach of the media. The best matches are the most desirable objective that leads to better media group selection.

The most important point here is that the components of the media mix are decided on by the promotional objectives. Thus, the first two steps shown in Exhibit 12.1 are highly interdependent. This interdependency is in sequential order. Without clear promotional objectives, it becomes impossible to put together an effective promotional mix.

The second most important point to remember is that every retailer has a promotional mix. This implies the presence of multiple media. Retailers use a combination of mutually reinforcing promotional forms. Studies have shown that a combination of media is better than single medium advertising (Dickson 1974).

Size of the Trading Area

The size of the trading area has a definite impact on the promotional mix. All other considerations aside, the retail establishment will need the most appropriate coverage for its trading area. To the extent that the trading area is quite widespread, radio and TV become more viable, since newspapers may not cover large geographic areas. Furthermore, in such situations outdoor advertising, namely, billboards, can become important.

The smaller the trading area, the greater the dependence on store appearance, direct mail, and outside promotional activity. The smallness of the trading area is usually related to the size of the retail establishment. Small trading area retailers are not likely to be able to afford expensive media such as TV or magazines.

The Message and the Product

There is need for basic congruence between the message and the media. As an example, take the retail firm that is establishing its credibility and is positioning itself. If the medium it uses does not possess the kind of credibility the message is trying to get across, then it cannot be used. Similarly, the retail store that is trying to establish a liberal, forward looking, special image should not advertise on TV next to or during a conservative political or semireligious TV program.

If the message needs visual effect, certain types of media (for example, radio) cannot be used. Similarly, if color is important for the message, then media such as newspapers cannot be used.

In addition to congruence between message and media, congruence between product and media is also important. Certain products such as fashion goods need visual impact; therefore, only newspapers, TV, or other print media can be utilized. Some well-known brand appliances do not need visual effect; hence, a special sale of these products can easily be advertised on the radio.

Although each case is unique and must be considered on its own merits, generalizations such as those presented here are useful to increase the decision maker's awareness of the factors relating to the promotional mix. Each retail store must find the most suitable promotional mix for itself.

Relative Cost

Cost is always one of the most important factors in making media decisions. Most advertising books deal with the measures of relative cost. The two measures are milline rate and cost per thousand (Berman and Evans 1983). All things being equal, the choice is always to use the lowest relative costs.

Amount of Lead Time

For many retail advertisements timing is very important, and usually there is little lead time to prepare the ads. The supermarket ads, for instance, appear in local newspapers one day and are expected to create traffic the next day; moreover, the sales of that week are different from those of the previous week. Thus, most grocery retailers and others who promote special sales need to use local media that do not need much lead time to prepare ads. For image-building or long-lasting impact, as well as for those types of retailers who need illustrations and color, a long lead time is necessary. Sears catalogs, advertisements in major magazines, or TV commercials all require a long lead time.

General Trade Practices

Trade practices inevitably influence the retailers' promotion mix. In most cases, retailers feel obligated to match or excel their competitors. If the competitors are advertising heavily in the local print media, retailers will often do the same. When McDonald's is engaged in massive television advertising, Burger King and Wendy's follow the same pattern.

Thus, these seven factors are instrumental in determining the promotional mix for the retail establishment. There is no research indicating the relative importance of these factors. Although they have not been prioritized here, some of them are more important than others. Until significant research findings are put to use, however, each retail establishment will have to decide on an individual basis.

MULTIATTRIBUTE PROMOTION VERSUS SINGLE-ATTRIBUTE PROMOTION

The retail store that wants to establish a far-reaching and longer lasting impression which will also manipulate the overall store image opts for a multiattribute promotional effort. A multiattribute advertising message includes more than one single message. It may indicate, for instance, that the store has totally unique sports clothing as well as formal wear. In both cases, the store excels because it carries the best brands, and this is what distinguishes it from its competitors. Under such an approach, therefore, some image building, some differential advantage establishment, and some comparative advertising are all packed into one (Lincoln and Samli 1981).

In such cases, credibility or believability becomes particularly important. If the retailers' claims are not believable and cannot be supported, then the whole promotional effort can backfire and become a liability (Lincoln and Samli 1981). Comparative advertising that lacks credibility is likely to support the leader rather than creating gains for the challenger. Single-attribute promotion, on the other hand, may be necessary for immediate sales results. Advertising a special anniversary sale, for example, may not do much in terms of manipulating the retail store image in the long run. However, it can yield immediate sales results. Thus, single-attribute advertising has a special role to play in the overall retail promotional mix.

THE PROMOTIONAL BUDGET

Once the promotional objectives are established and are interpreted in terms of a media mix, it is not difficult to put cost tags on each component of the media mix. But calculating the total the budget is established. This is a "buildup" budget rather than a "breakdown" budget. Typically, most retailers and most retailing texts follow the breakdown type of budget. Unlike the buildup budget, first a total advertising budget figure is established and then it is allocated among different media. Such a budget may be appropriate in terms of the total sum, but it does not fulfill the goals. When a total budget figure is established early in the process, the effect is almost to ignore the firm's objectives. The buildup approach is also called the task-objective or research-objective technique of establishing the advertising budget, which is preferred by most advertising scholars (Gilson and Berkman 1987, Berman and Evans 1986).

THE REVIEW PROCESS

Once the budget is tentatively decided on, a review and revision process follow. The review may, for instance, indicate that the components add up to more than what the company can afford. In such a case, the corporate promotional objectives may be questioned. Of the specific components of the preliminary budget, a few may either be eliminated or reduced. As an alternative, all items may be scaled down proportionately.

The review process takes place against the background of the seven factors used to develop the promotional mix. If there are inconsistencies in the sense that one factor indicates the use of TV alone and the other only billboards, the review process implies prioritization of the seven factors to be used in developing the promotional mix.

The review process is necessarily followed by revisions. Once all of the revisions are completed, the budget is developed and an overall check of the budget is performed. Not only overall size but also inconsistencies, competitive compatibility, and particularly appropriateness for strategic promotional objectives must be evaluated.

Two additional considerations are extremely important in the review and revision process: compatibility with store image and coordination of promotional efforts.

Compatibility with Store Image. In earlier chapters, image development and image manipulation are discussed. Promotional efforts have significant influence in developing, manipulating, and communicating the image (Hartley 1975). If the store wants to project its image as pacesetter, it cannot advertise imitating its competitors. It cannot use the media that are used mostly by the ''me too'' merchandising retailers. Similarly, it cannot allow the media to carry out a message that would make the store look like a ''pace taker'' rather than ''setter.''

Coordination of Promotional Efforts. When certain promotional efforts are to be made, in-store backup is needed. When certain merchandise is featured, sufficient quantities of that particular product or product category must be available in the store. Similarly, if the promotional campaign is going to create unusually heavy traffic, then an adequate number of salespeople, cash registers, bags, and other support materials and services are required so that the payoff from the promotional efforts can materialize fully (Hartley 1975).

IMPLEMENTATION

Unless properly implemented, no promotional plan has any significance. Therefore, implementation programs are needed which specify the temporal dimension of the advertising plans. They also single out what needs to be done and by whom.

Exhibit 12.3 illustrates the buildup process in the task objective method of developing the budget. Regardless of whether or not this budget is accepted as is, it needs to be tied into specific time dimensions. Thus, a budget and schedule are the key tools of implementation. These tools also lead to the implementation of a control mechanism.

THE CONSISTENCY THEORY

The consistency theory in retail promotion posits the existence of commercial and noncommercial retail promotional messages. The commercial messages are all part of the total promotional mix. They are planned and implemented. The noncommercial messages, however, are not part of the overall planned promotional activity. Retail establishments knowingly or unknowingly are involved in public relations activities. From buying uniforms for a junior bowling league to being honored by the city fathers as the company of the year, the company is involved in a large variety of activities and gets much recognition. Thus, the company starts developing a public-civic image.

The consistency theory maintains that, if the commercial promotion of the retail establishment is not consistent with its emerging public-civic image, most of the promotional effort is wasted. Hence, a large proportion of the promotional budget is also wasted. Ideally speaking, if the commercial promotional plans are prepared and implementation details are worked out, the emergence of a public-civic image based on noncommercial messages will yield the optimum results. The retail establishment must try to exert some degree of pressure on noncommercial communications. This can be achieved in at least two ways. First, the retail firm can manipulate certain social and civic activities just enough

Exhibit 12.3
An Illustrative Task-Objective-Based Promotional Budget for a Differentiator

Objective	Task	Cost
Gain awareness of professional women	Use 16 quarter-page ads in four separate, four successive Sunday editions of local papers. Artist's conception.	$8,000
Gain awareness of upper middle class	Four 45-second spots on local TV; heavy image symbols	$10,000
Appeal to regular good customers	Direct mail color brochures with special discounts	$7,000 $3,000
Overall image continuity	2 local newspaper and 2 magazine ads combined with improved interior and outside sign	$6,000
Special strategic seasonal advertising	Four seasonal promotional push combination of flyers. Four newspaper spreads and four promotional TV spots	$3,000 $2,000 $4,000
	TOTAL BUDGET	**$43,000**

to implant a certain type of noncommercial messages. For instance, Stix Baer and Fuller used to sponsor youth dances and organize dancing contests in St. Louis. Assuming that the company wants to establish a dynamic and youthful overall image, we may conclude that such a noncommercial promotional activity contributes significantly to the aspired image.

Second, the retail firm, by using effective marketing research, monitors its public-civic image which has been emerging through noncommercial communications. If the end result of this monitoring indicates a trend in the negative direction so that the firm is developing a social-civic image that is going to counteract its intended image, then the firm tries to manipulate not only the noncommercial but also commercial messages simultaneously.

Although the consistency theory is being utilized, and had been tested in political science and in communication areas, it has not been used in retailing. As a theory in planning retail marketing strategy, it needs to be tested. This type of research not only will test the overall theory, but will also spell out its ramifications. As such, the research will identify the specifics of how this theory can be operationalized. Hence, these research efforts will produce valuable information in the area of effective retail communication.

CONTROL

The control mechanism is based on an information system concept. This system includes a continuous collection of both primary and secondary data, statistical tools that put the data into useful form and evaluate them, and decision-oriented models that make the data useful. There are three specific steps: (1) continuous data collection, (2) statistical techniques, and (3) decision-oriented models. In controlling the promotional activity, measures of effect are essential. Although some of this activity takes place before all the promotional activity plans are implemented, much of it is done after the fact (*Business Week* 1976; *Marketing News* 1980).

In recent years, unique simulation models have been developed that can provide control not only "before" or "after," but also *during*. One such technique is GERTS (Graphic Evaluation Review Technique Simulation). Originally based on the PERT (Project Review and Evaluation Technique) process but improved and revised, GERTS enables the decision maker to simulate the whole advertising network and establish probabilities for failure or success. As the advertising activity commences and as data start coming in, the simulation is rerun. If there are significant areas of deviations from the original network, then revisions in the schedule, plans, and budgets may be initiated (Samli and Bellas 1973).

ATMOSPHERICS AS A RETAIL PROMOTIONAL TOOL

As stated by Philip Kotler (1973–1974), consumers buy the total product. The total product implies the *physical entity and plus*. The plus, among other things, includes the atmosphere of the store. Kotler maintained that in some cases, the place, more specifically the atmosphere of the place, is more influential than the product itself in the purchase decision. In fact, in some cases, the atmosphere is the primary product. From Kotler's perspective, the atmosphere implies the aesthetic factor in consumption. It communicates in a "silent language." Thus, in communicating with its markets, the retail establishment cannot ignore the silent language aspect of its communication which will appeal to the customer's perception.

Atmospherics is a particularly important tool when retail establishments are aiming at the same socioeconomic class and their merchandise-service mixes are basically the same. Bloomingdale's and Woodward and Lothrop have similar merchandise mixes. However, their respective clienteles are very loyal to these stores primarily because of their respective atmospherics. Or consider, for instance, the female apparel store that carries the same good merchandise as its immediate competitors but employs some of the town's well-known socialites on a part-time basis. They are very well dressed and have good taste in apparel,

and so they are considered the *opinion leaders* in fashion. The store offers coffee
or special tea, sometimes home-baked cake, and on special occasions some wine.
The atmosphere is elegant but very relaxed, and customers feel that the salespeople are trying their best to satisfy them. Such an atmosphere is difficult to
beat. Thus, the retail establishment must consider allocating a portion of its
promotional budget to atmospherics.

As stated earlier, the communication mix of the retail store must be consistent
within itself. However, additional consistency is needed between the store atmosphere and its communication mix. Unfortunately, research on this topic is
less than adequate. There is no information, for instance, on how much atmospherics mean in the promotional budget opposed to other elements of the mix.
What are the key elements of atmospherics? Do they vary from one type of
retailing to another? What is the relative weight of each element in atmospherics
in regards to the store's effective communication with its markets? Some of
these questions need to be explored in the near future.

SUMMARY

A six-step promotional model is presented in this chapter. These steps are:
(1) determine promotional objectives, (2) establish the components of the mix,
(3) develop an overall promotional budget, (4) review, revise, and finalize, (5)
develop a program of implementation, and (6) control. In this chapter the advertising budget is advocated to be a task-objective type. Hence, it has to follow
steps 1 and 2.

The reviewing, revising, and finalizing process follows the budgeting activity.
It is the completion of the total communication activity of the retailer with its
prospective (and/or actual) market(s). Since the completeness or comprehen-
siveness of the total program does not mean much without implementation, an
implementation plan is based on time, effort, and money. Hence, scheduling,
programming, and budgeting are all tools of implementation.

Finally, control is related to information in-flow on effectiveness. Such feedback can be used before, during, or after the advertising activity in order to
redirect it and hence to improve its effectiveness.

The consistency theory purports that the informal and noncommercial communication of retail establishments must be consistent with their formal and
commercial communication efforts.

REFERENCES

"Advertising for Small Business." *Bank of America Small Business Reporter*, 15, No.
    2 (1981).
"Attitude Share of Market Predicts Better Than Behavioral Measures." *Marketing News*,
    May 16, 1980, p. 7.
Bendell, C. "Looking at the Retail Ads." *Advertising Age* 19, January 13, 1958.

Berman, Barry, and Joel R. Evans. *Retail Management*. New York: Macmillan, 1986.

Burton, Philip Ward. *Retail Advertising for the Small Store*. New York: Prentice-Hall, 1951.

Cremin, S. "Stores Urged to Project a Style in Their Ads." *Editor and Publisher* 112, January 27, 1979.

Dickson, J. P. "Retail Media Combination Strategy." *Journal of Retailing* (Summer 1974): 61–69.

Eaton, K. "Retailers Disagree on Ad Philosophy." *Advertising Age* 51, March 17, 1980.

Edwards, Charles M., Jr., and William H. Howard. *Retail Advertising and Sales Promotion*. New York: Prentice-Hall, 1939.

Gilson, Christopher, and Harold W. Berkman. *Advertising*. New York: Random House, 1985.

Gloede, B. "Department Stores Are Coming Home to Newspapers." *Editor and Publisher* 112, December 29, 1979, p. 64.

Gore, B. "Fifty Years of Retail Advertising; Aim More Direct, Graphics Improve." *Advertising Age* 51, April 30, 1980, pp. 194–198.

Hartley, Robert F. *Retailing*. Boston: Houghton Mifflin, 1975.

Henderson, D. E. "Radio-Print Ad Mix Could Be Ideal for Retailers." *Advertising Age* 50, May 21, 1979.

Kamerzura, P. "Retailers Ask Audio-visual to Show Way to Higher Sales." *Advertising Age* 51, June 23, 1980.

Kotler, Philip. "Atmospherics as a Marketing Tool." *Journal of Retailing* (Winter 1973–1974): 48–64.

Larson, Carl M., Robert E. Weigand, and John S. Wright. *Basic Retailing*. Englewood Cliffs, N.J.: Prentice-Hall, 1982.

Levine, Harold. "Agency Head Urges Retailers to Shift Focus to Marketing." *Advertising Age* 50, October 19, 1979.

Lincoln, Douglas and A. C. Samli. "Assessing the Usefulness of Attribute Advertising." *Journal of Advertising* 3 (1981): 25–34.

Mandell, Maurice I. *Advertising*. 2nd ed. Englewood Cliffs, N.J.: Prentice-Hall, 1974.

Marquardt, Raymond A., James C. Makens, and Robert G. Roe. *Retail Management*. Hinsdale, Ill.: Dryden Press, 1975.

Mason, Joseph B., and Morris L. Mayer. *Modern Retailing*. Dallas: Business Publications, 1982.

"Measuring How Well Ads Sell." *Business Week*, September 13, 1976, pp. 104, 107–8.

Moore, Charles Thomas, and T. R. Martin. *The Extent of Retail Advertising as a Management Tool . . . Its Scope and Importance in Small Business*. University of Nevada, 1961.

"N. Y. B. B. B. Crack Down on Retailer." *Advertising Age* 50, September 24, 1979.

Radolf, A. "Retailer Seeks Better Service from Newspaper." *Editor and Publisher* 112, February 3, 1979, p. 10.

Ray, Michael L. *Advertising and Communication Management*. Englewood Cliffs, N.J.: Prentice-Hall, 1982.

"Retail Chains Overlook Co-op Pluses, Study Finds." *Advertising Age* 50 July 16, 1979, p. 14.

"Retailers Exhibit Clout in Europe." *Advertising Age* 50, July 16, 1979.

"Retailing Shifts, New Dimensions in Marketing Challenge Agencies." *Advertising Age* 29, June 30, 1958, p. 1.

Samli, A. C. "The Illusive Senior Citizen Market." *Washington Business Review* (February 1966): 31–44.

————, and Carl Bellas. "Improving New Product Planning with GERT Simulation." *California Management Review* (Summer 1973): 14–21.

————, and N. Windeshausen. "Teen-Agers as a Market." *University of Washington Business Review* (February 1965): 53–68.

Sandage, C. H., Vernon Fryburger, and Kim Rotzoll. *Advertising Theory and Practice.* Homewood, Ill.: Richard D. Irwin, 1979.

Sloan, P. "Soft Sales Continue to Befuddle Retailers." *Advertising Age* 50, July 23, 1979, p. 3.

————. "Store Boost Direct Mail, Eye Cable." *Advertising Age* 51, May 26, 1980, p. 4.

Thomas, L. "Retailers Fight for Competitive Edge." *Advertising Age* 50, September 24, 1979, p. S–12.

"Top Retailers Increase Ad Outlay by 9%." *Advertising Age* 50, October 29, 1979, p. S–1.

"Two-Minute T.V. Commercials Help Retailer Bolster Image." *Chair Store Age Executive* 54 (January 1978): 16.

Yovovich, B. G. "Retailers Wed in-Store Direct Marketing Sales." *Advertising Age* 51, January 21, 1980, p. S–26–S–28.

13 Merchandise Mix Planning Management and Control

Retail firms thrive on selling goods and services to specific customers within their trading area. In order to survive, firms must manage their merchandise mix well. Managing the merchandise mix is called merchandising, an operation that is composed of a set of activities related to product assortment decisions (Markin 1971). Included in this definition are at least three components: buying, planning, and control. Buying involves acquiring the necessary merchandise; planning involves developing a balanced assortment of merchandise offering; and control procedures are developed and used to facilitate the whole process. This chapter discusses these three components as they relate to merchandise mix management. Much planning goes into the buying activity, for it is also an important function in itself. The discussion is divided into three parts: (1) the buying function; (2) planning for buying as well as overall merchandise planning for depth, width, breadth, and consistency in the overall stocks of the retail establishment; and (3) the control function which, as discussed here and elsewhere in this book, implies feedback and corrective action regarding the merchandise mix.

BUYING: THE OTHER LIFE BLOOD OF RETAILING

Traffic (and therefore location) is customarily said to be the life blood of retailing. Indeed, without traffic, a retailer cannot survive, but all the same there must be something to sell to that traffic. Having appropriate goods and services to sell is a function of effective buying. Thus, here the buying function is considered to be the other life blood of retailing. Without appropriate goods and services to sell, the retail establishment loses its reason for existence. In order to be effective in buying, first the critical characteristics of buying must be explored, and then the skills of the buyers must be examined. There are at least four objectives in managing a merchandise mix effectively: (1) providing a highly desirable merchandise mix, (2) adjusting the mix to changing consumer needs, (3) maintaining an internal consistency, and (4) taking into consideration the external variables.

Providing a Highly Desirable Merchandise Mix. This objective is the main given in the overall merchandise management. The *raison d'être* of a retail establishment is to provide a highly desirable merchandise mix. As noted earlier, without such a mix, the retail store cannot survive. The high degree of desirability implies a number of features:

1. It must be different from those of the competitors; otherwise, the retail firm cannot establish a differential advantage leading to differential congruence.

2. Having a different merchandise mix is only partially sufficient. That particular mix must be appropriate for the market segment to which the retail firm is aiming. In fact, this appropriateness is one of the most important causes of the congruence between the customer's self-image and the perceived store image by the same customer. This congruence leads to customer satisfaction and subsequently to customer loyalty.

3. Not only should the merchandise mix be different and appropriate, but it must also have features observed in terms of five continuums: depth, width, breadth, consistency, and flexibility (Berman and Evans 1986; Mason and Mayer 1987; Lusch 1982).

> Depth: refers to the number of brands and styles within a particular generic class of product. A drug outlet carrying a candy selection of 10 to 15 types of candy bars has a relatively ''shallow'' assortment as compared to the store with a relatively ''deep'' assortment of 40 to 50 types.
>
> Width: refers to the number of different generic classes of products which a store may carry. For example, a store selling only boats has a ''narrow'' line as opposed to a retail firm carrying boats, hunting equipment, golfing equipment, sporting footwear, and so on. The second store is carrying ''wider'' lines.
>
> Breadth: refers to the number of units in each brand and style within given generic classes of products. The store that carries 10 each of the different types of candy bars has more breadth than the one with only 4 of each.
>
> Consistency: refers to the degree to which the different types of products that comprise the merchandise assortment are related. Merchandise assortments are highly consistent when all merchandise is closely related in use, value, appeal, and perceived brand images (Markin, 1971).
>
> Flexibility: refers to the ability to take advantage of good merchandise buys (distress or fire sale, special lots, remnants, etc.) by a department or a store regardless of the merchandise that may be found.

These five merchandise mix continuums are not value judgments in the sense that there is only one way of managing merchandise. Different options are available, and some options are more appropriate for specific types of retail establishments. Even the consistency versus inconsistency continuum does not imply a good or bad merchandising policy as much as just identifying the retailer's options.

Within the given overall retail marketing strategies, any two of these continuums account for a merchandise mix policy. There are at least six such policies:

1. Deep and narrow assortments. They reflect specialty store philosophy. A specialty store must have numerous brands and styles of the specialty area it represents.

2. Deep and wide assortments. They suggest the general store merchandising philosophy which features good selections of diverse product lines.

3. Shallow and narrow assortments. They follow the concept of the convenience stores, such as Hop-Ins or Seven Elevens which sell only frequently needed lines with little selection or depth in any given line.

4. Shallow and wide assortments. They reflect the five-and-dime type of store philosophy. Discount stores typically carry a few brands and styles of a large variety of generic product classes.

5. Consistent assortments. They imply that within a department or among departments as well as within the store as a whole, quality, class, and selection of merchandise are consistent. There are no extremely good and extremely bad product lines and/or departments. In other words they are all compatible.

6. Flexible assortments. They typify any type of bargain basement or bargain type of store such as army surplus stores. Furthermore, they typify decentralized buying such as is displayed by Kroger stores. These stores have very good produce departments that buy the best a community offers.

The retail marketing strategies discussed earlier in this book are partially implemented by these merchandise mix policies. This implementation process takes very specific forms so that the policies can partially fulfill a company's goals via its properly implemented retailing strategies. Certainly, Macy's cannot have a shallow and narrow assortment when it is trying to differentiate itself as the merchandise haven for the upper-middle-class shopper. Similarly, Tiffany's must have a deep and narrow assortment reflecting the specialty store characteristics and an effective philosophy of segmentation.

Adjusting the Mix to Changing Consumer Needs. This second objective seeks to develop the ability to reflect changes taking place in the market. This must be done at an early stage in the game.

Exhibit 13.1 illustrates some of the consumer trends and commensurate retailing activities of the past two decades or so. The future clearly illustrates how retailers must understand the specific trend and act accordingly. Retailers who are too old-fashioned to pay attention to such trends or who cannot understand them are practically doomed. In an era of leisure and informality, a formal wear store will have to carefully ascertain whether the market is large enough for it to survive. Otherwise, it must take drastic measures such as totally changing its product lines and perhaps becoming a sportswear store.

How can retailers be sure that they are detecting the trends and making a

Exhibit 13.1
Some Key Consumer Trends and Their Impact on Retailing

Consumer/trends	Impact on Retailing
Time consciousness	Need for efficient products and more efficient store procedures to get the customers in and out quickly.
Less formal	More room for casual products in the inventory, e.g., more sport goods than formal wear.
Leisure oriented	More emphasis on leisure-related products, e.g., hobbies, sports, and good educational products.
Health care	More emphasis on sports and exercise-related products, health foods, other related products.
More do it yourself	Need for household type of tools and other supplies.
More personal appearance consciousness	Personal grooming, apparel, and other related products and services.

proper attempt to remain abreast of changes in the market? Of course, keeping up with the market here implies adjusting the merchandise mix to the changing needs. This objective can be fulfilled through effective feedback and control functions, which are discussed elsewhere in this book. However, a brief discussion is presented here to reinforce the concept of keeping abreast of the market in regard to the merchandise mix. Maintaining up-to-date knowledge of the market is accomplished by merchandise mix preplanning analyses as seen in Exhibit 13.2.

MERCHANDISE MIX PREPLANNING

In developing an appropriate merchandise mix, changes in the market must be assessed and be *fed forward*. This is called preplanning for the merchandise mix. As seen in Exhibit 13.2, before the following season's (or year's) merchandise mix is planned, two items of information are needed: assessment of the past year's merchandise mixes and evaluation of the forces affecting the market. Merchandise mixes of past years show some subtle and obvious changes. It is necessary to examine the fast moving, slow moving, more popular, and less popular items and to ascertain the strengths and weaknesses of recent merchandise mixes.

Similarly, the retailer must know the growth components and declining com-

Exhibit 13.2
Merchandise Mix Preplanning Analyses

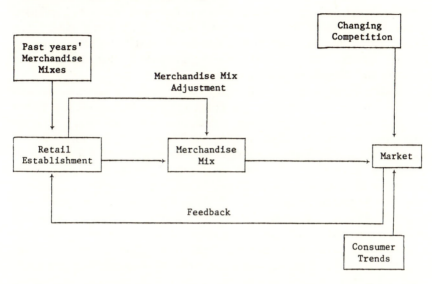

ponents of the merchandise mix. If, for instance, a bookstore's most noticeable growth has been in the area of fantasy-fiction and greatest decline in cookbooks and related topics, the retailer must decide to allocate more space and resources to carry more and better fantasy-fiction selections. The resources may be reallocated from the cookbooks section to this new growth area.

As seen in Exhibit 13.2, two groups of factors influence the market. Consumer trends and changing competition have already been discussed. When the trends are surfacing, the retailer must go along with them, for resisting the tide in retailing is suicidal. Let us now return to our earlier example. If people are becoming more casual, the formal wear store cannot wait and see if this trend is only a passing fancy. It must change along with consumer preferences. However, at least one more important factor must be taken into consideration within the context of the market. This factor is competition. Any change in competition and the changing competitive position of other retailers imply some necessary changes in the store's merchandise mix. If, for instance, a new competitor appears to be capturing the women's apparel market because the town's women are predominantly professionals and this new store has the most complete line of professional women's outfits, existing retail stores must make adjustments in their merchandise mixes. They may try to be as good or better, or may abandon this line completely.

By establishing the directions in which the merchandise mix is to be adjusted on the basis of deviations from the past, changing trends, and changing competition, merchandise mix planning is effectively facilitated. One of the most critical points in Exhibit 13.2 is where the retail establishment fits into the total picture. As preplanning for the coming year's merchandise mix is considered, the actual image and expected image changes of the store need to be considered so that the merchandise mix can be adjusted accordingly. If a retail apparel shop considers changing its image from "formal, stuffy and expensive" to more "casual, attractive and very good values for the money," then it must plan its inventory mix changes with extreme care.

Adjusting the merchandise mix to changes and trends in the market is extremely important for the retail firm's survival. However, those retail establishments that can play an active role in generating these changes and trends are assured better odds for survival as well as greater prospects for prosperity. In other words, in adjusting the merchandise mix, the retailer can be a *leader* or a *follower*. To the extent that the retailer is the leader and, hence, initiates the changes in the adjustment process, the retail establishment will not only survive but will also prosper more than an average store will. Being a pacesetter is not an easy task. It needs first to be established as an objective, and the retail marketing strategy must be developed around such an objective.

Maintaining an Internal Consistency. Throughout this book, differential congruence has been dealt with as the central theme of retail marketing strategy. In achieving and maintaining this congruence, the retailer must pay particular attention to the merchandise mix. The merchandise mix is one of the retailer's most significant extrinsic cues for developing an image which in turn will be instrumental in achieving the desired differential congruence.

Once again it must be reiterated that the effectiveness of the extrinsic cues is subject primarily to the internal consistency that the retail store achieves between its merchandise mix and other variables. If, for instance, the retail store is handling the most up-to-date fashion lines, but its salespeople are all middle aged and not very well dressed, the store's interior is extremely conservative, and customer services such as credit, merchandise adjustment, or liberal return policy are not appropriately administered, then the retail store does not have the internal consistency essential to achieving the desired differential congruence. The retail store is therefore sending conflicting cues to the market. Similar and perhaps more alarming situations can occur if a store's departments lack internal consistency. While one department may be known for its good values, high prices, and fashionable merchandise, another may develop a reputation for poor quality and cheap merchandise. Again, the retail store is sending conflicting cues to the market and hurting its chances of developing a synergistic effect achieved through a uniform image.

Taking into Consideration the External Variables. In achieving differential congruence, as retailers send out extrinsic cues through their merchandise mix, they must be cognizant of external variables and the store's efforts to develop an image. If, for example, in the short run a store is still making money by selling formal attire but in the long run the society tends to be more casual, then

Exhibit 13.3
A Partial List of External Variables

Factor	Merchandise Mix Adjustment
Increasing Competition	Place more emphasis on product differentiation leading to different congruence.
Worsening Economic Conditions	Streamline the merchandise mix. Change merchandise mix composition in terms of having more economical and lower priced products.
Changing Import Restrictions	Reassess the imported and importable components of the overall merchandise mix.
Major Population Movements in or out of the trading area (excessive outshopping)	Readjust the merchandise mix. Provide more attractive quality and variety. Differentiate to make your store more attractive. Consider relocation.

the store must start diversifying its merchandise mix so that the "formal" image will in time be relaxed (May 1974).

The retail establishment must, as was discussed earlier, understand external trends and changing needs. Furthermore, it must assess each of the trends and needs as they influence the store's well-being. In addition to the changing consumer needs discussed earlier, the retailer must be aware of at least four external variables and react to them swiftly. Ignoring these changes is especially detrimental to small retailers who always live dangerously anyway. These four variables are (1) increasing competition, (2) worsening economic conditions, (3) changing import restrictions—in other words increasing international competition, and (4) major population movements. These variables as well as possible merchandise mix adjustment policies are depicted in Exhibit 13.3.

BUYING THE PROPER MERCHANDISE MIX

Once the features of an attractive and adequate merchandise mix are determined, they must be explored from the perspective of differential congruence objectives and implementation. Two groups of considerations are particularly important: store-related aspects of buying and buyer-related aspects of buying (Exhibit 13.4)

Exhibit 13.4 begins where Exhibit 13.2 left off. In buying, perhaps the most important consideration is the continuity (if that is what is needed) in the store

Exhibit 13.4
Merchandise Mix Buying Factors

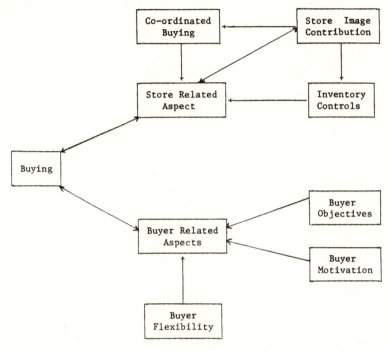

image or revision of this image according to the feedback and control functions. Even though the buying function in retailing is a personal creative expression, this display of creativity cannot be moving in a direction different from those efforts trying to build up the desired differential congruence.

As seen in Exhibit 13.4, there are three critical store-related aspects of buying. First is the store image contribution and continuation. As mentioned earlier, the merchandise mix is an important contributor to the store image. Hence, as the merchandise mix is planned and replenished, the consistency with the desired store image must be evaluated and the actual contribution to the overall store image must be assessed periodically.

The second store-related factor is inventory controls. There are various ways of controlling inventory, some of which are discussed in this chapter. Inventory must be controlled within a given context. Cost constraints, time limits, and, above all, store image goals are among these constraints. Inventory feedback is extremely important in fulfilling the buying function. Consider, for instance, the following:

XYZ store is a very elegant and rather expensive men's clothing store. Inventory controls indicated a shortage in their lower price line merchandise. This was just before Christmas season. The buyer found a bargain lot from a local K-Mart which was going out of business. Although it did not fit XYZ's image and was larger than the store's needs, the buyer purchased the lot. The company's open to buy budget was spent, and the newly acquired lot took up large space in the store. The company lost large sums because it was not ready for the Christmas season, and the newly acquired merchandise altered the store's image.

As can be seen, the buying function must be within budgetary and image constraints.

The third factor is coordinated buying. Assume, for instance, that the XYZ store discussed above has three separate buyers. These buyers have a completely different perception of XYZ's image. While one of them is buying bargain merchandise, the second one is buying only the most expensive formal wear and the third buyer feels that XYZ's lines should be competing with K-Mart lines. Unless the buying function is coordinated among the three buyers and they understand the store's present image and its image goals, XYZ cannot expect to be able to establish a differential advantage and a differential congruence.

BUYER-RELATED ASPECTS OF MERCHANDISE MIX

Buyer-related aspects of merchandise mix acquisition are based on three factors: buyer flexibility, buyer motivation, and buyer objectives.

Buyer Flexibility

All buyers must be flexible as to the sources, quality, and styles of merchandise. In retailing, the buyer is the person who pursues the fine art and science of buying the merchandise that will fulfill the store's objectives. It is termed the fine art of buying because good merchandise has many aesthetic features. Color, style, and fashion are some of the names attached to these aesthetic features. Not only must the buyer have good taste, but also the taste must reflect the taste of the store's customers. Furthermore, if the store employs multiple buyers, their tastes must not be too different from each other; otherwise, it would be almost impossible for the store to manipulate or to maintain a consistent image.

The scientific aspect of buying is reflected in the knowledge and use of certain merchandise planning tools such as stock lists, markups, markdowns, expense control factors, contribution returns, stock turnover analyses, return on merchandise investment and capital turnover, Gross Margin Return Per Dollar Cost of Inventory (GMROI) (Sweeney 1973; McGinnis et al. 1984), weighting technique, open-to-buyer computations, and others. These tools are discussed later in this chapter.

Exhibit 13.5
Some Key Buyer Motivation Factors

Factor	Brief Description
High morale	Favorable balance of work life and private life. Positive work conditions and market conditions, e.g. good company name, good merchandise to work with, good vendors to deal with.
Reasonable remuneration	A reasonable income with some bonus and other incentives. Knowing that the company takes care of the individual.
Interaction with management	Good working relationships with immediate supervisor and with other buyers. Good communication with department managers.
Seeing the results of efforts	Being able to work with department managers in terms of providing inputs as to the department's overall merchandise mix. Knowing the results of selling efforts.
Positive feedback	The manager's, other buyers and sales people's careful approach to make changes (if necessary) or providing praise (if and when possible).
Adequate training	The buyer's training in terms of acquiring necessary skills such as communication skills and ability to negotiate.
Proper information for buyers	Information for buyers as to how the market is doing, how the most recent merchandise lot purchased by the buyer has performed and existing options as to sources of merchandise.

Buyer Motivation

Buyer motivation is extremely important in acquiring the most desirable merchandise mix. Motivating buyers is not a simple task. Exhibit 13.5 illustrates six motivation factors for buyers. The retail manager must make sure that these factors are all present and do not counteract each other. Depending on the type of retail establishment, there may be more or fewer factors. However, the important point is that if the buyer is not properly motivated, his or her resultant deficient performance will be reflected in all phases of the retail function. If, for instance, the retail establishment is suffering from a questionable image and the buyer is painfully aware of this flaw, it is difficult for the buyer to be motivated.

Similarly, if the buyer is not paid adequately, he or she may be more concerned with trying to make ends meet than with turning in a good performance. Having a boss who is not understanding or not being in touch with other buyers and department managers is likely to be devastating to the buyer's morale.

Seeing the results of efforts in terms of the reactions of both management and store personnel is likely to be a positive motivator for buyers. Seeing the merchandise which they purchased displayed and promoted properly or seeing customers' positive reaction to this merchandise because it is properly displayed and sold effectively is a very important signal of immediate success.

If the manager of a retail establishment and/or departmental managers provide positive reinforcements for buyers, such as saying that the new merchandise lots are "very good," "well liked," or "very promising," the results are likely to be a very high level of motivation for buyers.

Like other professionals in retailing and elsewhere, buyers must be well trained and must be updated periodically. They also need to possess certain critical skills such as ability to communicate with the key persons in the vendors' places of business or with departmental managers as well as salespeople. Similarly, the ability to negotiate and to establish strong relationships with people is extremely important for the success of buyers and hence for their motivation.

Finally, a well-informed buyer is a highly motivated buyer. Specific information imparted by the retail establishment will motivate the buyer. Among other bits of information, the condition of the market, the behavior of competitors, and new and changing sources of merchandise are all essential ingredients in the buyer's satisfactory performance.

Buyer Objectives

A close relationship exists between buyer motivation and buyer objectives. As individual professionals buyers have some clear-cut objectives. They must understand that their personal objectives have a significant impact on the well-being of the retail establishment.

Congruence between the buyer's self-image and store image has an interesting twist in this context. Buyers reflect their art and science through their performance. This performance is consistent with the buyer's objectives. If the buyer has clear-cut professional objectives such as seeing that his or her institution achieves greater recognition or obtains a greater return on investment, then the buyer has higher probabilities of being successful. In this case success implies well-being for both the buyer and the retail store. Thus, at least in one sense, the retail store's well-being is a direct function of the buyer's degree of professionalism.

To the extent that the buyer is a mature professional, he or she is properly motivated and has mature personal objectives of advancement and success. Exhibit 13.6 illustrates the buyer's degree of professionalism in his or her objectives and the store's success.

Exhibit 13.6
Buyer's Professionalism and Store's Success

Since buyer motivation and objectives are so important to the well-being of the retail store and both motivation and objectives are partially a function of the buyer's degree of professionalism, the retail establishment must make a special effort to play an important role in the buyer's professional maturation process. The retail organization must see that its buyers go through periodic short courses and special programs to become better professionals. Much research is needed to determine the factors that influence the professionalization process of buyers.

In this professionalization process the special skills important for the buyers must be given special attention. Among these special skills are (1) communication skills, (2) the art of negotiation, (3) an understanding of the importance of acquiring knowledge for alternatives, (4) an ability to prioritize the store needs and alternative merchandise sources and categories, (5) an understanding of trends, styles, and fashions, and (6) merchandise knowledge. All are important training areas for successful buyers, but discussion of these areas is not within the scope of this chapter. The reader can develop his or her programs for a given store or a research situation according to the particular situation involved.

PLANNING THE MERCHANDISE MIX

As discussed earlier in this chapter, development of a successful merchandise mix is related to effective buying, planning, and control. After discussing effective buying, this section deals with merchandise mix planning, an internal process that deals with the quantities and mixture of the total merchandise within given periods of time for given sums of money.

Retail goals, retail strategies, and merchandise policies are all established at this point. Implementation of all concepts is largely a function of a successfully maintained effective merchandise mix. This hierarchical order is illustrated in Exhibit 13.7. (Here the reader must review the first chapter.) In this section the tools of merchandise planning are discussed. Certainly, the effectiveness of these tools and rigorous use of them are extremely important for the retail establishment to fulfill its goals. Three special merchandise lists are used in planning the merchandise mix: basic stock lists, model stock lists, and never-out lists.

Basic stock lists include the items that have a stable sales pattern. Because these patterns are often predictable, these lists are very specific and detailed.

Model stock lists are constructed primarily for certain shopping goods and fashion merchandise. Because their sales are not as predictable as the stable

Exhibit 13.7
Hierarchical Order of Retail Goal Implementation

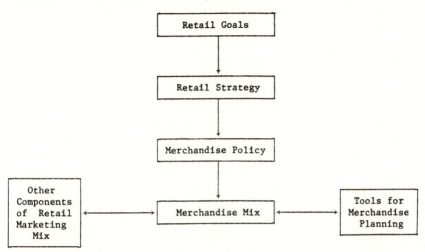

products, model stock lists are not nearly as detailed as basic stock lists. They are merely skeletons indicating the size, price, quality, and color groups rather than the specific products.

Never-out lists deal with products the store must keep on hand at all times. These products either are the core of the store's product line, or at least partially gave the retail establishment its image (Hartley 1975). Customers may equate the retail establishment with these products, and if the store is out of these products it may create a credibility gap.

Based on these lists and a great deal of additional information, a general merchandise plan can be prepared. This additional information is in the form of sales, end of the month inventory, reductions, beginning of the month inventory, and open-to-buy.[1] Typically, the average merchandise plan covers a six-month period. By constructing such a plan, a merchant can physically see relationships and associations among various product categories and other variables (Golden and Zimmerman 1980).

Merchandise plans are formulated by using six steps (Berman and Evans 1986): (1) selection of control units, (2) sales forecasts, (3) inventory level planning, (4) reduction planning, (5) planning purchases, and (6) planning profit margins. Of these the first five are pertinent here and are discussed briefly.

Control units can be selected by using department-wide classifications such as jewelry and sports goods in a department store. In addition, not only department-wide classifications but also within-department classifications can be used. The jewelry department may feature fashion jewelry, gold jewelry, dia-

---

[1] The reader is referred to any basic retailing test for a detailed discussion of these terms. Only one of these, open-to-buy, is discussed in this chapter.

monds and other valuable stones, watches, and the like. As opposed to departments in smaller stores, standard merchandise classifications may be used as
control units. Every retail establishment has its own merchandise classification.
However, for typical retail stores some commonly accepted merchandise classifications may be considered standard. At no time should a retail establishment
rely solely on its own internal classifications. Even small retail establishments
should seek information from outside, for example, other data classification and
trade association data. The national Retail Merchants Association provides a
standard merchandise classification for all types of retail operations.

Sales forecasts, as discussed in an earlier chapter, are necessary in preparing
a general merchandise plan. There are many different forecasting techniques.
Without getting into the discussion of various techniques, we can state that the
retailer has to look at three separate groups of indicators. First, external factors
such as changing personal income in the trading area or changing population of
the trading area may be utilized. Second, internal factors such as changing total
sales in dollars or units must be considered. Finally, the seasonality factor must
be considered. Seasonality is more important for some retail businesses than for
others. Thus,

$$S = f(X, Y, Z)$$

where

S = Sales volume.
X = external factors.
Y = internal factors.
Z = seasonal variations.

This formula implies that the store's sales volume is a function of external
factors, internal factors, and seasonal variations. Individual retailers have their
own sales volumes which interact differently with these variables. It is of the
utmost importance that they identify these relationships and use them for predicting in the future.

Similarly, the retailer can estimate future sales by analyzing past trends and
future growth. However, such forecasts must be revised and further adjusted on
the basis of subjective evaluations and expected changes. The retail establishment, for instance, may have experienced the situation displayed in Exhibit 13.8.
The illustration includes only a few critical product lines. Forecasts are based
on an expected 8-percent growth in the economy combined with the average
growth each product has experienced. However, they are further adjusted on the
basis of subjective criteria. Since overcoat sales have been shrinking, plans were
made to maintain the inventory at the same level. Suits are scaled downward

Exhibit 13.8
A Clothing Store Example[a]

Key Product Lines (Partial)	Five Years Average Sales Quarterly	Average Increase or Decrease %	Expected Growth in The Local Economy	Additional Subjective Adjustments
Overcoats	30,000	-2.0	32,400	30,000
Suits	50,000	3.0	55,500	53,000
Sport Jackets	35,000	5.0	45,000	48,000
Slacks	25,000	7.0	28,750	30,000
Sweaters	10,000	0.0	10,800	10,000

[a]Based on an estimated 8 percent growth adjusted to past experiences.

because of increased local competition. Sport jackets and slacks have shown particularly noticeable increases. Therefore, the forecasts are adjusted upward, and sweaters are expected to maintain their sales level in this store.

Inventory level planning is an essential component of merchandise plans. If a retail store does not have adequate stocks, it loses; however, if it is overstocked, it also loses. Hence, any retailer who can develop a system to plan purchases on time and in adequate quantities is likely to be ahead of the competition and to be more profitable than average.

In planning the inventory, three concepts are important: (1) average monthly stock, which implies that portion of the total inventory plan expected to be on hand; (2) Average monthly sales, based on actual sales data; and (3) planned monthly sales. These latter are derived from forecasts. Planned inventory is calculated on the basis of planned monthly sales and basic stock. The concept can be illustrated as follows:

$$PI = PMS + BS$$
$$BS = AMS - AMS_a$$

Therefore

$$PI = PMS + (AMS_t - AMS_a)$$

where

PI = Planned inventories.
PMS = Planned monthly sales.
BS = Basic stock.
AMS_t = Average monthly stock.
AMS_a = Average monthly sales.

Clearly, all retailers need a great deal of sophistication to develop effective inventory plans. They must have on hand carefully developed analyses of the average monthly stock and average monthly sales. Furthermore, they must have developed reasonable forecasts from which planned monthly sales can be derived. Despite the rich literature available, small retail firms are likely to approach these issues in a relatively pragmatic manner. Further research is needed to develop these concepts for the particular use of small retail firms or for formulation of similar concepts for easy planning, again, on the part of the small retail establishment.

Reduction planning is discussed in Chapter 14 in the section on markdowns. Suffice it to say here that some reduction in retailing is always necessary. Every retailer must use variable markdowns for effective marketing and particularly for effective promotion. Thus, most retailers not only use reductions but also even plan them.

Another type of reduction is planned reduction in the planned inventories. If the firm can develop logistics sophistication which will help reduce inventories without losing sales, then the retail establishments plan such reductions not for promotional purposes but for financial efficiency.

A third type of reduction is one that is imposed on the retailer. This form of reduction is shoplifting. It has been estimated that shoplifting accounts for 30 percent of stock shortages (Rothman 1980). Discussing this aspect of "merchandise reduction" is not within the scope of this book; the reader is therefore referred to standard retailing textbooks.

Planning purchases is a continuation of the four points discussed in this section. In addition to planned sales and planned inventories, planned reductions must also be calculated. Thus, planned sales can be illustrated as follows:

$$PP = AMS_t + PMS + PMR$$

where

PP = Planned purchases.
AMS_t = Average monthly stock.
PMR = Planned monthly reductions.
PMS = Planned monthly sales.

Perhaps one of the most important concepts related to purchase plans is open-to-buy (OTB). This concept depicts the difference between planned purchases and actual purchase commitments made by a buyer during the month. It is important that each buyer has some degree of flexibility by commending reasonable sums of OTB. The buyer will not only maintain a healthy dose of flexibility in terms of taking advantage of special opportunities, but will also feel more involved in the well-being of the retail store and therefore, be highly motivated.

ECONOMIC CONSTRAINTS

As plans for purchase are developed, some criteria must be established in reordering the merchandise that has been sold. Certain economic constraints must be considered in reordering. Retailers likes to order in large quantities because it enables them to reduce the cost of reordering and capitalizing on quantity discounts. On the other hand, ordering in small quantities will reduce the excessive costs of carrying large inventories. These two key constraints are brought forth and minimized by the concept of economic order quantity (EOQ) which can be illustrated by the following formula (Berman and Evans 1983).

$$EOQ = \frac{2DS}{PC}$$

where

EOQ = Economic order quantity in units.

D = Annual demand in units.

S = Costs to place an order.

P = Percentage of annual carrying cost to unit cost.

C = Unit cost of an item.

Such a formula may facilitate attempts to optimize the buying efforts by minimizing overstocking and understocking episodes. As estimated demand and costs change, EOQ is revised periodically.

MERCHANDISE CONTROLS

Most aspects of planning explored in this chapter also provide criteria for controls. Each time a financial criterion such as planned monthly sales or a quantitative criterion such as a model stock plan is discussed for planning purposes, control criteria are also established. This is due to the fact that planning criteria set forth certain limits, and control is comparing the difference between the planned and the actual. Thus, whereas model stock lists, basic stock lists, and never-out lists provide unit control criteria, the five-step merchandise mix planning process discussed in this chapter provides financial control criteria. Exhibit 13.9 illustrates the merchandise control process.

If, for instance, the retail establishment has been cultivating the image of an elegant but medium-priced apparel specialty shop, and research shows that the market views the present merchandise as too high class and extremely expensive, the retail establishment may be forced to provide a larger space in the model stock plan for lower priced products. The purchase plan will be adjusted accordingly, and more purchases reductions will be planned for these products.

Exhibit 13.9
Merchandise Control Process

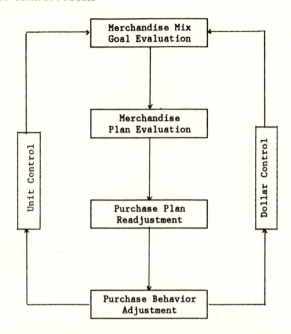

Finally, in order to obtain these products, the buyers may not only have to change vendors but may also have to change their behavior in that the new group of vendors may respond to different interaction patterns. For example, the sellers of very expensive merchandise may have somewhat of a "snob" behavior and the retail buyer may not treat them as peers. However, the sellers of more modest merchandise lines may expect to be treated as peers.

THE ROLE OF BRANDS

All products have a name and some type of identity called brand. In retailing, brands play varying roles. Retailers can, therefore, utilize brands in different ways in their constant attempt to achieve and maintain a state of differential congruence. In order to assess the different possibilities open to retailers in terms of their use of brands, we must understand the types of brands and their possible use. Three types of brands are distinguished in the marketing literature: national brands, private brands, and generic products.

From the retailer's perspective, national brands are manufacturers' brands. They carry a national and uniform identity in that they are known throughout the country and consumers have a reasonably uniform image of these products, even though they may be located in different corners of the country. All the Ford products are quite well known throughout the United States. Canon cameras or Anacin are similarly well known. National brands carry themselves. They are promoted by the manufacturer, and retailers can see them rather easily. Although they can promote the retailer's overall business, for the average retailer the profit margin for national brands is lower than that for other private brands, and sometimes certain strings are attached in promoting or simply carrying the product in a retail store. The retailer may be required to place the merchandise in a specific way or display the merchandise according to certain specifications, such as preparing special displays, arranging gondolas, or using other types of point-of-purchase promotion techniques.

Private brands are either wholesalers' or retailers' brands. In retailing, the use of private brands can be a major part of strategic efforts to establish differential congruence and hence to enjoy a competitive edge in the marketplace.

Retailers have many reasons to develop a private brand line, notably:

1. The retailer may already have a large captive audience. When Sears entered the automotive market with Allstate lines, it was enjoying the recognition and loyalty of large markets.

2. There may be certain product innovations that do not exist at the present time. Curtis Mathis appliances and particularly the warranty program that accompanies them provide a slightly better quality and customer assurance than those that exist in the market.

3. Having a private brand line cuts costs. Perhaps because the retailer has a very efficient distribution and delivery system or perhaps because the retailer can promote the product very effectively, it may be reasonable to use its own private brands.

4. There may be certain obvious gaps in the market between the best and second best auto tires, thereby justifying K-Mart to enter the market and position its tire lines at that level. These reasons and perhaps some others are not mutually exclusive. They may all exist simultaneously and, therefore, justify the use of private brands.

In addition to the uniqueness of a private brand that can improve the retailer's competitive edge, retailers can offer products at cheaper prices. It has been estimated that private brands are about 15 percent cheaper than national brands.

A third situation, which is not strictly generic but has the same type of retailing impact, is the situation in which the brand does not play any role at all in the sale of the product. When the tourists in Waikiki, Hawaii pass by ABC discount convenience stores, they do not care much about the brand of the T-shirts or Sushi's. Frequently, many convenience products are not pulled by their brand name as much as by the location and characteristics of retail establishments. Thus, in establishing a differential congruence and a competitive edge, the retail store may be using product-pull or store-image-pull as alternatives.

Finally, generic products imply that there is no brand or that the brand does not play a role in the sale of the product. Some products are brand ineffective, particularly if not having a brand means a lower price. During the stagflation of the late 1970s and early 1980s many no-brand products emerged. A simple white label on the container said "SOUP" or "PEANUT BUTTER." In addition to

Exhibit 13.10
Product Image Versus Store Image

	High Product-Image-Pull Low	
High Store Image Pull	Ideal	Emphasis on Store Image Management
Low	Emphasis on Product provides a boost for the store	Rethink Avoid Divest
	High Low	Low

this kind of generic concept, there is the one that applies to a widely known product. For example, if one asks for ''generic'' aspirin rather than Bayer aspirin, the cost is substantially cheaper. In either case of generic examples, these products are 10 to 15 percent cheaper than private brand products. Generic products tend to be quite popular when the economy is in a recession; they are not quite as popular in good economic times.

STORE-IMAGE-PULL VERSUS PRODUCT-PULL

Although store image is partially determined by the product mix, many more dimensions are involved. This section explores the interrelationship between the store image and product mix as two critical strategic tools. Consider the following two situations.

ABC discount stores which are part of a large chain of convenience stores catering almost exclusively to tourists in Honolulu, Hawaii. ABC stores decide to attract more customers and upgrade their image by carrying a sporty line of Calvin Klein's. Since they are a discount store they decide to sell the line below the manufacturers' suggested price.

Neiman-Marcus Co. decides to boost its men's wear sales by carrying a large line of Fruit-of-the-Loom men's underwear.

In both cases, there is a poor match between store image and product image. The ABC discount stores do not likely enhance their image by carrying just one prestige line. One the contrary, the chances are that they will be ''trading down'' the Calvin Klein name.

Similarly, the Neiman-Marcus store name and image carry much more of an ''elite'' appeal than the Fruit-of-the-Loom brand implies. Exhibit 13.10 illustrates the alternatives for retailers in using product image and store image as pivotal tools for their strategic plans.

The ideal situation is depicted by the upper-left-hand quadrant. Here the Calvin

Klein line may have found a strong home in Neiman-Marcus. The two may be complementing each other and be taking the store's competitive edge to a higher plateau.

In certain situations store-image-pull may not be very strong, and so products with substantial pull may be appropriate. A small middle-class chain of department stores may announce, for instance, that they carry exclusively the Estee Lauder line. This situation is illustrated in the lower left quadrant of Exhibit 13.10

A third situation is depicted in the upper-right-hand quadrant. Here the store has a strong image. It can use products without strong brand image and can push such products. In addition, in this case the store's use of its private brands is quite desirable. A specialty store with a strong image can have many convenience products treated as specialty goods. Thus, a manufacturer who has numerous products but has weak or no brand image can be quite successful if these products are carried by a number of specialty stores with strong store images. In such situations, to emphasize or to reinforce the store image is a stronger retail strategy than trying to find new products with strong images. Much of the time Neiman-Marcus carries products with quite nondescript or unknown brands. However, customers rely on the store's name and reputation rather than on the brand itself. In the fourth situation in Exhibit 13.10, neither the store nor the product has any pull. In such a situation, people will buy a product from a store, but they are hardly familiar with the store nor do they know anything about a product. As long as enough people patronize the store and buy some products, the store can survive. Many small gift shops or tourist traps in coastal cities or major beach or recreation areas belong to this category. In terms of controlling its destiny and being active in retail management, the retailer may rethink the situation and in many cases may avoid this type of arrangement.

As seen in Exhibit 13.10, in three out of four cases brand name and brand image play a very important role in retailing. Hence, the retailer needs to know the relative importance of different brand images. In order for a product to carry an image that will give the retailer some competitive edge, that product needs to be the "awareness" set as opposed to the "unawareness" set of the consumers (Narayana and Markin, 1975).

AWARENESS AND UNAWARENESS SETS

Some years ago Narayana and Markin (1975) pointed out that the relationship between consumer behavior and product performance could be most effectively explained by classifying existing brands into awareness and unawareness sets (Samli et al. 1978).

The awareness set represents those brands that the consumers know and might be inclined to purchase. The unawareness set, on the other hand, implies that the product is not known to the consumer, or the brand does not play an important role in the purchase process.

Exhibit 13.11
Different Alternatives of Brand Performance

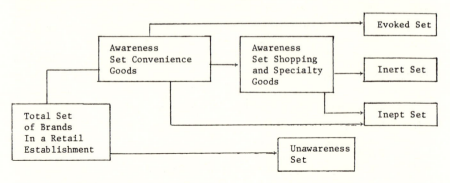

Source: Adapted and revised from Samli et al. 1978.

Of course, the retailer would prefer that all components of the merchandise mix be in the awareness set of the store's target market customers (Samli et al. 1978). Narayana and Markin (1975) have subdivided the awareness set into three subsets: evoked set, inert set, and inept set. They define the evoked set as the group of a few select brands which consumers consider in their purchase choice (Exhibit 13.11). The inert set, on the other hand, consists of those brands for which the consumer has neither a positive nor a negative evolution. Finally, the inept set includes those brands that are reflected by the consumer because of unpleasant experiences or negative feedback received from others (Samli et al. 1978).

Narayana and Markin reported that consumers do indeed attempt to simplify their decision-making process almost automatically by categorizing the existing brands. In this process, they accept a few, reject a few, and appear to ignore the rest of the brands. Consumers have their own rationalization in categorizing the products. Narayana and Markin tested and confirmed their theory in the convenience goods category. Samli et al. expanded the theory into shopping and specialty products. Since consumers spend more time and effort in purchasing shopping and specialty goods, there appears to be a larger number of brands in the evoked set brands in the shopping-specialty spectrum as opposed to the convenience goods. Similarly, analyses of the inept sets indicate that there are many more inept convenience goods brands than those of shopping and specialty goods. Thus, consumers tend to simplify their lives by ignoring or eliminating many brands. For obvious reasons, no significant gains are possible from switching brands in convenience product categories. With regard to shopping and specialty goods, simplifying life (convenience) is replaced by economic benefit and psychological satisfaction. Consumers generally gather more information on these products, and as a result they have stored a larger variety of brands in their evoked sets (Samli et al. 1978; Narayana and Markin 1975).

As part of their feedback activity to maintain a highly desirable merchandise mix, retailers may have to determine the relative position of the brands they carry. Some products may move from evoked to inert or inept sets. Similarly, many brands may gradually shift from awareness to unawareness sets, or vice versa. Retailers may periodically reconsider checking some of the brands in the merchandise mix and may accordingly have to adjust the promotional activity or the merchandise mix itself.

SUMMARY

This chapter posits that effective merchandise mix management means effective buying through planning and careful control. It is further emphasized that buying is the other life blood of retailing. The four objectives of merchandise mix management are identified as (1) providing a highly desirable merchandise mix, (2) adjusting the mix to changing needs, (3) maintaining an internal consistency, and (4) considering external variables. Five specific merchandise policies are discussed: (1) deep and narrow assortment, (2) deep and wide assortment, (3) shallow and narrow assortment, (4) shallow and wide assortment, and (5) consistent and flexible assortment.

Merchandise mix is first preplanned on the basis of external variables such as changes in competition, consumer trends, and past performances. On the basis of the preplanned merchandise mix, certain buying factors are singled out: namely, stock-related and buyer-related factors.

Of these factors, seven that motivate buyers are particularly important: (1) high morale, (2) reasonable remuneration, (3) interaction with management, (4) recognition of the results of efforts, (5) positive feedback, (6) adequate training, and (7) proper information for buyers.

In planning the merchandise mix, a five-step process is presented: (1) selection of control units, (2) sales forecasts, (3) inventory control, (4) reduction planning, and (5) planning purchases.

Merchandise mix controls are classified as financial and unit controls. It is emphasized that the control function has a hierarchical effect, and therefore the whole merchandise mix system must be controlled rather than simply constitute one or two steps in the total hierarchy.

In the merchandise mix management and control areas, the role of brands must be considered carefully. The retailer can use product or brand image as a force to establish a competitive edge or may use the store's own image. Variations of these two strategic tools provide numerous alternatives for the retailer.

Finally, it is suggested that the retailer must be concerned with the "awareness" or "unawareness" status of consumer goods. The awareness set of brands implies that consumers are familiar with these products. The awareness set is broken down into three subsets: evoked set, inert set, and inept set. The retailer would like to see all the brands in the merchandise mix in the evoked set.

REFERENCES

Berman, Barry, and Joel Evans. *Retail Management*. New York: Macmillan, 1986.

Darlymple, Douglas J. and Donald L. Thompson. *Retailing: An Economic View*. New York: Free Press, 1969.

Departmental and Specialty Store Merchandising and Operating Results. New York: National Retail Merchants Association, Published Annually.

Gist, Ronald R. *Retailing: Concepts and Decisions*. New York: John Wiley, 1968.

Golden, Lawrence, and Donald A. Zimmerman. *Effective Retailing*. Skokie, Ill.: Rand McNally, 1980.

Hartley, Robert F. *Retailing: Challenge and Opportunity*. Boston: Houghton Mifflin, 1975.

Lusch, Robert F. *Management of Retail Enterprises*. Boston: Kent Publishing, 1982.

McGinnis, Michael A., Myron Gable, and R. Burt Madden. "Improving the Profitability of Retail Merchandising Decisions—Revisited." *Journal of the Academy of Marketing Science* (Spring 1984): 49–57.

Markin, Rom J., Jr. *Retailing Management*. New York: Macmillan, 1971.

Mason, J. Barry, and Morris L. Mayer. *Modern Retailing*. Plains, Tex.: Business Publications, 1987.

May, Elenor G. "Practical Applications of Recent Retail Image Research." *Journal of Retailing* (Winter 1974–1975): 15–20.

Narayana, Chem L., and Rom J. Markin. "Consumer Behavior and Product Performance: An Alternative Conceptualization." *Journal of Marketing* (October 1975).

Rothman, Marion Burk. "EAS for All." *Stores* (June 1980): 31.

Samli, A. Coskun, Glen Riecken, and Carolyn W. Salmon. "Narayana-Markin Consumer Behavior and Product Performance Model: A New Dimension." In *Developments in Marketing Science*, Academy of Marketing Science, 1978, pp. 47–49.

Staples, William A. and Robert Suerdlow. "Planning and Budgeting for Effective Retail Merchandise Management." *Journal of Small Business* (January 1978): 1–6.

Staple Stock Replenishment. Dayton, Ohio: National Cash Register Co., 1970.

Sweeney, Daniel J. "Improving the Profitability of Retailing Merchandising Decisions." *Journal of Marketing* (January 1973): 60–68.

Wingate, John W., Elmer O. Schaller, and F. Leonard Miller. *Retail Merchandise Management*. Englewood Cliffs, N.J.: Prentice-Hall 1976.

14 Retail Pricing Strategy

Although retail pricing is important in itself, its role in the overall retail marketing strategy is of particular note. Most retailers do not understand pricing, and, hence, they adopt a rather simplistic orientation toward how their prices are established. Often, pricing is not utilized as part of the overall marketing strategy; rather, it is maintained in a situation of neutrality, with the prices determined on a cost-plus basis or by utilizing the manufacturers' suggested prices. In either case, pricing plays an active role in the retailer's overall marketing strategy.

In order to develop a pricing strategy to support the retailer's overall marketing strategy, it is first necessary to identify and understand the external and internal factors influencing retail pricing.

EXTERNAL FACTORS

Since the retailing process takes place in the market, certain factors prevailing in the market directly influence retail prices, including demand, price elasticity, competition, and price perceived quality.

Demand

Demand is reflected in the ability and willingness to buy the products the retail store is selling. If no potential can be actualized in terms of sales, the retail store does not have a chance to survive. However, if there is potential, its actualization in terms of being converted into sales is substantial, depending on the store's pricing strategy. All other factors being equal, if the retail store charges the "right" price, then it will sell more. The concept of right price, however, is subject to careful scrutiny.

Exhibit 14.1
Price Range Included Demand Function Versus Conventional Demand Function

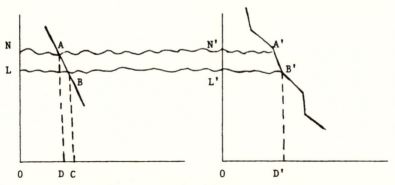

Consumers have a mental picture of the value of a product. This mental picture includes a range as well as a psychological dimension. It has been maintained that consumers think in terms of a price range rather than one single price. These price ranges are likely to vary on the basis of how much importance is attached to the product as well as the consumers' socioeconomic backgrounds. Thus, instead of the demand curve customarily illustrated in economics texts, the demand curve for the retailer is likely to be a disjointed rather than a continuous demand function. As seen in Exhibit 14.1, if a retailer were to raise prices from L to N in the conventional demand curve, a volume loss equivalent to D C would materialize. On the other hand, if the price range theory were accepted, the retailer could raise the price from L to N without losing any volume. Hence, the total revenue for the retailer would be substantially greater than the conventional demand function.

The range concept is related to an individual's psyche. To the extent that an individual would like to buy a certain brand or to patronize a retail store, he or she will not have one specific price in mind. Within reason, this individual will not insist on one price but will be willing to pay a little more or less to buy that product or to buy in that particular store. The individual's brand loyalty or store loyalty is part of his or her psyche. Another pricing concept that enters the individual's psyche is labeled psychological pricing. It has been suggested that odd prices are psychologically more attractive to customers. Thus, consumers typically opt for a product priced at $5.99 as opposed to the even price of $6.00 (Berman and Evans 1986, Hawkins 1957). This psychological point is important only if demand for the product or the retail store exists.

Price Elasticity

Price elasticity, though discussed in marketing literature, is rarely practiced by the practitioner and rarely advocated by marketing academics as an important pricing tool because it is too difficult to compute.

As a concept, price elasticity implies the consumer's reaction to price changes. It may be defined as the change in quantity demanded which is attributable to a 1-percent change in price. If the quantity demanded exceeds percentage, demand is considered to be price elastic, but if it is smaller than 1 percent, demand is considered to be price inelastic. It is calculated as:

$$\frac{\% \, \Delta \, Q}{\% \, \Delta \, P}$$

where % Δ Q = percent change in quantity demanded.
        % Δ P = percent change in price.

Any standard economics text presents a fair treatment of the concept (Samuelson, Reynolds, McConnell). From a retailing perspective, elasticity is important as an indicator of the store's competitive advantage or monopolistic power.

If the demand that a retail store commands is such that price increases yield a less than proportionate decline in quantities, then it is implied that the demand is inelastic and that the store has a substantial degree of monopoly power. In such cases, the retail establishment does not have to be engaged in price competition. Rather, it may be more readily engaged in nonprice competition, emphasizing other variables of the marketing mix.

It is dangerous for any firm to experiment with this kind of marketing behavior without measuring the demand elasticity. Texts discuss experimental research to determine price elasticity. Such experiments are expensive and time consuming (Berman and Evans 1983). Perhaps a better orientation is to approximate the demand elasticity by using a series of factors, including (1) competition, (2) importance of the products, (3) urgency of need, (4) ease of want satisfaction, (5) impact of total price (Lynn 1967), and (6) economic conditions. First a summary of these factors is presented.

1. *Competition*: Competition implies the availability of close substitutes. If the store's product line has close substitutes or, in general, the store has some very close competitors that are quite similar to itself, then it can be deduced that customers of the store could easily go to the competitors' stores. Therefore, the demand is elastic.

2. *Importance of products*: If the store's products are important to customers or if the store, in general, is very important to customers, then in the minds of consumers neither the store or its products can have substitutes. Therefore, the demand is inelastic.

3. *Urgency of need*: Even though the products of the store such as medicine or parts for an imported sports car may not be very important in absolute terms, because of the urgency of need the demand for the store could be inelastic. The whole line of Seven-Elevens or Hop-Ins is enjoying such need urgency based on convenience which is preferred over relatively higher prices.

4. *Ease of want satisfaction*: If the store's products are dealing with consumer wants that are readily satisfied, then the demand cannot be expanded by lower prices and, as such, demand is inelastic.

5. *Impact of total price*: If the prices of the store as a whole or the prices of some products in the store become too high, the customer may be forced to find substitutes; hence, at a certain price level, demand can become elastic.

6. *Economic conditions*: In recession years, demand may be somewhat price elastic in terms of price increases and price inelastic in terms of reductions. In other words, consumers may cut down their purchases but are not unlikely to increase their purchases.

These factors are discussed in more detail in the following section.

Competition

Directly or indirectly, competition has a profound impact on the firm's price elasticity. It plays an additional role in the pricing process. No matter how strong the image of the firm and no matter how inelastic its demand is, the retail establishment has to pay attention to actual as well as potential competition.

Depending on the degree of competitiveness, that is, the extent to which the competing store is considered to be a very close substitute, prices need to be kept within a reasonable range. The store's prices cannot overly exceed the competitors' prices. Thus, dynamic retailers perform regular comparative pricing research, so that they keep themselves within a predetermined price range determined by the difference between their own and competitors' average prices.

Even if at present there is no competition that is alarming the retail establishment, the store must be mindful of potential future competition. If conditions are suitable for entry and if the retail store has been charging exorbitant prices and taking advantage of a strong monopoly position, it is easy to deduce that in a very short period of time there will be increased competition. Thus, the retail store may consider the reduction of present profits through the reduction of its prices and opt for restricting undesirable future competition. Or it may consider that the present monopoly situation will yield enough revenue to make increased future competition tolerable. Seven-Eleven stores, for instance, opt for the latter alternative. Because of their convenient location, they charge higher prices than their competition. Because of their optimal location, they rely on the fact that competition is not likely to get keener and the store's demand is inelastic.

Importance of Products

In many towns usually one or two major apparel stores set the fashions. These stores are very well known and well established. They are upper-end specialty stores and have the best access to the high-fashion shoppers (Mills 1985). In the eyes of consumers, these stores and their products have almost no substitutes. Within reasonable ranges, their demand is inelastic. The "within reasonable" phrase is important here because any store can price itself out of a market by thinking that it has no competition or that it is extremely unique. At a certain point, the inelasticity diminishes, and the store loses its competitive edge by charging exorbitant prices.

Urgency of Need

For consumers with an urgent need for a product, the demand is likely to be inelastic. If party supplies prove to be less than adequate in quantity or in variety, then the host or hostess will go to the nearest Seven-Eleven or Hop-In and buy whatever is there. If the person is already in a drugstore and the aspirin there is 15 percent more expensive than in most other stores, the person will not go to the trouble of finding another place. Similarly, people in a resort hotel will pay $5.00 for a $2.00 can of tennis balls rather than seek them out in a series of unknown places, perhaps without suitable transportation. Thus, if the consumers feel that their need is urgent, the store as a whole or many generic products (headache remedies in general, soft drinks, party supplies, and so on) will experience an inelastic demand.

Ease of Want Satisfaction

Most products sold in a hardware store are of such a nature that trying to sell two, three, or four units at a lower price is not conducive to the customer. For example, two water hoses for the price of one has limited appeal, and the person who needs a hammer will not buy two if the price is reduced. Many product groups have similar features. Because they want the product and this want is rather easy to satisfy, demand is not elastic. Price reductions are not likely to cause individuals to eat more salt.

Impact of Total Price

Price inelasticity is not a continuous function. That is, if prices were to reach a certain unacceptable level, consumers, regardless of their attachment to the store or specific products, would switch to other substitutes. In fact, even if the product does not have close substitutes at certain price levels, all products are substitutable. An avid Porsche owner may decide to buy a mink coat for his wife instead of replacing his present car if the prices for the new models have become exorbitant. Thus, at certain price levels all products and all stores have substitutes. Therefore, demand becomes elastic.

Economic Conditions

When economic conditions become adverse, consumers become more careful with their money. Thus, reduced prices may imply substantial increases in quantities demanded. If, for instance, during a recession, a person needs to buy a suit, that person may look for a lower price suit. However, if the prices are reduced to half, he will not buy two suits. Thus, demand is relatively inelastic, and price reduction will not increase the purchase volumes more than proportionately. On the other hand, if in recession years, retailers were to increase their prices, they would experience a more than proportionate decrease in sales

Exhibit 14.2
Conditions Dictating Price-Level Strategies

	Price Strategy		
	Below Market	Market	Above Market
Low Competition	-	+	+
High-level product importance	-	+	+
Urgent needs	-	+	+
Easy to satisfy wants	-	+	-
Total prices are reasonable	-	+	-
Economy is experiencing a recession	-	+	-
High Competition	+	+	-
Low level product importance	+	+	-
Needs are not urgent	+	+	-
Wants are not easy to satisfy	+	-	-
Total prices are too high	+	-	-
Economy is experiencing a boom	+	-	-

volumes. Thus, while demand is elastic when prices are raised, it is inelastic when prices are reduced. We may conclude that within certain price ranges during recessions demand is inelastic. Exhibit 14.2 illustrates these conditions as they affect retail price-level strategies.

Price-Perceived Quality

A number of pricing studies indicate that price perception does not always mean cost or sacrifice to the consumer (Monroe 1978). In fact, these studies have shown that a perceived quality is implied by price and, in some cases, buyers tend to prefer higher priced products (Monroe 1978). The second tendency is particularly valid when consumers do not have any other information besides the price (Monroe 1979). The key question is whether or not the same situation can be applied to retailing.

It can be argued that the answer to this question lies in the concept of "price thresholds." As discussed earlier, consumers have limits for prices, and accordingly, they exhibit varying degrees of responsiveness to price changes. The Weber-Fechner law posits that if some lower price thresholds are established below the actual low prices, consumers will think that perhaps the product is undesirable for purchase (Uhl 1979). Hence, consumers will opt for higher prices if these products are sold in certain retail establishments. In marketing terms, if certain convenience goods, for example, canned peas, are sold in convenience stores such as a supermarket, the consumer will not attach much special value to them. However, another convenience good, such as men's underwear, privately branded and sold at Neiman-Marcus has a special value that may be reflected in a higher price. Thus, price-perceived quality reinforced by the retail store's reputation or image is a plausible proposition in retailing. Certain specialty goods, namely, expensive appliances or jewelry, may gain price-perceived value as their prices are raised within a certain range. The price-perceived value is related to price-perceived quality. In other words, as price goes up, the perceived quality of the product increases proportionately. Increased perceived quality further accelerates the perceived value.

INTERNAL FACTORS

Three groups of factors influence the retail prices internally: (1) price objectives, (2) strategic alternatives, and (3) goal-related strategies.

Price Objectives

Although in the final analysis the firm uses pricing to fulfill its objectives, in the interim, its pricing objectives differ noticeably. At least four price objectives can be cited: achieving (1) a certain sales volume, (2) a certain amount of profit in terms of dollars, (3) certain expected returns on investment, and (4) early recovery of cash for improving cash flow.

Achieving a certain sales volume has been and remains a strong objective for many retailers. For years A & P tried to achieve the number one position by achieving the largest sales volume.

Many retailers use pricing in order to attain a certain profit level in dollar terms. For example, a company may be determined to make $1 million in profits that year. An expected return on investment can be achieved by pricing. Thus, the company may be manipulating its prices to reach the desired return on investment (ROI).

Finally, for many retailers, particularly during recessions, cash flows are critical for survival. Retailers can facilitate or supplement their cash flow position by using special prices. For instance, by providing cash discounts and lowering prices, the retailer can facilitate the cash flow and eliminate the cash flow problems common during recessions.

Strategic Alternatives

Regardless of the strategic alternative being used, retail pricing is an important tool to fulfill the retailer's particular strategic alternative. If, for example, the store is exercising a segmentation strategy, its prices must reflect this strategic preference. For example, K-Mart caters to the lower middle class and to the middle class for whom price-perceived quality is not that relevant. However, Bloomingdale's and Neiman-Marcus will also position themselves within a given segment (primarily upper-upper and lower-upper) where price-perceived quality is very pertinent.

Similarly, store strategies related to life cycle can also be implemented with significant help from pricing. Sears, particularly during its growth era, promoted its pricing as the most reasonable for the product value received.

Goal-Related Strategies

In order to fulfill corporate objectives, goals are established which, in turn, are interpreted as pricing strategies. At least two types of pricing strategies can be identified in this context: price strategy related to market level and price strategy related to leadership.

Pricing strategy related to market level implies being above, at, or below the market level. Above the market indicates that the retailers set many prices above the competitors' level. This strategy is appropriate if the retailer deals with market segments where above price-perceived quality is prevalent. Once again, profit maximization is achieved by establishing a strong price-perceived quality relationship for the particular retail store.

Most big name stores in retailing such as Neiman-Marcus, Bloomingdale's, Bullocks, and I Magnin's at least partially practice above the market price policy. The store's image is so highly regarded and accepted that customers feel they are receiving something more than just the merchandise. They are not buying just a necktie but the Neiman-Marcus image. In common economic parlance, the situation implies that the store's demand curve is relatively inelastic, and the customers display a strong degree of store loyalty. Bloomingdale's, for example, enjoys a big spending, small socioeconomic group by providing "ego-trips into a discriminating world of fashion" (Cohen and Jones 1978).

The middle-class general merchandise department and discount department stores opt for meeting the competition type of pricing policy. Sears, Ward's, and Thalheimer's all belong to this category. The general orientation is primarily toward a low profile on prices and heavy emphasis on nonprice competition. Position is often exercised by pointing out that the retailer offers strong price/value relationships as opposed to some exorbitant brands and prices. Both Penney's and Sears are middle-of-the-road retailers. As they position themselves against each other, they position themselves primarily below very high and prestigious name brands (Birnbaum 1981; Cohen and Jones 1978).

Finally, below the market policy is emphasized by those discount stores and discount chains that cater to lower middle-class market segments. For K-Mart, Hills, and others in this category, the emphasis is on price competition, with few or no frills regarding customer services and sales promotion. They do not promote labels or brands. Instead, they emphasize cash only, returns and exchanges are limited, and no delivery services exist. They emphasize low-cost practices (Britten 1978, 1982).

A comparative analysis of pricing strategy related to market level is presented in Exhibit 14.3. Ten variables to be used in the analyses are identified and these ten are grouped into four categories: merchandise-related, service-related, store atmospherics-related, and general strategy-related factors.

Whether or not the retailer has some degree of leadership in the marketplace may imply that the store has options to use variable markups. Markup policies are also used to fulfill certain goals. If the retail store pursues a general merchandiser strategy, it tries to appeal to all segments, which implies a rather flexible pricing policy. Price flexibility means flexible and variable markup practices. Flexible markup suggests that either the store has numerous special sales where markups are all adjusted or the store is somewhat amenable to haggling. Haggling is much more common in Third World countries than in the United States. Variable markup, on the other hand, means using different markups for different products or product lines. The basic principle is low markup for fast-moving merchandise. Slow-moving merchandise has high markups which may be changed periodically for some big sales. Variable markup policy provides better opportunity to appeal to different markets more effectively and establish some degree of market leadership position.

Many retail establishments segment the market strategically. One very successful chain has segmented the market on the basis of some specific benefit-convenience. Seven-Eleven stores use a single markup approach across the board for all of their products. Such stores have performed particularly well in the marketplace, their number increasing from 500 in 1957 to 27,000 in 1976 (*Progressive Grocer*, April 1977). Thus, as noted earlier, it can be stated that for small items many consumers prefer convenience over price.

THE TWO STRATEGIC TOOLS

Although retailing scholars tend to classify pricing on the basis of demand-oriented pricing and cost-oriented pricing (Berman and Evans 1983; Alpert, 1971), for a retailer who understands, the market price orientation becomes rather unrealistic. Because competition in retailing is very keen and consumers are rather changeable, the retailers' emphasis on cost becomes the wrong focal point.

Strategically speaking, whether prices are raised or lowered is the most important point to be emphasized. Here, two factors need to be carefully examined: markups and markdowns. Of the two, markups are perhaps more demand and market oriented, and markdowns are more internal or cost oriented. The reason for this distinction is that price level faces more consumer and competitor retaliation. Markdowns are considered to be tactical and are used primarily to move merchandise that has not been moving satisfactorily.

In most textbooks, discussion revolves around the arithmetic of markups and markdowns (Mason and Mayer 1987; Berman and Evans 1986; Rosenbloom 1980). Here the emphasis is on the general strategic picture within which markups and markdowns are important. When both of these concepts are placed in proper context, their relative role within the overall retail strategy becomes more explicit.

Markups: The margin between the cost and the retail price is extremely important because, in terms of overall volume of the store, it is the success of

Exhibit 14.3
Market-Level-Related Pricing Strategy

Retail Mix Variable	Pricing Below the Market	Pricing at the Market	Pricing Above the Market
Merchandise Related:			
Product assortment	concentration on best-sellers	Medium Assortment	Broad and deep assortment
Merchandise lines carried	Private labels name-brand close-outs, small manu-facturers' products	Name brands	Exclusive brands
Merchandise Differentiation	Undifferentiated merchandise emphasis on price competition	Differentiated mer-chandise	Highly differentiated merchandise based on exclusivity
Role of fashion assortment	Fashion follower, conservative	Concentration on accepted best-sellers	Fashion leader
Service Related:			
Personal service	Self service little product knowledge on part of salespeople, no displays	Moderate assistance by sales personnel	High levels of personal selling, delivery, liberal exchanges, alterations adjustments, etc.
Special services	Cash and carry	Not available or extra charge to customers	Included in price
Store Atmospherics Related:			
Location	Poor, Inconvenient site	Close to competitors	Absence of strong competi-tors convenient to consumers

270

Retail Mix Variable	Pricing Below the Market	Pricing at the Market	Pricing Above the Market
Merchandise Related:			
Atmosphere	Inexpensive fixtures, little or no carpeting no paneling, racks for merchandise	Moderate atmosphere neutral and somewhat attractive	Very attractive, pleasant decor with many creative displays
Image	Store is known for its bargains and low prices	Store is known for price-quality combination; considered a middle-class place	Store is known for its exclusivity; it appeals to upper economic class
External appearance	Modest and unassuming	Reasonably nice but not very flashy	Very flashy
General Strategy Related:			
Key strategy emphasis	Mass merchandiser with limited differentiation and segmentation	Mass merchandiser with heavy emphasis on differentiation	Heavy segmenter and positioner

Source: Adapted and expanded from Berman and Evans 1986.

effective markup which will provide the effective price. As opposed to an internal markup orientation which, unfortunately, is quite widespread among retail practitioners, markup must be based primarily on external factors. An increase in markup is illustrated in Exhibit 14.4. Three general external factors are of special interest: first, the total market potential in general; second, demand elasticity; and third, competitors' expected reaction. What will be the market's long-range reaction? Is the demand inelastic enough to raise the price by increasing the markup? And, finally, will competitors retaliate by not raising their prices or even lowering their prices? Without appropriate answers to these questions, it will not pay to raise the price through an increased markup.

Markdowns: As was posited earlier, unlike markups, markdowns are likely to be internally oriented. They are utilized more readily for internal reasons in order to take care of internal merchandising problems. However, their excessive use or abuse has significant implications for external pricing strategy.

Markdowns are widespread in retailing. Some merchandise will not sell at the original price and sooner or later will have to be marked down. Many retailers use markdowns not only to (1) remedy buying errors, (2) compensate for changes in customer needs, or (3) retaliate against competitors' actions (Rosenbloom 1981), but also as a principal feature of a promotional event. Many retailers have regular promotional events such as inventory reduction sales, end of season clearance sales, or preseason sales during which time markdowns become the focal point of total activity. In such cases, markdowns help to:

Move merchandise that is not moving fast enough.

Attract customers who are attracted to special sales.

Build customer loyalty among these groups of customers.

Sell other merchandise not marked down.

Stimulate excitement about the store.

Using markdowns in such cases is an ongoing activity. Exhibit 14.5 illustrates this process. Perhaps the most important activity relating to markdown decisions is the continuous scrutiny of the merchandise to distinguish the unsold items from those that are selling well and then to determine why these items or lines are not selling.

Options to be used need to be related to the reasons why the products are not sold. If, for instance, there are promotional errors, they may not be corrected by markdowns. Similarly, certain external factors such as the consumer's total antipathy to the product line may necessitate discarding or giving the product to charity (Exhibit 14.5). The illustration shows how to make key decisions as to how long the markdowns should be used in one given situation and what the scope of the markdown should be, that is, how large should it be. In this respect, Yoram Kingberg et al. (1974) have developed a model to determine the optional size of a markdown. This model is based on the premise that each individual

Exhibit 14.4
A Decision Flowchart of Price Increase

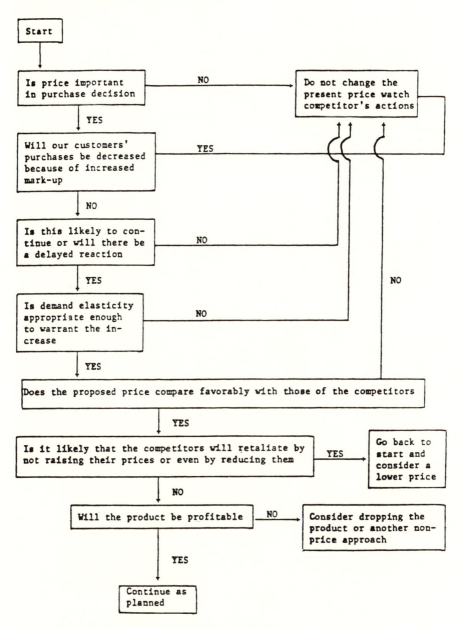

Exhibit 14.5
Markdown Decision Flow

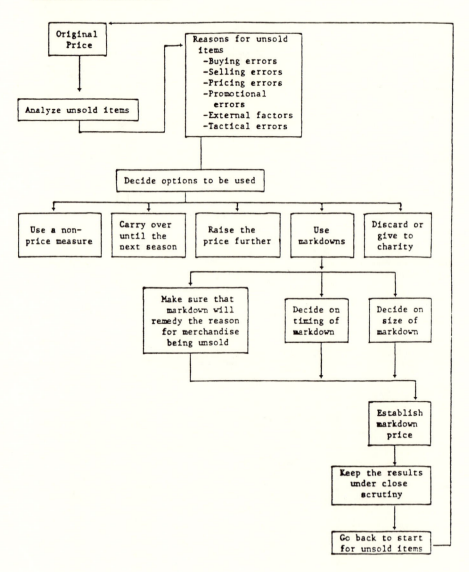

has a range of acceptable prices for any given product, with price above this range making the product too expensive and a price below the range inferring inferior quality (Gabor and Granger 1966; Monroe and Della Bitta 1978). Thus, intuitively or through research, the retail decision maker must approximate this range.

Finally, Exhibit 14.5 emphasizes that, after the specified time for the markdown, the whole situation is again reviewed and a decision on further markdowns is made. One important aspect of the exhibit is that it demonstrates the continuity of the process.

RETAIL PRICING STRATEGY IN AN ERA OF STAGFLATION

During the late 1970s and early 1980s, the American economy was very sluggish. This sluggishness was particularly reflected in the presence of simultaneous inflation and recession. This situation is termed stagflation. When stagflation prevails, conditions for retailers particularly deteriorate. During the prolonged American stagflation, many small retailers went bankrupt (Haberler 1977). Although at the writing of this book stagflation is not in existence, it can return. Therefore, it is extremely important that retail executives know enough about this economically devastating condition.

In order to avoid such a dramatic end as failure, the retailer must understand the nature of stagflation. With such an understanding, the retailer may then make effective decisions to counteract it and even benefit from it.

Conditions Under Stagflation

During stagflation, prices tend to go up while the total business volume is shrinking. Under these circumstances, the retailers' corrective action typically worsens the situation. As a result of stagflation, they find themselves in at least two adverse situations: (1) declining sales and (2) a worsening profit picture. For those who do not connect retailing's internal conditions to the adversities of the environment, the quickest solution follows such logic as: ''since I cannot increase the sales volume in the midst of this stagflation, I may be able to recoup my losses by cutting down my expenses as much as I can and raise my prices as well.'' The outcome of this orientation is twofold:

1. Retailers will try to cut down their expenses by reducing promotional activities, streamlining inventories, and decreasing the sales effort.
2. Retailers will raise their prices on a cost plus basis or at times simply indiscriminately. Sometimes the prices are raised on the basis of national consumer price index type of criteria.

When retailers decrease their efforts to sell more by cutting down their expenses and raise their prices further, the result is excess unused capacities and further reduction in sales volume. As was discussed earlier in this chapter, many retailers do not bring demand elasticity and other external factors into their pricing practices. However, most retailing activity and many retail product lines face elastic demand. By raising prices when demand is elastic and economic conditions are not up to par (recession), retail volume declines. Decreased retail volume reduces total revenues and creates additional excess retailing capacity (Shama 1978, 1980; Weiss 1975; Ramon 1980).

Remedial Pricing

The above discussion makes it obvious that reduced volume and increasingly unused capacities in retailing become devastatingly dangerous for the retailer in an era of stagflation. Business failures in these times increase in great proportions.

The strategic retailing options available to cope with stagflation, as has been implied thus far, are proper utilization of promotional activity, pricing, and product-service adjustments. First, retailers must try to overcome the adverse external conditions by expanding the business. This means that they do not reduce promotional activity; on the contrary, they try to expand promotion with the hope of increasing sales volume too.

Second, and most important, retailers try not to raise prices, even though they may not be making as much money on each unit sold. What they may be losing on each unit sold is more than compensated by increasing the sales volume more than proportionately. Thus, even though the markup for each unit is shrinking in a stagflation situation, retailers do not raise prices. In fact, they may reduce prices and increase volume.

Third, retailers should consider changing the product service mix to accommodate consumer needs and changing attitudes during stagflation. It has been posited that during stagflation consumer needs change. Many consumers opt for cheaper, more economic-oriented products and ease off expensive services. They buy products and services more frequently and carefully.

SUMMARY

This chapter emphasizes the role of pricing as a part of the overall retail marketing strategy.

In analyzing retail pricing, we must first be concerned with external factors, namely demand, price elasticity, competition, and price-implied quality. The second group of factors identified in this chapter are internal factors, three of which are explored: price objectives, strategic alternatives, and goal-related strategies.

Finally, two strategic tools, markups and markdowns, are examined. Although both have internal and external implications, markups are assumed to be more externally oriented than markdowns.

REFERENCES

Alpert, Mark I. *Pricing Decision*. Glenview, Ill.: Scott, Foresman, 1971.

Berman, Barry, and Joel Evans. *Retail Management*. 3rd ed. New York: Macmillan, 1986.

Birnbaum, Jeffrey. "Pricing of Products Is Still an Art." *The Wall Street Journal*, November 30, 1981.

Britten, Arthur B. "Off-Price Strategy." *Stores* (June 1978): 46.

———. "Off-Price." *Stores* (March 1982): 9–14.

Cohen, Arthur, and Ana Laid Jones. "Brand Marketing in the New Retail Environment." *Harvard Business Review* (September-October 1978): 140–46.

Gabor, Andre, and Clive Granger. "Price as an Indicator of Quality." *Economica* (February 1966): 43–70.

Haberler, Gottfried. "The Problems of Stagflation." *AEI Studies of Contemporary Economic Problems* (1977): 255–72.

Hawkins, Edward R. "Methods of Estimating Demand." *Journal of Marketing* (April 1957).

Kingberg, Yoram, Ambar Rao, and Melvin Shakun. "A Mathematical Model for Price Promotions." *Management Science* (February 1974): 948–59.

Lunstrom, William J. "Supermarket Patronage in a Highly Priced Cognitive Market: Does Environment Influence Decision Factors." In R. L. King, ed., *Retailing: Theory and Practice for the 21st Century*. Academy of Marketing Science, 1986, pp. 139–42.

Lynn, R. A. *Price Policies and Marketing Management*. Homewood, Ill.: Richard D. Irwin, 1967.

Mason, Barry, and Morris L. Mayer. *Modern Retailing*. Plains, Tex.: Business Publications, 1987.

Mills, Michael K. "Strategic Retail Fashion Marketing Positioning: A Comparative Analysis." *Journal of the Academy of Marketing Science* (Summer 1985): 212–25.

Monroe, Kent B., and Albert J. Della Bitta. "Models for Pricing Decision." *Journal of Marketing Research* (August 1978): 413–28.

Progressive Grocer. "44th Annual Report of the Grocery Industry." Vol. 56 (April 1977): 23.

Ramon, Murry. "Survival at Your Fingertips." *Sales and Marketing Management* (June 1980): 33–64.

Rosenbloom, Bert. *Retail Marketing*. New York: Random House, 1981.

Shama, Avraham. "Management and Consumers in an Era of Stagflation. "*Journal of Marketing* (July 1978): 43–52.

———. *Marketing in a Slow Growth Economy* New York: Praeger Publishers, 1980.

Uhl, Joseph U. "Consumer Perception of Retail Food Price Changes." In Kent B. Monroe, ed., *Pricing*. New York: McGraw-Hill, 1979.

Weiss, E. B. "New Marketing Tactics Battle the Shortage of Liquid Capital." *Advertising Age*, September 1975, pp. 38–39.

15 The Store Loyalty Concept: Dimensions and Measurement

M. Joseph Sirgy and A. Coskun Samli

Retailers work to create and maintain a desirable level of store loyalty toward their stores from the target market. Store loyalty is a highly technical measurement problem that can be more readily illustrated than described. This chapter, therefore, presents specific methodologies in order to explain this concept. In addition to discussing different alternatives on store loyalty measurements, it elaborates on various factors that cause store loyalty. These factors are assessed as predictors of loyalty.

Store loyalty is perhaps the single most important concept for the retailer. It indicates the "differential advantage" in Aldersonian terminology or "the monopoly power" in Chamberlainian terminology. If retailers could determine the nature and degree of loyalty, they could attempt to develop better retail strategies to increase or maintain satisfactory levels of store sales.

Numerous efforts have been made to identify retail market segments (Frank et al. 1972; Frank et al. 1969; Martineau 1958; Samli 1975). Traditionally, identifying the market segment that patronizes a retail store along a store loyalty factor has been construed as an effective method of market segmentation. The general theme of differential congruence has been discussed throughout this book. The only true measure of successful differential congruence is store loyalty. Thus, proper store loyalty measurement is extremely important from a retail marketing strategy perspective. Differential congruence and its measurement are covered elsewhere in this book; this chapter tackles the all-important concept of store loyalty.

The chapter partially draws from M. Joseph Sirgy and A. Coskun Samli, "A Path Analytic Model of Store Loyalty Involving Self-Concept, Store Image, Geographic Loyalty, and Socioeconomic Status," *Journal of Academy of Marketing Science* (June 1985).

In recent years, a number of attempts have been made to analyze store loyalty based on a unidimensional perspective. F. D. Reynolds, W. B. Darden, and W. S. Martin (1974), for instance, found out that store loyalty is related to psychographic variables. They state that a store's loyal customers are time conscious, are exposed to entertainment media, and are likely to shop locally. Other attempts have related store loyalty to socioeconomic characteristics (Enis and Paul 1968; Mason and Mayer 1970; Samli 1979; Samli and Sirgy 1981). These studies have indicated that certain socioeconomic criteria analyzed individually or combined in an index form may indicate store patronage and loyalty. Among the salient socioeconomic criteria used are income, education, occupation, and ownership of various luxury items. These have been found to be strong discriminating factors of store patronage and loyalty.

The third research trend involving the determinants of store loyalty is store image (Hirschman 1981). Perhaps the earliest and most widely cited works in this area were generated by Pierre Martineau (1958). He maintained that store loyalty is a function of store image. If individuals have a favorable image of the store, they are likely to develop a degree of loyalty commensurate with the favorableness of the image. Following Martineau's footsteps, a large variety of studies have been conducted exploring the finer points (Jacoby and Kyner 1973; Kelly and Stephenson 1967; Lessig 1973).

More recently, attempts have been made to establish a relationship between self-concept and store image interaction and between store patronage and loyalty (Sirgy 1982). B. L. Stern, R. F. Bush, and J. F. Haire (1977) demonstrated that consumers shop at stores whose images are similar to their own actual and ideal self-images. In another study, D. N. Bellinger, E. Steinberg, and W. W. Stanton (1976) found that self-image/store image congruity is a significant predictor of store loyalty. R. J. Dornoff and R. L. Tatham (1972) found that the shoppers' ideal self-image was more important in the selection of a department store than their actual self-image and their image of "best friend." The actual self-image was shown to be more influential in the choice of a supermarket, and the image of "best friend" to be most predictive for specialty stores.

Still another research track in store patronage/loyalty involves geographic factors. Samli (1979) examined intermarket shopping—or "outshopping"—in two surveys conducted seven years apart. The findings indicated that consumers residing in a small college town were "more satisfied" with their local shopping facilities after construction of a new shopping mall. John R. Nevin and Michael J. Houston (1980) worked with travel distance as a key variable in determining attraction to intraurban shopping areas; they also studied shopping area image in predicting affect for the shopping area.

Samli and Sirgy (1981) conducted a study to test the multidimensionality of store loyalty. Specifically, store loyalty was regressed on a self-image/store image congruity (social and ideal social congruities),[1] evaluation of store image,[2] socioeconomic status, area loyalty, and shopping complex loyalty.[3] The results showed that store image evaluations accounted for a major portion of the predicted

Exhibit 15.1
Satisfaction with Retail Store

Factors Behind Satisfaction	Measurement Criteria
Habit (simplified store loyalty)	Frequency Shopping around Proportion of total purchases Preference
Specific Store Attributes	Functional image components
Activity Generating Practices	Information provided by the store during the shopping process
Inertia	Loyalty to the area Loyalty to a specific shopping complex
Social Class	Segmentation Index
Self-Image Store Image Congruence	Individual self-image store-image measurement

variance in store loyalty. The tendency to shop in specific geographic regions (area loyalty and shopping complex loyalty) was found to be a significant predictor of store loyalty but accounted for only a negligible portion of the predicted variance. However, inspection of the pattern of correlations revealed that, although self-image/store image congruity failed to significantly predict store loyalty scores, the congruity variables (social congruity and ideal social congruity) were significantly correlated with store image evaluations. In addition, socioeconomic status was found to correlate significantly with the variables involved in the tendency to shop in specific geographic regions (area loyalty and shopping complex loyalty).

Based on the findings of the Samli and Sirgy study (1981), a path analytic model of store loyalty was proposed. The purpose of this chapter is (1) to formally introduce the ''causal'' model of store loyalty and argue its logical ramifications, (2) to test the model using a path analytic technique, and (3) to provide further validation of the model by conducting a replication study.

FACTORS BEHIND STORE LOYALTY

Store loyalty is the single most important factor in retailing success and longevity. Without loyalty toward the retail establishment, differential congruence for which management is striving does not exist and the store is doomed to fail.

Store loyalty is a function of customer satisfaction with the retail store. At least six factors underlie satisfaction. Any one or any combination of them can create different degrees of store satisfaction which, in turn, is converted into store loyalty. Exhibit 15.1 illustrates the factors involved in retail store satisfaction and measurement criteria. These factors are discussed within the context of an in-depth study discussed throughout this chapter.

LOYALTY MEASUREMENT

In an effort to determine the degree of store loyalty, a basic measure of loyalty needs to be established. A number of variables can be used for that purpose. Among the variables that have been used are: (1) the total volume purchased in the store, (2) the frequency with which the store has been visited, (3) the number of stores visited before the customer goes back to the store, (4) the proportion of total purchases that has taken place in that store, (5) whether the customers go back to the store, (6) whether customers would recommend it to their friends and, finally, (7) to what extent the individual is willing to go back to the same store whenever the need arises.

CRITERIA FOR A CHOICE

If the store is primarily a major product line store such as groceries or apparel, the total volume purchased in the store or the proportion of total purchases that took place in that store may be the best criteria. However, for a department store or a large discount store where a large variety of products are sold, the frequency with which the store has been visited or the number of stores visited before the customer goes back to the store is a better criterion. In all cases, whether the customer would go back to the store or would recommend the store to others is a good criterion and can be used as a measure of store loyalty.

Two or more of these criteria may be used. It is important to point out that we have no research findings showing which or what combination of them should be used for store measurement.

THE MODEL

Exhibit 15.2 illustrates the basic model used in this study. As can be seen, the model posits that store loyalty is determined primarily by functional store evaluation and by shopping complex loyalty, and, in turn, functional store image evaluation is determined by self-image/store image congruity, whereas shopping complex loyalty is determined by area loyalty and socioeconomic status.

Definitions of the Model's Constructs

Symbolic Store Image. This construct refers to the stereotypic personality images which people may have of a particular store. Among these images are traditional versus modern, classy versus folksy, friendly versus formal, and high status versus low status (Martineau 1958). The symbolic images should be differentiated from those functional images which shoppers may have of a particular

Exhibit 15.2
A "Causal" Model of Store Loyalty

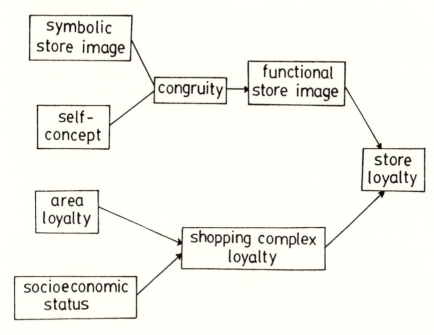

store. Functional store images are characterized by those aspects of the store that are mostly reflected in the tangible characteristics of the store such as clean versus dirty, quiet versus noisy (Samli and Sirgy 1981).

Self-Concept. This variable usually refers to more than one different self-perspective. Self-concept investigators have used this construct to denote actual self-image (how a person sees himself or herself), ideal self-image (how a person would like to see himself or herself), social self-image (how others see him or her), ideal social self-image (how a person would like others to see him or her). (See Sirgy 1982.)

Self-Image/Store Image Congruity. This concept refers to the match or mismatch of one or more actual self-image, ideal self-image, social self-image, or ideal social self-image with the corresponding personality images of the designated store. The match between actual self-image and store image (or product image) has been referred to as "self-congruity"; that between ideal self-image and store image as "ideal congruity"; that between social self-image and store image as "social congruity"; and the match between ideal social self-image and store image as "ideal social congruity" (Sirgy 1982). The congruence between these two sets of constraints (store or product image and self-concept) has been modeled using a variety of distance measures such as the Euclidean distance, absolute difference, simple difference, and difference squared indices (Birdwell

1968; Dolich 1969; Ross 1971; Schewe and Dillon 1978; Sirgy 1980; Sirgy and Danes 1982).

Evaluation of Functional Store Image. This construct denotes a summative attitudinal disposition toward the perceived functional images of a particular store. As previously stated, functional store images refer to those images encoded in the shopper's mental framework based on those functional attributes of the store (i.e., store pricing, product variety, and personnel treatment) (Lindquist 1974–1975). B. Weale (1961) defined this construct in terms of how well the store met the customer's aspiration level with regard to price, quality, and service. A. R. Oxenfeldt (1974–1975) considers the image to be a "combination of factual and emotional" attributes. This viewpoint, which parallels Martineau's (1958) definition, stresses that many shoppers will hold factually based opinions about a store and also feel certain ways toward it. Store image, as an aggregation of all consumer images of a particular store, has been used repeatedly by retail investigators such as Samli (1968, 1975, 1976), Berry (1969), Jenkins and Forsythe (1980) and Wyckham (1967).

Socioeconomic Status. This construct refers to social class which is defined as relatively permanent and homogeneous divisions in a society in which individuals or families sharing similar values, lifestyles, interests, and behaviors can be categorized (Coleman and Rainwater 1978).

Area Loyalty and Shopping Complex Loyalty. The tendency to shop in a specific geographic region describes a shopper's propensity to limit his or her shopping in a specific area (town or city or a specific portion of a city such as a particular suburb) and/or a specific shopping complex (e.g., shopping mall or surrounding stores). Therefore, one can further subdivide geographic loyalty into area loyalty and shopping complex loyalty. These constructs have not been previously used by retail investigators.

Store Loyalty. This is defined as a biased, behavioral response, expressed over time by some decision-making unit, with respect to one or more alternative stores out of a set of such stores, and as a function of psychological process (Jacoby and Kyner 1973). In other words, consistent repurchase by itself may not be a sufficient indicator of loyalty. Some form of psychological commitment on the part of the customer is also a necessary ingredient of true store loyalty. Other researchers maintain that frequency of patronage and recentness of store visits are sufficient indicators in the measurement of store loyalty (Samli 1975).

HYPOTHESIZED CAUSAL RELATIONS

> *Hypothesis 1*: Store image evaluation is a positive function of self-image/store image congruity (social congruity and ideal social congruity).
>
> *Hypothesis 2*: Store loyalty is a positive function of store image evaluation.

The model posits that the match or congruity between a particular store's symbolic image and a shopper's self-image (actual self, ideal self, social self, or ideal social self) resulting in self-image/store image congruity will bias the shopper's perception and evaluation of the store's functional image. The more conscious evaluation of the functional attributes of a particular store will in turn affect the shopper's loyalty to that store. In other words, the self-image/store image congruity effect is argued to operate at a more implicit or less *conscious* level, which affects the shopper's conscious perception and evaluation of the store's functional attributes (Mason and Mayer 1970).

Hazel Markus (1980) argued that personality images associated with the individual self (self-perceptions) and others (person-perception) are cognitive schemas that are organized at higher levels in the cognitive hierarchy. The cognitive schemas that are high on this hierarchy are referred to as abstract schemas, and those that are low on the same hierarchy are referred to as concrete schemas (Abelson 1976; Anderson 1980; Neisser 1976). Abstract schemas are more accessible and become easily activated under conditions of high familiarity. The allocation of cognitive processing or effort for abstract schemas is minimal relative to concrete schemas (Alderson 1957; Wyer and Carlson 1979). Once an abstract schema is activated and processed, the same schema can be subjected to a decompositional procedure in which less abstract and more concrete schemas are generated from the more abstract ones.

This social cognition theory can, therefore, be used to explain the relationship between self-image/product image congruity, functional store image evaluation, and store loyalty. The self-image/product image congruity variable involves abstract cognitive schemas that become activated and processed at a less conscious level. This is then followed by the decompositional process during which specific functional store image attributes are generated and subsequently evaluated. The overall evaluation of the store's functional attributes may, in turn, determine store loyalty behavior.[4]

Therefore, a positive relationship is expected between ideal social congruity (and social congruity) and functional store image evaluation. In addition, positive relationship is expected between functional store image evaluation and store loyalty (Mason and Mayer 1970).

> *Hypothesis 3*: Shopping complex loyalty is a positive function of area loyalty and a negative function of socioeconomic status.
> *Hypothesis 4*: Store loyalty is a positive function of shopping complex loyalty.

With respect to the theoretical justification of the interrelationship of socioeconomic status, area loyalty, shopping complex loyalty, and store loyalty, it has been demonstrated that lower socioeconomic consumers may express more loyalty to specific in-town shopping complexes than higher socioeconomic consumers do (Samli 1979). That is, lower socioeconomic consumers cannot afford to ''out shop'' and therefore are more restricted in terms of geographic mobility. This proposition is also supported by social class theory (Coleman and Rainwater 1978). Higher social class people exhibit greater social (geographic mobility included) mobility than lower social class people. Therefore, a negative relationship between socioeconomic status and shopping complex loyalty is expected.

Shopping complex loyalty can also be argued to be determined by area loyalty. This is simply due to the containment variation. Those who express high loyalty to a specific geographic region (e.g., town) may also express loyalty to a specific shopping complex. The same argument can be applied to the relationship between shopping complex loyalty and loyalty to a specific store within that shopping complex facility. The same phenomenon was observed between store loyalty and brand loyalty. R. E. Frank, W. F. Massey, and Thomas M. Lodahl (1969) and Frank (1967) studied the toilet-tissue purchasing behavior of 3,206 members of a panel and found a relationship between brand loyalty and store loyalty (Carmen 1970).

A positive relationship is expected between area loyalty and shopping complex loyalty, and between shopping complex loyalty and store loyalty.

Summary of Definitions of Model's Constructs

1. Symbolic store image: stereotypic image of the generalized (typical) user of a particular retail store.
2. Self-concept: a variety of self-perspectives such as actual self-image, ideal self-image, social self-image, and ideal social self-image.
3. Social self-image: how the consumer believes others view him or her.
4. Ideal social self-image: how the consumer would like others to view him or her.
5. Self-image/store image congruity: the degree of match between the symbolic store image and a given self-perspective (e.g., social self-image) along one or more image dimensions.
6. Social congruity: the degree of match between the symbolic store image and social self-image along one or more image dimensions.
7. Ideal social congruity: the degree of match between the symbolic store image and ideal social self-image along one or more image dimensions.
8. Store image evaluation: the summative attitude toward the functional or utilitarian attributes of a particular store.
9. Socioeconomic status: the social class position of consumers.
10. Area loyalty: the disposition of consumers to shop repeatedly in a given community.
11. Shopping complex loyalty: the disposition of consumers to shop repeatedly in a given shopping complex.
12. Store loyalty: the disposition of consumers to shop repeatedly in a given store.

METHODOLOGY

Two data sets were gathered from two different stores located in a southern university town. The first set was collected from an intercepted sample of people who patronized a discount department store (Study I). The second came from an intercept sample of shoppers who patronized a clothing department store (Study II–replication).

Sample Population and Sampling Method

A systematic sample was taken of 256 adult shoppers who were intercepted and interviewed as they came out of the discount department store. The sample was taken by interviewing every third customer. The interviews were spaced throughout the week and at various times of day to maximize sample representativeness.

The replication study involved 115 respondents who were interviewed as they were entering or leaving a specialty clothing store in the same southern university town. The same sampling procedure was used in the replication study.

The Functional Store Image Measures

F. F. Kelley and R. Stephenson (1967) first proposed the use of the semantic differential in the measurement of store image. Many investigators followed their lead in this area (Albaum and Dickson 1977; Lincoln and Samli 1979; McDougall and Fry 1974–1975; Pathak, Crissy, and Sweitzer 1974–1975; Samli and Sirgy 1981; Wyckham 1967).

The functional store image construct was measured by using a measure previously used by Samli (1976), Lincoln (1978) and Samli and Sirgy (1981). This measure consists of general store characteristics, physical characteristics, price, personnel, promotion, convenience, and product and services. Twenty semantic differential scales were used to measure these seven factors. Although the reliability and validity of this measure had been demonstrated by Lincoln, Samli, and Samli and Sirgy, further analyses were undertaken in the present study to reexamine the reliability and validity of the factor structure of this scale. A varimax factor analysis was conducted on the two data sets. The results of this analysis were mostly consistent with the hypothesized factor structure with minor deviations. A Chronbach Alpha reliability analysis was conducted on each factor containing two or more indicators, and the results from the two data sets were generally supportive of the internal consistency of the factors. Reliability coefficients varied from 0.56 to 0.87.

To determine the overall functional store image evaluation score per respondent, we used a summative index. In doing so, all the semantic differential scales were transformed in such a way that the positive poles of the scales indicated a favorable image. Therefore, the sum total score reflects the extent to which a given respondent has a favorable or unfavorable evaluation of the store based on the store's functional attributes.

The Symbolic Store Image Measure

In a preliminary procedure, we compiled a list of approximately 50 possible personality attributes associated with general retail stores from a convenience sample of eight subjects. Subjects were asked to write down the personality traits of shoppers who frequently patronized the two stores selected for this study. Their responses were then subjected to a content analysis. The four most consensual and nonredundant attributes were accordingly selected: modern versus traditional, friendly versus formal, classy versus folksy, and casual versus sophisticated.

These bipolar adjectives were then used in a semantic differential format to measure the symbolic store image. A factor analysis was performed to test the factor independence of these attributes. The results based on the two data sets showed that the modern versus traditional attribute was highly loaded with the friendly versus formal on one factor, and the classy versus folksy and the casual versus sophisticated were highly loaded on another factor. This method of measuring symbolic store image (and symbolic product image) was used in many self-concept investigations (Sirgy 1982).

The validity of this measure rests primarily on the nomological testing of the model. That is, empirical support for the hypotheses would automatically lend nomological validity to the measures employed. In the context of this study, it can be argued that the symbolic store image measure has nomological validity.

The Self-Concept Measures

In using the well-established procedure in self-concept investigations, we made use of the same attributes used to measure the symbolic store image. The two self-perspectives employed in this study were social self-image and ideal social self-image. The same form of semantic differential scales was used twice—once to measure social self-image and another time to measure ideal social self-image.

The verbal cue for measuring social self-image was: "To what extent do you think people see you as being . . . " The verbal cue used for measuring ideal social self was: "To what extent would you *like* people to see you as being . . . "

No internal consistency testing was considered or administered for these measures because theory does not warrant this kind of testing. Remember that we are interested in the congruity between the self-concept measures and the symbolic store image measures, and not exclusively the self-concept measures. From this theoretical perspective, the internal consistency type of reliability testing is senseless. Temporal stability as a measure of reliability is the ideal form of reliability testing under these conditions. However, because of the nature of the sample and cost constraints, a test–retest type of procedure was out of the question.

Therefore, the only criterion for reliability and validity we are left with in relation to the self-concept measures is nomological validity. And in this case, we *did* have it.

Self-Image/Store Image Congruity

Based on the works of Sirgy (1979, 1980, 1982) in the area of consumer self-concept, the generalized absolute difference congruence model has been demonstrated to be most predictive of product preference and purchase intention compared to other distance models. Therefore, the generalized absolute difference congruence model was used to obtain scores for social congruity (comparison between symbolic store image and social self-image—the lower the score the higher the congruity and vice versa) and ideal social congruity (comparison between symbolic store image and ideal social self-image).

Social congruity was calculated by the sum of the absolute differences between symbolic store images (STI) and social self-images (SSI). Mathematically formulated, a social congruity score (SC) for an individual respondent (k) was derived as follows:

$$SC_k = \sum_{i=1}^{i} |\, STI_{ik} - SSI_{ik} \,|.$$

Ideal Social Congruity (ISCK), representing the interaction between symbolic store image (STIi) and ideal social self-image (ISSI), was similarly formulated as

$$ISC_k = \sum_{i=1}^{i} |\, STI_{ik} - ISSI_{ik} \,|.$$

Socioeconomic Status Measures

Socioeconomic status in this study was measured by the Segmentation Index (SI) (Samli 1968, 1975, 1976) used in Samli's studies from which the SI measures of reliability and validity were already demonstrated. Following the basic pattern of earlier studies, an SI score was developed by using the sum of income level, luxury items, house payments, credit cards, hobbies, and occupation. Differential weights were assigned to each factor, and an SI score was calculated for each respondent.

Area Loyalty Measures

We used one indicator of area loyalty in this study. The respondents were asked to state the percentage of their total retail purchasing done in the area. Responses were recorded on a four-point rating scale ranging from less than 25 percent to more than 75 percent. Because of the single indicator measure of area loyalty, no reliability testing (internal consistency) was performed. It was assumed to be high. However, we can rely in part on the nomological validity of this measure.

Shopping Complex Loyalty Measure

Shopping complex loyalty was assessed by using a measure similar to area loyalty but directed at the shopping complex, not the town area. Again, as with the area loyalty measure, only one indicator was used in the measurement of this variable, and as a result, no internal consistency type of reliability was ascertained. As with the area loyalty measure, unfortunately, we have to rely on the measure's nomological validity.

Store Loyalty Measures

We measured store loyalty by using two indicators. The first indicator measured the frequency of shopping visits to the particular store. A five-point rating scale varying from twice a week or more to less frequently (than once a month) was used. It was assumed that the people who visit a store more often are more loyal to that store. The other indicator measured the consumer's willingness to go to that specific store whenever the need arises on a five-point Likert scale. It was assumed that high willingness to revisit the same store whenever the need arises is indicative of store loyalty (Bellinger, Steinberg, and Stanton 1976). These two indicators were equally weighted and summed to determine each respondent's general loyalty to the store in question. The correlation among these two indicators was high for both sets ($r = .603$ for Study I and $r = .725$ for Study II).

Design and Analysis

Through path analysis, a systematic and simultaneous evaluation of a system of nonmanipulated variables that are suspected to exhibit causality can be accomplished. Path analysis, though based on correlations, allows us to evaluate a system of nonmanipulated variables measured in their naturalistic setting from which "causal" inferences might be approximated. In this respect, path analysis performs several functions.

First, it attempts to find out whether a hypothesized cause does in fact have an effect. This is done by computing path coefficients (r) between the cause variable(s) and the effect variable. Path coefficients are estimated by partial standardized regression coefficients.

Second, path analysis analyzes the correlation between the cause and effect variables into its component causal direct effects, causal indirect effects, and noncausal effects. Indirect effects may occur in several ways. For example, when causes are correlated, each cause has a direct effect on the dependent variable as well as an indirect effect through correlations with other causes.

Third, path analysis is also used for theory testing. Through its application, one can determine whether or not a pattern of correlations for a set of observations is consistent with a specific theoretical formulation. As shown above, a correlation between two variables can be expressed as a composite of direct and indirect effects of one variable on the other. When we use coefficients, it is therefore possible to reproduce the correlation matrix (R) for all the variables in the system. By deleting certain paths, the researcher is offering a more parsimonious causal model. If after the deletion of some paths it is possible to reproduce the original R matrix, or closely approximate it, then the conclusion will be that the pattern of correlations in the data is consistent with the more parsimonious model (Kerlinger and Pedhazer 1973).

The investigators did *not* use LISREL to conduct the path analytic procedure because of the possible confusion stemming from underidentification associated with the lack of multiple indicators. In this study, except for the two indicators of store loyalty, most of the model's constructs were measured multidimensionally with each dimension having *one* indicator.

The testing of the store loyalty model through path analysis was performed in two stages. Stage 1 involved setting up the full model (i.e., model with all possible connections) and deriving the path coefficients for all possible links. Then, those paths that showed nonsignificant path coefficients were deleted. The trimmed (parsimonious) model was expected to closely correspond to the proposed store loyalty model.

Stage 2 of the analysis involved obtaining path coefficients for the proposed model (which is hopefully the same or close to the trimmed model) and subjecting those path coefficients to a decompositional analysis into direct and indirect causal effects and noncausal association. The total predicted effects (reproduced correlations) were then compared with the obtained or zero-order correlations to test the model for a goodness-of-fit. A theoretically sound model was expected to show nonsignificant discrepancies between the predicted and obtained correlations.

Results

Exhibit 15.3 shows a correlation matrix as well as other descriptive statistics involving the model variables. These are store loyalty (SL), socioeconomic status (SES), social congruity (SC), ideal social congruity (ISC), area loyalty (AL), shopping complex loyalty (SCL), and store image evaluation (SIE). Exhibit 15.4 shows the same statistics involving the replication study.

Exhibit 15.5 represents a path model involving all causal relations based on the full model (SL as a function of SC, ISC, AL, SES, SIE, and SCL; SL as a function of SIE and SCL; SIE as a function of SC, ISC, AL, and SES; and SCL as a function of SC, ISC, AL and SES). The results show that 28.5 percent of

Exhibit 15.3

Zero-Order Correlations, Means, and Standard Deviations of Variables Involved in Study I (N = 256)

Zero-Order Correlations

Variables	SL	SES	SC	ISC	AL	SCL	SIE	Means	Std. Dev.
SL		-.124	-.249**	-.306***	.183*	.173*	.493***	5.832	1.938
SES			.107	.075	.044	-.181*	-.121	25.562	9.302
SC				.776***	-.012	-.126	-.298***	4.269	2.609
ISC					-.124	-.092	-.424***	5.078	2.913
AL						.434***	.057	2.730	1.165
SCL							.080	1.820	.974
SIE								67.660	10.011

Note: SL   =   Store Loyalty   *p<.10
        SES =   Socioeconomic Status   **p<.05
        SC   =   Social Congruity   ***p<.01
        ISC =   Ideal Social Congruity
        Al   =   Area Loyalty
        SCL =   Shopping Complex Loyalty
        SIE =   Store Image Evaluation

the total variance in SL scores was accounted for by SC, ISC, AL, SES, SIE, and SCL. Of those, only SIE and ISC were significant ($p < .05$). The results of the replication study provided further substantiation for this finding. SL was found to be significantly and strongly predicted by SIE and SCL ($p < .05$) but not by SC, ISC, AL, and SES.

As expected, SIE was found to be significantly influenced by ISC ($r = -.400$, $p < .01$) but not SC, AL, and SES ($r = .177$, $r = -.070$, $r = -.043$, respectively, and all nonsignificant, $p > .10$). ISC accounted for .080 r^2 change in the .085 total predicted variance in SIE scores. The replication study produced a similar pattern of results. The replication study also showed that SIE was primarily predicted by ISC ($r = -.395$, $p < .01$).

Also as expected, SCL was found to be significantly influenced by AL ($r = .628$, $p < .01$) and SES ($r = -.141$, $p < .01$), whereas the ISC and SC variables were nonsignificant ($r = .069$ and $r = -.002$, respectively, $p > .10$). The replication study added further support to this finding (AL: $r = .457$, $p < .01$; and SES: $r = -.189$, $p < .05$; ISC: $r = .143$, $p > .10$; SC: $r = -.211$, $p < .10$).

These results involving Stage 1 of the analysis provided strong support for the proposed model. Stage 2 of the analysis involved the decompositional analysis

Exhibit 15.4

Zero-Order Correlations, Means, and Standard Deviations of Variables Involved in Replication Study (N = 115)

<table>
<tr><td colspan="8" style="text-align:center">Zero-Order Correlations</td><td></td><td></td></tr>
<tr><th>Variables</th><th>SL</th><th>SES</th><th>SC</th><th>ISC</th><th>AL</th><th>SCL</th><th>SIE</th><th>Means</th><th>Std. Dev.</th></tr>
<tr><td>SL</td><td>.024</td><td>-.106</td><td>-.080</td><td>.106</td><td>.239*</td><td>.393***</td><td>5.232</td><td>1.633</td><td></td></tr>
<tr><td>SES</td><td></td><td>.064</td><td>-.016</td><td>-.079</td><td>-.191*</td><td>-.020</td><td>27.183</td><td>4.780</td><td></td></tr>
<tr><td>SC</td><td></td><td></td><td>.806***</td><td>.129</td><td>.126</td><td>-.157*</td><td>4.704</td><td>2.442</td><td></td></tr>
<tr><td>ISC</td><td></td><td></td><td></td><td>.120</td><td>.146</td><td>-.265***</td><td>4.548</td><td>2.352</td><td></td></tr>
<tr><td>AL</td><td></td><td></td><td></td><td></td><td>.647***</td><td>-.095</td><td>2.496</td><td>1.079</td><td></td></tr>
<tr><td>SCL</td><td></td><td></td><td></td><td></td><td></td><td>.007</td><td>2.035</td><td>.917</td><td></td></tr>
<tr><td>SIE</td><td></td><td></td><td></td><td></td><td></td><td></td><td>73.000</td><td>10.144</td><td></td></tr>
</table>

Note: SL = Store Loyalty   *p<.10
      SES = Socioeconomic Status   **p<.05
      SC = Social Congruity   ***p<.01
      ISC = Ideal Social Congruity
      Al = Area Loyalty
      SCL = Shopping Complex Loyalty
      SIE = Store Image Evaluation

performed on the proposed model (and, in this case, according to the results of Stage 1 analysis, is fairly equivalent to the trimmed or empirically derived model). The path coefficients of the proposed model are shown in Exhibit 15.6.

The proposed parsimonious model posits that SL is a function of SIE and SCL where SIE is a function of ISC and SCL is a function of AL and SES. This parsimonious model is tested by decomposing the correlations among the parsimonious model variables and comparing the predicted total association (sum of causal and noncausal association) with that of the obtained association (zero-order correlations). The parsimonious model is determined to be successful only when the predicted total association based on the relations presented in the parsimonious model are not found to diverge significantly from the obtained zero-order correlations. This is accomplished in Exhibit 15.7 for the first study and in Exhibit 15.8 for the replication study.

As shown in Exhibits 15.7 and 15.8, the reproduced (or predicted) correlations are not very different from the obtained zero-order correlations. However, we do not have to count on the mere inspection of the difference; we can test whether these discrepancies are significantly different from zero. This is done by using

Exhibit 15.5
The Full Model

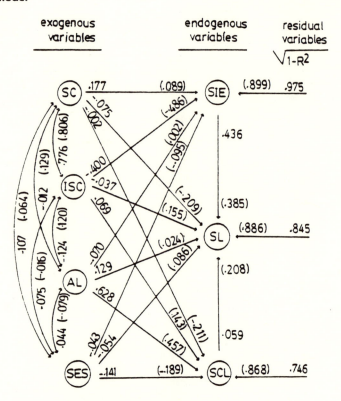

NOTE: coefficients in parentheses
belong to replication study

the chi-square test for assessing whether the discrepancy between estimated (predicted) and obtained correlations for the parsimonious model as a whole is beyond chance.[5] In this case, the computed chi-square was X^2 (6) = 10.5 and 8.0 for Study I and Study II, respectively ($p > .05$). Therefore, it can be said that the parsimonious model does fairly well. SL was found to be "caused" *essentially* by SIE ($r = .482, p < .01$ for study I and $r = .373, p < .01$ for the replication study) and SCL ($r = .135, p < .10$ for Study I and $r = .204$, $p < .05$ for the replication study), together accounting for 26.1 percent (and 19.6 percent for the replication study) of the total variance. SIE was found to be "causally influenced" by ISC ($r = -.424, p < .01$ for Study 1 and $r = -.265, p < .01$ for the replication study) accounting for 18 percent (and 7 percent for the replication study) of the total variance in SIE scores. In addition, SCL was found to be "causally" determined by AL ($r = .443, p < .01$ for

Exhibit 15.6
The Parsimonious Model

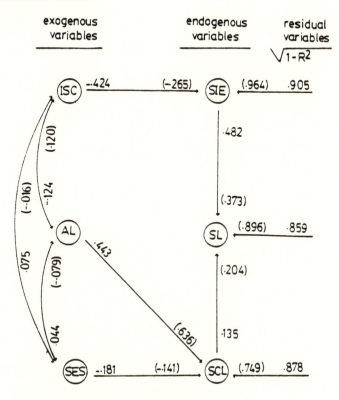

NOTE : coefficients in parentheses
belong to replication study

Study l and r $= .636$, $p < .01$ for the replication study) SES ($r = -.181$, $p < .05$ for Study l and r $= -.141$, $p < .10$ for the replication study), together accounting for 22.9 percent (and 43.9 percent for the replication study) of the total variance.

DISCUSSION AND CONCLUSION

This study demonstrates that store loyalty is determined by a set of highly interrelated variables. The interrelationship among store loyalty determinants is examined conceptually and empirically. A "causal" model was formulated to describe the interrelationships among the factors that determine store loyalty. This model suggests that store loyalty is influenced by store image evaluation and shopping complex loyalty. Store image evaluation is in turn influenced by self-image/store image congruity. Shopping complex loyalty is influenced by area loyalty and socioeconomic status.

Exhibit 15.7
Decomposition of Correlations Among Parsimonious Model Variables of Study I (N = 256)

	Causal Association	+ Noncausal Association = Total Association		
Variables	[Direct + Indirect = Total] +	[$\sum$ Components = Total]	= Predicted	Obtained
SIE/ISC	$P_{SIE/ISC}$ + ___ = -.424 + (-.424)	_____ = -.424	-.424	-.424
SCL/AL	$P_{SCL/AL}$ + ___ = .443 + (.443)	$r_{AL/SES}P_{SCL/SES}$ = -.008 = (.044) (-.181)	.435	.434
SCL/SES	$P_{SCL/SES}$ + ___ = -.181 + (-.181)	$r_{SES/AL}P_{SCL/AL}$ = .019 = (.044) (.443)	-.162	-.181
SL/SIE	$P_{SL/SIE}$ + ___ = .482 + (.482)	$r_{SIE/SCL}P_{SL/SCL}$ = .011 = (.080) (.135)	.493	.460
SIE/AL	___ + ___ = ___ +	$r_{AL/ISC}P_{SIE/ISC}$ = .053 = (-.124)(-.424)	.053	.057
SIE/SES	___ + ___ = ___ +	$r_{SES/ISC}P_{SIE/ISC}$ = -.032 = (.075) (-.424)	-.032	-.121
SL/ISC	___ + ___ = ___ +	$r_{ISC/SIE}P_{AL/SIE}$ (-.424)(.482) $r_{ISC/SCL}+P_{SL/SCL}$ = -.216 = (-.092) (.135)	-.216	-.272
SL/AL	___ + ___ = ___ +	$r_{AL/SIE}P_{SL/SIE}$ (.057) (.482) $+$ $r_{AL/SCL}$ $P_{SL/SCL}$ = .086 = (.434) (.135)	.086	.166
SL/SES	___ + ___ = ___ +	$r_{SES/SIE}P_{SL/SIE}$ (-.121) (.482) $+$ $r_{SES/SCL}P_{SL/SCL}$ = -.082 =	-.082	-.118
SCL/ISC	___ + ___ = ___ +	$r_{ISC/AL}P_{SCL/AL}$ (-.124)(.443) $+$ $r_{ICS/SES}SCL/SES$ = -.068 = (.075) (-.181)	-.068	-.092

Exhibit 15.8
Decomposition of Correlations Among Parsimonious Model Variables of Replication Study (N = 115)

	Causal Association	+	Noncausal Association	= Total Association
Variables	$[$ Direct + Indirect = Total $]$ +	$[$ Σ Components = Total $]$	= Predicted	Obtained
SIE/ISC	$P_{SIE/ISC}$ (-.265) + ___ = -.265 +	_____	= -.265	-.265
SCL/AL	$P_{SCL/AL}$ (.636) + ___ = .636 +	$r_{AL/SES} P_{SCL/SES}$ = .011 (-.079)(-.141)	= .647	.647
SCL/SES	$P_{SCL/SES}$ (-.141) + ___ = -.141 +	$r_{SES/AL} P_{SCL/AL}$ = -.050 (-.079)(.636)	= -.191	-.191
SL/SIE	$P_{SCL/SES}$ (.373) + ___ = .373 +	$r_{SIE/SCL} P_{SL/SCL}$ = .001 (.007)(.204)	= .374	.382
SL/SCL	$P_{SL/SCL}$ (.204) + ___ = .204 +	$r_{SCL/SIE} P_{SL/SIE}$ = .003 (.007)(.204)	= .207	.209
SIE/AL	___ + ___ = ___ +	$r_{AL/ISC} SIE/ISC$ = -.032 (.120)(-.265)	= -.032	-.095
SL/ISC	___ + ___ = ___ +	$r_{ISC/SIE} P_{SL/SIE}$ = -.069 (-.265)(.373) $+$ $r_{ISC/SCL} P_{SL/SCL}$ (.146)(.204)	= -.069	-.088
SL/AL	___ + ___ = ___ +	$r_{AL/SIE} P_{SL/SIE}$ = .097 (-.095)(.373) $+$ $r_{AL/SCL} P_{SL/SCL}$ (.647)(.204)	= .097	.047
SL/SES	___ + ___ = ___ +	$r_{SES/SIE} P_{SL/SIE}$ = -.046 (-.020) $+_p$ (.373) $r_{SES/SCL} P_{SL/SCL}$ (-.191)(.204)	= -.046	.017
SCL/ISC	___ + ___ = ___ +	$r_{ISC/AL} P_{SCL/AL}$ = .079 (.120) $+$ (.636) $r_{ISC/SES} P_{SCL/SES}$ (-.016)(-.141)	= .079	.146

This model was subjected to testing through a path analytic procedure in two independent studies. The results of both studies provide validational support for the "causal" model as developed in this chapter. Although the interrelationships among store loyalty determinants were delineated in this model, the results showed that the task of identifying the major determinants of store loyalty are far from complete as indicated by the magnitude values of the residual variables. Further conceptualizations and testing of store loyalty determinants need to be completed.

Research Implications

Although the path analytic findings of the proposed store loyalty model are strong, further study is needed to resolve some troublesome issues. Among these issues are the following.

1. It is not clear whether self-image/store image congruity causally affects store image evaluations. Store image evaluations may influence the congruity process. For example, a shopper may be familiar only with the store range of product prices. Based on this functional store image attribute, the shopper may infer the stereotypic or symbolic image associated with the store and not vice versa. These two competing hypotheses should be tested at a future date.

2. It is also not clear whether *either* or *both* self-image/store image congruity and functional store image evaluations causally determine store loyalty. According to Daryl Bem's (1967) self-perception theory, it is conceivable that both symbolic and functional store images have been determined by attributing the causes of one's shopping behavior to those symbolic and/or functional store images. These causal attributions may have accounted for subjects' responses to the store loyalty measures. Future research might also address this issue.

3. The use of the semantic differential technique to measure self-concept, and symbolic and functional store images is plagued with problems. First, equal weights are assumed for all attributes. Second, the salience of attributes might not be high across respondents and across stores. Finally, responses might be affected by halo effects (Sirgy 1982). Other types of measurements should be used in future research.

4. Based on the percentage of predicted variance in store loyalty scores, it is obvious that other unforeseen factors should be included in the model. These factors may include loyalty to specific product brands which a store might not carry (*brand loyalty*) and the extent to which the store is new or has been in the market for some time (*store life cycle*). Future research may incorporate these variables into the proposed store loyalty model.

Managerial Implications

The managerial implications of this study are clear-cut.

1. The retail manager must know how consumers perceive the functional as

well as the symbolic characteristics of the store. This knowledge can be obtained through research on store image.

2. Those functional store image characteristics found to be poorly evaluated by the majority of the respondents should be the basis for retail strategy development. These strategies should be developed to affect the consumers' image of the store and therefore increase store patronage and store loyalty.

3. The retail manager must also realize that those symbolic images of the store (which most retailers pay hardly any attention to) play a significant role in store patronage and loyalty behaviors. The retailer is therefore also advised to gather information about how consumers see the store in personality terms. Is the store a friendly store? A formal store? A classy store? In addition, the retailer should know something about how consumers see themselves. If the personality of the store seems to coincide with the personality of most of the target customers, then the retailer can rest assured that he or she has won half the battle. If the retailer finds out that most of the target customers have different personality images from those propagated by the store, then it is time for action. Through various promotional efforts, the retailer should be able to change those symbolic store images in the direction of his or her target customers. This is essential since self-image/store image congruity effects as demonstrated by this study do affect how customers perceive the functional store attributes.

4. It is not enough for the retail manager to watch out for the store without paying any regard to what is happening with the immediate surrounding stores. Based on this study, shopping complex loyalty is a significant determinant of store loyalty. If the customers are not pleased with the surrounding stores for one reason or another, their loyalty to the store will decline. Therefore, the retail manager must see that the neighboring stores are using wise and sound strategies to maintain a satisfactory level of store patronage and loyalty. This undoubtedly entails cooperation and establishing harmonious relations with neighboring retail managers. In doing so, retail managers in the immediately surrounding areas have to develop promotional strategies to enhance shopping complex loyalties. This can be accomplished by considering area loyalty and socioeconomic status as significant influences on shopping complex loyalty. To increase shopping complex loyalty, retail managers have to appeal to those customers who are basically loyal to the general area where the shopping complex is located and to those customers whose socioeconomic status matches the pricing policies and social class image portrayed by this unified entity of stores.

SUMMARY

This chapter explores the store loyalty concept. First, it is posited that different researchers relate store loyalty to different variables. Although some researchers associate store loyalty with psychographic variables, others believe there is a relationship between socioeconomic characteristics and store loyalty. Still others have attempted to single out store image variables as the major force behind the store image congruence is a key factor, a theme that is pursued throughout this book. However, this chapter suggests that store image is a multidimensional concept. Hence, one set of variables may not fully explain it. In this book, self-image and store image congruence is seen not only as a cause but also as an effect. The congruence is present because customers are satisfied and because the store has a desirable image.

A path analytic model is presented in order to examine the concept of store loyalty. Based on this model, data were gathered and a study test-retest situation was pursued. Study findings indicate that store loyalty is indeed a multidimensional phenomenon. Different dimensions may play varying predictor roles for different stores under given conditions.

It is extremely important for retailers to study the particular predictor variables indicating their customers' loyalty to their stores. It is maintained that early predictions of changes in store loyalty are likely to provide important managerial alternatives for retailers who would like to maintain the health and stability of their stores.

NOTES

1. Social congruity is defined as the match between symbolic (i.e., personality related—"friendly," "unfriendly," "formal") store image and shoppers' social self-image ("the image of myself as seen by others"). Ideal social congruity is defined as the match between symbolic store image and the shopper's ideal social self-image ("the image of myself as I would like to be seen by others").

2. Evaluation of store image was construed to be an attitude toward the store as determined by the perception and evaluation of the store's functional attributes (i.e., store's product variety, store's prices, and store's location).

3. Area loyalty and shopping complex loyalty are defined as behavioral tendencies to shop in a particular shopping mall or a small surrounding one where most of the stores are conglomerated (shopping complex loyalty). To the best of our knowledge, these two constructs are new to the retailing literature.

4. Of course, the same theory can be used to argue that store loyalty is determined by other factors (perhaps sheer habit), and what is really occurring here in the model depicted in Exhibit 15.2 is a store loyalty *attribution* process.

5. However, C. Fornell and D F. Larcker (1981) argue that the chi-square test may provide misleading results; therefore, they offer the F-test to be applied on each endogenous variable.

$$F_q, (N-q-1)[R^2 (N-q-1)]/[(1-R^2)q]$$

where q = number of observed independent variables, and R^2 = perception of variance accounted for in a specific endogenous variable. Following these suggestions, three F-tests were conducted for each of the SIE, SL, and SCL variables. The results were as follows:

Study I	Replication Study
SIE--F(1,255) = 55.970**	SIE--F(1,114) = 8.581*
SL --F(2,253) = 36.052**	SL --F(2,112) = 88.815*
SCL--F(2,253) = 38.018**	SCL--F(2,112) = 43.822**

*p < .01 **p > .001

REFERENCES

Abelson, R. P. "A Script Theory of Understanding, Attitude, and Behavior." In J. Carroll and T. Payne, eds., *Cognition and Social Behavior*. Hillsdale, N.Y.: Erlbaum, 1976.

Albaum, G., and J. Dickson, "A Method for Developing Tailormade Semantic Differentials for Specific Marketing Content Areas." *Journal of Marketing Research* 14 (February 1977): 87–91.

Alderson, W. *Marketing Decision and Executive Action*. Homewood, Ill.: Richard D. Irwin, 1957.

Anderson, John R. *Cognitive Psychology and Its Implications*. San Francisco: Freeman, 1980.

Bellinger, D. N., E. Steinberg, and W. W. Stanton. "The Congruence of Store Image and Self-Image." *Journal of Retailing* 52 (1976): 17–32.

Bem, Daryl. "Self-Perception: An Alternative Interpretation of Cognitive Dissonance Phenomena." *Psychological Review* 74 (1967): 183–200.

Berry, L. L. "The Components of Department Store Image: A Theoretical and Empirical Analysis." *Journal of Retailing* (Spring 1969): 3–20.

Birdwell, A. "A Study of Influence of Image Congruence on Consumer Choice." *Journal of Business* 41 (1968): 76–88.

Carman, James M. "Concepts of Brand Loyalty: Some Positive Results." *Journal of Marketing Research* 7 (February 1970): 67–76.

Chamberlain, E. *The Theory of Monopolistic Competition*. Cambridge, Mass.: University Press, 1933.

Coleman, R. P., and L. Rainwater. *Social Standing in America: New Dimensions of Class*. New York: Basic Books, 1978.

Dolich, I. J. "Congruence Relationship Between Self-Images and Product Brands." *Journal of Marketing Research* 6 (1969): 80–84.

Dornoff, R. J., and R. L. Tatham. "Congruence Between Personal Image and Store Image." *Journal of Market Research Society* 14 (1972): 45–52.

Enis, B. M., and G. W. Paul. "Store Loyalty Characteristics of Shoppers and Switchers." *Southern Journal of Business* 3 (1968): 266–76.

Fornell, C., and D. F. Larcker. "Evaluating Structural Equation Models with Unobservable Variables and Measurement Error." *Journal of Marketing Research* 17 (1981): 39–50.

Frank, R. E. "Corrolates of Buying Behavior for Grocery Products." *Journal of Marketing* 31 (October 1967): 48–53.

———, W. F. Massey, and Thomas M. Lodahl. "Purchasing Behavior and Personal Attributes." *Journal of Advertising Research* 9 (December 1969): 15–24.

———, W. F. Massey, and Y. Wind. *Market Segmentation.* Englewood Cliffs, N.J.: Prentice-Hall, 1972.

Hirschman, Elizabeth. "Retail Research and Theory." In Ben M. Enis and Kenneth J. Roering, eds., *Review of Marketing 1981.* Chicago: American Marketing Association, 1981.

Jacoby, J., and D. B. Kyner. "Brand Loyalty Versus Repeat Purchase Behavior." *Journal of Marketing Research* 10 (1973): 1–9.

Jenkins, R. L., and S. M. Forsythe. "Retail Image Research: State of the Art Review with Implications for Retail Strategy." In V. V. Bellur and B. G. Gnaudi, eds., *Developments in Marketing Science.* Miami: Academy of Marketing Science, 1980, pp. 189–93.

Kelley, R. G., and R. Stephenson. "The Semantic Differential: An Informative Source for Designing Retail Patronage Appeals." *Journal of Marketing* 31 (December 1967): 43–47.

Kerlinger, F. N., and E. J. Pedhazer. *Multiple Regression in the Behavioral Sciences.* New York: Holt, Rinehart and Winston, 1973.

Lessig, Y. P. "Consumer Store Image and Store Loyalties." *Journal of Marketing* (October 1973).

Lincoln, D. J. "The Effects of Comparative Advertising on the Department Store Image: An Experimental Analysis." Ph.D. diss. Marketing Department, Virginia Tech, Blacksburg, Virginia.

———, and A. C. Samli. "Retail Store Image: Definitions and Measurement." In *Proceedings of Southern Marketing Association* (1979):

Lindquist, J. D. "Meaning of Image." *Journal of Retailing* 50 (Winter 1974–1975): 29–38.

McDougall, G. H. G., and J. N. Fry. "Combining Two Methods of Image Measurement." *Journal of Retailing* 50 (Winter 1974–1975): 53–56.

Markus, Hazel. "The Self in Thought and Memory." In Daniel M. Wegner and Robin R. Vallacher, eds., *The Self in Social Psychology.* New York: Oxford University Press, 1980.

Martineau, P. "The Personality of the Retail Store." *Harvard Business Review* 36 (1958): 47–55.

Mason, J. B., and M. L. Mayer. "The Problem of the Self-Concept in Store Studies." *Journal of Marketing* 34 (1970): 67–69.

Neisser, U. *Cognition and Reality: Principles and Implications of Cognitive Psychology.* San Francisco: Freeman, 1976.

Nevin, John R., and Michael J. Houston. "Image as a Component of Attraction to Intraurban Shopping Areas." *Journal of Retailing* 56 (Spring 1980): 77–93.

Nisbett, Richard, and Lee Rosee. *Human Inference: Strategies Shortcomings of Social Judgement.* Englewood Cliffs, N.J.: Prentice-Hall, 1981.

Oxenfeldt, A. R. "Developing a Favorable Price-Quantity Image." *Journal of Retailing* 50 (Winter 1974–1975): 7.

Pathak, D. S., W. J. Crissy, and R. W. Sweitzer. "Customer Image Versus the Retailer's Anticipated Image." *Journal of Retailing* 50 (1974–1975).

Plummer, J. T. "The Concept and Application of the Life Style Segmentation." *Journal of Marketing* 38 (Winter 1974): 21–28.

Reynolds, F. D., W. B. Darden, and W. S. Martin. "Developing an Image of the Store-Loyal Customer." *Journal of Retailing* (Winter 1974): 73–84.

Ross, I. "Self-Concept and Brand Preference." *Journal of Business of the University of Chicago* 44 (1971): 38–50.

Samli, A. C. "Segmentation and Carving a Niche in the Market Place." *Journal of Retailing* (Summer 1968): 35–45.

———. "Use of Segmentation Index to Measure Store Loyalty." *Journal of Retailing* (Spring 1975): 51–60.

———. "Segmentation Index and Store Image in Retail and Service Establishments: A New Direction in Marketing Research for Retailers." In *Research That Works for Today's Marketing Problems.* Proceedings of ESOMAR Conference, Venice, Italy, 1976, pp. 143–55.

———. "Some Observations on Intermarket Shopping Behavior as It Relates to the Spatial Dimension." Proceedings, National Educators' Conference. Chicago: American Marketing Association, 1979, pp. 408–10.

———, and M. J. Sirgy. "A Multidimensional Approach to Analyzing Store Loyalty: A Predictive Model." In Ken Bernhardt and Bill Kehoe, eds., *The Changing Marketing Environment: New Theories and Applications.* Chicago: American Marketing Association, 1981.

Schewe, C. D., and W. R. Dillon. "Marketing Information System Utilization: An Application of Self-Concept Theory." *Journal of Business Research* 6 (1978): 67–69.

Sirgy, M. Joseph. "Self-Concept in Consumer Behavior." Ph.D. diss., University of Massachusetts, Amherst, 1979.

———. "Self-Concept in Relation to Product Preference and Purchase Intention." In V. V. Bellur, ed., *Developments in Marketing Science,* vol. 3. Marquette: Academy of Marketing Science, 1980.

———. "Self-Concept in Consumer Behavior: A Critical Review." *Journal of Consumer Research* 9 (December 1982): 287–300.

———, and Jeffrey A. Danes. "Self-Image/Product-Image Congruence Models: Testing Selected Mathematical Models." In Andrew Mitchell, ed., *Advances in Consumer Research,* vol. 9. Ann Arbor, Mich.: Association for Consumer Research, 1982.

Stern, B. L., R. F. Bush, and J. F. Haire, Jr. "The Self-Image/Store Image Matching Process: An Empirical Test." *Journal of Business* 50 (1977): 63–69.

Weale, B. "Measuring the Customer's Image of a Department Store." *Journal of Retailing* 37 (Summer 1961): 40–48.

Wyckham, R. G. "Aggregate Department Store Image: Social and Experimental Factors." Proceedings of the American Marketing Association Conference, Chicago, 1967, p. 333.

Wyer, Robert S., Jr., and Donald E. Carlson. *Social Cognition, Inference, and Attribution.* Hillsdale, N.J.: Erlbaum, 1979.

Appendix 1

CRITERIA USED IN THIS STUDY TO IDENTIFY THE PERCEIVED IMAGE OF CONSUMERS

General Characteristics

Well known	Unknown
Well established	Not well established

Physical Characteristics

Clean	Dirty
Quiet	Noisy
Elegant interior	Plain interior

Price

Prices too high	Prices low
Wide price range	Limited price range
Too high price for the value purchased	Reasonable price for the value purchased

Personnel

Personnel are courteous	Personnel are not courteous
Personnel have nice appearance	Personnel have questionable appearance
Personnel are knowledgeable	Personnel are not knowledgeable

Promotion

Store is highly recommended by your friends	Store is poorly recommended by your friends
Store uses good promotional devices	Store uses poor promotional devices
Store advertising is highly believable	Store advertising is highly misleading

Convenience

Store is located conveniently	Store is located inconveniently
It is easy to find a parking place	It is difficult to find a parking place

Product and Services

Product selection is wide	Product selection is narrow
Product quality is high	Product quality is low
Product information is dependable	Product information is not dependable
Credit service is good	Credit service is poor

Appendix 2

CRITERIA USED IN THE SEGMENTATION INDEX

Categories	Weighted by	Categories	Weighted by
1. Income	1-8	5. Credit cards	
		Diner's Club	6
2. Education	1-8	Gasoline	1
		American Express	5
3. Luxury items		Visa	4
Stereo console	2	Master Charge	3
AM/FM radio	1	Store Credit Card	2
Central air		Carte Blanche	7
conditioning	4		
Color TV console	3	6. Hobbies	
Wall-to-wall carpeting	5	Expensive hobbies	5
Boat 14 feet or less	6	Moderately expensive	
Boat 15 feet or more	7	hobbies	3
		Cheap hobbies	1
4. House payments			
$10–125		7. Occupation	
$126–300		Blue collar	1
Above 300		White collar	3

16 Retail Information Management Systems (RIMS): A New Tool for Successful Retailing

Retailing is perhaps the most dynamic sector in the American economy. The average life span of retail firms was once estimated to be five years, and there is hardly any reason to assume that this situation has changed significantly. Furthermore, earlier studies indicated that more than 30 percent of retail establishments fail in less than six months. Thus, survival is a prime concern, particularly among small retailers. However, survival is not the only goal, since in itself it does not imply growth and profitability. The firm must also grow and prosper over and beyond survival.

Not unlike manufacturers, today's retailers operate in an environment whose characteristics make survival and profitability goals difficult to achieve. In general, retail life cycles are getting shorter and retail failure percentages are high. Technological innovations, evolving socioeconomic trends, and emerging new lifestyles have accelerated the complexity and speed of change in the retailer's environment (Bates 1977; Berman and Evans 1986).

Survival, growth, and profitability are accounted for by the increasing proficiency of the retail establishment which may be enumerated in terms of at least three specific activities: (1) the limited resources of retailers must be effectively allocated; (2) both in functional and planning areas, management must utilize time effectively; and (3) strategic decisions must be made successfully. In all of these cases, an effective decision-making process must take place. Such a decision-making process consists of identifying goals, determining alternatives, deciding on the expected outcome of each alternative, and, finally, making a decision. The process is common to both small and large retailers. In order to function properly, the above decision-making process constantly requires information. In essence, effective management is managing information well, and this principle is applicable to both large and small retailers. Thus, a Retail Information Management System (RIMS) is essential in all retailing.

This chapter emphasizes the need for retailers to manage their information. This management process includes all activities from data gathering to information processing. The chapter describes RIMS which can provide such information management.

MARKETING RESEARCH BY RETAILERS

With the exception of some major chains and large department stores, research traditionally has not been the forte of small retailers for a number of reasons:

Lack of resources to do research.
Lack of expertise to engage in research.
Less than adequate understanding of what research can do.
Intense involvement in day-to-day activities allowing no time to do anything else.
Inability to use research findings.
Consideration of research as a luxury activity.

In addition, it has been suggested that the techniques are not quite developed, and data collection and analysis are very complicated (Lesser and Stearns 1986). Thus, it is safe to assert that, traditionally, small retailers have not been active in research areas, and are woefully unaware of their need for information and how to use it.

Because of the vulnerability created by internal lacks such as management skills or finances and because of adverse external conditions, retailers must learn to develop and use an information system. Such a system will be keyed to providing routine and recurrent as well as ad hoc information, which is essential for retailers to enter the market, self-perpetuate, and prosper. This particular system provides the necessary ingredients for management to allocate resources, use time, and make strategic decisions successfully. In a nutshell, the system must coordinate the total information-gathering efforts of the firm so that relevant and timely information can be captured, organized, and delivered when needed. This chapter presents a general model of RIMS in an effort to publicize its conceptual construct. Thus, the chapter seeks to identify information sources, types of information, the information flow process, and the component of RIMS within the context of a five-stage development: (1) idea planning and feasibility, (2) definition of requirements, (3) design, (4) implementation, and (5) evaluation. This five-stage development is necessary for RIMS to become functional and viable.

BACKGROUND

A RIMS can be viewed as a specifically applied version of a Management or Marketing Information System (MIS). Such a system has been typically defined as a "system of people, equipment, procedures, documents, and communications that collects, retrieves, and presents data for use in planning, budgeting, accounting, controlling, and other management processes" (Eldin and Croft, 1974). Simply put, a MIS is an integrated person–machine system for providing information to support the operation, management, and decision-making functions of an organization. The word *machine* in the definition does not refer to the computer only; rather, it implies systematic processing of certain information.

A MIS should be a well-planned and organized effort and should provide managers at different levels with relevant, reliable, timely, and economic information that is gathered from both internal and external resources. MIS also needs to be flexible, responsible, and usable. To be of real value to decision makers, it should be management oriented and should embody management science techniques.

RETAIL INFORMATION MANAGEMENT SYSTEMS (RIMS)

A RIMS can be viewed as a specialized MIS with a prime focus on the retailing industry. Its major objective is to create a better flow of needed information to make decisions. Therefore, RIMS is considered a subsystem within a certain retailing institution with a basic function of optimum decision making through integration, feedback, and control.

RIMS may be of two types: computer and noncomputer based. In this chapter, a special attempt is made to aid the retailer in establishing a computer-based system. However, a better understanding and appreciation of computer-based systems may be made possible by first providing a brief overview of noncomputer-based systems.

Noncomputer-based RIMS. Prior to the invention and use of the computer, both manual and mechanical means were employed to gather, process, store, and retrieve information. In fact, a firm need not have a computer to have a RIMS. An example is the newsstand proprietor who could have a RIMS, using his own memory as a data storage and his own logical and mathematical abilities as a means of processing the data (McLeod 1987). However, such simple manual information systems are rarely found, except for very small business organizations. Even in small retail firms it is not uncommon to have cash registers and/ or adding machines. Therefore, it can be stated that almost every RIMS combines both manual and mathematical techniques to accomplish its goals. Size of organization, amount of information, economies of processing, and value of speed are among the factors in the tradeoffs between humans and machines within these systems.

A RIMS of this nature is likely to suffer from distintegration between functions, duplication of work, limitations in processing large amounts of data, and lack of precision. Perhaps the greatest deficiency of noncomputerized RIMS is their inability to distinguish between the different types of information needed by management at different levels.

The above points support the need for the use of computer-based RIMS. In addition, the recent introduction of several low-cost mini- and microprocessor computer-based RIMS has made the process simple. There is no consensus among practitioners or academicians regarding the number and types of stages involved in creating an information system. Regardless of the stages, it is important first to observe the nature and characteristics of a RIMS. Exhibit 16.1 illustrates a relatively simple RIMS model. The model indicates the process from data gathering to information formulation for management decisions. The model displays the presence of four components: the data-gathering component, the data processing component, a management information base, and the feedback unit (Samli 1980). These four components generate and facilitate an overall information flow.

Information Flow. RIMS is designed for management use, and in that capacity, it produces three distinctively different outputs: (1) standard reports, (2) answers to special problems, and (3) special assessment and evaluation (Dalton 1976; Dearden and Anthony 1976).

Standard Reports. These are generated by internal information. Reports on merchandising, operations, finances, personnel, and sales promotion are typical in retailing, regardless of size. Information regarding the general operations of the retail establishment is the basis for evaluation, planning, and control.

Answers to Special Problems. Special problems may vary from adding a new line or a new department to changing the internal layout or the image of the store. Adding new and more profitable merchandise lines and deleting those that are not being profitable are among the most important concerns of retail establishments. A strong and effectively functioning RIMS must cater to this type of need. Similarly, if the store needs to change its image, it is extremely important that RIMS facilitates such an activity by providing information on the strengths and weaknesses of the present image and on what the nature, characteristics, and direction of the new image should be.

Special Assessment. Not totally independent from the first two types of outputs, various types of evaluations are a very important output of RIMS. In order to make plans for the future or to establish certain controls, various types of assessments may be required. If, for instance, the RIMS can assess the market potential and expected change in the clientele of a restaurant as it moves away from being a family place, it can enable management to offer a new elaborate menu with a bar of mixed drinks. On another occasion, the retail establishment may consider the merits of relocating in a newly developed mall as opposed to a semi-defunct downtown. A simpler decision relating to changing advertising media may be based on information on the effectiveness of the existing media.

Exhibit 16.1 illustrates the types of outputs that RIMS uses as it provides proper outputs for management's use. One category, random information, has not been discussed. Not all informational inputs in RIMS are deliberate. If, for instance, the management of a mall department store becomes aware of a study that was done externally for another purpose and if it reports that the area needs

**Exhibit 16.1
RIMS Flow Process**

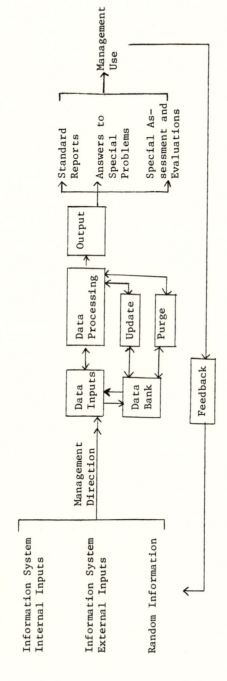

Source: Adapted and revised from O'Brien 1970.

a furniture outlet, such a random information input may be processed in the RIMS, leading to a new furniture department in the store (Schaffir and Trentin 1973).

Data Processing. The middle part of Exhibit 16.1 depicts the data processing aspects of RIMS. It can be seen that, in order for RIMS to provide proper information, it should have a data bank and a retrieval system.

The nature of the data bank depends on the size and degree of sophistication of the retail establishment. Ideally, the system is fully computerized aided by marketing research as well as market intelligence services. The system can be totally computerized, partially computerized, or totally noncomputerized. In all cases, not only the presence of a data bank but also its quality is important The quality of the data bank is related to (1) its scope, (2) the ability to update it, and, finally, (3) the retrievability of its data. First, if the data bank does not have the width and breadth of data called for, it is not likely to be very functional. Second, if the data are not updated so that new and fresh information is always available for the decision makers, the whole concept becomes self-defeating. Finally, no matter how good the data bank might be in terms of its scope and its timeliness, if it does not have the versatility to provide management with any and all types of information generated through its retrieval system, the whole concept becomes a total failure.

Finally, Exhibit 16.1 illustrates the presence of a feedback module. This module provides a built-in quality control and improvement mechanism that will be further discussed toward the end of this chapter.

COMPUTER-BASED RIMS: A DEVELOPMENT PROCEDURE

McLeod (1987) suggests a four-stage development process for RIMS, whereas Schafer (1972) recommends a seven-stage process. The following proposed development cycle combines McLeod's and Schafer's plans and thus utilizes the advantages of each while minimizing their disadvantages. A suggested RIMS development cycle is presented in Exhibit 16.2 and is discussed below (Samli 1980).

Step 1: Idea, Planning, and Feasibility

Whenever the need to construct a RIMS arises, management should ascertain that this need is real and that having such a system is justified. Medium or large retail establishments may use a management team representing different managerial functions. The team should answer a series of questions: What about existing information systems, if any? What about the proposed RIMS: Can it be done? Is it practical? Is it economical? How should it be done? The point to be emphasized is that managers tend to overlook existing systems in an attempt to acquire newer ones.

Exhibit 16.2
Suggested RIMS Development Cycle

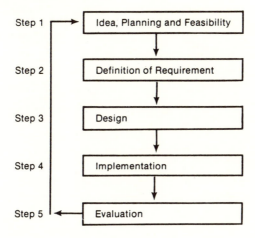

After any existing information system has been thoroughly investigated and the need to acquire a new system is certain, the team proceeds to examine available alternatives. A feasibility study of any proposed system is of crucial value since a considerable investment may be involved. The study helps management to identify potential problem areas and provides an objective basis for decision making rather than depending on management wishes to have a new RIMS because it is fashionable. Exhibit 16.3 shows the complexities involved in this stage as exemplified by the number of steps needed (Schafer 1972).

As the exhibit suggests, the team needs to compare existing and proposed systems based on costs and benefit analysis for each system. In addition, the team needs to know the relationship between the value of information and its determinant factors, since cost of information is a function of accuracy, speed, time response, person-machine mix, completeness, and brevity.

Step 2: Definition of Requirements

The main purpose of this stage is to define needed information. This will serve as a guide for the design of the central data base which is a major component of the RIMS. As the committee in charge, the team is also required to make a decision regarding the equipment to be used. Normally, it will have a number of alternatives from which to select based on the firm's needs and capabilities. Therefore, the success of the team is contingent on inclusion of management representatives, users (middle management in medium and large organizations), and specialists.

At this stage in the game, it is necessary to decide how RIMS will be manned and where it will be located in the organization. Many firms that have some

Exhibit 16.3
RIMS Feasibility Study Procedure

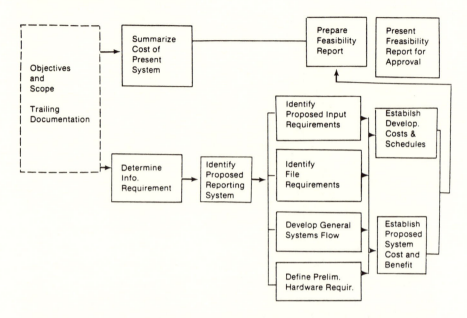

facsimile of RIMS have made the mistake of putting the system within either the personnel or accounting department which limits its performance to a great extent. Therefore, it is generally wiser to establish a separate department for RIMS which reports either to the executive vice-president or the president. At this stage of development, performance criteria also are to be established. They will serve as a basis of control and evaluation.

Information Needs and Sources

In order to identify the information sources, both the internal and external environments of retailing have to be examined. Exhibit 16.4 presents some of the information sources a retailer might deal with. As can be seen, the sources are classified as internal and external.

An information management system for retailers has to be simple and sensitive to local changes. The simplicity and sensitivity become greater as the retail establishment becomes smaller. Thus, the smallest retailer has to have the smallest and most sensitive RIMS. Furthermore, RIMS must not be too costly. Smaller retailers in particular do not have the means to develop an elaborate RIMS. On the basis of these criteria, the most important source of information is internal.

Internal Sources and Types of Information

Internal sources of information, particularly in small-scale retailing, are extremely valuable. First, they provide a vital set of facts; second, the information

Exhibit 16.4
RIMS Information Sources

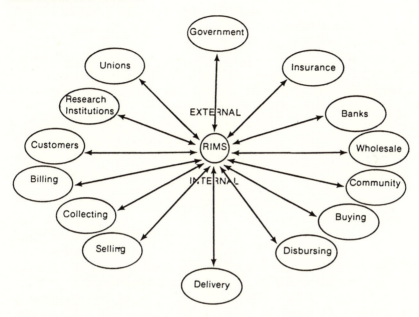

is easy to gather; and third, it is relatively less costly to gather internal information (O'Brien 1970).

Financial Control may include the responsibility center, budget data, cost data, revenue data, customer data if possible, schedule data, sales, receivables, purchases data, personnel and payroll, securities data (if any), data on debt, asset data, creditors data, and tax data. Data are gathered from books, transaction records, and management reports or plans.

The Transaction File may include receipts, payments, bank accounts, discounts, dates of transaction, amount of cash, description of securities, sales, purchases, and similar items. Sources of information are receipts, authorization slips, vouchers payable, and other financial statements. These can be broken down by departments, product lines, and personnel. The Human Resources File may include names of employees, their social security numbers, departments, job classification, original hiring date, seniority, characteristics (such as sex, race, and religion), and merit plan ratings, if applicable. Sources of data include personnel files and respective department periodic reports. This source yields additional information on different compensation programs, scheduling, and staff requirements as well as personnel selection.

The Sales File may include a breakdown by product, product line, customer class, cost center, region, or salesperson. The problem here is that most retailers deal in small quantities and with a large number of customers. Therefore, it is very difficult to include the name and address of each customer (an exception may be credit customers) as industrial firms do. However, it is possible to summarize the observation of salespersons regarding who shops at this store or to carry out marketing research frequently. In such a case, market research findings are added to the data base for future use.

Accounts Receivable and Customer Files provide information about service charges, aging analyses, collection performances, bill adjustments, and customer complaints. This is one of the most important information sources in determining performance effectiveness in the marketplace.

A Data Base Sales File can be a vital tool to competition, since it enables management to compare products and understand trends. It can also help management to carry out analyses of product life cycles and to make conclusions regarding the profitability of each product, salesperson, or customer class. This also aids forecasting.

All of these information sources can be tapped by those who are involved in the types of activities to which these sources are related. The person, for instance, who is in charge of merchandising will be the most natural choice to provide the necessary information for the RIMS.

Whether or not the information will be in an informal or formal form would depend on the retail establishment's size and degree of sophistication. If it is quite sizable and there are a number of layers between the top decision-making level and the accountant or the merchandising manager, then the information could take a formal report form. In such cases, the sophistication level of the specialists at different managerial levels is also high, which further facilitates the presence of formal information format. In addition to formal reports, the information system is likely to be computerized in these firms. In smaller and less sophisticated firms, a more informal approach is likely to be used, consisting primarily of semiformal reports and word-of-mouth information flow.

External Sources and Types of Information

Exhibit 16.4 illustrates some of the most important external sources of information. Exhibit 16.5 identifies four more specific types of information based on the sources identified in Exhibit 16.4. As can be seen, neither the sources nor the types of information are difficult to gain access to. However, the simplistic nature of the sources and information does not imply that the information is not very important. On the contrary, this type of information is vital to the well-being of both small and large retailers. Some scholars have suggested more elaborate and complex external information systems based on shopping behavior theory (Lesser and Stearns 1986). Edgar A. Pessemier (1980) has suggested that such a system is necessary to develop an effective store image and to manipulate the position of the store accordingly. J. Barry Mason and Morris Mayer (1980) go further, suggesting that retail merchandise information systems are to be used for critical strategic decision making.

Exhibit 16.5 identifies four general types of information from four specific

Exhibit 16.5
Specific Types of External Information for Small Businesses

A. Population Movements

    1. Would the key institutions continue growing? What are the prospects for new business in town?

    2. New land zoning decisions.

        a. newly expected residential areas
        b. newly zoned commercial areas
        c. highway and road construction

B. Town Ordinances

    1. New licensing rulings

    2. Permits for new businesses

    3. Town plans for growth and stabilization

    4. Town council's changing attitude toward supporting businesses

        a. energy-related
        b. transportation facilities
        c. warehousing facilities

C. Competition

    1. Changing nature of competition

        a. What is the relative image compared to that of the competition?
        b. What are the changes in market share?
        c. What is the degree of ease of entry?

    2. What are the key changes expected in the near future?

        a. Is the market attractive enough for large national chains to enter?
        b. Is there an expected change in the profile of one of the retail complexes in town?

D. External Support Systems

    1. Will there be a critical change in the local money market?

        a. change in money supply
        b. change in interest rates
        c. more stringent terms of lending
        d. changing attitudes of banks

    2. What is the sentiment of real estate owners?

        a. Will absentee owners take care of their properties?
        b. Do local owners have enough empathy?

sources. As can be seen, the sources are not difficult to gain access to, and the types of information obtained from them are rather simplistic. However, these types of information are vital, particularly to the well-being of small retailers.

In a small town, for instance, where a number of businesses thrive on the traffic passing through the main interstate highway, plans relating to creating a bypass can be extremely important for the future of these businesses. With the incoming bypass, many of these businesses either would have to relocate or change their marketing strategy in an effort to appeal to the endogenous market segments of that town.

Again, if the town has changed the licensing requirements for new businesses making it easier to open a new retail establishment, obviously existing retailers will have to change their strategies to keep competition out.

The changing nature of competition has a significant impact on retail strategies. If competition has become keener, substantial differentiation or segmentation may take place on the part of the existing retailers so that additional competitive advantage is gained. Finally, external support systems in terms of finances, taxes, and real estate property owners' attitudes all play decisive roles in retail marketing strategy. Numerous examples could be given for each and every item of Exhibit 16.5. However, most of the types of information presented in the illustration are self-explanatory regarding their impact on retail marketing strategies.

Step 3: RIMS Design and Engineering

Once the decisions have been made regarding data needs and data scope, the nature of the company has to be considered for the RIMS design and engineering. Exhibit 16.6 indicates some specifics in the data base. Needless to say, internal and external data have to be gathered for planning, control risk avoidance, and opportunity assessment.

The preparation of internal and external data in the total RIMS is at least partially dependent on the level at which the managerial decision is made. Lower level managerial decisions are mostly programmed and routine and, hence, are mostly based on internal information. As the level at which decisions are made rises, the need for and dependency on external information become very real, emphasizing once again the fact that a good RIMS gathers its information both from internal and external sources. Exhibit 16.7 illustrates these relationships.

These interrelationships and the specific RIMS designs vary from one company to another. Some major retailers have devised RIMS-like systems that are unique because of their particular needs.

Sears' $750 million RIMS presents the best example of how a national chain can utilize these systems. Ten thousand POS (point of sale) registers are linked to the main computer at Sears' Chicago headquarters. The POS devices report in-store computers that are linked to headquarters that report to the main quarters.

The May Company Department Store uses a Mark 2000 to ensure a two-way

Exhibit 16.6
RIMS Database

	Internal							External					
Source / Orientation	Finance	Selling	Purchase	Inventory	Delivery	Personnel	Wholesale	Research	Customers	Community	Banks	Govern.	Unions
Planning													
Control													
Risk													
Opportunities													

Data Base

communication system with in-store and regional computers. The system has error-detecting and correcting capabilities.

In 1970 Montgomery Ward opened what was then considered the nation's largest computer-operated store in Rockford, Illinois. The computerized RIMS was responsible for creating seasonal merchandise plans, writing all purchase orders, noting color, size, and style trends, and handling all customer accounts, recordkeeping, and billing. At the end of the day, the information is sent to headquarters.

A mail order company based in Washington, D.C., used a RIMS to process orders, decide inventory, and plan its purchases. A similar concept was employed recently when a new retailing store used thousands of terminals to receive orders from customers and help them get the product at the cheapest price offered anywhere in the United States.

Many supermarkets and specialty stores have used RIMS primarily in inventory management and product line assortments. These stores are perhaps more apt to utilize EPOS (electronic point of sale). Very recently, however, they extended their utilization of the system to verify credit. One store, for example, used 50 NCR retail terminals which perform as cash registers to report information to a control office to verify credit. Credit decisions were made in seconds.

The New York-based Brooks Fashion Store, with 325 branches, has modified its eight-year-old electronic data processing to focus on Purchase Order Management to meet the demands of this large chain. Thus, the electronic data processing system was converted to RIMS.

Exhibit 16.7
RIMS Database Dependencies

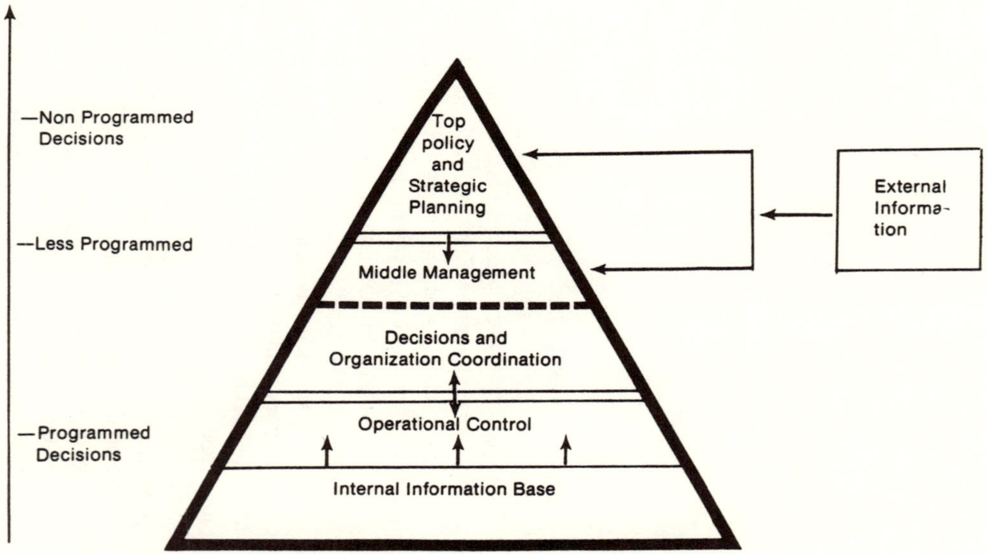

External Information

Top policy and Strategic Planning

Middle Management

Decisions and Organization Coordination

Operational Control

Internal Information Base

—Non Programmed Decisions

—Less Programmed

—Programmed Decisions

Exhibit 16.8
RIMS Implementation Activities

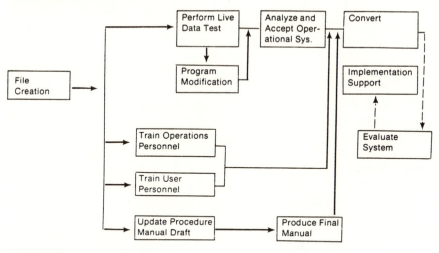

Exhibit 16.9
RIMS Evaluation Activities

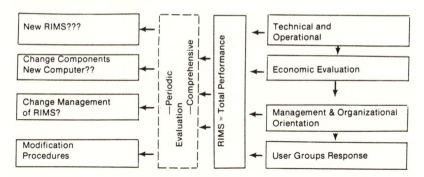

Step 4: Implementation and System Support

Implementation of RIMS takes two separate paths simultaneously: information and personnel. One without the other is not effective. Hence, as the system is being operationalized in terms of information gathering, processing, and retrieval, the people responsible for the systems are trained (Gibson et al. 1973; McLeod 1987). Thus, the two components have to be developed and balanced properly. Exhibit 16.8 illustrates the balance between the two. As the system is developed, all the procedures regarding personnel are also developed in the form of manuals.

Implementation support for RIMS is related to the personnel. Hence, conversion of RIMS from an idea to a full-fledged system becomes a reality through the people responsible for its functioning.

Information flow of the RIMS calls for special attention (Samli 1980). RIMS is designed for management use, and as discussed earlier, in that capacity it produces at least three distinctively different outputs: (1) standard reports, (2) answers to special problems, and (3) special assessment and evaluation (Exhibit 16.1) (Dalton 1976; Dearden and Anthony 1976).

Step 5: Evaluation

Evaluation is the final step in the RIMS development cycle. If RIMS is to perform effectively, it has to be evaluated. Two types of evaluation are identified: periodic evaluation and total performance evaluation. Exhibit 16.9 illustrates the evaluation process. Periodic evaluation involves (1) overhauling the whole system, (2) changing its components, (3) changing its management, or (4) modifying the procedures. Total performance evaluation also has at least four components: (1) technical evaluation, (2) economic evaluation, (3) management evaluation, and (4) group response.

Evaluation is closely related to quality control and improvement mechanisms. This whole activity comes under the feedback component of RIMS. In order for RIMS to function as an effective system, it has to have a built-in quality control and improvement mechanism. This mechanism is depicted by its feedback component. When management is using the output of RIMS, it has to keep track of how much output is utilized, how often it is utilized, whether it is in proper form to be used, if the output needs to be changed, how, and finally, if additional output is needed, what kinds? All this information needs to be brought back to the information system level. If, for instance, rapidly changing prices require that a gift shop install an inventory control system based on units rather than on prices, management's needs are used as feedback to change that portion of RIMS (Samli 1980).

ENTERPRISE LIFE CYCLE AND RIMS

The life cycle of the retail establishment, just like that of a new product, has four distinct phases: introduction, growth, maturity, and decline (Alderson and Shapiro 1963). RIMS will have to provide some standard and some special types of information just because of the changing information needs relating to the stage of the life cycle. Exhibit 16.10 illustrates some of the changing information needs. The list is illustrative rather than exhaustive. As can be seen, many of the information needs are satisfied by standard reports, but in each stage, some special problem areas and/or information needs arise. Consider, for instance, the following episodes: XYZ Company was considering opening up a complete health care complex in a small college town. Although the population base was narrow, the quality and sophistication of the market were such that actual potential was very high.

ABC Company was an elegant gift shop of imported goods. Business was not

Exhibit 16.10
Partial RIMS Information Components Throughout the Life Cycle

Introduction

    Market Potential
    Feasibility
    Cash Flow Needs
  - Promotional Information
  - Standard Operational Expenditures

Growth

  - Changes in the Market
    Market segment Information
    Image Analysis
  - Promotional Information
  - Operational Expenditures
  - Operational Controls

Maturity

  - Changes in the Market
    Market segment Information
    Image Analysis
  - Promotional Information
  - Operational Expenditures
  - Operational Controls

Decline

  - Changes in the Market
    Market segment Information (for new markets)
    Image Analysis
  - Promotional Information
  - Operational Expenditures
  - Operational Controls
    Information for Diversification
    New Market Feasibility Information

  - Standard Report

very good. Market analyses indicated that there was a special elite market for ABC. However, the mass media market exposure of the elite market was completely different from ABC's media mix. The end result was that nobody knew ABC existed.

KIM Company handled office supplies at retail and wholesale. The company put most of its efforts into the retail aspects of the business. However, business in general was not yielding a reasonable return. When the transactions and profits were analyzed, it was found that, whereas retail activity was losing substantial amounts of money, wholesale activity, despite the lack of emphasis, appeared to be extremely profitable. The company discontinued the retail activity and became very successful (Samli 1980).

SUMMARY

Retailers, like manufacturers, continually face obstacles in their attempts to achieve success. Basically, this success depends on the retailer's ability to manage information. Effective decision making cannot occur unless proficient information management takes place. This basic notion is the crux of this chapter. The Retail Management Information System (RIMS) was introduced for that purpose. Five phases of a RIMS development cycle are discussed in this chapter: (1) idea, planning and feasibility, (2) definition of requirement, (3) design, (4) implementation, and (5) evaluation. Each phase is discussed in detail in order to enable the reader to understand the basics of developing a RIMS.

REFERENCES

Alderson, Wroe, and Stanley Shapiro, eds. *Marketing and the Computer*. Englewood Cliffs, N.J.: Prentice-Hall, 1963.

Bates, Albert. "Ahead—The Retrenchment Era. "*Journal of Retailing* 53 (Fall 1977): 29–45.

Berman, Barry, and Joel R. Evans. *Retail Management*. 3rd ed. New York: Macmillan, 1986.

Cox, Donald F., and Robert E. Good. "How to Build a Marketing Information System." *Harvard Business Review* 45 (May 1967): 145–71.

Dalton, Alan. "How Management Information Systems Work." *Supervisory Management* (January 1976).

Dearden, Johnny, and Robert Anthony. *Management Control Systems*. Homewood, Ill.: Robert Irwin, 1976.

Eldin, Hamed K., and May Croft. *Management Information Systems: Management Science Approach*. New York: Petrocelli, 1974.

Gibson, Lawrence D., Charles S. Mayer, Christopher E. Nugent, and Thomas E. Vollman. "An Evolutionary Approach to Marketing Information Systems." *Journal of Marketing* 37 (April 1973): 2–6.

Lesser, Jack A., and James M. Stearns. "The Development of Retailing Information Systems Based on Shopping Behavior Theory." In Naresh Malhotra, ed., *Advances in Marketing Science*. Academy of Marketing Science, 1986.

Mcleod, Raymond, Jr. *Management Information Systems*. Chicago: Science Research Associates, 1987.

Mason, J. Barry, and Morris Mayer. "Retail Merchandise Information System for the 1980s." *Journal of Retailing* (Spring 1980): 56–76

O'Brien, James J. *Management Information Systems*. New York: Van Nostrand, 1970.

Pessemier, Edgar A., "Store Image and Positioning." *Journal of Retailing* (Spring 1980): 94–106.

Porter, M. E., and V. E. Miller. "How Information Gives You Competitive Advantage." *Harvard Business Review* (July-August 1985): 149–160.

Samli, A. Coskun. "Retailing Information Management Systems: An Introduction to RIMS." In Proceedings of ESOMAR Seminar on Information Systems in Action, Amsterdam: 1980, pp. 63–73.

Schafer, Edward A. "Management Control Over the Computer Activity." *Data Management* 10 (September 1972): 45–55.

Schaffir, Kurt, and H. George Trentin. *Marketing Information Systems*. New York: AMACOM, 1973.

Zmud, R. W., and M. R. Lind. "The Use of Formal Mechanics for Linking the Information Systems Function with End-Users." In M. Jarke, ed., *Managers, Mi... and Main Frames; Integrating Systems for End-Users*. New York: John W... 1986.

17 Control Function in Retailing

A retail establishment can be defined as a merchandise control system. As such, this system has what customers want, when they want it, and minimal sales because of stockouts. Because of the wide range in types of retailing firms, control methods vary from systems using calculated risks to rigid and costly operations involving total control. Although this chapter makes some comments on the total control systems in retailing, the focus is on some specific key areas of control, especially inventory control, accounting control, budget control, and control of sales transactions with an electronic sales-recording system.

With the increasing number and size of competitors, better informed and particular consumers, and high costs in expanding sales, more and more retail managers are relying on computerized sensing and monitoring mechanisms. Total comprehensive systems are needed to integrate regional operations with branch units. Such systems will enable retail managers to tighten up control efforts over operating expenses. In order for such control systems to function effectively, rapid communication and feedback of results are needed, as well as a shorter lead time for implementing corrective measures into the system. Thus, a subtle distinction is being made between feedback and control. Although feedback implies ability to monitor activities and events, unless it is transformed into corrective and redirective action, it is not control.

THE PURPOSE OF CONTROL FUNCTIONS

In general, the concept of control implies the process of taking steps to bring actual results and desired results closer together (Kotler 1980; Aipi 1970). Exhibit 17.1 illustrates this concept. As can be seen, analysis of retail functions is partially based on feedback of actual results. This analysis is used to formulate spective. Both illustrations attempt to focalize the control function in the broadest possible sense. In the Retail Plan Analysis type of activity, the opposite is true. It is based on the detailed marketing plan, and the marketing plan is analyzed from its most specific points to its most general premises. While the "no" answers lead the analyst to move to the next most general question, "yes" answers will indicate the triggering of the control mechanism. If, for instance, the strategy is at fault, then the control mechanism will trigger some activity to rectify this problem as quickly and effectively as possible. It must be reiterated that Exhibit 17.6 indicates four components of the retail planning process: analysis, planning, operations, and control. Although other models have different numbers of components, the basic orientation is likely to remain the same.

Corrective Action

Corrective action follows the results of audits and is triggered by the control mechanism (Davis 1981). In essence, it puts an element of the firm's overall marketing activity back into line, or it alters the current position of that element within the overall marketing strategy in order to achieve adjusted goals. Such a change can range from a method of implementation to a change in the actual goals based on the analyses. Thus, the final word on the control function in retailing is based on the corrective action. The feedback information and audit have to trigger the corrective action mechanism. It is essential that the total system of the retail establishment function like an open system, so that the corrective action mechanism can function effectively in terms of making necessary adjustments.

SUMMARY

Control function brings the desired and actual results of the retail function closer together. It is supported by systematic monitoring and adjusting of the retail firm's internal and external environments. Monitoring is facilitated by feedback and audit functions. The audit function takes the form of continuous audits of limited form or general retail marketing audits. These first audit the environment. Then internally they explore the organization, information system, planning system, objectives, and strategies of the retail establishment. The retail audit next explores pricing and advertising. The crux of the control function lies in continuous controls of adjusting standards, adjusting measurements, and adjusting goals. All of these make it possible for corrective action to be taken and properly implemented. In order for the control mechanism to work, the retail establishment's total system must remain open.

REFERENCES

Aipi, Bo. *Planning and Control Through Marketing Research*. London: Hutchinson, 1970.

Berman, Barry, and Joel Evans. *Retail Management*. New York: Macmillan, 1986.

Davis, Kenneth. *Marketing Management*. 4th ed. New York: John Wiley, 1981.

Hartley, Robert F. *Retailing: Challenge and Opportunity*. Boston: Houghton Mifflin, 1975.

Kelly, Eugene, and William Lazer. "The Retailing Mix: Planning and Management." *Journal of Retailing* (Spring 1961).

Kotler, Philip. *Marketing Management Analysis Planning and Control*. Englewood Cliffs, N.J.: Prentice-Hall, 1980.

Kusche, Robert H., and Michael B. Russell. "The Marketing Audit: New Dynamics in Loan Assessment." *Journal of Commercial Bank Lending* (March 1970): 53–58.

Lazer, William. *Marketing Management, a Systems Perspective*. New York: John Wiley, 1971.

Lusch, Robert F. *Management of Retail Enterprises*. Boston: Kent, 1982.

————, and Ray Serpkenci. "The New Model Offers Retailers a Realistic Estimate of Gross Margin Return from Merchandise Lines." *Marketing News* (February 18, 1983): 6.

Mahaian, Vigaz, Stuart I. Bretschneider, and John W. Bradford. "Feedback Approaches to Modeling Shifts in Market Response." *Journal of Marketing* (Winter 1980): 69–74.

Monroe, Kent. *Pricing: Making Profitable Decisions*. New York: McGraw-Hill, 1979.

Naylor, John, and Alan Wood. *Practical Marketing Audits: A Guide to Increased Profitability*. London: Associated Business Programmes, 1978.

Stores 42, No. 2 (February 1980).

Wilson, K. M. S. *Management Controls and Marketing Planning*. London: Redwood Burn Ltd., 1979.

18 Future Outlook and Areas of Further Exploration

All disciplines need periodic self-assessment, and retailing is no exception. This final chapter takes a critical look at the retailing literature and attempts to identify the surpluses and deficiencies in the literature on retail management. As is true of any review effort of this kind, this chapter cannot avoid a degree of subjectivity. However, this subjectivity tends to lessen somewhat as the author's familiarity with the subject matter area increases. In analyzing a discipline's progress by evaluating the literature in that discipline, numerous approaches may be taken. The following approach is used in this chapter: (1) the discipline's major research frontiers are identified; (2) each frontier is examined in terms of its research ferment; (3) each area's research is assessed on the basis of excessive coverage or desperate need of research; and (4) each area's research is evaluated on the basis of the availability of recent research information.

SURPLUS AREAS

Exhibit 18.1 and 18.2 identify the retailing areas in which research information is rather ample. Exhibit 18.1 illustrates the areas that may have been somewhat overstudied. Recent "fads" or "trends" can be determined by examining the second column in the illustration. Store image studies and merchandise control research have been quite widespread during the past decade or so. It can also be seen that, although there is a rich literature on the topic of "trading area and market potentials," this information is becoming somewhat outdated. It is up to the research scholar to determine whether the time gap can also cause a credibility gap.

Exhibit 18.2 deals with more mature rather than overcrowded areas. Again, recent trends in retail buying practices and store loyalty can be detected. As can

Exhibit 18.1
Overcrowded Research Areas and Recency of Research

Topic	Recency
Location Research	Combination
Trading Area Analysis and Market Potentials	Somewhat aged
Store Image Studies	Recent
Merchandise Control	Recent

In this figure and subsequent figures in the Recency column, the following evaluative criteria are utilized: Combination means partly recent and partly aging. One has to go back some years to assess the full impact of the overall research effort in this area; somewhat aged means there has not been any ferment in this area during the past three or four years. The researcher must go back some years if he or she wants to assess research efforts in this area; recent means that all that is available has been done in recent years. There will be almost nothing available on this topic if the researcher goes back a few years.

Exhibit 18.2
Mature Areas of Retailing Research and Recency of Research

Topic	Recency
Retail Competition	Combination
Downtown Versus Shopping Centers	Somewhat Aged
Retail Buying	Recent
Store Layout	Somewhat Aged
Fashion Merchandising	Somewhat Aged
Store Loyalty	Recent

be seen, store layout research raises a serious question as to whether or not the information accumulated in the past is still relevant. Similarly, fashion merchandising, particularly in relationship to strategy development in retailing, has not been adequately researched in recent years.

DEFICITS IN RETAIL RESEARCH

Exhibits 18.3, 18.4, and 18.5 indicate different degrees of deficits in retail research. Exhibit 18.3 illustrates nominal deficits. Information on consumer behavior and retailing is still somewhat lacking. Much of the information in this area is very recent, and if this volume of research continues, the deficiency will soon be eliminated. Retail pricing policies and practices represent areas in need of more research, but the information that exists is not quite up to date. Thus, a negative trend may be keeping research away from retail pricing.

The topics listed in Exhibit 18.4 are more critical. Although the available information is recent in all of the areas specified, the exhibit indicates some critical areas in retail management that have been dormant. This illustration may indicate the beginnings of some major research trends, but it will take some time

Exhibit 18.3
Slightly Under-Researched Key Retailing Areas and Recency of Research

Topic	Recency
Retail Pricing Policies and Practices	Somewhat Aged
Retail Advertising Policies and Practices	Combination
Retailing Research	Combination
Consumer Behavior and Retailing	Recent
Retail Institutions and Evolution	Combination

Exhibit 18.4
Substantially Neglected Retailing Research Areas and Recency of Research

Topic	Recency
Consumer Self Image and Store Image	Recent
Retail Planning	Recent
Retail Administration and Personnel	Recent
Retail Strategy Development	Recent

Exhibit 18.5
Retailing Areas That Need Immediate Attention and Recency of Available Research

Topic	Recency
Store Image Versus Brand Image Interface	Combination
Retail Non-Financial Controls	Recent
Retail Feedback	Recent
Efficiency in Retailing	Somewhat Aged

before each of the four areas listed in Exhibit 18.4 provides a good information base. Of the topics listed, retail strategy development is perhaps the most critical. This is one of the reasons why the present book was written.

Exhibit 18.4 indicates the broadness of the retail research spectrum in need of research. On one end of the spectrum is retail strategy development, and on the other is retail administration and personnel. The latter is one of the major means of implementing the overall strategic plans. It also is woefully neglected.

Finally, Exhibit 18.5 lists the areas that are in greatest need of research. The lack of information in these areas is very costly to practitioners as well as to consumers. Hence, any research in this area is likely to have far-reaching benefits for society.

Since this is the most needy area, a brief description of the specific topics to be researched is of particular importance (Lindquist and Samli 1985):

1. The store image versus brand image controversy goes back to the late 1960s and early 1970s. The relative roles of store image versus brand image in providing differential advantage for the retailer are not well understood. When Louis P. Bucklin (1963) classified retail stores as specialty stores selling specialty goods, specialty stores selling shopping goods, and so on, he alluded to the fact that brand and store images (particularly in the case of specialty goods) go hand in hand and are at least additive, if not multiplicative. However, this and many related issues that could be extremely valuable in retail management have not been carefully researched up to this point.

2. Retail controls traditionally have been financial. They are established and implemented by retail accountants or financial analysts. However, many non-financial controls, for example, changes in store image or store clientele or changes in customer purchase behavior, could not only be early indicators of some critical changes but could also lead to effective control by facilitating critical corrective action early in the game. Chapter 17 posits a series of assertions that may provide guidance for future research in this area.

3. Closely related to nonfinancial controls is retail feedback, which is a critical area that has not been developed adequately. Neither the theory nor the practice of retail feedback has been researched in a systematic and an ongoing manner. A sound theory and practice of retail feedback developed by the aid of good systematic research will provide further flexibility to retail management in activating the corrective action and control mechanisms. Furthermore, such feedback activity will enhance the effectiveness of the sector as a whole as well as of individual retail establishments. The RIMS concept developed in this book provides a model for future research in this area.

4. Efficiency in retailing is a particularly neglected area. Perhaps this is mainly because people-related service-type industries do not lend themselves to efficiency and productivity analyses as well as other production-related industries. Some earlier attempts (Hollander 1965; Beckman 1955) have not been followed through, and retail productivity and efficiency concepts are still a mystery. This

research area provides perhaps the most important direction in retailing research since its outcome can be especially beneficial at the societal level.

FUTURE RESEARCH IN RETAILING

As has been presented in this chapter, the deficit areas indicate not only good opportunities for research but also socially worthwhile project avenues. Almost all areas presented in Exhibits 18.4 and 18.5 are likely to make both micro and macro contributions. The research areas, almost by their very nature, imply the utilization of complex and sophisticated research methodologies. It is also implied that the data will be generated from retail practices as well as from consumer behavior or attitudes. Thus, some behavioral research specialists are urged to enter into the neglected but very challenging retailing field.

None of the five illustrations in this chapter makes a reference to computer simulation. As discussed in Chapter 5, simulation in retailing is a good possibility. Unfortunately, however, little, if any, work has yet been done in applying different simulation models to retail marketing strategy development.

Finally, in addition to retailing scholars, a few words must be directed to the retailing practitioner. In this day and age of ever increasing competition, differential congruence and the resultant competitive edge can be achieved not only through hard work but also through research. In other words, hard work without research is likely to fall short of achieving differential congruence. The smart retailer not only should follow the literature very carefully but also conduct his or her own research. The retail establishment needs to be evaluated and to adjust to constantly changing market conditions. Thus, a carefully designed feedback and control system is a must for every well-managed retail establishment. All retail establishments give certain indications of good or poor health. These indicators must be regularly examined, and the necessary adjustments must be made accordingly. Thus, the retail executive must not only be a good administrator, but also a "doer" or at least a "user" of research. Each retail establishment must develop and execute its own research program.

SUMMARY

This brief chapter attempts to assess the state of the art in retailing research. The discipline's major research frontiers are identified on the basis of the present author's values. Although some areas are identified as surplus areas, it is posited that there are four important research avenues in the retail marketing strategy development area: (1) store image versus brand image interface, (2) retail nonfinancial controls, (3) retail feedback, and (4) efficiency in retailing.

The chapter reflects the author's subjective evolution system as well as his personal biases.

REFERENCES

Beckman, Theodore N. ''The Value Added Concept as Applied to Marketing and Its Implications.'' In Stewart H. Rwoldt, ed., *Frontiers of Marketing*. Bloomington, Ind.: Bureau of Business Research, 1955.

Bucklin, Louis P. ''Retail Strategy and Classification of Consumer Goods.'' *Journal of Marketing* (January 1963): 53–54.

Hollander, Stanley C. ''Measuring the Cost and Value of Marketing.'' *Business Topics* (Autumn 1965): 25–35.

Lindquist, Jay D., and A. Coskun Samli. ''Retailing Management Research and Theory Development: Surpluses and Shortfalls.'' *Journal of the Academy of Marketing Science* (Summer 1985): 147–160.

Index

About the Author

DR. A. COSKUN (JOSH) SAMLI is Research Professor of Marketing and International Business at the University of North Florida. He received his bachelor's degree from Istanbul Academy of Commercial Science, his MBA from the University of Detroit, and his Ph.D. from Michigan State University. As a Ford Foundation Fellow, he has done post-doctoral work at UCLA, The University of Chicago, and as an International Business Program Fellow at New York University.

In 1974–75 Dr. Samli was Sears-AACSB Federal Faculty Fellow in the Office of Policy and Plans, U.S. Maritime Administration. In 1983, he was invited to New Zealand as the Erskine Distinguished Visiting Scholar to lecture and undertake research at Canterbury University. In 1985 Dr. Samli was a Fulbright Distinguished Lecturer in Turkey and was selected as the Beta Gamma Sigma, L. J. Buchan Distinguished Professor for the academic year 1986–87.

Dr. Samli is the author or coauthor of more than 150 scholarly articles, 3 books, and 30 monographs. A large proportion of his writings, research, and consulting have been devoted to small- and medium-sized retailing enterprises.